Expert Performance Indexing for SQL Server 2012

Jason Strate
Ted Krueger

Apress®

Expert Performance Indexing for SQL Server 2012

Copyright © 2012 by Jason Strate and Ted Krueger

ISBN 978-1-4302-3741-9   ISBN 978-1-4302-3742-6 (eBook)

DOI 10.1007/978-1-4302-3742-6

Trademarked names, logos, and images may appear in this book. Rather than use a trademark symbol with every occurrence of a trademarked name, logo, or image we use the names, logos, and images only in an editorial fashion and to the benefit of the trademark owner, with no intention of infringement of the trademark.

The use in this publication of trade names, trademarks, service marks, and similar terms, even if they are not identified as such, is not to be taken as an expression of opinion as to whether or not they are subject to proprietary rights.

While the advice and information in this book are believed to be true and accurate at the date of publication, neither the authors nor the editors nor the publisher can accept any legal responsibility for any errors or omissions that may be made. The publisher makes no warranty, express or implied, with respect to the material contained herein.

President and Publisher: Paul Manning
Lead Editor: Jonathan Gennick
Technical Reviewers: Jorge Segarra and Ken Simmons
Editorial Board: Steve Anglin, Ewan Buckingham, Gary Cornell, Louise Corrigan, Morgan Ertel, Jonathan Gennick,
    Jonathan Hassell, Robert Hutchinson, Michelle Lowman, James Markham, Matthew Moodie, Jeff Olson, Jeffrey
    Pepper, Douglas Pundick, Ben Renow-Clarke, Dominic Shakeshaft, Gwenan Spearing, Matt Wade, Tom Welsh
Coordinating Editor: Debra Kelly
Copy Editors: Mary Bearden and Mary Behr
Compositor: SPi Global
Indexer: SPi Global
Artist: SPi Global
Cover Designer: Anna Ishchenko

Distributed to the book trade worldwide by Springer Science+Business Media New York, 233 Spring Street, 6th Floor, New York, NY 10013. Phone 1-800-SPRINGER, fax (201) 348-4505, e-mail orders-ny@springer-sbm.com, or visit www.springeronline.com.

For information on translations, please e-mail rights@apress.com, or visit www.apress.com.

Apress and friends of ED books may be purchased in bulk for academic, corporate, or promotional use. eBook versions and licenses are also available for most titles. For more information, reference our Special Bulk Sales–eBook Licensing web page at www.apress.com/bulk-sales.

Any source code or other supplementary materials referenced by the author in this text is available to readers at www.apress.com. For detailed information about how to locate your book's source code, go to www.apress.com/source-code.

To Sarah, who missed too many walks and movies and learned more about SQL Server and indexing that she ever thought she would.

– Jason Strate

In memory of Benelli, who was lost during the writing of this book. Always a part of our family and in our hearts

– Ted Krueger

Contents at a Glance

About the Author xv

About the Technical Reviewer xvii

Acknowledgments xix

Introduction xxi

■Chapter 1: Index Fundamentals 1

■Chapter 2: Index Storage Fundamentals 15

■Chapter 3: Index Statistics 51

■Chapter 4: XML, Spatial, and Full-Text Indexing 91

■Chapter 5: Index Myths and Best Practices 121

■Chapter 6: Index Maintenance 135

■Chapter 7: Indexing Tools 165

■Chapter 8: Index Strategies 187

■Chapter 9: Query Strategies 235

■Chapter 10: Index Analysis 249

Index...325

Contents

About the Author xv

About the Technical Reviewer xvii

Acknowledgments xix

Introduction xxi

■Chapter 1: Index Fundamentals 1

Why Build Indexes? 1

Major Index Types 2

    Heap Tables 2

    Clustered Indexes 2

    Nonclustered Indexes 3

    Column Store Indexes 3

Other Index Types 4

    XML Indexes 4

    Spatial Indexes 4

    Full-Text Search 5

Index Variations 5

    Primary Key 5

    Unique Index 5

    Included Columns 6

    Partitioned Indexes 6

    Filtered Indexes 6

Compression and Indexing 7

Index Data Definition Language 7

    Creating an Index 8

    Altering an Index 10

    Dropping an Index 10

Index Meta Data 11

    sys.indexes 11

    sys.index_columns 12

    sys.xml_indexes 12

    sys.spatial_indexes 12

    sys.column_store_dictionaries 12

    sys.column_store_segments 12

Summary 12

■Chapter 2: Index Storage Fundamentals 15

Storage Basics 15

    Pages 15

    Extents 16

Page Types 17

    File Header Page 18

    Boot Page 19

    Page Free Space Page 19

    Global Allocation Map Page 19

    Shared Global Allocation Map Page 20

    Differential Changed Map Page 20

    Bulk Changed Map Page 20

    Index Allocation Map Page 21

    Data Page 21

    Index Page 21

    Large Object Page 21

Organizing Pages 22

    Heap Structure 22

    B-Tree Structure 24

    Column Store Structure 25

Examining Pages 27

    DBCC EXTENTINFO 27

    DBCC IND 31

    DBCC PAGE 35

Page Fragmentation 43

    Forwarded Records 44

    Page Splits 45

Index Characteristics 48

    Heap 48

    Clustered Index 48

    Non-Clustered Index 48

    Column Store Index 49

Summary 49

■Chapter 3: Index Statistics 51

Index-Level Statistics 51

    DBCC SHOW_STATISTICS 51

    Catalog Views 56

    STATS_DATE 57

    Statistics DDL 57

    Index-Level Statistics Summary 57

Usage Statistics 57

    Header Columns 58

    User Columns 58

    System Columns 64

    Index Usage Stats Summary 66

Operational Statistics 66

    Header Columns 67

    DML Activity 67

    SELECT Activity 70

    Locking Contention 72

    Latch Contention 76

    Page Allocation Cycle 80

    Compression 82

    LOB Access 83

    Index Operational Stats Summary 85

Physical Statistics 85

    Header Columns 86

    Row Statistics 87

    Fragmentation Statistics 88

    Index Physical Stats Summary 89

Summary 89

■Chapter 4: XML, Spatial, and Full-Text Indexing 91

XML Indexing 91

    Benefits 91

    Categories 92

    Creating an XML Index 92

    Effects on Execution Plans 95

Spatial Data Indexing 101

    How Spatial Data Is Indexed 101

    Creating Spatial Indexes 102

    Supporting Methods with Indexes 107

    Understanding Statistics, Properties, and Information 109

    Restrictions on Spatial Indexes 111

Full-Text Indexing 112

    Creating a Full-Text Example 112

    Creating a Full-Text Catalog 113

Creating a Full-Text Index 113

Full-Text Search Index Catalog Views and Properties 118

Summary 120

■Chapter 5: Index Myths and Best Practices 121

Index Myths 121

Myth 1: Databases Don't Need Indexes 122

Myth 2: Primary Keys Are Always Clustered 123

Myth 3: Online Index Operations Don't Block 125

Myth 4: Any Column Can Be Filtered In Multicolumn Indexes 127

Myth 5: Clustered Indexes Store Records in Physical Order 129

Myth 6: Fill Factor Is Applied to Indexes During Inserts 130

Myth 7: Every Table Should Have a Heap/Clustered Index 131

Index Best Practices 132

Use Clustered Indexes on Primary Keys by Default 133

Balance Index Count 133

Fill Factor 133

Indexing Foreign Key Columns 134

Index to Your Environment 134

Summary 134

■Chapter 6: Index Maintenance 135

Index Fragmentation 135

Fragmentation Operations 135

Fragmentation Issues 144

Defragmentation Options 146

Defragmentation Strategies 149

Preventing Fragmentation 156

Index Statistics Maintenance 158

Automatically Maintaining Statistics 158

Manually Maintaining Statistics 159

Summary 163

■**Chapter 7: Indexing Tools** **165**

Missing Index DMOs 165

    Explaining the DMOs... 166

    Using the DMOs... 169

Database Engine Tuning Advisor 172

    Explaining DTA.. 173

    Using the DTA GUI... 174

    Using the DTA Utility... 178

Summary 186

■**Chapter 8: Index Strategies** **187**

Heaps 187

    Temporary Objects.. 187

    Other Heap Scenarios... 189

Clustered Indexes 190

    Identity Column... 191

    Surrogate Key... 192

    Foreign Key... 194

    Multiple Column.. 198

    Globally Unique Identifier... 202

Non-Clustered Indexes 204

    Search Columns.. 205

    Index Intersection 207

    Multiple Columns.. 210

    Covering Index.. 211

    Included Columns 212

    Filtered Indexes 216

    Foreign Keys 219

ColumnStore Index 223

Index Storage Strategies 225

    Row Compression... 226

    Page Compression.. 228

Indexed Views 231

Summary 234

■Chapter 9: Query Strategies 235

LIKE Comparison 235

Concatenation 238

Computed Columns 240

Scalar Functions... 242

Data Conversion 244

Summary 247

■Chapter 10: Index Analysis...249

Indexing Method... 249

Monitor 250

Performance Counters.. 251

Dynamic Management Objects.. 256

SQL Trace.. 274

Analyze 279

Review of Server State 279

Schema Discovery... 309

Database Engine Tuning Advisor... 315

Unused Indexes 318

Index Plan Usage 318

Implement 320

Communication.. 320

Deployment Scripts 322

Execution 323

Repeat 323

Summary.. 324

Index 325

About the Authors

Jason Strate is a database architect and administrator consultant for Digineer with more than 15 years of experience. He has been a recipient of Microsoft's "Most Valuable Professional" designation for SQL Server since July 2009. His experience includes design and implementation of both OLTP and OLAP solutions, as well as assessment and implementation of SQL Server environments for best practices, performance, and high availability solutions.

Jason is an active member of the SQL Server community. He currently serves as Regional Mentor for the North Central PASS region, helping community members and chapters connect with each other. In the community, he presents on SQL Server and related topics at local, regional, and national events including SQL Saturdays and the PASS Summit. He also blogs at www.jasonstrate.com and www.sqlkaraoke.com, and can be contacted on Twitter as @stratesql.

Ted Krueger is a SQL Server consultant for a highly respected consulting company and Microsoft Partner, Magenic. A Microsoft MVP, he has worked with SQL Server for more than a decade, focusing on high availability, disaster recovery, replication, scalability, and SSIS. Ted tirelessly contributes to the community through many channels. He is a forum administrator, blogger, speaker, volunteer, and a PASS Regional Mentor. He is a co-founder and co-owner at LessThanDot.com, a highly respected technical resource. You can follow him as @onpnt on Twitter. On the side, he also enjoys fishing and golf.

About the Technical Reviewers

Jorge Segarra is a DBA-turned-BI consultant for Pragmatic Works Consulting and a SQL Server MVP.

In addition to being a member of the Jacksonville SQL Server User Group, he is a Regional Mentor for PASS. Jorge co-authored the Apress book *SQL 2008 Pro Policy-Based Management* as well as the upcoming title *SQL Server 2012 Bible* and was a Red Gate Software Exceptional DBA of the Year 2010 finalist. He also founded SQL University, a community project aimed at helping people learn SQL Server from the ground up, which you can find at http://sqluniversity.org.

Ken Simmons is a database administrator and developer specializing in Microsoft SQL Server. He is an author for multiple SQL Server web sites and books including *Pro SQL Server 2008 Administration*, *Pro SQL Server 2008 Mirroring*, *Pro SQL Server 2008 Policy-Based Management*, and *Pro SQL Server 2012 Administration*. He currently holds certifications for MCP, MCAD, MCDBA, MCTS for SQL Server 2005, and MCITP for SQL Server 2008.

Acknowledgments

A few years ago, I asked Lara Rubbelke if she knew if anyone was working on any sort of indexing data warehouse or a process to index a SQL Server environment as a whole. Her reply was, "You are." At the time, I hadn't actually considered writing a book; I was just looking for a tool. After thinking about it for a few years, that conversation served as the inspiration for this book.

Writing a book is long process. During the writing of this book, a lot happened: I got married, moved the wife from Wisconsin to Minnesota, bought a house, and moved into the new house. Thanks to Sarah for being there while I wrote this book and for reading this book from cover to cover several times. Thanks to Nikolai, Aspen, and Dysin for having the patience to wait some nights when I needed to work on the book. Thanks also to Michael and Grace for allowing me the time on weeknights to work on the book.

Thanks to Kevin Kline for helping me connect with Apress and thanks to the editors and staff at Apress for helping me get this book together. There is a lot more that goes into the writing a book than just the writing. I'm glad there are people to put together things like the index of the book, so that all the work didn't fall to me.

Thanks to my co-workers at Digineer for letting me bounce ideas off of them and reading through a number of the chapters. These include Ben Thul, Aaron Drinkwine, Stan Sajous, Mark Vaillancourt, and Eric Strom.

Speaking of which, I'd like to thank Ted for agreeing to help out on the book. It was much more work than I thought it would be and you bailed me out a few times.

Lastly, I feel I need to acknowledge that Tim is short, like garden gnome short.

-Jason Strate

When Jason first told me about his concept of writing a book completely focused upon SQL Server indexing, I knew it was going to be an immediate success and great resource for anyone working with SQL Server. There simply was not one single resource that was only about indexing and everything that goes into it. Later, when Jason asked if I would help write content for the book, I was ecstatic and honored to be part of it. Jason is a true mentor and friend, and giving me the chance to work with him on this book is truly a highlight of my career.

Writing any amount of content for a book is a very time-consuming task. The only way that Jason and I could accomplish the task of putting the time and devotion into this book was in large part thanks to our families. Without the understanding of my wife, Michelle, and sons Ethan and Cameron, the book may never have been finished.

Without family, we have little motivation to learn and share what we know. My family helps me in doing this, but the SQL community also plays a large part in my motivation. The SQL community is a resource that relies a great deal on the power of knowledge transfer, mentorship, and unselfish assistance. I'd like to thank everyone who makes the SQL community what it is and for allowing me to be a part of it for so many years.

I'd also like to thank the technical editors of the book and the Apress staff. The book had critical deadlines that had to be met in order to be printed on schedule. Without all of their help and patience, we never would have made it.

-Ted Krueger

Introduction

Indexes are important. Not only that, they are vastly important. No single structure aids in retrieving data from a database more than an index. Indexes represent both how data is stored and the access paths by which data can be retrieved from your database. Without indexes, a database is an unordered mess minus the roadmap to find the information you seek.

Throughout my experience with customers, one of the most common resolutions that I provide for performance tuning and application outages is to add indexes to their databases. Often, the effort of adding an index or two to the primary tables within a database provides significant performance improvements—much more so than tuning the database on statement. This is because an index can affect the many SQL statements that are being run against the database.

Managing indexes may seem like an easy task. Unfortunately, their seeming simplicity is often the key to why they are overlooked. Often there is an assumption from developers that the database administrators will take care of indexing. Or there is an assumption by the database administrators that the developers are building the necessary indexes as they develop features in their applications. While these are primarily cases of miscommunication, people need to know how to determine what indexes are necessary and the value of those indexes. This book provides that information.

Outside of the aforementioned scenarios is the fact that applications and how they are used changes over time. Features created and used to tune the database may not be as useful as expected, or a small change may lead to a big change in how the application and underlying database are used. All of this change affects the database and what needs to be accessed. As time goes on, databases and their indexes need to be reviewed to determine if the current indexing is accurate for the new load. This book also provides information in this regard.

From beginning to end, this book provides information that can take you from an indexing novice to an indexing expert. The chapters are laid out such that you can start at any place to fill in the gaps in your knowledge and build out from there. Whether you need to understand the fundamentals or you need to start building out indexes, the information is available here.

Chapter 1 covers index fundamentals. It lays the ground work for all of the following chapters. This chapter provides information regarding the types of indexes available in SQL Server. It covers some of the primary index types and defines what these are and how to build them. The chapter also explores the options available that can change the structure of indexes. From fill factor to included columns, the available attributes are defined and explained.

Chapter 2 picks up where the previous chapter left off. Going beyond defining the indexes available, the chapter looks at the physical structure of indexes and the components that make up indexes. This internal understanding of indexes provides the basis for grasping why indexes behave in certain ways in certain situations. As you examine the physical structures of indexes, you'll become familiar with the tools you can use to begin digging into these structures on your own.

Armed with an understanding of the indexes available and how they are built, Chapter 3 explores the statistics that are stored on the indexes and how to use this information; these statistics provide insight into how SQL Server is utilizing indexes. The chapter also provides information necessary to decipher why an index may not be selected and why it is behaving in a certain way. You will gain a deeper understanding of how this information is collected by SQL Server through dynamic management views and what data is worthwhile to review.

Not every index type was fully discussed in the first chapter; those types not discussed are covered in Chapter 4. Beyond the classic index structure, there are a few other index types that should also be considered when performance tuning. These indexes are applicable to specific situations. In this chapter, you'll look into these other index types to understand what they have to offer. You'll also look at situations where they should be implemented.

Chapter 5 identifies and debunks some commonly held myths about indexes. Also, it outlines some best practices in regards to indexing a table. As you move into using tools and strategies to build indexes in the chapters that follow, this information will be important to remember.

With a firm grasp of the options for indexing, the next thing that needs to be addressed is maintenance. In Chapter 6, you'll look at what needs to be considered when maintaining indexes in your environment. First you'll look at fragmentation.

SQL Server is not without tools to automate your ability to build indexes. Chapter 7 explores these tools and looks at ways that you can begin build indexes in your environment today with minimal effort. The two tools discussed are the Missing Index DMVs and the Database Engine Tuning Advisor. You'll look at the benefits and issues regarding both tools and get some guidance on how to use them effectively in your environment.

The tools alone won't give you everything you need to index your databases. In Chapter 8, you'll begin to look at how to determine the indexes that are needed for a database and a table. There are a number of strategies for selecting what indexes to build within a database. They can be built according to recommendations by the Query Optimizer. They can also be built to support metadata structures such as foreign keys. For each strategy of indexing there are a number of considerations to take into account when deciding whether or not to build the index.

Part of effective indexing is writing queries that can utilize an index on a query. Chapter 9 discusses a number of strategies for indexing. Sometimes when querying data the indexes that you assume will be used are not used after all. These situations are usually tied into how a query is structured or the data that is being retrieved. Indexes can be skipped due to SARGability issues (where the query isn't being properly selective on the index). They can also be skipped over due to tipping point issues, such as when the number of reads to retrieve data from an index potentially exceeds the reads to scan that or another index. These issues effect index selection as well as the effectiveness and justification for some indexes.

Today's DBA isn't in a position where they have only a single table to index. A database can have tens, hundred, or thousands of tables, and all of them need to have the proper indexes. In Chapter 10, you'll learn some methods to approach indexing for a single database but also for all of the databases on a server and servers within your environment.

As mentioned, indexes are important. Through the chapters in this book you will become armed with what you need to know about the indexes in your environment. You will also learn how to find the information you need to improve the performance of your environment.

CHAPTER 1

Index Fundamentals

The end goal of this book is to help you improve the performance of your databases through the use of indexes. Before we can move toward that end, we must first understand what indexes are and why we need them. We need to understand the differences between how information on a clustered index and heap table is stored. We'll also look at how nonclustered and column store indexes are laid out and how they rely on other indexes. This chapter will provide the building blocks to understanding the logical design of indexes.

Why Build Indexes?

Databases exist to provide data. A key piece in providing the data is delivering it efficiently. Indexes are the means to providing an efficient access path between the user and the data. By providing this access path, the user can ask for data from the database and the database will know where to go to retrieve the data.

Why not just have all of the data in a table and return it when it is needed? Why go through the exercise of creating indexes? Returning data when needed is actually the point of indexes; they provide that path that is necessary to get to the data in the quickest manner possible.

To illustrate, let's consider an analogy that is often used to describe indexes—a library. When you go to the library, there are shelves upon shelves of books. In this library, a common task repeated over and over is finding a book. Most often we are particular on the book that we need, and we have a few options for finding that book.

In the library, books are stored on the shelves using the Dewey Decimal Classification system. This system assigns a number to a book based on its subject. Once the value is assigned, the book is stored in numerical order within the library. For instance, books on science are in the range of 500 to 599. From there, if you wanted a book on mathematics, you would look for books with a classification of 510 to 519. Then to find a book on geometry, you'd look for books numbered 516. With this classification system, finding a book on any subject is easy and very efficient. Once you know the number of the book you are looking for, you can go directly to the stack in the library where the books with 516 are located, instead of wandering through the library until you happen upon geometry books. This is exactly how indexes work; they provide an ordered manner to store information that allows users to easily find the data.

What happens, though, if you want to find all of the books in a library written by Jason Strate? You could make an educated guess, that they are all categorized under databases, but you would have to know that for certain. The only way to do that would be to walk through the library and check every stack. The library has a solution for this problem—the card catalog.

The card catalog in the library lists books by author, title, subject, and category. Through this, you would be able to find the Dewey Decimal number for all books written by Jason Strate. Instead of wandering through the stacks and checking each book to see if I wrote it, you could instead go to the specific books in the library written by me. This is also how indexes work. The index provides a location of data so that the users can go directly to the data.

Without these mechanisms, finding books in a library, or information in a database, would be difficult. Instead of going straight to the information, you'd need to browse through the library from beginning to end to find what you need. In smaller libraries, such as book mobiles, this wouldn't be much of a problem. But as the library gets larger and settles into a building, it just isn't efficient to browse all of the stacks. And when there is research that needs to be done and books need to be found, there isn't time to browse through everything.

This analogy has hopefully provided you with the basis that you need in order to understand the purpose and the need for indexes. In the following sections, we'll dissect this analogy a bit more and pair it with the different indexing options that are available in SQL Server 2012 databases.

Major Index Types

You can categorize indexes in different ways. However, it's essential to understand the three categories described in this particular section: heaps, clustered indexes, and nonclustered indexes. Heap and clustered indexes directly affect how data in their underlying tables are stored. Nonclustered indexes are independent of row storage. The first step toward understanding indexing is to grasp this categorization scheme.

Heap Tables

As mentioned in the library analogy, in a book mobile library the books available may change often or there may only be a few shelves of books. In these cases the librarian may not need to spend much time organizing the books under the Dewey Decimal system. Instead, the librarian may just number each book and place the books on the shelves as they are acquired. In this case, there is no real order to how the books are stored in the library. This lack of a structured and searchable indexing scheme is referred to as a *heap*.

In a heap, the first row added to the index is the first record in the table, the second row is the second record in the table, the third row is the third record in the table, and so on. There is nothing in the data that is used to specify the order in which the data has been added. The data and records are in the table without any particular order.

When a table is first created, the initial storage structure is called a heap. This is probably the simplest storage structure. Rows are inserted into the table in the order in which they are added. A table will use a heap until a clustered index is created on the table (we'll discuss clustered indexes in the next section). A table can either be a heap or a clustered index, but not both. Also, there is only a single heap structure allowed per table.

Clustered Indexes

In the library analogy, we reviewed how the Dewey Decimal system defines how books are sorted and stored in the library. Regardless of when the book is added to the library, with the Dewey Decimal system it is assigned a number based on its subject and placed on the shelf between other books of the same subject. The subject of the book, not when it is added, determines the location of the book. This structure is the most direct method to find a book within the library. In the context of a table, the index that provides this functionality in a database is called a *clustered index*.

With a clustered index, one or more columns are selected as the key columns for the index. These columns are used to sort and store the data in the table. Where a library stores books based on their Dewey Decimal number, a clustered index stores the records in the table based on the order of the key columns of the index.

The column(s) used as the key columns for a clustered index are selected based on the most frequently used data path to the records in the table. For instance, in a table with states listed, the most common method of finding a record in the table would likely be through the state's abbreviation. In that situation, using the state abbreviation for the clustering key would be best. With many tables, the primary key or business key will often function as the clustered index clustering key.

Both heaps and clustered indexes affect how records are stored in a table. In a clustered index, the data outside the key columns is stored alongside the key columns. This equates to the clustered index as being the physical table itself, just as a heap defines the table. For this reason, a table cannot be both a heap and a clustered index. Also, since a clustered index defines how the data in a table is stored, a table cannot have more than one clustered index.

Nonclustered Indexes

As was noted in our analogy, the Dewey Decimal system doesn't account for every way in which a person may need to search for a book. If the author or title is known, but not the subject, then the classification doesn't really provide any value. Libraries solve this problem with card catalogs, which provide a place to cross reference the classification number of a book with the name of the author or the book title. Databases are also able to solve this problem with nonclustered indexes.

In a nonclustered index, columns are selected and sorted based on their values. These columns contain a reference to the clustered index or heap location of the data they are related to. This is nearly identical to how a card catalog works in a library. The order of the books, or the records in the tables, doesn't change, but a shortcut to the data is created based on the other search values.

Nonclustered indexes do not have the same restrictions as heaps and clustered indexes. There can be many nonclustered indexes on a table, in fact up to 999 nonclustered indexes. This allows alternative routes to be created for users to get to the data they need without having to traverse all records in a table. Just because a table can have many indexes doesn't mean that it should, as we'll discuss later in this book.

Column Store Indexes

One of the problems with card catalogs in large libraries is that there could be dozens or hundreds of index cards that match a title of a book. Each of these index cards contains information such as the author, subject, title, International Standard Book Number (ISBN), page count, and publishing date; along with the Dewey Decimal number. In nearly all cases this additional information is not needed, but it's there to help filter out index cards if needed. Imagine if instead of dozens or hundreds of index cards to look at, you had a few pieces of paper that only had the title and Dewey Decimal number. Where you previously would have had to look through dozens or hundreds of index cards, you instead are left with a few consolidated index cards. This type of index would be called a *column store index*.

Column store indexes are completely new to SQL Server 2012. Traditionally, indexes are stored in row-based organization, also known as *row store*. This form of storage is extremely efficient when one row or a small range is requested. When a large range or all rows are returned, this organization can become inefficient. The column store index favors the return of large ranges of rows by storing data in column-wise organization. When you create a column store index, you typically include all the columns in a table. This ensures that all columns are included in the enhanced performance benefits of the column store organization. In a column store index, instead of storing all of the columns for a record together, each column is stored separately with all of the other rows in an index. The benefit of this type of index is that only the columns and rows required for a query need to be read. In data warehousing scenarios, often less than 15 percent of the columns in an index are needed for the results of a query.[1]

Column store indexes do have a few restrictions on them when compared to other indexes. To begin with, data modifications, such as those through INSERT, UPDATE, and DELETE statements, are disallowed. For this reason, column store indexes are ideally situated for large data warehouses where the data is not changed that frequently. They also take significantly longer to create; at the time of this writing, they average two to three times longer than the time to create a similar nonclustered index.

Even with the restrictions above, column store indexes can provide significant value. Consider first that the index only loads the columns from the query that are required. Next consider the compression improvements that similar data on the same page can provide. Between these two aspects, column store indexes can provide significant performance improvements. We'll discuss these in more depth in later chapters.

---

[1] http://download.microsoft.com/download/8/C/1/8C1CE06B-DE2F-40D1-9C5C-3EE521C25CE9/Columnstore%20Indexes%20for%20Fast%20DW%20QP%20SQL%20Server%202011.pdf.

Other Index Types

Besides the index types just discussed, there are a number of other index types available. These are XML, spatial, and full-text search indexes. These don't necessarily fit into the library scenario that has been outlined so far, but they are important options. To help illustrate, we'll be adding some new functionality to the library. Chapter 4 will expand on the information presented here.

XML Indexes

Suppose we needed a method to be able to search the table of contents for all of the books in the library. A table of contents provides a hierarchical view of a book. There are chapters that outline the main sections for the book; which are followed by subchapter heads that provide more detail of the contents of the chapter. This relationship model is similar to how XML documents are designed; there are nodes and a relation between them that define the structure of the information.

As discussed with the card catalog, it would not be very efficient to look through every book in the library to find those that were written by Jason Strate. It would be even less efficient to look through all of the books in the library to find out if any of the chapters in any of the books were written by Ted Krueger. There are probably more than one chapter in each book, resulting in multiple values that would need to be checked for each book and no certainty as to how many chapters would need to be looked at before checking.

One method of solving this problem would be to make a list of every book in the library and list all of the chapters for each book. Each book would have one or more chapter entries in the list. This provides the same benefit that a card catalog provides, but for some less than standard information. In a database, this is what an *XML index* does.

For every node in an XML document an entry is made in the XML index. This information is persisted in internal tables that SQL Server can use to determine whether the XML document contains the data that is being queried.

Creating and maintaining XML indexes can be quite costly. Every time the index is updated, it needs to shred all of the nodes of the XML document into the XML index. The larger the XML document, the more costly this process will be. However, if data in an XML column will be queried often, the cost of creating and maintaining an XML index can be offset quickly by removing the need to shred all of the XML documents at runtime.

Spatial Indexes

Every library has maps. Some maps cover the oceans; others are for continents, countries, states, or cities. Various maps can be found in a library, each providing a different view and information of perhaps the same areas. There are two basic challenges that exist with all of these maps. First, you may want to know which maps overlap or include the same information. For instance, you may be interested in all of the maps that include Minnesota. The second challenge is when you want to find all of the books in the library that where written or published at a specific place. Again in this case, how many books were written within 25 miles of Minneapolis?

Both of these present a problem because, traditionally, data in a database is fairly one dimensional, meaning that data represent discrete facts. In the physical world, data often exist in more than one dimension. Maps are two dimensional and buildings and floor plans are three dimensional. To solve this problem, SQL Server provides the capabilities for *spatial indexes*.

Spatial indexes dissect the spatial information that is provided into a four-level representation of the data. This representation allows SQL Server to plot out the spatial information, both geometry and geography, in the record to determine where rows overlap and the proximity of one point to another point.

There are a few restrictions that exist with spatial indexes. The main restriction is that spatial indexes must be created on tables that have primary keys. Without a primary key, the spatial index creation will not succeed. When creating spatial indexes, they are restricted utilizing parallel processing, and only a single spatial index can be built at a time. Also, spatial indexes cannot be used on indexed views. These and other restrictions are covered in Chapter 4.

Similar to XML indexes, spatial indexes have upfront and maintenance costs associate with their sizes. The benefit is that when spatial data needs to be queried using specific methods for querying spatial data, the value of the spatial index can be quickly realized.

Full-Text Search

The last scenario to consider is the idea of finding specific terms within books. Card catalogs do a good job of providing information on find books by author, title, or subject. The subject of a book isn't the only keyword you may want to use to search for books. At the back of many books are keyword indexes to help you find other subjects within a book. When this book is completed, there will be an index and it will have the entry full-text search in it with a reference to this page and other pages where this is discussed in this book.

Consider for a moment if every book in the library had a keyword index. Furthermore, let's take all of those keywords and place them in their own card catalog. With this card catalog, you'd be able to find every book in the library with references to every page that discusses full-text searches. Generally speaking, this is what an implementation of a full-text search provides.

Index Variations

Up to this point, we've looked at the different types of indexes available within a SQL Server. These aren't the only ways in which indexes can be defined. There are a few index properties that can be used to create variations on the types of indexes discussed previously. Implementing these variations can assist in implementing business rules associated with the data or to help improve the performance of the index.

Primary Key

In the library analogy, we discussed how all of the books have a Dewey Decimal number. This number identifies each book and where it is in the library. In a similar fashion, an index can be defined to identify a record within a table. To do this, an index is created with a primary key to identify a record within a table. There are some differences between the Dewey Decimal number and a primary key, but conceptually they are the same.

A primary key is used to identify a record within a table. For this reason none of the records in a table can have the same primary key value. Typically, a primary key will be created on a single column, though it can be composed of multiple columns.

There are a few other things that need to be remembered when using a primary key. First, a primary key is a unique value that identifies each record in a table. Because of this, all values within a primary key must be populated. No null values are allowed in a primary key. Also, there can only be one primary key on a table. There may be other identifying information in a table, but only a single column or set of columns can be identified as the primary key. Lastly, although it is not required, a primary key will typically be built on a clustered index. The primary key will be clustered by default, but this behavior can be overridden and will be ignored if a clustered index already exists. More information on why this is done will be included in Chapter 5.

Unique Index

As mentioned previously, there can be more than a single column or set of columns that can be used to uniquely identify a record in a table. This is similar to the fact that there is more than one way to uniquely identify a book in a library. Besides the Dewey Decimal number, a book can also be identified through its ISBN. Within a database, this is represented as a *unique index*.

Similar to the primary key, an index can be constrained so that only a single value appears within the index. A unique index is similar in that it provides a mechanism to uniquely identify records in a table and can also be created across a single or multiple columns.

One chief difference between a primary key and a unique index is the behavior when the possibility of null values is introduced. A unique index will allow null values within the columns being indexed. A null value is considered a discrete value, and only one null value is allowed in a unique index.

Included Columns

Suppose you want to find all of the books written by Douglas Adams and find out how many pages are in each book. You may at first be inclined to look up the books in the card catalog, and then find each book and write down the number of pages. Doing this would be fairly time-consuming. It would be a better use of your time if instead of looking up each book you had that information right on hand. With a card catalog, you wouldn't actually need to find each book for a page count, though, since most card catalogs include the page count on the index card. When it comes to indexing, including information outside the indexed columns is done through *included columns*.

When a nonclustered index is built, there is an option to add included columns into the index. These columns are stored as nonsorted data within the sorted data in the index. Included columns cannot include any columns that have been used in the initial sorted column list of the index.

In terms of querying, included columns allow users to lookup information outside the sorted columns. If everything they need for the query is in the included columns, the query does not need to access the heap or clustered index for the table to complete the results. Similar to the card catalog example, included columns can significantly improve the performance of a query.

Partitioned Indexes

Books that cover a lot of data can get fairly large. If you look at a dictionary or the complete works on William Shakespeare, these are often quite thick. Books can get large enough that the idea of containing them in a single volume just isn't practical. The best example of this is an encyclopedia.

It is rare that an encyclopedia is contained in a single book. The reason is quite simple—the size of the book and the width of the binding would be beyond the ability of nearly anyone to manage. Also, the time it takes to find all of the subjects in the encyclopedia that start with the letter "S" is greatly improved because you can go directly to the "S" volume instead of paging through an enormous book to find where they start.

This problem isn't limited to books. A problem similar to this exists with tables as well. Tables and their indexes can get to a point where their size makes it difficult to continue to maintain the indexes in a reasonable time period. Along with that, if the table has millions or billions of rows, being able to scan across limited portions of the table vs. the whole table can provide significant performance improvements. To solve this problem on a table, indexes have the ability to be partitioned.

Partitioning can occur on both clustered and nonclustered indexes. It allows an index to be split along the values supplied by a function. By doing this, the data in the index is physically separated into multiple partitions, while the index itself is still a single logical object.

Filtered Indexes

By default, nonclustered indexes contain one record in them for every row in the table for which the index is associated. In most cases, this is ideal and provides the index an opportunity to assist in selectivity for any value in the column.

There are atypical situations where including all of the records in a table in an index is less than ideal. For instance, the set of values most often queried may represent a small number of rows in a table. In this case, limiting the rows in the index will reduce the amount of work a query needs to perform, resulting in an improvement in the performance of the query. Another could be where the selectivity of a value is low compared to the number of rows in the table. This could be an active status or shipped Boolean values; indexing on these values wouldn't drastically improve performance, but filtering to just those records would provide a significant opportunity for query improvement.

To assist in these scenarios, nonclustered indexes can be filtered to reduce the number of records they contain. When the index is built, it can be defined to include or exclude records based on a simple comparison that reduces the size of the index.

Besides the performance improvements outlined, there are other benefits in using filtered indexes. The first improvement is reduced storage costs. Since filtered indexes have fewer records in them, due to the filtering, there will be less data in the index, which requires less storage space. The other benefit is reduced maintenance costs. Similar to the reduced storage costs, since there is less data to maintain, less time is required to maintain the index.

Compression and Indexing

Today's libraries have a lot of books in them. As the number of books increases, there comes a point where it becomes more and more difficult to manage the library with the existing staff and resources. Because of this, there are a number of ways that libraries find to store books, or the information within them, to allow better management without increasing the resources required to maintain the library. As an example, books can be stored on microfiche or made available only through electronic means. This provides the benefits of reducing the amount of space needed to store the materials and allows library patrons a means to look at more books more quickly.

Similarly, indexes can reach the point of becoming difficult to manage when they get too large. Also, the time required to access the records can increase beyond acceptable levels. There are two types of compression available in SQL Server: row-level and page-level compression.

With *row-level compression*, an index compresses each record at the row level. When row-level compression is enabled, a number of changes are made to each record. To begin with, the metadata for the row is stored in an alternative format that decreases the amount of information stored on each column, but because of another change it may actually increase the size of the overhead. The main changes to the records are numerical data changes from fixed to variable length and blank spaces at the end of fixed-length string data types that are not stored. Another change is that null or zero values do not require any space to be stored.

Page-level compression is similar to row-level compression, but it also includes compression across a group of rows. When page-level compression is enabled, similarities between string values in columns are identified and compressed. This will be discussed in detail in Chapter 2.

With both row-level and page-level compression, there are some things to be taken into consideration. To begin with, compressing a record takes additional central processing unit (CPU) time. Although the row will take up less space, the CPU is the primary resource used to handle the compression task before it can be stored. Along with that, depending on the data in your tables and indexes, the effectiveness of the compression will vary.

Index Data Definition Language

Similar to the richness in types and variations of indexes available in SQL Server, there is also a rich data definition language (DDL) that surrounds building indexes. In this next section, we will examine and discuss the DDL for building indexes. First, we'll look at the CREATE statement and its options and pair them with the concepts discussed previously in this chapter.

For the sake of brevity, backward compatible features of the index DDL will not be discussed; information on those features can be found in Books Online for SQL Server 2012. XML and spatial indexes and full-text search will be discussed further in later chapters.

Creating an Index

Before an index can exist within your database, it must first be created. This is accomplished with the CREATE INDEX syntax shown in Listing 1-1. As the syntax illustrates, most of the index types and variations previously discussed are available through the basic syntax.

Listing 1-1. CREATE INDEX Syntax

```
CREATE [ UNIQUE ] [ CLUSTERED | NONCLUSTERED ] INDEX index_name
  ON <object> ( column [ ASC | DESC ] [ ,…n ] )
  [ INCLUDE ( column_name [ ,…n ] ) ]
  [ WHERE <filter_predicate> ]
  [ WITH ( <relational_index_option> [ ,…n ] ) ]
  [ ON { partition_scheme_name ( column_name )
    | filegroup_name
    | default
    }
  ]
  [ FILESTREAM_ON { filestream_filegroup_name | partition_scheme_name | "NULL" } ]
[ ; ]
```

The choice between CLUSTERED and NONCLUSTERED indexing determines whether an index will be built in based on one of those two basic types. Excluding either of these types will default the index to nonclustered.

The uniqueness of the index is determined by the UNIQUE keyword, including it within the CREATE INDEX syntax will make the index unique. The syntax for creating an index as a primary key will be included later in this chapter.

The <object> option determines the base object over which the index will be built. The syntax allows for indexes to be created on either tables or views. The specification of the object can include the database name and schema name, if needed.

After specifying the object for the index, the sorted columns of an index are listed. These columns are usually referred to as the *key columns*. Each column can only appear in the index a single time. By default, the columns will be sorted in the index in ascending order, but descending order can be specified instead. An index can include up to 16 columns as part of the index key. The data in key columns, also, cannot exceed 900 bytes.

As an option, Included columns can be specified with an index, which are added after the key columns for the index. There is no option for either ascending or descending since Included columns are not sorted. Between the key and nonkey columns, there can be up to 1,023 columns in an index. The size restriction on the key columns does not affect Included columns.

If an index will be filtered, this information is specified next. The filtering criteria are added to an index through a Where clause. The Where clause can use any of the following comparisons: IS , IS NOT , = , <> , != , > , >= , !> , < , <= , and !<. Also, a filtered index cannot use comparisons against a Computed column, a user-defined type (UDT) column, a Spatial data type column, or a HierarchyID data type column.

There are a number of options that can be used when creating an index. In Listing 1-1, there is a segment for adding index options, noted by the tag <relational_index_option>. These index options control both how indexes are created as well as how they will function in some scenarios. The DDL for the available index options are provided in Listing 1-2.

Listing 1-2. Index Options

```
  PAD_INDEX = { ON | OFF }
| FILLFACTOR = fillfactor
| SORT_IN_TEMPDB = { ON | OFF }
| IGNORE_DUP_KEY = { ON | OFF }
| STATISTICS_NORECOMPUTE = { ON | OFF }
| DROP_EXISTING = { ON | OFF }
```

```
| ONLINE = { ON | OFF }
| ALLOW_ROW_LOCKS = { ON | OFF }
| ALLOW_PAGE_LOCKS = { ON | OFF }
| MAXDOP = max_degree_of_parallelism
| DATA_COMPRESSION = { NONE | ROW | PAGE}
  [ ON PARTITIONS ( { <partition_number_expression> | <range> }
  [ , ...n ] ) ]
```

Each of the options allows for different levels of control on the index creation process. Table 1-1 provides a listing of all of the options available for CREATE INDEX. In later chapters, examples and strategies for applying them are discussed. More information on the CREATE INDEX syntax and examples of its use can be found in Books Online for SQL Server 2012.

Table 1-1. *CREATE INDEX Syntax Options*

Option Name	Description
FILLFACTOR	Defines the amount of empty space to leave in each data page of an index when it is created. This is only applied at the time an index is created or rebuilt.
PAD_INDEX	Specifies whether the FILLFACTOR for the index should be applied to the nonleaf data pages for the index. The PAD_INDEX option is used when data manipulation language (DML) operations that lead to excessive nonleaf level page splitting need to be mitigated.
SORT_IN_TEMPDB	Determines whether to store temporary results from building the index in the tempdb database. This option will increase the amount of space required.
IGNORE_DUP_KEY	Changes the behavior when duplicate keys are encountered when performing inserts into a table. When enabled, rows violating the key constraint will fail. When the default behavior is disabled, the entire insert will fail.
STATISTICS_NORECOMPUTE	Specifies whether any statistics related to the index should be re-created when the index is created.
DROP_EXISTING	Determines the behavior when an index of the same name on the table already exists. By default, when OFF, the index creation will fail. When set to ON, the index creation will overwrite the existing index.
ONLINE	Determines whether a table and its indexes are available for queries and data modification during index operations. When enabled, locking is minimized and an Intent Shared is the primary lock held during index creation. When disabled, the locking will prevent data modifications to the index and underlying table for the duration of the operation. ONLINE is an Enterprise Edition only feature.
ALLOW_ROW_LOCKS	Determines whether row locks are allowed on an index. By default, they are allowed.
ALLOW_PAGE_LOCKS	Determines whether page locks are allowed on an index. By default, they are allowed.
MAXDOP	Overrides the server-level maximum degree of parallelism during the index operation. The setting determines the maximum number of processors that an index can utilize during an index operation.
DATA_COMPRESSION	Determines the type of data compression to use on the index. By default, no compression is enabled. With this, both Page and Row level compression types can be specified.

Altering an Index

After an index has been created, there will be a need, from time to time, to modify the index. There are a few reasons to alter an existing index. First, the index may need to be rebuilt or reorganized as part of ongoing index maintenance. Also, some of the index options, such as the type of compression, may need to change. In these cases, the index can be altered and the options for the indexes are modified.

To modify an index the ALTER INDEX syntax is used. The syntax for altering indexes is shown in Listing 1-3.

Listing 1-3. ALTER INDEX Syntax

```
ALTER INDEX { index_name | ALL }
  ON <object>
  { REBUILD
    [ [PARTITION = ALL]
     [ WITH ( <rebuild_index_option> [ ,…n ] ) ]
     | [ PARTITION = partition_number
         [ WITH ( <single_partition_rebuild_index_option>
             [ ,…n ] )
         ]
       ]
    ]
  | DISABLE
  | REORGANIZE
    [ PARTITION = partition_number ]
    [ WITH ( LOB_COMPACTION = { ON | OFF } ) ]
  | SET ( <set_index_option> [ ,…n ] )
  }
[ ; ]
```

When using the ALTER INDEX syntax for index maintenance, there are two options in the syntax that can be used. These options are REBUILD and REORGANIZE. The REBUILD option re-creates the index using the existing index structure and options. It can also be used to enable a disabled index. The REORGANIZE option resorts the leaf level pages of an index. This is similar to reshuffling the cards in a deck to get them back in sequential order. Both of these options will be discussed more thoroughly in Chapter 6.

As mentioned above, an index can be disabled. This is accomplished through the DISABLE option under the ALTER INDEX syntax. A disabled index will not be used or made available by the database engine. After an index is disabled, it can only be reenabled by altering the index again with the REBUILD option.

Beyond those functions, all of the index options available through the CREATE INDEX syntax are also available with the ALTER INDEX syntax. The ALTER INDEX syntax can be used to modify the compression of an index. It can also be used to change the fill factor or the pad index settings. Depending on the changing needs for the index, this syntax can be used to change any of the available options.

It is worth mentioning that there is one type of index modification that is not possible with the ALTER INDEX syntax. When altering an index, the key and included columns cannot be changed. To accomplish this, the CREATE INDEX syntax is used with the DROP_EXISTING option.

For more information on the ALTER INDEX syntax and examples of its use, you can search for it in Books Online.

Dropping an Index

There will be times when an index is no longer needed. The index may no longer be necessary due to changing usage patterns of the database, or the index may be similar enough to another index that it isn't useful enough to warrant its existence.

To drop, or remove, an index the DROP INDEX syntax is used. This syntax includes the name of the index and the table, or object, that the index is built against. The syntax for dropping an index is shown in Listing 1.4.

Listing 1-4. DROP INDEX Syntax

```
DROP INDEX
    index_name ON <object>
  [ WITH ( <drop_clustered_index_option> [ ,…n ] ) ]
```

Besides just dropping an index, there are a few additional options that can be included. These options primarily apply to dropping clustered indexes. Listing 1-5 details the options available to use for a DROP INDEX operation.

Listing 1-5. DROP INDEX Options

```
MAXDOP = max_degree_of_parallelism
  | ONLINE = { ON | OFF }
  | MOVE TO { partition_scheme_name ( column_name )
      | filegroup_name
      | "default"
      }
  [ FILESTREAM_ON { partition_scheme_name
      | filestream_filegroup_name
      | "default" } ]
```

When a clustered index is dropped, the base structure of the table will change from clustered to heap. When built, a clustered index defines where the base data for a table is stored. When making a change from the clustered to the heap structure, SQL Server needs to know where to place the heap structure. If the location is anywhere other than the default file group, it will need to be specified. The location for the heap can be a single file group or defined by a partitioning scheme. This information is set through the MOVE TO option. Along with the data location, the FILESTREAM location may also need to be set through these options.

The performance impact of the drop index operation may be something that you need to consider. Because of this, there are options in the DROP INDEX syntax to specify the maximum number of processors to utilize along with whether the operation should be completed online. Both of these options function similar to the options of the same name in the CREATE INDEX syntax.

For more information on the DROP INDEX syntax and examples of its use, you can search in Books Online.

Index Meta Data

Before going too deep into indexing strategies, it is important to understand the information available in SQL Server on the indexes. When there is a need to understand or know how an index is built, there are catalog views that can be queried to provide this information. There are four catalog views available for indexes. Every user and system database has these catalog views in them and will only return specific indexes that are unique to each database in which they are queried. Each of these catalog views provides important details for each index.

sys.indexes

The sys.indexes catalog view provides information on each index in a database. For every table, index, or table-valued function there is one row within the catalog view. This provides a full accounting of all indexes in a database.

The information in sys.indexes is useful in a few ways. First, the catalog view includes the name of the index. Along with that is the type of the index, identifying whether the index is clustered, nonclustered, and so forth. Along with that information are the properties on the definition of the index. This includes the fill factor, filter definition, the uniqueness flag, and other items that were used to define the index.

sys.index_columns

The sys.index_columns catalog view provides a list of all of the columns included in an index. For each key and included column that is a part of an index, there is one row in this catalog view. For each of the columns in the index, the order of columns is included along with the order in which the column is sorted in the index.

sys.xml_indexes

The catalog view sys.xml_indexes is similar to sys.indexes. This catalog view returns one row per XML index in a database. The chief difference with this catalog view is that it also provides some additional information. The view includes information on whether the XML index is a primary or secondary XML index. If the XML index is a secondary XML index, the catalog view includes a type for the secondary index.

sys.spatial_indexes

The sys.spatial_indexes catalog view is also similar to sys.indexes. This catalog view returns one row for every spatial index in a database. The main difference with this catalog view is that it provides additional information on spatial indexes. The view includes information on whether the spatial index is a geometric or geographic index.

sys.column_store_dictionaries

The sys.column_store_dictionaries catalog view is one of the new catalog views that supports columnstore indexes. This catalog view returns one row for each column in a columnstore index. The data describes the structure and type of dictionary built for the column.

sys.column_store_segments

The sys.column_store_segments catalog view is another of the new catalog views that support columnstore indexes. This catalog view returns at least one row for every column in a columnstore index. Columns can have multiple segments of approximately one million rows each. The rows in the catalog view describe base information on the segment (for example, whether the segment has null values and what the minimum and maximum data IDs are for the segment).

Summary

This chapter presented a number of fundamentals related to indexes. First, we looked at the type of indexes available within SQL Server. From heaps to nonclustered to spatial indexes, we looked at the type of the index and related it to the library Dewey Decimal system to provide a real-world analogy to indexing. This example helped illustrate how each of the index types interacted with the others and the scenarios where one type can provide value over another.

Next, we looked at the data definition language (DDL) for indexes. Indexes can be created, modified, and dropped through the DDL. The DDL has a lot of options that can be used to finely tune how an index is structured to help improve its usefulness within a database.

This chapter also included information on the metadata, or catalog views, available on indexes within SQL Server. Each of the catalog views provides information on the structure and makeup of the index. This information can assist in researching and understanding the view that are available.

The details in this chapter provide the framework for what will be discussed in later chapters. By leveraging this information, you'll be able to start looking deeper into your indexes and applying the appropriate strategies to index your databases.

■ ■ ■

CHAPTER 2

Index Storage Fundamentals

Where the previous chapter discussed the logical designs of indexes, this chapter will dig deeper into the physical implementation of indexes. An understanding of the way in which indexes are laid out and interact with each other at the implementation and storage level will help you become better acquainted with the benefits that indexes provide and why they behave in certain ways.

To get to this understanding, the chapter will start with some of the basics about data storage. First, you'll look at data pages and how they are laid out. This examination will detail what comprises a data page and what can be found within it. Also, you'll examine some DBCC commands that can be used diagnostically to inspect pages in the index.

From there, you'll look at the three ways in which pages are organized for storage within SQL Server. These storage methods relate back to heap, clustered, non-clustered, and column store indexes. For each type of structure, you'll examine how the pages are organized within the index. You'll also examine the requirements and restrictions associated with each index type.

Missing from this chapter is a discussion on how full-text, spatial, and XML indexes are stored. Those topics are briefly covered in Chapter 4. Since those topics are wide enough to cover entire books on their own, we recommended the following Apress books: *Pro Full-Text Search in SQL Server 2008*, *Pro SQL Server 2008 XML*, *Beginning Spatial with SQL Server 2008*, and *Pro Spatial with SQL Server 2012*.

You will finish this chapter with a deeper understanding of the fundamentals of index storage. With this information, you'll be better able to deal with, understand, and expect behaviors from the indexes in your databases.

Storage Basics

SQL Server uses a number of structures to store and organize data within databases. In the context of this book and chapter, you'll look at the storage structures that relate directly to tables and indexes. You'll start by focusing on pages and extents and how they relate to one another. Then you'll look at the different types of pages available in SQL Server and relate each of them back to indexes.

Pages

As mentioned in the introduction, the most basic storage area is a page. Pages are used by SQL Server to store everything in the database. Everything from the rows in tables to the structures used to map out indexes at the lowest levels is stored on a page.

When space is allocated to database data files, all of the space is divided into pages. During allocation, each page is created to use 8KB (8192 bytes) of space and they are numbered starting at 0 and incrementing 1 for every page allocated. When SQL Server interacts with the database files, the smallest unit in which an I/O operation can occur is at the page level.

There are three primary components to a page: the page header, records, and offset array, as shown in Figure 2-1. All pages begin with the page header. The header is 96 bytes and contains meta-information about the page, such as the page number, the owning object, and type of page. At the end of the page is the offset array. The offset array is 36 bytes and provides pointers to the byte location of the start of rows on the page. Between these two areas are 8060 bytes where records are stored on the page.

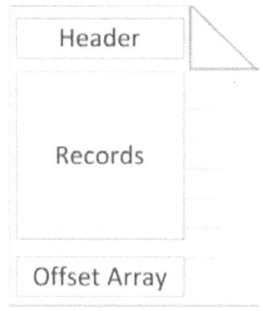

Figure 2-1. *Page structure*

As mentioned, the offset array begins at the end of the page. As rows are added to a page, the row is added to the first open position in the records area of the page. After this, the starting location of the page is stored in the last available position in the offset array. For every row added, the data for the row is stored further away from the start of the page and the offset is stored further away from the end of the page, as shown in Figure 2-2. Reading from the end of the page backwards, the offset can be used to identify the starting position of every row, sometimes referred to as a slot, on the page.

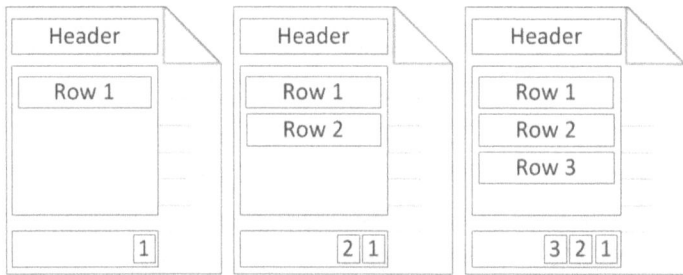

Figure 2-2. *Row placement and offset array*

While the basics of pages are the same, there are a number of different ways in which pages are useful. These uses include storing data pages, index structures, and large objects. These uses and how they interact with a SQL Server database will be discussed later in this chapter.

Extents

Pages are grouped together eight at a time into structures called *extents*. An extent is simply eight physically contiguous data pages in a data file. All pages belong to an extent, and extents can't have fewer than eight pages. There are two types of extents use by SQL Server databases: *mixed* and *uniform* extents.

In mixed extents, the pages can be allocated to multiple objects. For example, when a table is first created and there are less than eight pages allocated to the table, it will be built as a mixed extent. The table will use mixed extents as long as the total size of the table is less than eight pages, as show in Figure 2-3. By using mixed extents, databases can reduce the amount of space allocated to small tables.

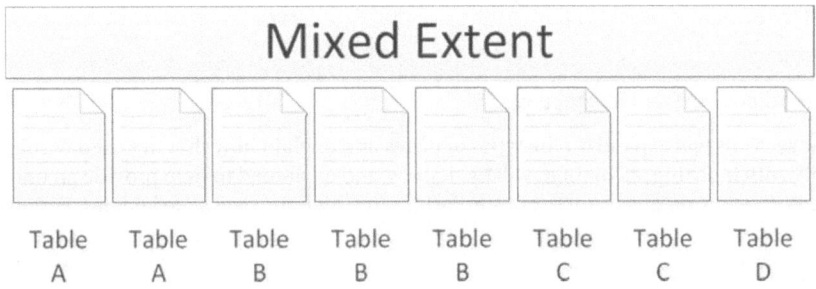

Figure 2-3. Mixed extent

Once the number of pages in a table exceeds eight pages, it will begin using uniform extents. In a uniform extent, all pages in the extent are allocated to a single object in the database (see Figure 2-4). Due to this, pages for an object will be contiguous, which increases the number of pages of an object that can be read in a single read. For more information on the benefits of contiguous reads, see Chapter 6.

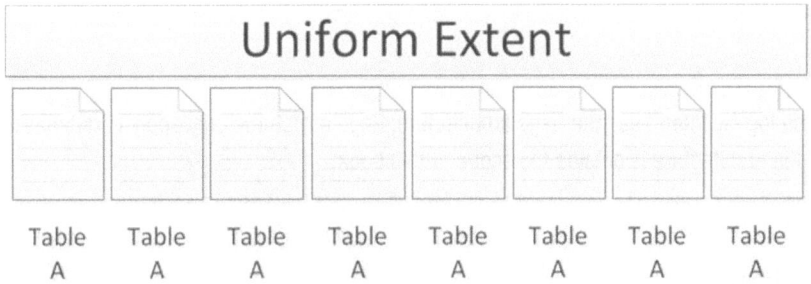

Figure 2-4. Uniform extent

Page Types

As mentioned, there are many ways in which a page can be used in the database. For each of these uses, there is a type associated with the page that defines how the page will be used. The page types available in a SQL Server database are

- File header page
- Boot page
- Page Free Space (PFS) page
- Global Allocation Map (GAM) page

- Shared Global Allocation Map (SGAM) page

- Differential Changed Map (DCM) page

- Bulk Changed Map (BCM) page

- Index Allocation Map (IAM) page

- Data page

- Index page

- Large object (Text and Image) page

The next few sections will expand on the types of pages and explain how they are used. While not every page type deals directly with indexing, all of them will be defined and explained to help provide an understanding of the total picture. With every database, there are similarities in which the pages are laid out. For instance, in the first file of every database the pages are laid out as shown in Figure 2-5. There are more page types available than the figure indicates, but as the examinations of each page type will show, only those in the first few pages are fixed. Many of the others appear in patterns that are dictated by the data in the database.

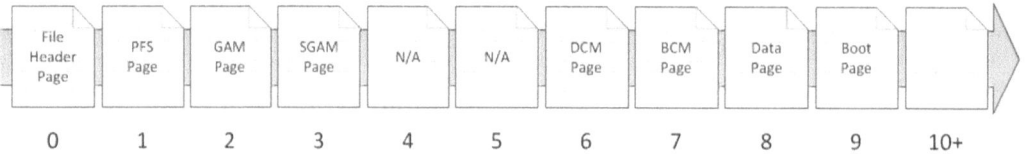

Figure 2-5. *Data file pages*

■ **Note**   Database log files don't use the page architecture. Page structures only apply to database data files. Discussion of log file architecture is outside the scope of this book.

File Header Page

The first page in any database data file is the file header page, shown in Figure 2-5. Since this is the first page, it is always numbered 0. The file header page contains metadata information about the database file. The information on this page includes

- File ID

- File group ID

- Current size of the file

- Max file size

- Sector size

- LSN information

There are a number of other details about the file on the file header page, but basically the information is immaterial to indexing internals.

Boot Page

The boot page is similar to the file header page in that it provides metadata information. This page, though, provides metadata information for the database itself instead of for the data file. There is one boot page per database and it is located on page 9 in the first data file for a database (see Figure 2-5). Some of information on the boot page includes the current version of the database, the create date and version for the database, the database name, the database ID, and the compatibility level.

One important attribute on the boot page is the attribute dbi_dbccLastKnownGood. This attribute provides the date that the last known DBCC CHECKDB completed successfully. While database maintenance isn't within the scope of this book, regular consistency checks of a database are critical to verifying that data remains available.

Page Free Space Page

In order to track whether pages have space available for inserting rows, each data file contains Page Free Space (PFS) pages. These pages, which are the second page of the data file (see Figure 2-5) and located every 8,088 pages after that, track the amount of free space in the database. Each byte on the PFS page represents one subsequent page in the data file and provides some simple allocation information regarding the page, namely, it determines the approximate amount of free space on the page.

When the database engine needs to store LOB data or data for heaps, it needs to know where the next available page is and how full the currently allocated pages are. This functionality is provided by PFS pages. Within each byte are flags that identify the current amount if space that is being used. Bits 0-2 determine whether the page is in one of the following free space states:

- Page is empty
- 1 to 50 percent full
- 51 to 80 percent full
- 81 to 95 percent full
- 96 to 100 percent full

Along with free space, PFS pages also contain bits to identify a few other types of information for a page. For instance, bit 3 determines whether there are ghost records on a page. Bit 4 identifies if the page is part of the Index Allocation Map, described later in this chapter. Bit 5 states whether the page is a mixed page. And finally, bit 6 identifies if a page has been allocated.

Through the additional flags, or bits, SQL Server can determine what and how a page is being used from a high level. It can determine if it is currently allocated. If not, is it available for LOB or heap data? If it is currently allocated, the PFS page then provides the first purpose described earlier in this section.

Finally, when the ghost cleanup process runs, the process doesn't need to check every page in a database for records to clean up. Instead, the PFS page can be checked and only those pages with ghost records need to be accessed.

■ **Note**   The indexes themselves handle free space and page allocation for non-LOB data and indexes. The allocation of pages for these structures is determined by the definition of the structure.

Global Allocation Map Page

Similar to the PFS page is the Global Allocation Map (GAM) page. This page determines whether an extent has been designated for use as a uniform extent. A secondary purpose of the GAM page is in assisting in determining whether the extent is free and available for allocation.

Each GAM page provides a map of all of subsequent extents in each GAM interval. A GAM interval consists of the 64,000 extents, or 4GB, that follow the GAM page. Each bit on the GAM page represents one extent following the GAM page. The first GAM page is located on page 2 of the database file (see Figure 2-5).

To determine whether an extent has been allocated to a uniform extent, SQL Server checks the bit in the GAM page that represents the extent. If the extent is allocated, then the bit is set to 0. When it is set to 1, the extent is free and available for other purposes.

Shared Global Allocation Map Page

Nearly identically to the GAM page is the Shared Global Allocation Map (SGAM) page. The primary difference between the pages is that the SGAM page determines whether an extent is allocated as a mixed extent. Like the GAM page, the SGAM page is also used to determine whether pages are available for allocation.

Each SGAM page provides a map of all of subsequent extents in each SGAM interval. An SGAM interval consists of the 64,000 extents, or 4GB, that follow the SGAM page. Each bit on the SGAM page represents one extent following the SGAM page. The first SGAM page is located on page 3, after the GAM page of the database file (see Figure 2-5).

The SGAM pages determine when an extent has been allocated for use as a mixed extent. If the extent is allocated for this purpose and has a free page, the bit is set to 1. When it is set to 0, the extent is either not used as a mixed extent or it is a mixed extent with all pages in use.

Differential Changed Map Page

The next page to discuss is the Differential Change Map (DCM) page. This page is used to determine whether an extent in a GAM interval has changed. When an extent changes, a bit value is changed from 0 to 1. These bits are stored in a bitmap row on the DCM page with each bit representing an extent.

DCM pages are used track which extents have changed between full database backups. Whenever a full database backup occurs, all of the bits on the DCM page are reset back to 0. The bit then changes back to 1 when a change occurs within the associated extent.

The primary use for DCM pages is to provide a list of extents that have been modified for differential backups. Instead of checking every page or extent in the database to see if it has changed, the DCM pages provide the list of extents to backup.

The first DCM page is located at page 6 of the data file. Subsequent DCM pages occur for each GAM interval in the data file.

Bulk Changed Map Page

After the DCM page is the Bulk Changed Map (BCM) page. The BCM page is used to indicate when an extent in a GAM interval has been modified by a minimally logged operation. Any extent that is affected by a minimally logged operation will have its bit value set to 1 and those that have not will be set to 0. The bits are stored in a bitmap row on the BCM page with each bit representing an extent in the GAM interval.

As the name implies, BCM pages are used in conjunction with the BULK_LOGGED recovery model. When the database uses this recovery model, the BCM page is used to identify extents that were modified with a minimally logged operation since the last transaction log backup. When the transaction log backup completes, the bits on the BCM page are reset to 0.

The first BCM page is located at page 7 of the data file. Subsequent BCM pages occur for each GAM interval in the data file.

Index Allocation Map Page

Most of the pages discussed so far provide information about whether there is data on the pages they cover. More important than whether a page is open and available, SQL Server needs to know whether the information on a page is associated to a specific table or index. The pages that provide this information are the Index Allocation Map (IAM) pages.

Every table or index first starts with an IAM page. This page indicates which extents within a GAM interval, discussed previously, are associated with the table or index. If a table or index crosses more than one GAM interval, there will be more than one IAM page for the table or index.

There are four types of pages that an IAM page associates with a table or index. These are data, index, large object, and small-large object pages. The IAM page accomplishes the association of the pages to the table or index through a bitmap row on the IAM page.

Besides the bitmap row, there is also an IAM header row on the IAM page. The IAM header provides the sequence number of IAM pages for a table or index. It also contains the starting page for the GAM interval that the IAM page is associated with. Finally, the row contains a single-page allocation array. This is used when less than an extent has been allocated to a table or index.

The value in understanding the IAM page is that it provides a map and root through which all of the pages of a table or indexes come together. This page is used when all of the extents for a table or index need to be determined.

Data Page

Data pages are likely the most prevalent type of pages in any database. Data pages are used to store the data from rows in the database's tables. Except for a few data types, all data for a record is located on data pages. The exception to this rule is columns that store data in LOB data types. That information is stored on large object pages, discussed later in this section.

An understanding of data pages is important in relationship to indexing internals. The understanding is important because data pages are the most common page that will be looked at when looking at the internals of an index. When you get to the lowest levels of the index, data pages will always be found.

Index Page

Similar to data pages are index pages. These pages provide information on the structure of indexes and where data pages are located. For clustered indexes, the index pages are used to build the hierarchy of pages that are used to navigate the clustered index. With non-clustered indexes, index pages perform the same function but are also used to store the key values that comprise the index.

As mentioned, index pages are used to build the hierarchy of pages within in index. To accomplish this, the data contained in an index page provides a mapping of key values and page addresses. The key value is the key value from the index that the first sorted row on the child table contains and the page address identifies where to locate this.

Index pages are constructed similarly to other page types. The page has a page header that contains all of the standard information, such as page type, allocation unit, partition ID, and the allocation status. The row offset array contains pointers to where the index data rows are located on the page. The index data rows contain two pieces of information: the key value and a page address (these were described earlier).

Understanding index pages is important since they provide a map of how all of the data pages in an index are hooked together.

Large Object Page

As previously discussed, the limit for data on a single page is 8 KBB. The max size, though, for some data types can be as high as 2GB. For these data types, another storage mechanism is required to store the data. For this there is a large object page type.

The data types that can utilize LOB Pages include text, ntext, image, nvarchar(max), varchar(max), varbinary(max), and xml. When the data for one of these data types is stored on a data page, the LOB page will be used if the size of the row will exceed 8 KBB. In these cases, the column will contain references to the LOB pages required for the data and it will be stored on LOB pages instead (see Figure 2-6).

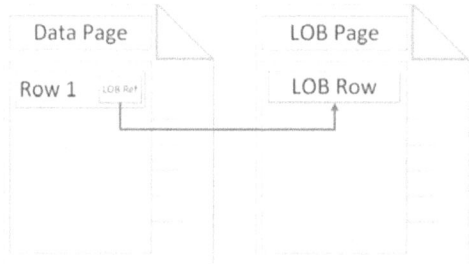

Figure 2-6. *Data page link to LOB page*

Organizing Pages

So far you've looked at the low level components that make up the internals for indexing. While these pieces are important to indexing, the structures in which these components are organized are where the value of indexing is realized. SQL Server utilizes a number of different organizational structures for storing data in the database.

The organizational structures in SQL Server 2012 are

- Heap

- B-Tree

- Columnar

These structures all map to specific index types that will be discussed later in this chapter. In this section, you'll examine each of the ways to organize pages to build that understanding.

■ **Note**   In the structures for organizing indexes, the levels of the index that contain index pages are considered non-leaf levels. When referencing levels that contain data pages, the levels are called leaf levels.

Heap Structure

The default structure for organizing pages is called a heap. Heaps occur when a B-tree structure, discussed in the next section, is not used to organize the data pages in a table. Conceptually, a heap can be envisioned to be a pile of data pages in no particular order, as shown in Figure 2-7. In the example, the only way to retrieve all of the "Madison" records is to check each page to see if "Madison" is on the page.

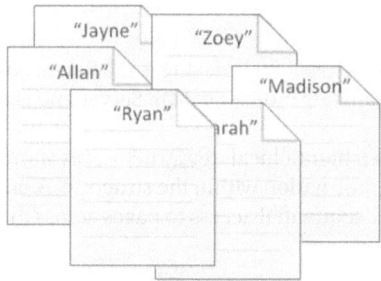

Figure 2-7. *Heap pile example*

From an internals perspective, though, heaps are more than a pile of pages. While unsorted, heaps have a few key components that organize the pages for easy access. All heaps start with an IAM page, shown in Figure 2-8. IAM pages, as discussed, map out which extents and single page allocations within a GAM interval are associated with an index. For a heap, the IAM page is the only mechanism for associating data pages and extents to a heap. As mentioned, the heap structure does not enforce any sort of ordering on the pages that are associated with the heap. The first page available in a heap is the first page found in the database file for the heap.

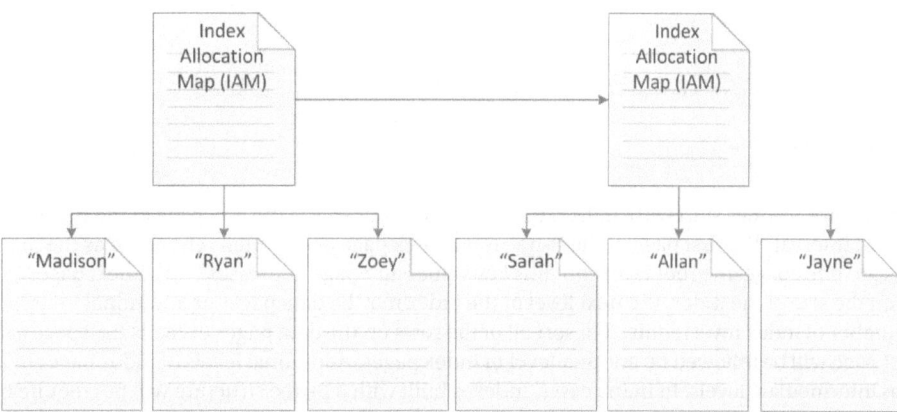

Figure 2-8. *Heap structure*

The IAM page lists all of the data pages associated with the heap. The data pages for the heap store the rows for the table, with the use of LOB pages as needed. When the IAM page has no more pages available to allocate in the GAM interval, a new IAM page is allocated to the heap and the next set of pages and their corresponding rows are added to the heap, as detailed in Figure 2-1. As the image shows, a heap structure is flat. From top to bottom, there is only ever one level from the IAM pages to the data pages of the structure.

While a heap provides a mechanism for organizing pages, it does not relate to an index type. A heap structure is used when a table does not have a clustered index. When a heap stores rows in a table, they are inserted without an enforced order. This happens because, as opposed to a clustered index, a sort order based on specific columns does not exist on a heap.

B-Tree Structure

The second available structure that can be used for indexing is the Balanced-tree, or B-tree, structure. It is the most commonly used structure for organizing indexes in SQL Server and is used by both clustered and non-clustered indexes.

In a B-tree, pages are organized in a hierarchical tree structure, as shown in Figure 2-9. Within the structure, pages sorted to optimize searches for information within the structure. Along with the sorting, relationships between pages are maintained to allow sequential access to pages across the levels of the index.

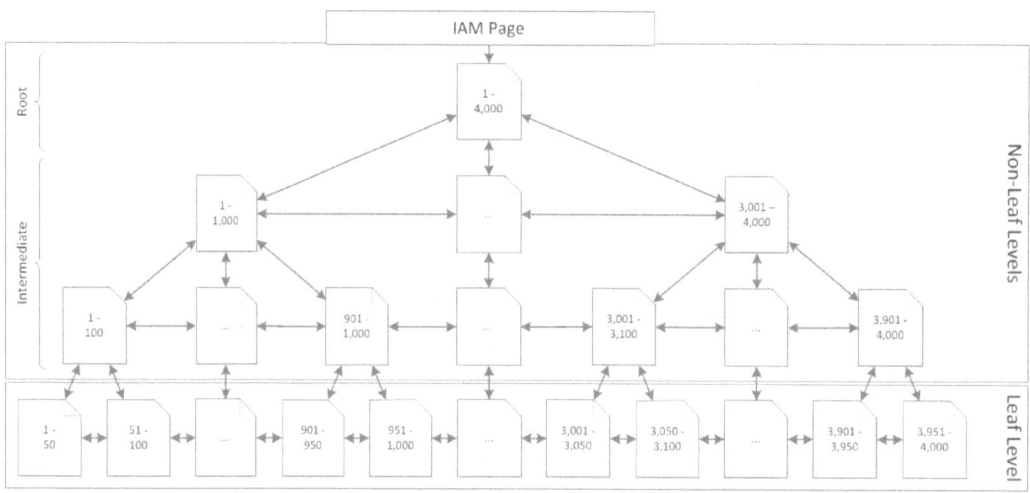

Figure 2-9. *B-tree structure*

Similar to heaps, B-trees start with an IAM page that identifies where the first page of the B-tree is located within the GAM interval. The first page of the B-tree is an index page and is often referred to as the root level of the index. As an index page, the root level contains key values and page addresses for the next pages in the index. Depending on the size of the index, the next level of the index may be data pages or additional index pages.

If the number of index rows required to sort all of the rows on the data pages exceeds the space available, then the root page will be followed by another level of index pages. Additional levels of index pages in a B-tree are referred to as intermediate levels. In many cases, indexes built with a B-tree structure will not require more than one or two intermediate levels. Even with a wide indexing key, millions to billions of rows can be sorted with just a few levels.

The next level of pages below the root and intermediate levels of the indexes, referred to as the *non-leaf levels*, is the *leaf level* (see Figure 2-9). The leaf level contains all of the data pages for the index. The data pages are where all of the key values and the non-key values for the row are stored. Non-key values are never stored on the Index pages.

Another differentiator between heaps and B-trees is the ability within the index levels to perform sequential page reads. Pages contain previous page and next page properties in the page headers. With index and data pages, these properties are populated and can be used to traverse the B-tree to find the next requested row from the B-tree without returning to the root level of the index. To illustrate this, consider a situation where you request the rows with key values between 925 and 3,025 from the index shown in Figure 2-9. Through a B-tree, this operation can be done by traversing the B-tree down to key value 925, shown in Figure 2-10. After that, the rows through key value 3,025 can be retrieved by accessing all pages after the first page in order, finishing the operation when the last key value is encountered.

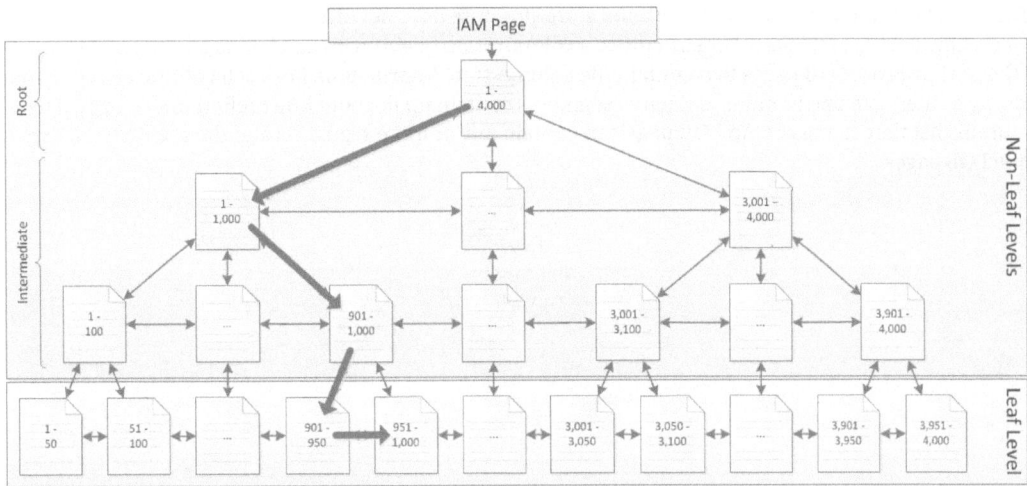

Figure 2-10. *B-tree sequential read*

One option available for tables and indexes is the ability to partition these structures. Partitioning changes the physical implementation of the index and how the index and data pages are organized. From the perspective of the B-tree structure, each partition in an index has its own B-tree. If a table is partitioned into three different partitions, there will then be three B-tree structures for the index.

Column Store Structure

SQL Server 2012 introduces a new organizational structure for indexes called column store, which is based on Microsoft's Vertipaq™ technology. This new structure is used by the new column store non-clustered index type. The column store structure makes a divergence from the traditional method of storing and indexing data from a row-wise to a column-wise format. This means that instead of storing all of the values for a row with all of the other values in the row, the values are stored with the values of the same column grouped together. For instance, in the example in Figure 2-11, instead of four row "groups" stored on the page, three column "groups" are stored.

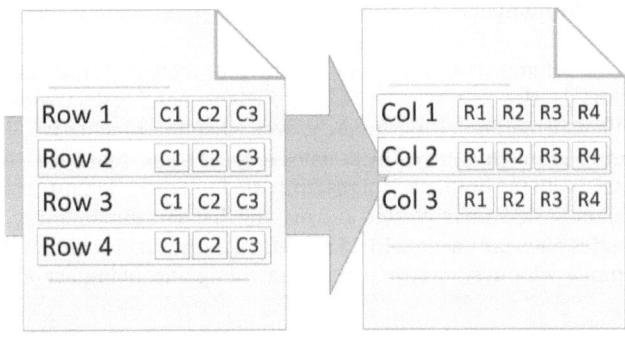

Figure 2-11. *Row-wise vs. column-wise storage*

The physical implementation of the column store structure does not introduce any new page types; it instead utilizes existing page types. Like other structures, a column store begins with an IAM page, shown in Figure 2-12. From the IAM page are LOB pages that contain the column store information. For each column stored in the column store, there are one or more segments. Segments contain up to about one million rows worth of data for the columns that they represent. An LOB page can contain one or more segments and the segments can span multiple LOB pages.

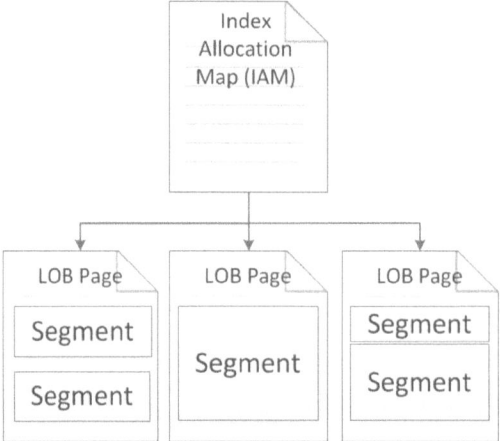

Figure 2-12. Column store structure

Within each segment is a hash dictionary that is used to map the data that comprises the segment of the column store. The hash dictionary also contains the minimum and maximum values for the data in the segment. This information is used by SQL Server during query execution to eliminate segments during query execution.

One of the advantages of the column store structure is its ability to leverage compression. Since each segment of the column store structure contains the same type of data both from a data type to a contents perspective, SQL Server has a greater likelihood of being able to utilize compression on the data. The compression used by the column store is similar to page level compression. It utilizes dictionary compression to remove similar values throughout the segment. There are two main differences between page and column store compression. First, while page compression is optional, column store compression is mandatory and cannot be disabled. Second, page compression is limited to compressing the values on a single page. Alternately, column store compression is for the entire segment, which may span multiple pages or could have multiple segments on the same page. Regardless of the number of pages or segments on a page, column store compression is contained to the segment.

Another advantage to the column store is that only the columns requested from the column store are returned. We often reprimand developers not to use SELECT * when querying databases; instead they are asked to request only the columns that are required. Unfortunately, even when this practice is followed, all of the columns for the row are still read from disk into memory. The practice reduces some network traffic and streamlines execution, but it doesn't assist with the bottleneck of reading data from disk. Column store addresses this issue by only reading from the columns that are requested and moving that data into memory. Along these same lines, according to Microsoft, queries often only access 10-15 percent of the available columns in a table[1]. The reduction in the columns retrieved from a column store structure will have a significant impact on performance and I/O.

---

[1] **Columnstore Indexes: A New Feature in SQL Server known as Project "Apollo,"** Microsoft SQL Server Team Blog, http://blogs.technet.com/b/dataplatforminsider/archive/2011/08/04/columnstore-indexes-a-new-feature-in-sql-server-known-as-project-apollo.aspx

---

■ **Note**   The column store structure and related column store index are only available in SQL Server 2012 Enterprise, Evaluation, and Developer editions.

Examining Pages

The first part of this chapter outlined the types of pages found in SQL Server databases. On top of that, you've looked at the structures available for organizing and managing the relationship between pages within your databases. In this next section, you are going to look at the tools available for examining pages in your database. The purpose of using these tools is to provide a foundation from which you'll be able to look at the behaviors of indexes in this chapter and throughout the rest of the book. Also, this will provide you with the knowledge to do your own exploring of indexes in your environment.

■ **Warning**   The tools used in this section are undocumented and unsupported. They do not appear in Books Online and their functionality can change without notice. That being said, these tools have been around for quite some time and there are many blog posts that describe their behavior. Additional resources for using these tools can be found at www.sqlskills.com.

DBCC EXTENTINFO

The DBCC command DBCC EXTENTINFO provides information about extents allocations that occur within a database. The command can be used to identify how extents have been allocated and whether the extents being used are mixed or uniform. The syntax for using DBCC EXTENTINFO is shown in Listing 2-1. When using the command, there are four parameters that can be populated; these are defined in Table 2-1.

Listing 2-1. DBCC EXTENTINFO Syntax

```
DBCC EXTENTINFO ( {database_name | database_id | 0}
  , {table_name | table_object_id}, { index_name | index_id | -1}
  , { partition_id | 0}
```

When executing DBCC EXTENTINFO, a dataset is returned. The results include the columns defined in Table 2-2. For every extent allocation, there will be one row in the results. Since extents are comprised of eight pages, there can be as many as eight allocations for an extent when there are single page allocations, such as when mixed extents are used. When uniform extents are used, there will be only one extent allocation and one row returned for the extent.

To demonstrate how the command works, let's walk through a couple examples to observer how extents are allocated. In the first example, shown in Listing 2-2, you will create a database named Chapter2Internals. In the database, you will create a table named dbo.IndexInternalsOne with a table definition that inserts one row per data page. Into the table you will first insert four records. The last statement in Listing 2-2 is DBCC EXTENTINFO command against dbo.IndexInternalsOne.

Table 2-1. *DBCC EXTENTINFO Parameters*

Parameter	Description
database_name | database_id	Specifies either the database name or database ID where the page will be retrieved. If the value 0 is provided for this parameter or the parameter is not set, then the current database will be used.
table_name | table_object_id	Specifies which table to return in the output by either providing the table name and object_ID for the table. If no value is provided, the output will include results for all tables.
index_name | index_id	Specifies which index to return in the output by either providing the index name or index_ID. If -1 or no value is provided, then the output will include results for all indexes on the table.
partition_id	Specifies which partition of the index to return in the output by providing the partition number. If 0 or no value is provided, then the output will include results for all partitions on the index.

Table 2-2. *DBCC EXTENTINFO Output Columns*

Parameter	Description
file_id	File number where the page is located.
page_id	Page number for the page.
pg_alloc	Number of pages allocated from the extent to the object.
ext_size	Size of the extent.
object_id	Object ID for the table.
index_id	Index ID associated with the heap or index.
partition_number	Partition number for the heap or index.
partition_id	Partition ID for the heap or index.
iam_chain_type	The type of IAM chain the extent is used for. Values can be in-row data, LOB data, and overflow data.
pfs_bytes	Bytes array that identifies the amount of free space, whether there are ghost records, if the page is an IAM page, if it is allocated, and if it is part of a mixed extent.

Listing 2-2. DBCC EXTENTINFO Example One

```
USE master
GO
CREATE DATABASE Chapter2Internals
GO
USE Chapter2Internals
GO
CREATE TABLE dbo.IndexInternalsOne
    (
    RowID INT IDENTITY(1,1)
```

```
    ,FillerData CHAR(8000)
    )
GO
INSERT INTO dbo.IndexInternalsOne DEFAULT VALUES
GO 4
DBCC EXTENTINFO(0, IndexInternalsOne, -1)
```

In the results from the DBCC command, shown in Figure 2-13, you can see that there were four pages allocated to the table. The items of interest in these results are the pg_alloc and ext_size columns. Both of these columns should have the number 1 in your results. This means that one page of the extent was allocated and used by the table. Even though pages 228, 230, and 231 are on the same extent, the pages are allocated separately because each insert was in a separate transaction. You can determine that the pages are on the same extent by dividing the page number by eight. In this case, pages 228, 230, and 231 are on the 28th extent in the database. The fourth page allocated to the table shows another interesting aspect of single page allocations. The page allocated is in the 33rd extent. This means that single page allocations to a table with less than eight pages may not be in the same extent in the database and may not even be on neighboring extents.

	file_id	page_id	pg_alloc	ext_size	object_id	index_id	partition_number	partition_id	iam_chain_type	pfs_bytes
1	1	228	1	1	245575913	0	1	72057594039042048	In-row data	0x6400000000000000
2	1	230	1	1	245575913	0	1	72057594039042048	In-row data	0x6400000000000000
3	1	231	1	1	245575913	0	1	72057594039042048	In-row data	0x6400000000000000
4	1	264	1	1	245575913	0	1	72057594039042048	In-row data	0x6400000000000000

Figure 2-13. DBCC EXTENTINFO for eight pages in dbo.IndexInternalsOne

Now you'll expand the example a bit further. For the second example, you'll perform two more sets of inserts into the table dbo.IndexInternalsOne, shown in Listing 2-3. In the first insert, you'll insert two records, which will require two pages. The second insert will insert another four rows, which will result in four additional pages. The final count pages for the table will be ten, which should change SQL Server from allocating pages via mixed extents to uniform extents.

Listing 2-3. DBCC EXTENTINFO Example Two

```
INSERT INTO dbo.IndexInternalsOne
VALUES ('Demo'),('Demo');
GO
INSERT INTO dbo.IndexInternalsOne DEFAULT VALUES
GO 4
DBCC EXTENTINFO(0, IndexInternalsOne, -1)
GO
```

The results from the second example, shown in Figure 2-14, show a couple of interesting pieces of information on how mixed and uniform extents are allocated. First, even though the first insert added two rows resulting in two new pages, numbered 265 and 266, these pages were still allocated one at a time, hence the term "single page allocation." Next is the insert that increased the size of the table by another four pages. Looking at the results, the four pages added were not allocated identically. The first two pages, numbered 267 and 268, were added as single page allocations. The other two pages, starting with page number 272, were added in an extent allocation that contained eight pages with two pages currently allocated, shown in columns ext_size and pg_alloc, respectively. One of the key takeaways in this example is that when the number of pages exceeds eight for a table or index, allocations change from mixed to uniform and previous allocations are not re-allocated.

	file_id	page_id	pg_alloc	ext_size	object_id	index_id	partition_number	partition_id	iam_chain_type	pfs_bytes
1	1	228	1	1	245575913	0	1	72057594039042048	In-row data	0x6400000000000000
2	1	230	1	1	245575913	0	1	72057594039042048	In-row data	0x6400000000000000
3	1	231	1	1	245575913	0	1	72057594039042048	In-row data	0x6400000000000000
4	1	264	1	1	245575913	0	1	72057594039042048	In-row data	0x6400000000000000
5	1	265	1	1	245575913	0	1	72057594039042048	In-row data	0x6400000000000000
6	1	266	1	1	245575913	0	1	72057594039042048	In-row data	0x6400000000000000
7	1	267	1	1	245575913	0	1	72057594039042048	In-row data	0x6400000000000000
8	1	268	1	1	245575913	0	1	72057594039042048	In-row data	0x6400000000000000
9	1	272	2	8	245575913	0	1	72057594039042048	In-row data	0x4444000000000000

Figure 2-14. DBCC EXTENTINFO for ten pages in dbo.IndexInternalsTwo

Now let's look at how to remove the initial single page allocations in the mixed extent from the table or index. Accomplishing this change is relatively simple: the table or index just needs to be rebuilt. The code in Listing 2-4 will rebuild the table dbo.IndexInternalsOne and then execute DBCC EXTENTINFO.

Listing 2-4. DBCC EXTENTINFO Example Three

```
ALTER TABLE dbo.IndexInternalsOne REBUILD
GO
DBCC EXTENTINFO(0, IndexInternalsOne, -1)
GO
```

In this third example, the rebuild of the table removed all of the single page allocations. Now instead of nine extent allocations, there are only two allocations (see Figure 2-15). Both allocations are for extents that contain eight pages. The one peculiar item in the results is the first allocation that has nine of eight pages allocated. The extra page allocated is the IAM page associated with the table or index. When a table or index begins with uniform extents, the IAM page is included in the count with the first extent. The reason that uniform extents are used is that SQL Server was able to determine during the insert that the number of pages allocated would exceed a single extent and skipped mixed extent allocations.

	file_id	page_id	pg_alloc	ext_size	object_id	index_id	partition_number	partition_id	iam_chain_type	pfs_bytes
1	1	280	9	8	245575913	0	1	72057594039107584	In-row data	0x4444444444444444
2	1	288	2	8	245575913	0	1	72057594039107584	In-row data	0x4444000000000000

Figure 2-15. DBCC EXTENTINFO for dbo.IndexInternalsOne after REBUILD

In the last three examples, you worked with an example that started with inserts that inserted one page per transaction. In the next example, you'll use DBCC EXTENTINFO to observe the behavior when more than eight pages are inserted into a table in the first transaction. Using the code in Listing 2-5, you'll build a new table named dbo.IndexInternalsTwo. Into this table, you'll insert nine rows, which will require nine pages to be allocated. Then you'll execute the DBCC command to see the results.

Listing 2-5. DBCC EXTENTINFO Example Four

```
CREATE TABLE dbo.IndexInternalsTwo
    (
    RowID INT IDENTITY(1,1)
    ,FillerData CHAR(8000)
    )
```

```
GO
INSERT INTO dbo.IndexInternalsTwo
VALUES ('Demo'),('Demo'),('Demo'),('Demo'),('Demo')
    ,('Demo'),('Demo'),('Demo'),('Demo');
GO
DBCC EXTENTINFO(0, IndexInternalsTwo, -1)
GO
```

As you can see in the results, shown in Figure 2-16, it doesn't matter how large the initial insert into a table is because the first pages allocated to the table or index will use single page allocation from mixed extents. Not until the ninth page is needed does the table make the switch from mixed to uniform extents, shown by the extent size of eight on the last row. Regardless of the size of the insert, extents are initially allocated one at a time.

	file_id	page_id	pg_alloc	ext_size	object_id	index_id	partition_number	partition_id	iam_chain_type	pfs_bytes
1	1	264	1	1	261575970	0	1	72057594039173120	In-row data	0x6400000000000000
2	1	266	1	1	261575970	0	1	72057594039173120	In-row data	0x6400000000000000
3	1	267	1	1	261575970	0	1	72057594039173120	In-row data	0x6400000000000000
4	1	268	1	1	261575970	0	1	72057594039173120	In-row data	0x6400000000000000
5	1	269	1	1	261575970	0	1	72057594039173120	In-row data	0x6400000000000000
6	1	271	1	1	261575970	0	1	72057594039173120	In-row data	0x6400000000000000
7	1	228	1	1	261575970	0	1	72057594039173120	In-row data	0x6400000000000000
8	1	229	1	1	261575970	0	1	72057594039173120	In-row data	0x6400000000000000
9	1	312	1	8	261575970	0	1	72057594039173120	In-row data	0x4400000000000000

Figure 2-16. *DBCC EXTENTINFO for dbo.IndexInternalsTwo*

As these examples have shown, DBCC EXTENTINFO can be extremely useful for investigating how pages are allocated to tables and indexes. Through the examples, you were able to verify the page and extent allocation information that was discussed earlier in this chapter. Using the DBCC command can be extremely useful when trying to investigate issues related to fragmentation and how pages have been allocated. In Chapter 6, you'll look at how to use this command to identify potential excessive use of extents.

DBCC IND

The next command that can be used to investigate indexes and their associated pages is DBCC IND. This command returns a list of all the pages associated with the requested object, which can be scoped to the database, table, or index level. The syntax for using DBCC IND is shown in Listing 2-6. When using the command, there are three parameters that can be populated; these are defined in Table 2-3.

Listing 2-6. DBCC IND Syntax

```
DBCC IND ( {'dbname' | dbid}, {'table_name' | table_object_id},
      {'index_name' | index_id | -1})
```

DBCC IND returns a dataset when executed. For every page that is allocated to the requested objects, one row is returned in the dataset; the columns are defined in Table 2-4. Unlike the previous DBCC EXTENTINFO, DBCC IND does explicitly return the IAM page in the results.

Within the results from DBCC EXTENTINFO results is a PageType column. This column identifies what type of page is returned through the DBCC command. The page types can include data, index, GAM, or any other of the page types discussed earlier in the chapter. A full list of the page types and the value identifying the page type is included in Table 2-5.

Table 2-3. *DBCC IND Parameters*

Parameter	Description
database_name | database_id	Specifies either the database name or database ID where the page list will be retrieved. If the value 0 is provided for this parameter or the parameter is not set, then the current database will be used.
table_name | table_object_id	Specifies which table to return in the output by either providing the table name or object_ID for the table. If no value is provided, the output will include results for all tables.
index_name | index_id	Specifies which index to return in the output by either providing the index name or index_ID. If -1 or no value is provided, the output will include results for all indexes on the table.

Table 2-4. *DBCC IND Output Columns*

Parameter	Description
PageFID	File number where the page is located.
PagePID	Page number for the page.
IAMFID	File ID where the IAM page is located.
IAMPID	Page ID for the page in the data file.
ObjectID	Object ID for the associated table.
IndexID	Index ID associated with the heap or index.
PartitionNumber	Partition number for the heap or index.
PartitionID	Partition ID for the heap or index.
iam_chain_type	The type of IAM chain the extent is used for. Values can be in-row data, LOB data, and overflow data.
PageType	Number identifying the page type. These are listed in Table 2-5.
IndexLevel	Level at which the page exists in the page organizational structure. The levels are organized from 0 to N, where 0 is the lowest level of the index and N is the index root.
NextPageFID	File number where the next page at the index level is located.
NextPagePID	Page number for the next page at the index level.
PrevPageFID	File number where the previous page at the index level is located.
PrevPagePID	Page number for the previous page at the index level.

Table 2-5. *Page Type Mappings*

Page Type	Description
1	Data page
2	Index page
3	Large object page
4	Large object page
8	Global Allocation Map page
9	Share Global Allocation Map page
10	Index Allocation Map page
11	Page Free Space page
13	Boot page
15	File header page
16	Differential Changed Map page
17	Bulk Changed Map page

The primary benefit of using DBCC IND is that it provides a list of all pages for a table or index with their locations in the database. You can use this to help investigate how indexes are behaving and where pages are ending up. To put this information into action, here are a couple demos.

For the first example, you'll revisit the tables created in the last section and examine the output for each of these in comparison to the DBCC EXTENTINFO output. The code example includes DBCC IND commands for IndexInternalsOne and IndexInternalsTwo, shown in Listing 2-7. The database ID passed in is 0 for the current database and the index ID is set to -1 to return pages for all indexes.

Listing 2-7. DBCC IND Example One

```
USE Chapter2Internals;
GO
DBCC IND (0, 'IndexInternalsOne',-1);
GO
DBCC IND (0, 'IndexInternalsTwo',-1);
```

In the DBCC EXTENTINFO examples, there were two extent allocations for the table IndexInternalsOne, shown in Figure 2-15. These results show that there were 11 pages allocated to the table. The DBCC IND results, shown in Figure 2-17, detail all of the pages that were part of the previous two extent allocations.

In these results, there was a single IAM page and ten Data pages allocated to the table. Where DBCC EXTENTINFO provided page 280 as the start of the extent allocations, containing nine pages, it was not possible to identify where the IAM page was based on that. It was instead in another extent that the results did not list, and the results for DBCC IND identify as being on page 270.

	PageFID	PagePID	IAMFID	IAMPID	ObjectID	IndexID	PartitionNumber	PartitionID	iam_chain_type	PageType	IndexLevel	NextPageFID	NextPagePID	PrevPageFID	PrevPagePID
1	1	270	NULL	NULL	245575913	0	1	72057594039107584	In-row data	10	NULL	0	0	0	0
2	1	280	1	270	245575913	0	1	72057594039107584	In-row data	1	0	1	281	0	0
3	1	281	1	270	245575913	0	1	72057594039107584	In-row data	1	0	1	282	1	280
4	1	282	1	270	245575913	0	1	72057594039107584	In-row data	1	0	1	283	1	281
5	1	283	1	270	245575913	0	1	72057594039107584	In-row data	1	0	1	284	1	282
6	1	284	1	270	245575913	0	1	72057594039107584	In-row data	1	0	1	285	1	283
7	1	285	1	270	245575913	0	1	72057594039107584	In-row data	1	0	1	286	1	284
8	1	286	1	270	245575913	0	1	72057594039107584	In-row data	1	0	1	287	1	285
9	1	287	1	270	245575913	0	1	72057594039107584	In-row data	1	0	1	288	1	286
10	1	288	1	270	245575913	0	1	72057594039107584	In-row data	1	0	1	289	1	287
11	1	289	1	270	245575913	0	1	72057594039107584	In-row data	1	0	0	0	1	288

Figure 2-17. *DBCC IND for dbo.IndexInternalsOne*

The next set of results from the example shows the output for DBCC IND against dbo.IndexInternalsTwo. These results, shown in Figure 2-18, are quite similar with the exception of the IAM page. Reviewing the results for the DBCC EXTENTINFO, in Figure 2-14, the extent allocations only account for nine pages being allocated to the table. In the results for dbo.IndexInternalsTwo, there are ten pages allocated, with one of them being the IAM page. The benefit of using DBCC IND for listing the page for an index is that you get the exact page numbers without having to make any guesses. Also, note that the index level in the results returns as level 0 with no intermediate levels. As stated earlier, heap structures are flat and the pages are in no particular order.

	PageFID	PagePID	IAMFID	IAMPID	ObjectID	IndexID	PartitionNumber	PartitionID	iam_chain_type	PageType	IndexLevel	NextPageFID	NextPagePID	PrevPageFID	PrevPagePID
1	1	265	NULL	NULL	261575970	0	1	72057594039173120	In-row data	10	NULL	0	0	0	0
2	1	264	1	265	261575970	0	1	72057594039173120	In-row data	1	0	0	0	0	0
3	1	266	1	265	261575970	0	1	72057594039173120	In-row data	1	0	0	0	0	0
4	1	267	1	265	261575970	0	1	72057594039173120	In-row data	1	0	0	0	0	0
5	1	268	1	265	261575970	0	1	72057594039173120	In-row data	1	0	0	0	0	0
6	1	269	1	265	261575970	0	1	72057594039173120	In-row data	1	0	0	0	0	0
7	1	271	1	265	261575970	0	1	72057594039173120	In-row data	1	0	0	0	0	0
8	1	228	1	265	261575970	0	1	72057594039173120	In-row data	1	0	0	0	0	0
9	1	229	1	265	261575970	0	1	72057594039173120	In-row data	1	0	0	0	0	0
10	1	312	1	265	261575970	0	1	72057594039173120	In-row data	1	0	0	0	0	0

Figure 2-18. *DBCC IND for dbo.IndexInternalsTwo*

As mentioned, the tables in the last example were organized in a heap structure. For the next example, you'll observe what the output from DBCC IND is when examining a table with a clustered index. In Listing 2-8, first the table dbo.IndexInternalsThree is created with a clustered index on the RowID column. Then, you'll insert four rows. Finally, the example executes DBCC IND on the table.

Listing 2-8. DBCC IND Example Two

```
USE Chapter2Internals
GO
CREATE TABLE dbo.IndexInternalsThree
    (
    RowID INT IDENTITY(1,1)
    ,FillerData CHAR(8000)
    ,CONSTRAINT PK_IndexInternalsThree PRIMARY KEY CLUSTERED (RowID)
    )
GO
INSERT INTO dbo.IndexInternalsThree DEFAULT VALUES
GO 4
DBCC IND (0, 'IndexInternalsThree',-1)
```

Figure 2-19 shows the results from this example involving dbo.IndexInternalsThree. Notice the change in how IndexLevel is being returned as compared to the previous example (Figure 2-18).

	PageFID	PagePID	IAMFID	IAMPID	ObjectID	IndexID	PartitionNumber	PartitionID	iam_chain_type	PageType	IndexLevel	NextPageFID	NextPagePID	PrevPageFID	PrevPagePID
1	1	273	NULL	NULL	277576027	1	1	72057594039238656	In-row data	10	NULL	0	0	0	0
2	1	272	1	273	277576027	1	1	72057594039238656	In-row data	1	0	1	275	0	0
3	1	274	1	273	277576027	1	1	72057594039238656	In-row data	2	1	0	0	0	0
4	1	275	1	273	277576027	1	1	72057594039238656	In-row data	1	0	1	276	1	272
5	1	276	1	273	277576027	1	1	72057594039238656	In-row data	1	0	1	277	1	275
6	1	277	1	273	277576027	1	1	72057594039238656	In-row data	1	0	0	0	1	276

Figure 2-19. *DBCC IND for dbo.IndexInternalsThree*

In this example, the index level for the third row in the results has an IndexLevel of 1 and also a PageType of 2, which is an index page. With these results, there is enough information to rebuild the B-Tree structure for the index, as seen in Figure 2-20. The B-Tree starts with the IAM page, which is page number 1:273. This page is linked to page 1:274, which is an index page at index level 1. Following that, pages 1:272, 1:275, 1:276, and 1:277 are at index level 0 and doubly linked to each other.

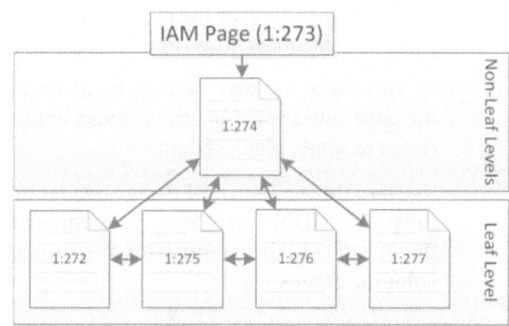

Figure 2-20. *DBCC IND for dbo.IndexInternalsThree*

Through both of these examples, you examined how to use DBCC IND to investigate the pages associated with a table or an index. As the examples showed, the command provides the information on all of the pages of the table or index, including the IAM page. These pages include the page numbers to identify where they are in the database. The relationships between the pages is also included, even the next and previous page numbers that are used to navigate the index for B-tree indexes.

DBCC PAGE

The last command available for examining pages is DBCC PAGE. While the other two commands provide information on the pages associate with tables and indexes, the output from DBCC PAGE provides a look at the contents of a page. The syntax for using DBCC PAGE is shown in Listing 2-9.

Listing 2-9. DBCC PAGE Syntax

```
DBCC PAGE ( { database_name | database_id | 0}, file_number, page_number
    [,print_option ={0|1|2|3} ])
```

The DBCC PAGE command accepts a number of parameters. Through the parameters, the command is able to determine the database and specific page requested, which is then returned in the requested format. The parameters for DBCC PAGE are detailed in Table 2-6.

Table 2-6. *DBCC PAGE Parameters*

Parameter	Description
database_name | database_id	Specifies either the database name or database ID where the page will be retrieved. If the value 0 is provided for this parameter or the parameter is not set, the current database will be used.
file_number	Specifies the file number for the data file in the database from where the page will be retrieved.
page_number	Specifies the page number in the database file that will be retrieved.
print_option	Specifies how the output should be returned. There are four print options available. **0 – Page Header Only:** Returns only the page header information. **1 – Hex Rows:** Returns the page header information, all of the rows on the page, and the offset array. In this output, each row is returned individually. **2 – Hex Data:** Returns the page header information, all of the rows on the page, and the offset array. Unlike option 1, the output shows all of the rows are single block of data. **3 – Data Rows:** Returns the page header information, all of the rows on the page, and the offset array. This option differs from the other options in that the data in the columns for the row are translated as listed with their columns names. This parameter is optional and 0 is used as the default when no option is selected.

■ **Note**   By default, the DBCC PAGE command outputs its messages to the SQL Server event log. In most situations, this is not the ideal output mechanism. Trace flag 3604 allows you to modify this behavior. By utilizing this trace flag, the output from the DBCC statements returns to the Messages tab in SQL Server Management Studio.

Through DBCC PAGE and its print options, everything that is on a page can be retrieved. There are a few reasons why you might want to look at the contents of a page. To start with, looking at an index or data page can help you understand why an index is behaving in one manner or another. You gain insight into how the data within the row is structured, which may cause rows to be larger than expected. The sizes of rows do have an important impact on how indexes behave, since as a row gets larger, the number of pages required to store the indexes increase. An increase in the number of pages for an index increases the resources required to use the index, which results in longer query times and, in some cases, a change in how or which indexes will be utilized. Another reason to use DBCC PAGE is to observer what happens to a data page when certain operations occur. As the examples later in this chapter will illustrate, DBCC PAGE can be used to uncover what happens during page splits and forwarded record operations.

To help demonstrate how to use DBCC PAGE, you'll run through a few demonstrations with each of the print options. These demos will be based on the code in Listing 2-10, which uses DBCC IND to identify page numbers for the examples. For each example, you'll look at some of the ways the results can differ between page types. While the page numbers in your database may differ slightly, the demos are based on an IAM page of 278, Index page of 279, and Data page of 296, as shown in Figure 2-21.

Listing 2-10. DBCC IND Query for DBCC PAGE Examples

```
USE [Chapter2Internals];
GO
CREATE TABLE dbo.IndexInternalsFour
    (
    RowID int IDENTITY(1,1) NOT NULL
    ,FillerData varchar(2000) NULL
    ,CONSTRAINT PK_IndexInternalsFour PRIMARY KEY CLUSTERED ([RowID] ASC)
    );
INSERT INTO dbo.IndexInternalsFour (FillerData)
VALUES (REPLICATE(1,2000)),(REPLICATE(2,2000)),(REPLICATE(3,2000))
    ,(REPLICATE(4,2000)),(REPLICATE(5,25));
GO
DBCC IND(0, 'dbo.IndexInternalsFour', -1);
GO
```

	PageFID	PagePID	IAMFID	IAMPID	ObjectID	IndexID	PartitionNumber	PartitionID	iam_chain_type	PageType	IndexLevel	NextPageFID	NextPagePID	PrevPageFID	PrevPagePID
1	1	278	NULL	NULL	293576084	1	1	72057594039304192	In-row data	10	NULL	0	0	0	0
2	1	277	1	278	293576084	1	1	72057594039304192	In-row data	1	0	1	296	0	0
3	1	279	1	278	293576084	1	1	72057594039304192	In-row data	2	1	0	0	0	0
4	1	296	1	278	293576084	1	1	72057594039304192	In-row data	1	0	0	0	1	277

Figure 2-21. DBCC IND results for dbo.IndexInternalsFour

Page Header Only Print Option

The first print option available for DBCC PAGE is the page header only where print_option equals 0. With this option, only the page header is returned in the output from the DBCC command. The page header is returned will all DBCC PAGE requests; using this option just limits the results to only the page header. Two sections are returned as part of the page header.

The first section returned is the buffer information. The buffer provides information on where the page is currently located in memory in SQL Server. In order to read a page, the page must first be retrieved from disk and placed in memory. This section provides the address that could be used to find the memory location of the page.

The second section is the actual page header. The page header contains a number of attributes that describe the page and the contents of the page. Not all of the attributes are currently in use by SQL Server, but there are a number of attributes that are worth understanding. These key attributes are listed and defined in Table 2-7.

To demonstrate the use of DBCC PAGE for the page header only option the code in Listing 2-11 can be used. Your results should be similar to those found in Figure 2-22. In these results, you can see the page number at the top of the page indicating that it is page 1:279. The m_type is 2, which translates to being an index page. The m_slotCnt shows that there are two rows on the page. Referring back to Figure 2-21, the row count would correlate to the two index records needed to map data pages 1:277 and 1:296 to the index. Finally, the allocations statuses show that the page is allocated on the GAM page, it is part of mixed extent (per PFS page), and the page has been changed since the last full backup (per the DCM page).

Table 2-7. *Page Header Key Attribute Definitions*

Attribute	Definition
m_pageId	File ID and page number for the page.
m_type	The type of page returned; see the page type list in Table 2-5.
Metadata: AllocUnitId	Allocation unit ID from that maps the catalog view sys.allocation_units.
Metadata: PartitionId	Partition ID for the table or index. This maps to partition_ID in the catalog view sys.partitions.
Metadata: ObjectId	Object ID for the table. This maps to the object_ID in the catalog view sys.tables.
Metadata: IndexId	Index ID for the table or index. This maps to the index_ID in the catalog view sys.indexes.
m_prevPage	Previous page in the index structure. This is used in B-tree indexes to allow reading sequential pages along index levels.
m_nextPage	Next page in the index structure. This is used in B-tree indexes to allow reading sequential pages along index levels.
m_slotCnt	Number of slots, or rows, on the page.
Allocation Status	Lists the locations of the GAM, SGAM, PFS, DIFF (or DCM), and ML (or BCM) pages for the page requested. It also includes the status for each from those metadata pages.

Listing 2-11. DBCC PAGE with Page Header Only Print Option

```
DBCC TRACEON(3604)
DBCC PAGE(0,1,279,0)
```

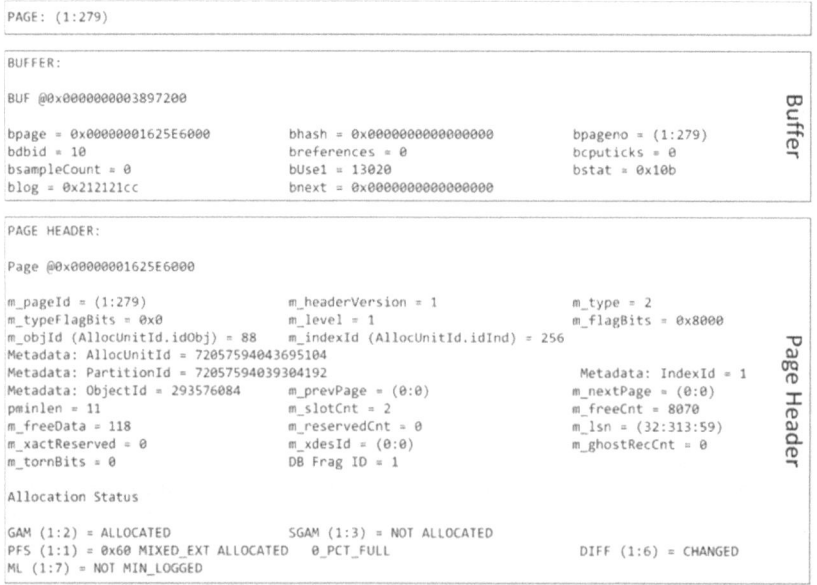

Figure 2-22. *DBCC PAGE output for page header only print option*

As the page header only option shows, there is a lot of useful information in the page header. In fact, you are provided enough information to envision how this page relates to the other pages in the index and the extent it occupies.

Hex Rows Print Option

The next print option available for DBCC PAGE is the hex rows print option, where print_option equals 1. This print option expands on the previous option adding into the output an entry for every slot on the page and the offset array that describes the location of each slot on the page.

The data section of the page repeats for every row that is on the page and contains all of the metadata and the data associated with that row. For the metadata, the row includes the slot number, page offset, record type, and record attributes. This information helps define the row and what contributes besides the size of the data to the row size. At the end of the slot is a memory dump of the row. The memory dump displays the row in a hex format that, while not easily read by humans, contains all of the data for the row. For more on the attributes and their definitions, see Table 2-8.

Table 2-8. *Hex Rows Key Attribute Definitions*

Attribute	Definition
Slot	The position of the row on the page. The count is 0 based and starts immediately after the page header.
Offset	Physical byte location of the row on the page.
Length	The length of the row on the page.
Record Type	The type of row. Some possible values are INDEX_RECORD and PRIMARY_RECORD.
Record Attributes	List of attributes on the row that contribute to the size of the row. These can include the NULL_BITMAP and the VARIABLE_COLUMNS array
Record Size	The length of the row on the page.
Memory Dump	The memory location for the data on the page. For the hex rows option, it is limited to the information in that slot. The memory address is provided and afterwards a hex dump of the data stored in the slot.

The offset array is the last section of information included in the hex row option results. The offset array contains two pieces of information for each row on the table. The first piece of information is the slot number with its hex representation. The second piece is the byte location for the slot on the page. With these two pieces of information, any row on the page can be located and returned.

For the hex rows example, you'll continue to investigate the index page (1:279) that you looked at in the last section. This time, you'll use the hex rows print option, which is when print_option of 1 is used in DBCC PAGE, as show in Listing 2-12.

The results for the DBCC PAGE command will be longer than the previous execution, since this time it includes the row data with the page header. To focus on the new information, the buffer and page header results have been excluded in the sample output in Figure 2-23. In the data section, there are two slots shown, slot 0 and slot 1. These slots map to the two index rows on the page, which can be verified through the record type of INDEX_RECORD for each of the rows. The hex data for the rows contains the page and range information for the index record, but that isn't translated with this print option. The last section has the offset table containing the slot information for both of the rows on the table. Note that the offset ends with 0 and counts up from the bottom. This matches to how the offset array was described earlier in the chapter. The rows start after the header incrementing up, while the offset array starts at the end of the page incrementing backwards. In this manner, new rows can be added to the table without reorganizing the page.

Listing 2-12. DBCC PAGE with Hex Rows Print Option

```
DBCC TRACEON(3604)
DBCC PAGE(0,1,279,1)
```

Figure 2-23. *DBCC PAGE output for hex rows print option*

The hex row print option is a bit more useful that the first print option. It includes the page header information but expands on it to provide insight into the actual rows on the page. This information can prove valuable when you want to look at a row to determine its size on the page and why it may be larger than expected.

Hex Data Print Option

The third print option available for DBCC PAGE is the hex data print option, where print_option equals 2. This print option, like the previous option, starts with the output from the page header only print option and adds on to it. The information added through this option includes the hex output of the data section of the page and the offset array. With the data section, the page is output complete and unformatted as it appears on the actual page. The output in this format can be useful when you want to see the page in its raw form.

To demonstrate the hex data print option, you'll use the script in Listing 2-13. In it the DBCC PAGE command is used to retrieve the page from `dbo.IndexInternalsFour` that contains the last row. This row contains 25 fives in the `FillerData` column.

Listing 2-13. DBCC PAGE with Hex Data Print Option

```
DBCC TRACEON(3604)
DBCC PAGE(0,1,279,2)
```

In the results, shown in Figure 2-24, the output contains a large block of characters in the data section. The block contains three components. On the far left is page address information, such as 0000000041438000. The page address identifies where on the page the information is located. The middle section contains the hex data that is contain in that section of the page. The right side of the character block contains the character representation of the hex data. For the most part, this data is not legible, except when it comes to character data being stored from character data types, such as `char` and `nchar`. The sixth row of the character data shows the start of the 25 fives with the value wrapping to the next line.

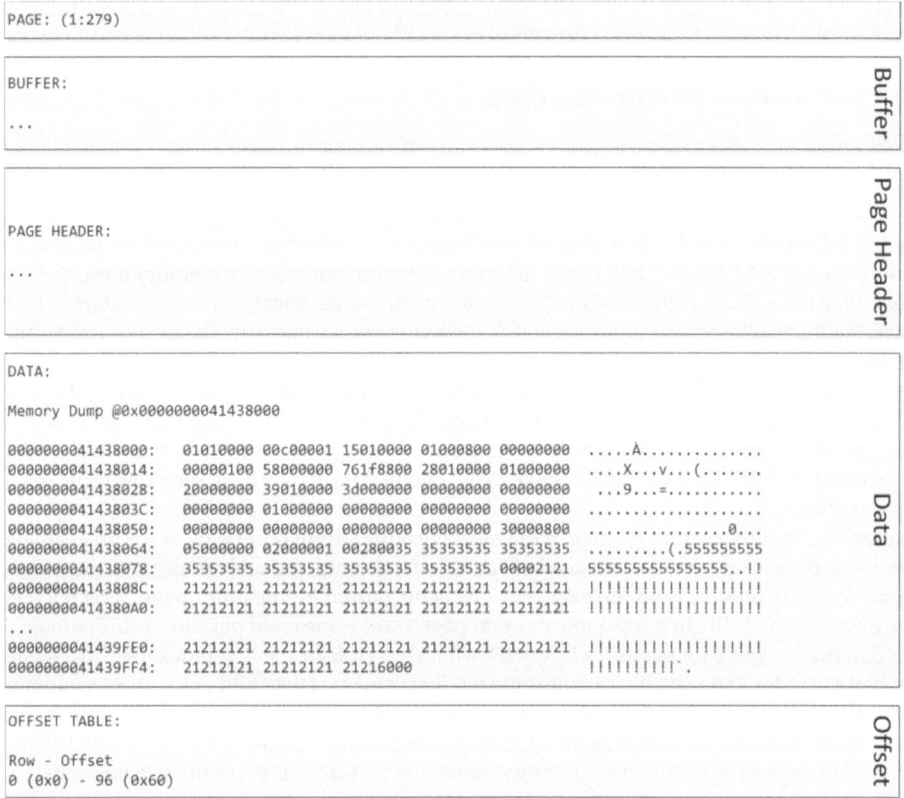

Figure 2-24. *DBCC PAGE output for Hex Data Only print option*

Initially, the hex data print option may seem less useful that the other print options. In many situations this will be the case. The true value in this print option is that it DBCC PAGE doesn't try to interpret the page for you. It displays the page as-is. With the other print options, the output will sometimes be reordered to conform to expect slot orders; an example of this is demonstrated in Chapter 5.

Row Data Print Option

The last print option available for DBCC PAGE is the row data print option, where print_option equals 3. The output from this print option can change depending on the type of page that is being requested. The basic information returned for most pages is identical to that returned from the hex rows print option: the data split per row in the hex format. The output varies, though, when it comes to data pages and index pages. For these page types, this print option provides some extremely useful information about the page.

■ **Note**   You can use the WITH TABLERESULTS option with DBCC PAGE to output the results from the command to a result set instead of messages. This option is useful when you want to insert the results returned from the DBCC command into a table.

To show the differences between the data and index page outputs, let's walk through another example. This example will use the table dbo.IndexInternalsFour that was created in Listing 2-10. In the demo for this print option, shown in Listing 2-14, you'll execute DBCC PAGE against one of the data pages and the index page for the table.

Listing 2-14. DBCC PAGE with Row Data Print Option

```
DBCC TRACEON(3604)
DBCC PAGE(0,1,296,3) -- Data page
DBCC PAGE(0,1,279,3) -- Index page
```

Comparing the results from the data page, shown in Figure 2-25, to the output from the hex data print option, shown in Figure 2-24, there is one major difference. Underneath the hex memory dump for the slot, all of the column details from the row are decode and presented in a legible format. It starts with Slot 0 Column 1, which contains the RowID column, which it shows to have a value of 5. The next column, Column 2, is the FillerData column, which contains 25 fives. For each of these columns, the physical length is noted along with the offset of the value within the row. The last value provided on the data section of the page is the KeyHashValue. This value isn't actually stored on the page. Instead it is a hash value that was created when the page was placed in memory based on the keys on the page. This value is shown in tools that are used by SQL Server to report information about pages back to the end user; you may have seen this value before while investigating deadlocks.

With the index page, there isn't a change in the message output from other page types. Instead, the difference with this page is the result set. Instead of just a message output, a table is also returned. The table returns one row for every index row on the page. Reviewing the output for the index page, shown in Figure 2-26, there are two rows returned. The first row indicates that page 1:277 is the child page to the index page. It also shows that the key value for the index is RowID, which is NULL for the first index row. This means that this is the start of the index and no values are limiting the first values on the child page. The second row maps to page 1:296 with a key value of 5. In this case, the key value indicates that the first row on the child page has a RowID of 5. Since the key value can change from index to index, the results from the DBCC PAGE command with these options will change as well. For every index variation, the output will return the relevant values for the index.

The row data print option is one of the most useful options for the DBCC PAGE command. For data pages, it provides total insight into the data stored on the page, how much space it takes up, and its position. This allows you a direct line into understanding why only certain rows may be fitting on the page and why, for instance, a page split may have occurred. The result set from the index page output is equally as useful. The ability to map the index rows to pages and return the key values can provide much insight into how the index is organized and how the pages are laid out.

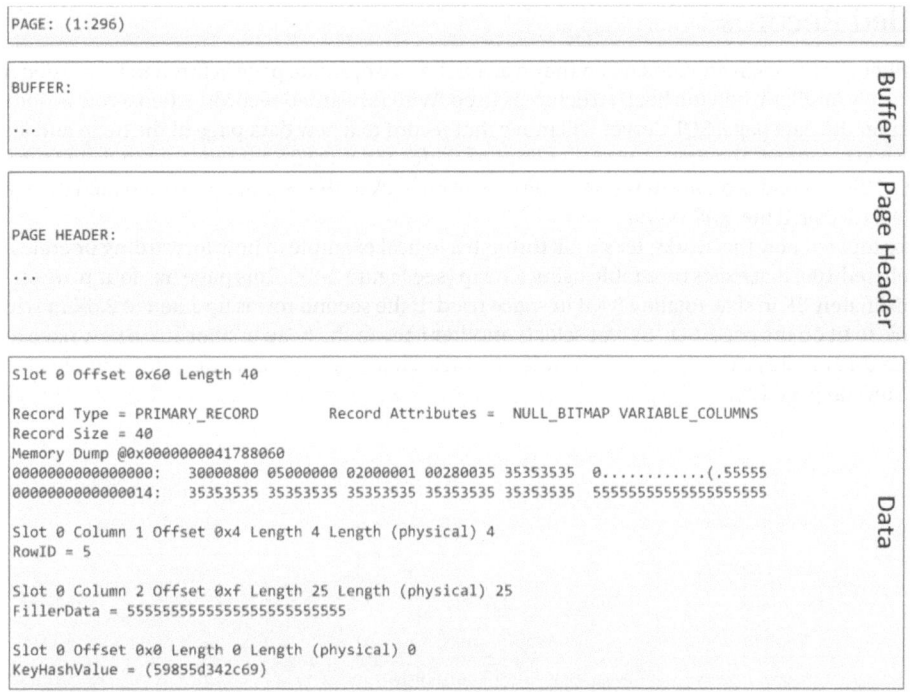

Figure 2-25. *DBCC PAGE output for row data print option for data page*

	FileId	PageId	Row	Level	ChildFileId	ChildPageId	RowID (key)	KeyHashValue	Row Size
1	1	279	0	1	1	277	NULL	NULL	11
2	1	279	1	1	1	296	5	NULL	11

Figure 2-26. *DBCC PAGE output for row data print option for index page*

Page Fragmentation

As discussed throughout this chapter, SQL Server stores information in the database on 8 KB pages. In general, records in tables are limited to that size; if they are smaller than 8 KB, SQL Server stores more than one record per page. One of the problems with storing more than a single record per page is handling situations where the total size of all of the records on a page exceeds more than 8 KB of space. In these situations, SQL Server must change how a the records on a page is stored. Depending on how the pages are organized, there are two ways in which SQL Server will handle the situations: forwarded records and page splits.

■ **Note**   This discussion does not consider two situations where single records can be larger than a page. These other situations are row overflow and large objects. With row overflow, SQL Server will allow a single record on a page to exceed the 8 KB in certain situations. Also, when large object values exceed the 8 KB size, they utilize LOB pages instead of data pages. These do not have a direct impact on the page fragmentation discussed in this section.

Forwarded Records

The first method for managing records when they exceed the size of a data page is through forwarded records. This method only applies when the heap structure is used. With forwarded records, when a row is updated and no longer fits on the data page, SQL Server will move that record to a new data page in the heap and add pointers between the two locations. The first pointer identifies on which the record now exists, often called the *forwarded record pointer*. The second is on the new page, pointing from back to the original page on which the forwarded record existed; it's called the *back pointer*.

As an example of how this works, let's walk through a logical example of how forwarding operates. Consider a page, numbered 100, that exists on a table using a heap (see Figure 2-27). This page has four rows on it and each row is approximately 2K in size, totaling 8 KB in space used. If the second row is updated to 2.5K in size, it will no longer be able to fit on the page. SQL Server selects another page in the heap or allocates a new page to the heap, page numbered 101 in this case. The second row is then written to that page and the pointer to the new page replaces the row on page 100.

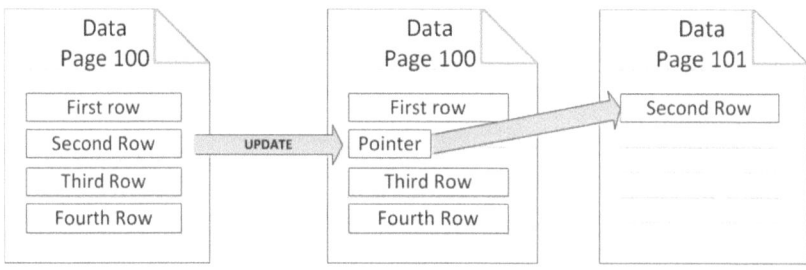

Figure 2-27. *Forward record process diagram*

Taking this logical example further, the next thing to do is examine how records are forwarded on a table. For the example, you'll create a table named dbo.HeapForwardedRecords, shown in Listing 2-15. To represent the rows from the logical example, you'll use the sys.objects table to add 24 rows to dbo.HeapForwardedRecords. Each of these rows has a RowID to identify the row and 2,000 characters, resulting in four rows per page in the table. Using sys.dm_db_index_physical_stats, you can verify (see Figure 2-28) that there are six pages in the table with a total of 24 records.

Listing 2-15. Forwarded Record Scenario

```
USE AdventureWorks2012
GO

CREATE TABLE dbo.HeapForwardedRecords
(
  RowId INT IDENTITY(1,1)
  ,FillerData VARCHAR(2500)
);

INSERT INTO dbo.HeapForwardedRecords (FillerData)
SELECT TOP 24 REPLICATE('X',2000)
FROM sys.objects;

DECLARE @ObjectID INT = OBJECT_ID('dbo.HeapForwardedRecords');

SELECT object_id, index_type_desc, page_count, record_count, forwarded_record_count
FROM sys.dm_db_index_physical_stats (DB_ID(), @ObjectID, NULL, NULL, 'DETAILED');
GO
```

	object_id	index_type_desc	page_count	record_count	forwarded_record_count
1	1956202019	HEAP	6	24	0

Figure 2-28. Physical state of dbo.HeapForwardedRecords before forwarding records

The next step in the demonstration is to cause forward records in the table. To do this, you'll update every other row in the table to expand the values FillerData from 2,000 to 2,500 characters, shown in Listing 2-16. As a result, two of the rows will be too large to fit in the space remaining on the pages where these rows are located. Instead of 8 KB of data, there will be about 9K being written to the 8 KB page.

As a result, SQL Server will need to move records off of the page to complete the updates. Since moving one of the records off of the page will leave enough room on the page for the second row, only one record will be forwarded. The output from sys.dm_db_index_physical_stats (see Figure 2-29) verifies that this is the case. The page count increases to nine and there six records are logged as being forwarded. One item of particular interest is the record count. While the number of rows in the table did not increase, there are now six additional records in the table. This is because the original record for the row is still in the original position with a pointer to another record elsewhere that contains the data for the row.

Listing 2-16. Script to Cause Forwarded Records

```
USE AdventureWorks2012
GO

UPDATE dbo.HeapForwardedRecords
SET FillerData = REPLICATE('X',2500)
WHERE RowId % 2 = 0;

DECLARE @ObjectID INT = OBJECT_ID('dbo.HeapForwardedRecords');
SELECT object_id, index_type_desc, page_count, record_count, forwarded_record_count
FROM sys.dm_db_index_physical_stats (DB_ID(), @ObjectID, NULL, NULL, 'DETAILED');
GO
```

	object_id	index_type_desc	page_count	record_count	forwarded_record_count
1	1956202019	HEAP	9	30	6

Figure 2-29. Physical state of dbo.HeapForwardedRecords after forwarding records

The problem with forwarded records is that it causes rows in the table to have records in two locations, resulting in an increase in the amount of I/O activity required when retrieving data from and writing data to the table. The larger the table and the higher the number of forwarded records, the more likely that forwarded records can have a negative impact on performance.

Page Splits

The second approach for handling pages where the size of the rows on the page exceeds the size of the page is the performing the page split. A page split is used on any index that is implemented under the B-tree index structure, which includes clustered and non-clustered indexes. With page splits, if a row is updated to a size that will no longer fit on the data page on which it currently exists, SQL Server will take half of the records on the page and place them on a new page. Then SQL Server will attempt to write the data for the row to the page again. If the data will then fit on the page, the page will be written. If not, then the process will be repeated until it fits on the page.

To explain how page splits operate, let's walk through an update that results in a page split. Similar to the last section, consider a table with a page numbered 100 (see Figure 2-30). There are four rows stored on page 100 and each is approximately 2K in size. Suppose that one of the rows, such as the second row, is updated to 2.5K in size. The data for the page will be 8.5K, which exceeds the available space, which causes a page split to occur. To split the page, a new page is allocated, numbered 101, and half of the rows on the page (the third and fourth row) are written to the new page. At this point, the second row can be written to the page, since there is now 4K of open space on the page.

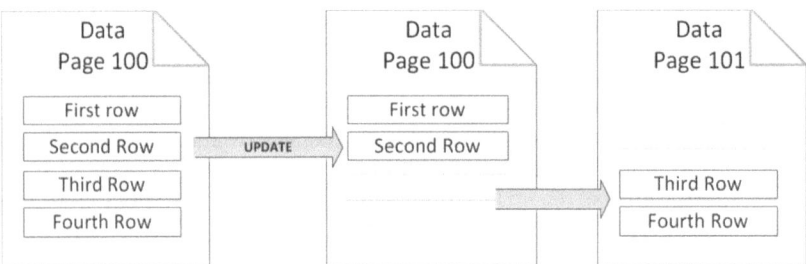

Figure 2-30. *Page split process diagram*

To demonstrate how page splits occur on a table, let's walk through an example similar to the one already described, which causes page splits to occur on the table. To start the example, create the table dbo. ClusteredPageSplits, provided in Listing 2-17. Into this table you'll insert 24 records that are about 2K in length. This should result in four rows per page and six data pages allocated to the table. Look at the information on index level 0, which is the leaf level. Since the table is using a B-tree, through the clustered index there will be an additional page that is used for the index tree structure. On index level one, there are six records, which reference the six pages in the index. You can confirm this information with Figure 2-31.

Listing 2-17. Page Split Scenario

```
USE AdventureWorks2012
GO

CREATE TABLE dbo.ClusteredPageSplits
(
   RowId INT IDENTITY(1,1)
  ,FillerData VARCHAR(2500)
  ,CONSTRAINT PK_ClusteredPageSplits PRIMARY KEY CLUSTERED (RowId)
);

INSERT INTO dbo.ClusteredPageSplits (FillerData)
SELECT TOP 24 REPLICATE('X',2000)
FROM sys.objects;

DECLARE @ObjectID INT = OBJECT_ID('dbo.ClusteredPageSplits');

SELECT object_id, index_type_desc, index_level, page_count, record_count
FROM sys.dm_db_index_physical_stats (DB_ID(), @ObjectID, NULL, NULL, 'DETAILED');
GO
```

	object_id	index_type_desc	index_level	page_count	record_count
1	2100202532	CLUSTERED INDEX	0	6	24
2	2100202532	CLUSTERED INDEX	1	1	6

Figure 2-31. *Physical state of dbo.ClusteredPageSplits before page splits*

Causing the page splits on the table can be done by updating some of the records to exceed the size of the page. You'll do this by issuing an UPDATE statements that increases the FillerData column in every other row from 2K to 2.5K characters in length, using the script in Listing 2-18. The resulting rows on each page will be 9K in size, which, like the previous example, exceeds the available page size, thus causing SQL Server to use page spits to free up space on the page.

Investigating the results (Figure 2-32) after the page splits have occurred shows the effect of the page splits on the table. For starters, instead of 6 pages at the leaf level of the index, at index level zero there are 12 pages. As mentioned, when a page split occurs, the page is split in half and a new page is added. Since all of the data pages were updated in the table, all of the pages were split resulting in a doubling of the pages at the leaf level. The only change at index level zero was the addition of six pages to reference the new pages in the index.

Listing 2-18. Script to Cause Page Splits

```
USE AdventureWorks2012
GO

UPDATE dbo.ClusteredPageSplits
SET FillerData = REPLICATE('X',2500)
WHERE RowId % 2 = 0;

DECLARE @ObjectID INT = OBJECT_ID('dbo.ClusteredPageSplits');
SELECT object_id, index_type_desc, index_level, page_count, record_count
FROM sys.dm_db_index_physical_stats (DB_ID(), @ObjectID, NULL, NULL, 'DETAILED');
GO
```

	object_id	index_type_desc	index_level	page_count	record_count
1	2100202532	CLUSTERED INDEX	0	12	24
2	2100202532	CLUSTERED INDEX	1	1	12

Figure 2-32. *Physical state of dbo.ClusteredPageSplits after page splits*

There are two distinctions between page splits and forwarded records that are worth mentioning. First, when the page splits occurred, the number of records on the data pages did not increase. A page split moves the location of records to make room for the records within the logical index ordering. The second is that page splits do not increase the record count. Since page splits have made room for the record, there is no need for an additional records to point to where data is stored.

Page splits can lead to performance issues similar to forwarded records. These performance issues occur both when the page split is occurring and afterwards. During the page splits, the page that is being split needs to be locked exclusively while the records are split between two pages. This means that there can be contention when someone needs to access a row other than the one being updated when the page split happens. After the page is split, the physical order of the data pages in the index are almost always not in their logical order within the index. This interrupts SQL Server's ability to perform contiguous reads, decreasing the amount of data that can be read in single operations. Also, the more pages that need to be read into memory for a query to execute, the slower the query will perform compared the same results on fewer pages.

Index Characteristics

The first part of this chapter discussed the physical structures that are used to store indexes. In those sections, a clear line between the types of indexes available and these structures was not defined. In this section, the main index types for SQL Server will be discussed, along with the indexing structure that they use. For each, you'll learn about the requirements and restrictions associated with the indexes.

Heap

The first index type to discuss is the heap. As pointed out earlier in the book, a heap is not actually a type of index. It is instead the result of the lack of a clustered index on a table. A heap index will, as the name implies, use the heap structure for organizing page in a table.

There is only a single requirement for creating a table with a heap. The requirement is that a clustered index can't already be created on the table. If there is a clustered index, then a heap will not be used. Heaps and clustered indexes are mutually exclusive. Also, provided there is not a clustered index, there can be only a single heap on a table. The heap is used to store the data pages for the index and this is done only once.

The primary concern when using heaps is the fact that the data in the heaps is not ordered. There is no column that determines the sort for the data on the pages. The result of this is that, without other supporting non-clustered indexes, queries will always be forced to scan the information in the table.

Clustered Index

The second index type is the clustered index. Clustered indexes utilize a B-tree for storing data. For all practical purposes, a clustered index is the opposite of a heap. When a clustered index is built on a table, the heap is replaced with the B-tree structure, organizing the pages according to the key columns of the clustering index. The B-tree for a clustered index includes data pages with all of the data for the rows in the table.

Clustered indexes have a few restrictions when considering the columns for the index. The first restriction is that the total length for the key columns cannot exceed 900 bytes. Second, the clustering key in a clustered index must be unique. If columns in a clustering key are not unique, the SQL Server will add a hidden uniquifier column to the row when it is stored. The uniquifier is a 4-byte numeric value that is added to non-unique clustering keys to enforce uniqueness. The uniquifier size is not considered part of the 900 byte limit.

When building clustered indexes, there are a few things to consider. First, there can be only a single clustered index per table. Since the clustered index is stored in the order of the clustering key and the data in the row is stored with the key, there can't be an alternative sort on top of the table sorting it in a second manner. Also, when building a clustered index on an existing table with a heap, be sure to have enough space available for a second copy of the data. Until the build of the index is completed, both copies of the data will exist.

As will be discussed in later chapters, it is often preferable to create clustered indexes on all tables. This preference is not an absolute, and there are situations where clustered indexes are not appropriate. You will need to investigate in your own databases to determine which structure is best. Simply use this preference as a starting point.

Non-Clustered Index

The next index type to discuss is the non-clustered index. Non-clustered indexes are similar to clustered indexes in a couple ways. For starters, non-clustered indexes use the B-tree structure for storing data. They are also limited to 900 bytes for their key columns.

Beyond the similarities to clustered indexes, there are some differences. First, there can be more than one non-clustered index on a table. In fact, there can be up to 999 non-clustered indexes on a table, each with no more than 16 columns. This upper limit isn't an invitation to create that many indexes, it is just an indication to the total number of non-clustered indexes that can be create. Though, with filtered indexes, it may sometimes be worthwhile to create more indexes on a table than was traditionally considered appropriate. Also, instead of having a leaf level where data is stored in the B-tree, non-clustered indexes have page references to the locations in either the heap or clustered index on the table where the data is located.

Column Store Index

The last index type discussed in this section is the column store index. Column store indexes use the column store structure, as the name implies.

There are two primary restrictions to consider when working with column store indexes. To begin with, a column store index is read-only. Once it has been created, there can be no data modifications to the data in the table. For this reason, it is often worthwhile to partition the underlying table to reduce the amount of data that needs to be contained in a column store index and to allow rebuilding of the index when new data is added to the table. Also, there can only be a single column store index on a table. This restriction is not a problem since it is advisable to include every column in a table in the column store index.

There are a few additional restriction that need to be considered with column store indexes. The first is that not all data types that are available to be used in column store indexes. The data types that cannot be used are `binary`, `varbinary`, `ntext`, `text`, `image`, `nvarchar(max)`, `varchar(max)`, `uniqueidentifier`, `rowversion`, `sql_variant`, `decimal` (with greater than 18 digits), `datetimeoffset`, `xml`, and CLR-based types. While all columns in a table should be added to a clustered index, there is a limit of 1,024 columns in a column store index. Also, due to the nature of column store indexes, the index cannot be unique, clustered, contain included columns, or have an ascending or descending order designated.

When using column store indexes, there are some features within SQL Server that it cannot be combined with. Since column store uses its own compression technology, it can't be combines with row or page compression. It can't be used with replication, change tracking, or change data capture. These technologies would not make sense with column store since they assist in read/write scenarios, while column store indexes are read-only. The last feature restrictions are filestream and filetable, which can't be used with column store.

Summary

In this chapter, you looked at the components that are used as the building blocks for indexes. Now you have the fundamental foundation necessary to create indexes that will behave in the ways that you expect and anticipate. To review, you looked at the different types of pages that SQL Server uses to store data in the database and how these pages are arranged together in extents. Then you looked at the available structures for organizing pages, not for physical storage but in a logical fashion in order to access the data on those pages. Then you looked the tools available for investigating the pages and structures of indexes through DBCC commands. The chapter concluded with a review of how the structures for indexes are associated with the available index types.

CHAPTER 3

■ ■ ■

Index Statistics

Now that you understand the logical and physical fundamentals of indexes, you should also look at the way in which statistics are stored for indexes. These statistics provide insight into how SQL Server can and is utilizing indexes. It also provides information needed to decipher why an index may not be selected and how it is behaving. This chapter will provide you with a deeper understanding about where and how this information is collected. You'll investigate some additional DBCC statements and Dynamic Management Objects (DMO) that are available and demonstrate how that information comes to be.

There are four domains of information that the statistics in this chapter will cover. The first domain is column-level statistics. This provides the query optimizer information on the population of data within a column and thus, an index. The next domain is index usage statistics. Information here provides insight into whether and how an index is being used. The third domain is operational statistics. This information is similar to usage statistics but provides deeper insight. The last domain of information is physical statistics and it provides insight into the physical characteristics of the index and how it is distributed within the database.

Index-Level Statistics

Without any more ado, let's begin by looking at the first domain of statistic information, index-level statistics. This area is one of the most important artifacts within SQL Server when it comes to indexes. Index-level statistics provide information on how data is distributed within an index. SQL Server uses this information to determine the anticipated frequency and distribution of values within an index; this is referred to as *cardinality*.

Through cardinality, the query optimizer develops cost-based execution plans to find the best execution plan for executing the submitted request. If the statistics for an index are incorrect or considered out of date, then the plan that is created will, likely, likewise be inefficient. It is important to understand, and be able to interact with, statistics in order to be certain that indexes in your environment not only exist but also provide their expected benefits.

There are many ways to interact with statistics within SQL Server. You'll review some of the most common mechanisms in the sections to follow. With each of these methods, you'll look what they are, what they provide, and the value in using the method.

DBCC SHOW_STATISTICS

The first, and likely most important, way to interact with statistics is through the DBCC command SHOW_STATISTICS. This command will return the current query optimization statistics for the requested database object, either a table or a view. The information returned is a statistics object that includes three different components: the header, histogram, and the density vector. Each of these components provides SQL Server an understanding of the data available in the index.

Returning the statistics object can be done with the DBCC syntax in Listing 3-1. This syntax accepts the name of the table or indexed view for the statistics and then the target is returned. The target is either the name of the index or the column-level statistics that were created.

Listing 3-1. DBCC SHOW_STATISTICS Syntax

```
DBCC SHOW_STATISTICS ( table_or_indexed_view_name, target )
[ WITH [ < options > ]
```

There are four options that can be included with the DBCC command: NO_INFOMSGS, STAT_HEADER, DENSITY_VECTOR, and HISTOGRAM. Any or all of these options can be included in a comma-separated list.

The option NO_INFOMSGS suppresses all informational messages when the DBCC command is executed. These are error messages generated with severity from 0 to 10, 10 being the highest severity error. In most cases, since these error messages are informational, they are not of value when using this DBCC statement.

The options STAT_HEADER, DENSITY_VECTOR, and HISTOGRAM limit the output from the DBCC command. If one or more of the options are included, then only the statistics components for the items included will be returned. If none of these are selected, then all of the components are included.

With the DBCC command defined, let's walk through each of the statistics components. Each will be defined and then an example of their contents from the AdventureWorks database will be explored. The results that you'll be reviewing can be created with Listing 3-2.

Listing 3-2. DBCC SHOW_STATISTICS for Index on Sales.SalesOrderDetail Table

```
DBCC SHOW_STATISTICS ( 'Sales.SalesOrderDetail'
, PK_SalesOrderDetail_SalesOrderID_SalesOrderDetailID )
```

Stats Header

The stats header is the metadata portion of the statistics object. These columns, listed in Table 3-1, are primarily informational. They inform on the number of rows that were considered when building the statistics and how those rows were selected through filtering. It also includes information on when the statistics where last updated, which can be useful when investigating potential issues with the quality of statistics.

Reviewing the stats header information for PK_SalesOrderDetail_SalesOrderID_SalesOrderDetailID on Sales.SalesOrderDetail, shown in Figure 3-1, shows a number of items of interest. First, since the Rows and Rows Sampled values are the same, you know that the statistics are not based on estimates. Next, the statistics were last updated on Jun 29, 2011 (though this value may differ in your database). Another item is that there are 154 steps, of a possible 200, in the statistics histogram. The number of steps is equal to ranges. In this case, 154 steps means there are 154 ranges, each with an upper bound value in the statistics. For example, step 154 may have an upper bound range of 124,000. If step 153 has an upper boundary of 110,000, step 154 covers the range from 110,001 to 124,000. Only those values would be contained in step 154. The last thing of note to point out is the lack of a filtered expression; neither the index nor statistics are filtering out rows.

Histogram

On the other end of the spectrum from the stats header is the histogram. The histogram provides the details of the statistics object that the query optimizer uses to determine cardinality. When building the histogram, SQL Server calculates a number of aggregates that are based on either a statistics sample or all of the rows in the table or view. The aggregates measure the frequency in which values occur and groups the values into no more than 200 segments, or steps. For each of these steps, a distribution of the statistics columns are computed that include the number of rows in the step, the upper bound of the step, number of rows matching the upper bound, distinct rows in the step, and average number of duplicate values in the step. The columns that match these aggregates are listed in Table 3-2. With this information, the Query Optimizer is able to estimate the number of rows returned for ranges of values in an index, thus allowing it to calculate a cost associated with retrieving the row.

Table 3-1. *Stats Header Columns from DBCC SHOW_STATISTICS*

Column Name	Description
Name	Name of the statistics object. For index statistics, this is the same name as the index.
Updated	Date and time that the statistics were last updated.
Rows	Total number of rows in the table or indexed view when the statistics were last updated. For filtered statistics or indexes, the count pertains to the number of rows that matched the filter criteria.
Rows Sampled	Total number of rows sampled for statistics calculations. Histogram and density values are estimates when the Rows Sampled value is less than the value in Rows.
Steps	Number of steps in the histogram. Each step spans a range of column values followed by an upper bound column value. The histogram steps are defined on the first key column in the statistics. The maximum number of steps is 200.
Density	Calculated as 1/distinct values for all values in the first key column of the statistics object, excluding the histogram boundary values. As of SQL Server 2008, this value is no longer used by SQL Server.
Average Key Length	Average number of bytes per value for all of the key columns in the statistics object.
String Index	Indicates whether the statistics object contains string summary statistics to improve the cardinality estimates for query predicates that use the LIKE operator.
Filter Expression	When populated, this is the predicate for the subset of table rows included in the statistics object.
Unfiltered Rows	Total number of rows in the table before applying the filter expression. If Filter Expression is NULL, Unfiltered Rows is equal to Rows.

	Name	Updated	Rows	Rows Sampled	Steps	Density	Average key length	String Index	Filter Expression	Unfiltered Rows
1	PK_SalesOrderDetail_SalesOrderID_SalesOrderDeta...	Jun 29 2011 10:50PM	121317	121317	154	0.2704914	8		NO	NULL	121317

Figure 3-1. *Stats header for index on Sales.SalesOrderDetail table*

Table 3-2. *Histograms Columns from DBCC SHOW_STATISTICS*

Column Name	Description
RANGE_HI_KEY	Upper-bound column value for a histogram step. The column value is also called a key value.
RANGE_ROWS	Estimated number of rows whose column value falls within a histogram step, excluding the upper bound.
EQ_ROWS	Estimated number of rows whose column value equals the upper bound of the histogram step.
DISTINCT_RANGE_ROWS	Estimated number of rows with a distinct column value within a histogram step, excluding the upper bound.
AVG_RANGE_ROWS	Average number of rows with duplicate column values within a histogram step, excluding the upper bound (RANGE_ROWS / DISTINCT_RANGE_ROWS for DISTINCT_RANGE_ROWS > 0).

As mentioned in the previous section, there are 154 steps in the histogram. In Figure 3-2, which includes a number of rows from the histogram, you can see how a few of the steps in Sales.SalesOrderDetail are aggregated. If you look at the second item in Figure 3-2, it shows the RANGE_HI_KEY of 43692; this means that all SalesOrderID values between 43660 and 43692 are included in these estimates. There are 283 rows in this series, based on the RANGE_ROWS value, with 33 distinct rows in the series. Translating these numbers to the SalesOrderDetail table, there are 33 distinct SalesOrderID values with 283 SalesOrderDetailID items between them. Lastly, there are 32 SalesOrderDetailID items for SalesOrderID 43692.

	RANGE_HI_KEY	RANGE_ROWS	EQ_ROWS	DISTINCT_RANGE_ROWS	AVG_RANGE_ROWS
1	43659	0	12	0	1
2	43692	282	28	32	8.8125
3	43898	716	28	205	3.492683
4	44079	403	27	180	2.238889
5	44288	766	34	208	3.682692
6	44488	570	27	199	2.864322
7	44538	614	35	49	12.53061
8	44570	370	32	31	11.93548
9	44758	409	27	187	2.187166
10	44801	504	26	42	12

Figure 3-2. Sample of the histogram for index on Sales.SalesOrderDetail table

This leaves one last column to look at: AVG_RANGE_ROWS. This column is often scrutinized and can result in a lot of pain when statistics are out of date. It states how many rows can be expected when any one value or range of values from the statistics are retrieved. To check the accuracy of the range average, execute Listing 3-3, which will aggregate some of the values in the second step. After it is complete, the results (shown in Figure 3-3) will show that the averages closely match the average range rows value of 8.8125.

Listing 3-3. Query to Check AVG_RANGE_ROWS Estimate

```
USE AdventureWorks2012
GO

SELECT (COUNT(*)*1.)/COUNT(DISTINCT SalesOrderID) AS AverageRows
FROM Sales.SalesOrderDetail
WHERE SalesOrderID BETWEEN 43672 AND 43677;

SELECT (COUNT(*)*1.)/COUNT(DISTINCT SalesOrderID) AS AverageRows
FROM Sales.SalesOrderDetail
WHERE SalesOrderID BETWEEN 43675 AND 43677;

SELECT (COUNT(*)*1.)/COUNT(DISTINCT SalesOrderID) AS AverageRows
FROM Sales.SalesOrderDetail
WHERE SalesOrderID BETWEEN 43675 AND 43680;
```

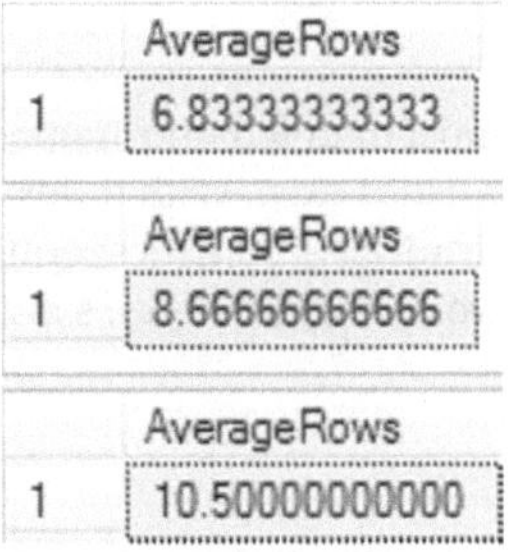

	AverageRows
1	6.83333333333

	AverageRows
1	8.66666666666

	AverageRows
1	10.50000000000

Figure 3-3. Results of AVG_RANGE_ROWS estimate validation

This histogram is a valuable tool to use when the statistics of an index are in question. If there is a need to determine why a query is behaving in a specific manner or you need to check why a query plan is estimating rows as it is, the histogram can be used to validate these behaviors and results.

Density Vector

The last portion of the statistics components is the density vector. The density vector describes the columns within a statistics object. There is a row for each key value in the statistics or index object. For instance, if there are two columns in an index named `SaleOrderID` and `SalesOrderDetailID`, there will be two rows in the density vector. The density vector will have a row for `SaleOrderID` and a row for `SaleOrderID` and `SalesOrderDetailID`, shown in Figure 3-4. There are three pieces of information available for density vector: the density, average length, and columns included in the vector (column names detailed in Table 3-3).

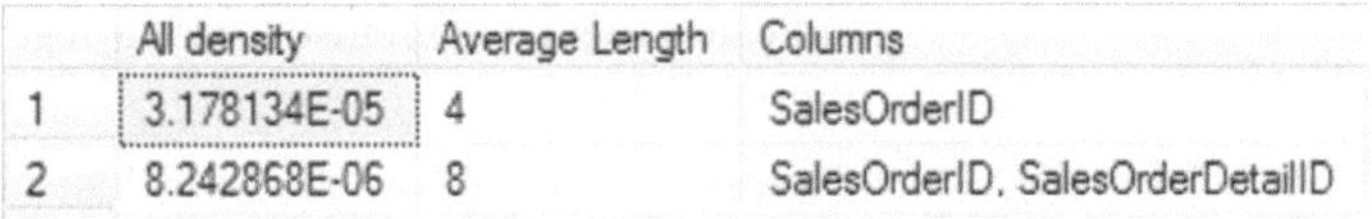

	All density	Average Length	Columns
1	3.178134E-05	4	SalesOrderID
2	8.242868E-06	8	SalesOrderID, SalesOrderDetailID

Figure 3-4. Sample of the density vector for index on Sales.SalesOrderDetail table

Table 3-3. Density vector columns from DBCC SHOW_STATISTICS

Column Name	Description
All Density	Returns the density for each prefix of columns in the statistics object, one row per density. The density is calculated as 1/*distinct column values*.
Average Length	Average length, in bytes, to store the column values for each level of the density vector
Columns	Names of columns in each density vector level.

The value of the density vector is that it helps the query optimizer adjust cardinality for multiple column statistics objects. Since the ranges within the histogram are based solely on the first column of the statistics object, the density provides an adjustment between when single or multi-column queries are executed.

Catalog Views

Using DBCC SHOW_STATISTICS provides the most detailed information on query optimization statistics. It does, however, rely on the user knowing that the statistics exist. With index statistics, it is easy to know about the statistics since all indexes have statistics. Column-level statistics require an alternative method for discovering the statistics. This is accomplished through two catalogue views: sys.stats and sys.stat_coumns.

sys.stats

The catalogue view sys.stats returns one row for every query optimization statistic object that exists within the database. Whether the statistic was created based on an index or column, the statistic object is listed in the view. The list of columns in sys.stats is shown in Table 3-4.

Table 3-4. *Columns for sys.stats*

Column Name	Data Type	Description
object_id	int	ID of the object to which these statistics belong.
name	sysname	Name of the statistics. This value must be unique for every object_id.
stats_id	int	ID of the statistics (unique within the object).
auto_created	bit	Statistics were auto-created by the query processor.
user_created	bit	Statistics were explicitly created by the user.
no_recompute	bit	Statistics were created with the NORECOMPUTE option.
has_filter	bit	Indicates whether the statistics are aggregated based on a filter or subset of rows.
filter_definition	nvarchar(max)	Expression for the subset of rows included in filtered statistics.

sys.stat_columns

As a companion to sys.stats, the catalogue view sys.stat_columns provides one row for every column within a statistics object. The columns in sys.stat_columns are listed in Table 3-5.

Table 3-5. *Columns for sys.stats*

Column Name	Data Type	Description
object_id	int	ID of the object of which this column is part
stats_id	int	ID of the statistics of which this column is part
stats_column_id	int	1-based ordinal within set of stats columns
column_id	int	ID of the column from sys.columns

STATS_DATE

As statistics age, they can sometimes become out of date. The STATS_DATE function provides the date of the most recent update to statistics. The syntax for the function, shown in Listing 3-4, accepts an object_id and stats_id. In the case of indexes, the stats_id is the same value as the index_id.

Listing 3-4. *STATS_DATE Syntax*

```
STATS_DATE ( object_id, stats_id )
```

Statistics DDL

We have primarily been discussing index level statistics in this chapter. Statistics can also created, and provide, significant value on non-indexed columns. Index statistics are automatically created when an index is created and automatically dropped when the index is dropped. When manually creating or dropping statistics on non-indexed columns, there are two DDL statements that can be used to accomplish this: CREATE and DROP STATISTICS; since they are outside the scope of this book, we will not be discussing them. The third DDL statement, UPDATE STATISTICS, applies to all statistics including the index-level statistics. Since UPDATE STATISTICS is primarily tied to index maintenance, it is discussed in Chapter 7.

Index-Level Statistics Summary

Query optimization statistics are a vital piece of indexing. They provide the information that the query optimizer requires in order to build cost-based query plans. Through this process, SQL Server can identify high quality plans through their calculated costs. In this section, you looked at how statistics are stored and the tools you can use in order to investigate and begin to understand the statistics that are stored for an index.

Usage Statistics

The next domain of information to take a look at is index usage stats. Index usage statistics are accumulated through the DMO sys.dm_db_index_usage_stats. This DMO returns counts of different types of index operations and when the operation was last performed. Through this information, you can discern how frequently an index is being used and how current that usage is.

The DMO sys.dm_db_index_usage_stats is a dynamic management view (DMV). Due to this, it does not require any parameters. It can be joined to other tables or views through any of the JOIN operators. Indexes appear within the DMV after the index has been used for the first time or since the reset of the statistics.

■ **Note** Along with restarting the SQL Server service, closing or detaching a database will reset all of the statistics for an index that have been accumulated in sys.dm_db_index_usage_stats.

Within the DMV sys.dm_db_index_usage_stats there are three types of data provided: header columns, user statistics, and system statistics. In the next few sections, you will explore each to gain an understanding of what information they hold and how you can use it.

Header Columns

The header columns for the DMV provide referential information that can be used to determine for which index the statistics were accumulated. The columns that are a part of this are listed in Table 3-6. These columns are primarily used to join the DMV to system catalog views and other DMOs.

Table 3-6. *Header Columns in sys.dm_db_index_usage_stats*

Column Name	Data Type	Description
database_id	smallint	ID of the database in which the table or view is defined
object_id	int	ID of the table or view in which the index is defined
index_id	int	ID of the index

One of the first things that can be done with sys.dm_db_index_usage_stats is to check to see if an index has been used since the last time the statistics in the DMV were reset. Using the header columns, similar to the T-SQL statement in Listing 3-5, can provide a list of the indexes that have not been used. If you are using the AdventureWorks database, your results will look similar to those in Figure 3-5. In these results, indexes that have not been used are returned.

Listing 3-5. Query for Header Columns in sys.dm_db_index_usage_stats

```
USE AdventureWorks2012
GO

SELECT TOP 10 OBJECT_NAME(i.object_id) AS table_name
    ,i.name AS index_name
    ,ius.database_id
    ,ius.object_id
    ,ius.index_id
FROM sys.indexes i
    LEFT JOIN sys.dm_db_index_usage_stats ius
        ON i.object_id = ius.object_id
        AND i.index_id = ius.index_id
        AND ius.database_id = DB_ID()
WHERE ius.index_id IS NULL
AND OBJECTPROPERTY(i.object_id, 'IsUserTable') = 1
```

This type of information can be useful for managing the indexes in your databases. It is an excellent resource for identify the indexes that have not been used in a while. This strategy of index management is discussed further in Chapter 10.

User Columns

The next set of columns in the DMV sys.dm_db_index_usage_stats is the user columns. The user columns provide insight into how indexes are being specifically used within query plans. The columns are listed in Table 3-7; they include statistics on the counts of how many of each operation occurred and the time in which the last one occurred.

	table_name	index_name	database_id	object_id	index_id
1	Store	PK_Store_CustomerID	NULL	NULL	NULL
2	Store	AK_Store_rowguid	NULL	NULL	NULL
3	Store	IX_Store_SalesPersonID	NULL	NULL	NULL
4	Store	PXML_Store_Demographics	NULL	NULL	NULL
5	ProductPhoto	PK_ProductPhoto_ProductPhotoID	NULL	NULL	NULL
6	ProductProductPhoto	NULL	NULL	NULL	NULL
7	ProductProductPhoto	PK_ProductProductPhoto_ProductID_ProductPhotoID	NULL	NULL	NULL
8	StoreContact	PK_StoreContact_CustomerID_ContactID	NULL	NULL	NULL
9	StoreContact	AK_StoreContact_rowguid	NULL	NULL	NULL
10	StoreContact	IX_StoreContact_ContactID	NULL	NULL	NULL

Figure 3-5. *sys.dm_db_index_usage_stats header columns query results*

Table 3-7. *User Columns in sys.dm_db_index_usage_stats*

Column Name	Data Type	Description
user_seeks	bigint	Aggregate count of seeks by user queries.
user_scans	bigint	Aggregate count of scans by user queries
user_lookups	bigint	Aggregate count of bookmark/key lookups by user queries
user_updates	bigint	Aggregate count of updates by user queries
last_user_seek	datetime	Date and time of last user seek
last_user_scan	datetime	Date and time of last user scan
last_user_lookup	datetime	Date and time of last user lookup
last_user_update	datetime	Date and time of last user update

There are four types of index operations that sys.dm_db_index_usage_stats monitors. These are represented through the columns user_seeks, user_scans, user_lookups, and user_updates.

The first of the index usage columns is user_seeks. The operations for this column occur whenever a query executes and returns a single row or range of rows for which it has a direct access path. For instance, if a query executes and retrieves all of the sales details records for a single order or a small range of orders, similar to the queries in Listing 3-6, the query plan for these would use a seek operation (see Figure 3-6).

Listing 3-6. Index Seek Queries

```
USE AdventureWorks2012
GO

SELECT * FROM Sales.SalesOrderDetail
WHERE SalesOrderID = 43659
GO

SELECT * FROM Sales.SalesOrderDetail
WHERE SalesOrderID BETWEEN 43659 AND 44659
GO
```

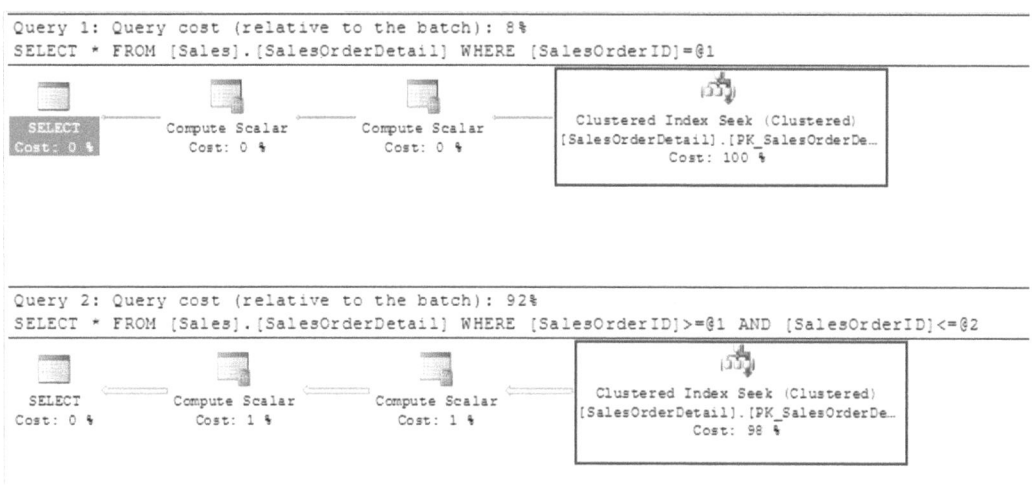

Figure 3-6. Query plans for seek queries

After running the queries from Listing 3-6, the DMV sys.dm_db_index_usage_stats will be counted into the user_seeks column. The query in Listing 3-7 provides a query to investigate this. If you are following along, you should see the results in Figure 3-7. As the results show, the value in the user_seeks column is 2, which matches the count of operations from Listing 3-6. Based on this, you know that two queries were executed using the index and both were able to utilize the index to go directly rows that were requested.

Listing 3-7. Query for index_seeks from sys.dm_db_index_usage_stats

```
USE AdventureWorks2012
GO

SELECT TOP 10
  OBJECT_NAME(i.object_id) AS table_name
  ,i.name AS index_name
  ,ius.user_seeks
  ,ius.last_user_seek
FROM sys.indexes i
  INNER JOIN sys.dm_db_index_usage_stats ius
          ON i.object_id = ius.object_id
          AND i.index_id = ius.index_id
          AND ius.database_id = DB_ID()
WHERE ius.object_id = OBJECT_ID('Sales.SalesOrderDetail')
  GO
```

	table_name	index_name	user_seeks	last_user_seek
1	SalesOrderDetail	PK_SalesOrderDetail_SalesOrderID_SalesOrderDet...	2	2011-08-07 22:57:52.950

Figure 3-7. Query results for index_seeks

The next usage column is `user_scans`. The value of this column is increased whenever a query executes and it must scan through every row of an index. For instance, consider a query on sales details is unfiltered and must return all records or a query that is filtered on a column that is unindexed. Both of these queries, shown in Listing 3-8 are asking SQL Server for either everything it has in a table or a few rows that it doesn't have a location on. The only way to accommodate this request would be through a scan of the `SalesOrderDetail` table. The execution plans for these two queries is show in Figure 3-8.

Listing 3-8. Index Scan Queries

```
USE AdventureWorks2012
GO

SELECT * FROM Sales.SalesOrderDetail
GO

SELECT * FROM Sales.SalesOrderDetail
WHERE CarrierTrackingNumber = '4911-403C-98'
GO
```

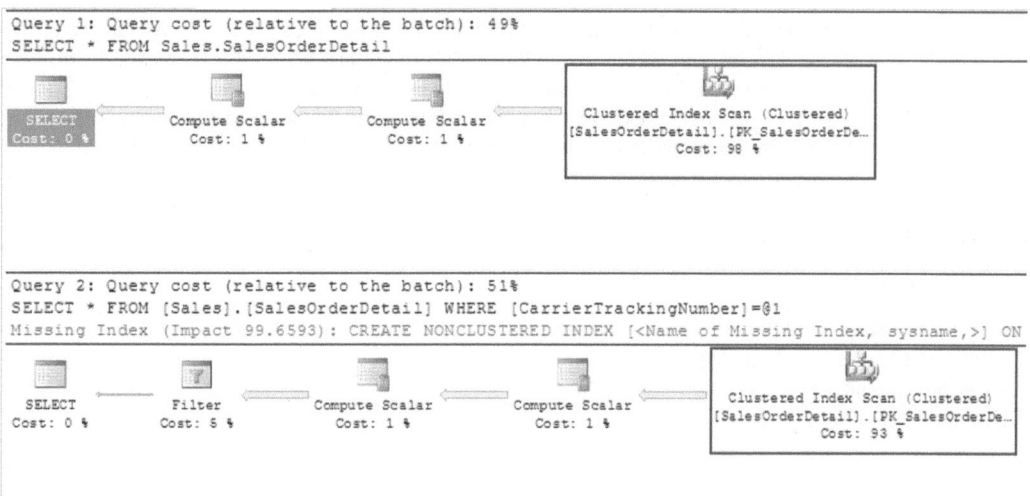

Figure 3-8. *Query plans for seek queries*

When index scans occur, they can be seen in `sys.dm_db_index_usage_stats`. The query in Listing 3-9 provides a view in the DMV to see the accumulation of the scans. Since there were two scans, one for each of the two queries, the results in Figure 3-9 show that there have been two operations under `user_scans`. This information can be useful when trying to troubleshoot situations where there are large numbers of scans on a table. By looking at this information, you are able to find the indexes with high scans and then begin to look at why queries using those indexes are using scans over more optimal operations like index seeks.

Listing 3-9. Query for index_scans From sys.dm_db_index_usage_stats

```
USE AdventureWorks2012
GO

SELECT TOP 10
  OBJECT_NAME(i.object_id) AS table_name
```

```
    ,i.name AS index_name
    ,ius.user_scans
    ,ius.last_user_scan
FROM sys.indexes i
  INNER JOIN sys.dm_db_index_usage_stats ius
            ON i.object_id = ius.object_id
            AND i.index_id = ius.index_id
            AND ius.database_id = DB_ID()
WHERE ius.object_id = OBJECT_ID('Sales.SalesOrderDetail')
  GO
```

	table_name	index_name	user_scans	last_user_scan
1	SalesOrderDetail	PK_SalesOrderDetail_SalesOrderID_SalesOrderDet...	2	2011-08-07 23:16:55.860

Figure 3-9. *Query results for index_scans*

The third column in the DMV is user_lookups. User lookups occur when a seek on a non-clustered index occurs but does not have all of the required columns in it to satisfy the query. When this happens, the query must look up the columns from the clustered index. An example would be a query against the SalesOrderDetail table that is returning ProductID and CarrierTrackingNumber that is filtered on ProductID; this query is shown in Listing 3-10 The query plan from this query is shown in Figure 3-10. The query plan shows a seek on the non-clustered index and a key lookup on the clustered index.

Listing 3-10. Index Lookup Query

```
USE AdventureWorks2012
GO

SELECT ProductID, CarrierTrackingNumber
FROM Sales.SalesOrderDetail
WHERE ProductID = 778
GO
```

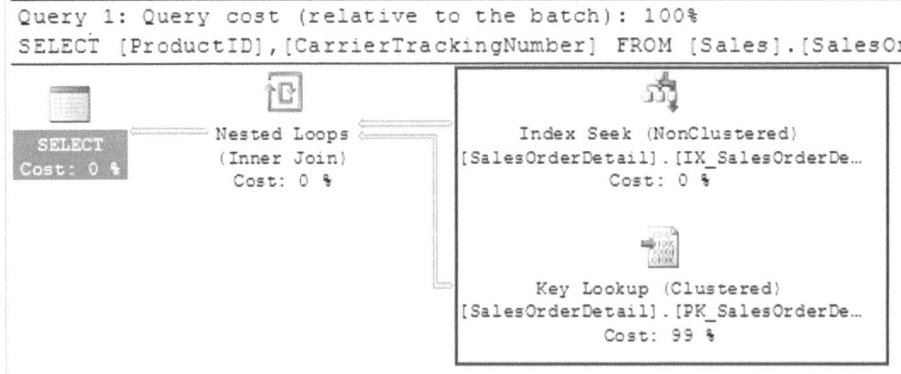

Figure 3-10. *Query plans for seek and key lookup*

In sys.dm_db_index_usage_stats, there will be a tally of one for both user_seeks and user_lookups. To access these values, use Listing 3-11, which will return the results in Figure 3-11. Patterns between these columns can help with determining proper clustering keys or identifying when to modify indexes to avoid the key lookups. Key lookups aren't necessarily bad but can be a performance bottleneck if overused and left unchecked. We'll discuss more on what to look for in regards to user_lookups in later chapters.

Listing 3-11. Query for index_lookups from sys.dm_db_index_usage_stats

```
SELECT TOP 10
  OBJECT_NAME(i.object_id) AS table_name
  ,i.name AS index_name
  ,ius.user_seeks
  ,ius.user_lookups
  ,ius.last_user_lookup
FROM sys.indexes i
  INNER JOIN sys.dm_db_index_usage_stats ius
            ON i.object_id = ius.object_id
            AND i.index_id = ius.index_id
            AND ius.database_id = DB_ID()
WHERE ius.object_id = OBJECT_ID('Sales.SalesOrderDetail')
```

	table_name	index_name	user_seeks	user_lookups	last_user_lookup
1	SalesOrderDetail	PK_SalesOrderDetail_SalesOrderID_SalesOrderDet...	0	1	2011-08-08 00:21:28.567
2	SalesOrderDetail	IX_SalesOrderDetail_ProductID	1	0	NULL

Figure 3-11. Query results for index_lookups

The last of the index operations is user_updates. The user_updates column is not limited to update operations on a table. In actuality, it covers all INSERT, UPDATE, and DELETE operations that occur on a table. To demonstrate this, you can execute the code in Listing 3-12. This code will INSERT a record into the SalesOrderDetail table, then UPDATE the record, and finally DELETE the record from the table. Since the execution plans for these are complex due to foreign key relationships, they have not been included in this example.

Listing 3-12. Index Lookup Query

```
USE AdventureWorks2012
GO

INSERT INTO Sales.SalesOrderDetail
(SalesOrderID, CarrierTrackingNumber, OrderQty, ProductID, SpecialOfferID, UnitPrice,
UnitPriceDiscount, ModifiedDate)
SELECT SalesOrderID, CarrierTrackingNumber, OrderQty, ProductID, SpecialOfferID, UnitPrice,
UnitPriceDiscount, GETDATE() AS ModifiedDate
FROM Sales.SalesOrderDetail
WHERE SalesOrderDetailID = 1;
GO
```

```
UPDATE Sales.SalesOrderDetail
SET CarrierTrackingNumber = '999-99-9999'
WHERE ModifiedDate > DATEADD(d, -1, GETDATE());
GO

DELETE FROM Sales.SalesOrderDetail
WHERE ModifiedDate > DATEADD(d, -1, GETDATE());
GO
```

At the completion of the execution of the code listing, there were three operations that occurred on the table. For each of these operations, sys_dm_db_index_usage_stats accumulated one tick in the user_updates column. Execute the code in Listing 3-13 to see the activity that occurred on the index. The results will be similar to those in Figure 3-12. Besides the changes made to the clustered index for SalesOrderDetail, the updates made to the non-clustered indexes are also included. Being able to see the effects of an insert, update, or delete on a table can help provide an understanding of the impact of users and the volatility of your data.

Listing 3-13. Query for index_lookups from sys.dm_db_index_usage_stats

```
SELECT TOP 10
    OBJECT_NAME(i.object_id) AS table_name
   ,i.name AS index_name
   ,ius.user_updates
   ,ius.last_user_update
FROM sys.indexes i
  INNER JOIN sys.dm_db_index_usage_stats ius
            ON i.object_id = ius.object_id
            AND i.index_id = ius.index_id
            AND ius.database_id = DB_ID()
WHERE ius.object_id = OBJECT_ID('Sales.SalesOrderDetail')
```

	table_name	index_name	user_updates	last_user_update
1	SalesOrderDetail	PK_SalesOrderDetail_SalesOrderID_SalesOrderDet...	3	2011-08-08 00:48:05.163
2	SalesOrderDetail	AK_SalesOrderDetail_rowguid	2	2011-08-08 00:48:05.163
3	SalesOrderDetail	IX_SalesOrderDetail_ProductID	2	2011-08-08 00:48:05.163

Figure 3-12. *Query results for index_updates*

System Columns

The last set of columns in sys.dm_db_index_usage_stats is the system columns. The system columns return the same general information as the user columns, except these values are from the perspective of background processes. Whenever something triggers within SQL Server, such as a triggered statistics update, that activity will be tracked through these columns. The system columns are listed in Table 3-8.

Table 3-8. *System Columns in sys.dm_db_index_usage_stats*

Column Name	Data Type	Description
system_seeks	bigint	Number of seeks by system queries
system_scans	bigint	Number of scans by system queries
system_lookups	bigint	Number of lookups by system queries
system_updates	bigint	Number of updates by system queries
last_system_seek	datetime	Time of last system seek
last_system_scan	datetime	Time of last system scan
last_system_lookup	datetime	Time of last system lookup
last_system_update	datetime	Time of last system update

For the most part, these columns can be ignored. It is good, though, to understand how they are aggregated. To see an example, execute the code in Listing 3-14. This will change a majority of the rows in the SalesOrderDetail table. Since more than 20 percent of the rows have changed, an automatic statistics update will be triggered. The statistics update is not directly related to user activity and is instead a background, or system, process.

Listing 3-14. Update for Sales.SalesOrderDetail

```
USE AdventureWorks2012
GO

UPDATE Sales.SalesOrderDetail
SET UnitPriceDiscount = 0.01
WHERE UnitPriceDiscount = 0.00
```

After the update has completed, run the T-SQL statements in Listing 3-15. This code will return all of the system columns. Within these is the system_scans column, shown in Figure 3-13. During the statistics update, SQL Server performed a scan twice on the table to retrieve the information necessary to complete the statistics update.

Listing 3-15. Query for System Columns in sys.dm_db_index_usage_stats

```
SELECT OBJECT_NAME(i.object_id) AS table_name
  ,i.name AS index_name
  ,ius.system_seeks
  ,ius.system_scans
  ,ius.system_lookups
  ,ius.system_updates
  ,ius.last_system_seek
  ,ius.last_system_scan
  ,ius.last_system_lookup
 ,ius.last_system_update
FROM sys.indexes i
  INNER JOIN sys.dm_db_index_usage_stats ius
            ON i.object_id = ius.object_id
            AND i.index_id = ius.index_id
            AND ius.database_id = DB_ID()
WHERE ius.object_id = OBJECT_ID('Sales.SalesOrderDetail')
```

Figure 3-13. *sys.dm_db_index_usage_stats header columns query results*

From a usefulness perspective, there isn't much of anything that can be gleaned from these columns. They are just the result of background processes and are more there to inform what is happening with indexes in the background.

Index Usage Stats Summary

In this section, we discussed the statistics found in DMV sys.dm_db_index_usage stats. This DMV provides some extremely useful statistics around how and if indexes are being used in the database. By monitoring these statistics over the long run, you will be able to understand which indexes are providing some of the most value. Strategies for using all of these columns to index for performance will be discussed in Chapter 8.

Operational Statistics

The third area of statistics to consider is index operational stats. These statistics are presented to users through the DMO sys.dm_db_index_operational stats. From a high level, this DMO provides low level information on I/O, locking, latching, and access methods that occur on indexes. Through this low-level information, you can identify indexes that may be encountering performance issues and start to understand what is leading to those performance issues. At the end of this section, you will understand the statistics provided in the DMO and know how to investigate indexes through these statistics.

Unlike the DMO in the last section, sys.dm_db_index_operational_stats is a dynamic management function (DMF). Due to this, the DMF requires a number of parameters to be supplied when it is used. The parameters for the DMF are detailed in Table 3-9.

Table 3-9. *Parameters for sys.dm_db_index_operational_stats*

Parameter Name	Data Type	Description
database_id	smallint	ID of the database where the indexes reside. Providing the values 0, NULL, or DEFAULT will return index information for all databases. The function DB_ID can be used in this parameter.
object_id	int	Object ID of the table or view for which statistics should be returned. Providing the values 0, NULL, or DEFAULT will return index information for all tables or views in database.
index_id	int	Index ID of the index for which statistics should be returned. Providing the values -1, NULL, or DEFAULT will return statistics for all indexes on the table or view.
partition_number	int	Partition number on an index in which statistics should be returned. Providing the values 0, NULL, or DEFAULT will return statistic information for all partitions on an index.

Through the parameters, statistics on indexes can be as widely or narrowly focused as necessary. This flexibility is useful since sys.dm_db_index_operational_stats does not allow the use of the CROSS APPLY or OUTER APPLY operators. When passing the parameters into the DMF, the syntax for doing so is defined in Listing 3-16.

Listing 3-16. Index Operational Stats Syntax

```
sys.dm_db_index_operational_stats (
    { database_id | NULL | 0 | DEFAULT }
    , { object_id | NULL | 0 | DEFAULT }
    , { index_id | 0 | NULL | -1 | DEFAULT }
    , { partition_number | NULL | 0 | DEFAULT }
)
```

■ **Note**   The DMF `sys.dm_db_index_operational` stats can accept the use of the Transact SQL functions `DB_ID()` and `OBJECT_ID()`. These functions can be used for the parameters `database_id` and `object_id`, respectively.

Header Columns

To start looking at the statistics, you need to identify the header columns that will be used with all of the resulting queries. For every row that is returned through the DMF, there will be a `database_id`, `object_id`, `index_id`, and `partition_number`. These columns are defined further in Table 3-10. As is implied through the `partition_number`, the granularity of the results for this DMF is at the partition level. For non-partitioned indexes, the partition number will be 1.

Table 3-10. *Header Columns in sys.dm_db_index_operational_stats*

Column Name	Data Type	Description
database_id	smallint	ID of the database on which the table or view is defined
object_id	int	ID of the table or view on which the index is defined
index_id	int	ID of the index
partition_number	int	1-based partition number within the index or heap

The header columns provide the basis for understanding to which indexes the statistics apply. This will help provide perspective regarding the statistics returned. Also, they can be used to join to catalogue views, such as sys.indexes, to provide the names of the indexes.

The useful statistical information in this DMF comes in the rest of the columns returned by the function. The information that can be returned provides insight into DML activity, the page allocation cycle, data access patterns, index contention, and disk activity. In the following sections, you'll look into the columns of the DMF that provide statistics for this information.

DML Activity

The place to begin when investigating the operation stats on an index is with the DML activity on the index. The columns that represent this activity are listed in Table 3-11. These columns provide a count of the number of rows that are affected by DML operations. The statistics that follow are similar to those in sys.dm_db_index_usage but with a few differences in perspective that will be discussed next.

Table 3-11. *DML Activity Columns in sys.dm_db_index_operational_stats*

Column Name	Data Type	Description
leaf_insert_count	bigint	Cumulative count of leaf-level rows inserted
leaf_delete_count	bigint	Cumulative count of leaf-level rows deleted
leaf_update_count	bigint	Cumulative count of leaf-level rows updated
leaf_ghost_count	bigint	Cumulative count of leaf-level rows that are marked to be deleted, but not yet removed
nonleaf_insert_count	bigint	Cumulative count of inserts above the leaf level. For heaps, this value will always be 0.
nonleaf_delete_count	bigint	Cumulative count of deletes above the leaf level. For heaps, this value will always be 0.
nonleaf_update_count	bigint	Cumulative count of updates above the leaf level. For heaps, this value will always be 0.

Within sys.dm_db_index_operational_stats there are two areas where DML activity that can be tracked. These are at the leaf and the non-leaf levels. These areas of DML activity were discussed in Chapter 2; for more information on leaf and non-leaf pages refer to that chapter.

The difference between these two types of data changes are important to help identify whether there are changes are a result of DML operations or an effect caused by DML operations. This means that leaf level DML activity is a direct result of INSERT, UPDATE, and DELETE statements. The non-leaf level DML activity happens when leaf level activity results in a change in how the index is structured and isn't something that can be directly impacted with an INSERT, UPDATE, or DELETE statement.

Both leaf and non-leaf level DML activity are broken apart into statistics based on the type of DML operation that has occurred. As previously indicated, DML activity monitors INSERT, UPDATE, and DELETE activity. For each of these operations, there is a column in sys.dm_db_index_operational_stats. Additionally, there is a column that counts records that have been ghosted off the leaf level DML activity.

During DELETE operations, rows affected by the statement are deleted in a two-phase operation. Initially, the records are marked for delete. When this occurs, the records are referred to as being ghosted; the rows in this state are counted in leaf_ghost_count. At regular intervals, a cleanup thread within SQL Server will go through and perform an actual delete operation on rows marked as ghosted. At that point, the records will be counted in the lead_delete_column. This process helps in the performance of delete operations, since the actual delete of a row happens after the transaction is committed. Also, in the event of transaction rollback, the ghost flag on a row is all that needs to change rather than an attempt to recreate the row in the table. This activity only occurs at the leaf level; non-leaf pages are deleted whenever all of the rows associated with the page have been deleted or otherwise removed.

As mentioned, this DML activity on this DMF is similar to that found in sys.dm_db_index_usage_stats. While it is similar, there are some very stark differences. The first difference is that the information in sys.dm_db_index_operational stats is much more granular than sys.dm_db_index_usage_stats. Operational stats report down to the leaf and non-leaf level; usage stats do not. Along with the granularity is the difference in how the counts are tabulated. Usage stats count one for every plan that performs the operation on the index, whether 0 or 100 rows, the stats are collected. Operational stats differ in that the count increments for every row that has the DML operation performed. To summarize the difference, usage stats aggregate when the index is used and operational stats aggregate based on how much of the index is used.

The code in Listing 3-17 illustrates how operational stats are tabulated. In the listing, 73 rows are added to the table dbo.KungFu. Then 23 rows are deleted from the table. This is followed by 50 rows being updated in the table. The last query returns operational stats based on the DML activity. The results of the final query are shown in Figure 3-14.

Listing 3-17. DML Activity Script

```
USE AdventureWorks
GO

IF OBJECT_ID('dbo.KungFu') IS NOT NULL
  DROP TABLE dbo.KungFu
GO

CREATE TABLE dbo.KungFu
(
 KungFuID INT
,Hustle BIT
,CONSTRAINT PK_KungFu_KungFuID PRIMARY KEY CLUSTERED (KungFuID)
)
GO

INSERT INTO dbo.KungFu
        SELECT ROW_NUMBER() OVER (ORDER BY t.object_id)
               ,t.object_id % 2
        FROM sys.tables t
GO

DELETE FROM dbo.KungFu
WHERE   Hustle = 0
GO

UPDATE dbo.KungFu
SET     Hustle = 0
WHERE   Hustle = 1
GO

SELECT OBJECT_SCHEMA_NAME(ios.object_id) + '.' + OBJECT_NAME(ios.object_id) AS table_name
        ,i.name AS index_name
        ,ios.leaf_insert_count
        ,ios.leaf_update_count
        ,ios.leaf_delete_count
        ,ios.leaf_ghost_count
FROM sys.dm_db_index_operational_stats(DB_ID(),NULL,NULL,NULL) ios
    INNER JOIN sys.indexes i
        ON i.object_id = ios.object_id
        AND i.index_id = ios.index_id
WHERE ios.object_id = OBJECT_ID('dbo.KungFu')
ORDER BY ios.range_scan_count DESC
```

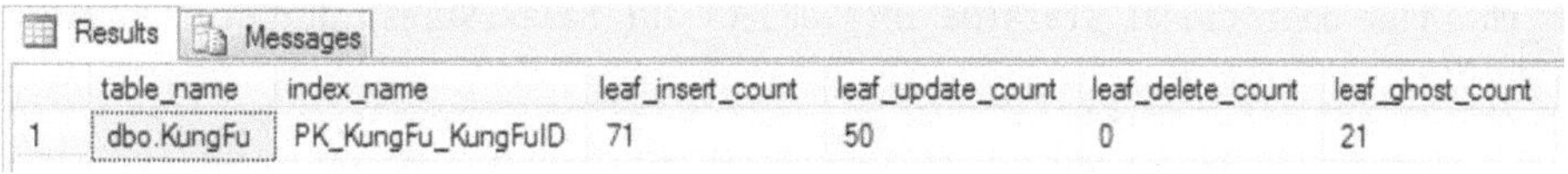

	table_name	index_name	leaf_insert_count	leaf_update_count	leaf_delete_count	leaf_ghost_count
1	dbo.KungFu	PK_KungFu_KungFuID	71	50	0	21

Figure 3-14. DML activity query results (result may vary on your system)

The value in looking at the DML activity in an index is to help you understand what is happening to the data in an index. For example, if a non-clustered index is being updated often, it may be beneficial to look at the columns in the index to determine if the volatility of the columns match the benefit of the index. It is good to look at the indexes with high amounts of DML activity and consider whether or not the activity matches your own understanding of the database platform.

SELECT Activity

After DML activity, the next area of information that can be looked at is the information on SELECT activity. The SELECT activity columns, shown in Table 3-12, identify the type of physical operation that was used when queries were executed. There are three types of access that SQL Server collects information on: range scans, singleton lookups, and forwarded records.

Table 3-12. *Access Pattern Columns in sys.dm_db_index_operational_stats*

Column Name	Data Type	Description
range_scan_count	bigint	Cumulative count of range and table scans started on the index or heap
singleton_lookup_count	bigint	Cumulative count of single row retrievals from the index or heap
forwarded_fetch_count	bigint	Count of rows that were fetched through a forwarding record

Range Scan

Range scans occur whenever a range of rows or a table scan is used to access data. When considering a range of rows, it can be anywhere from 1 to 1,000 or more rows. The number of rows in the range is not material in how SQL Server accesses the data. With table scans, the number rows is also not important but you already, likely, assume that it includes all records in the table. In sys.dm_db_index_operational_stats, these values are stored in the column range_scan_count.

To see this information collected in range_scan_count, execute the code in Listing 3-2 and Listing 3-4 from the previous section. In these two code samples, four queries will be executed. The first two will result in index seeks in the query plan, shown in Figure 3-2. And the second two queries result in index scans, as shown in the execution plans in Figure 3-4. Running the code in Listing 3-18 will show, as displayed in Figure 3-15, that all four queries used a range scan to retrieve the data from the table.

Listing 3-18. Query for range_scan_count from sys.dm_db_index_operational_stats

```
SELECT OBJECT_NAME(ios.object_id) AS table_name
      ,i.name AS index_name
      ,ios.range_scan_count
FROM sys.dm_db_index_operational_stats(DB_ID(),OBJECT_ID('Sales.SalesOrderDetail'),NULL,NULL) ios
    INNER JOIN sys.indexes i
      ON i.object_id = ios.object_id
        AND i.index_id = ios.index_id
ORDER BY ios.range_scan_count DESC
```

	table_name	index_name	range_scan_count
1	SalesOrderDetail	PK_SalesOrderDetail_SalesOrderID_SalesOrderDet...	4
2	SalesOrderDetail	AK_SalesOrderDetail_rowguid	0
3	SalesOrderDetail	IX_SalesOrderDetail_ProductID	0

Figure 3-15. *Query results for range_scan_count*

Singleton Lookup

The next statistics column collected on SELECT activity is singleton_lookup_count. Values in this column are increased whenever the key lookup, formerly bookmark lookup, is used. In general terms, this is the same type information as is collected in the column user_lookups in sys.dm_db_index_usage stats. There is a significant difference, though, between these user_lookups and singleton_lookup_count. When a key lookup is used, user_lookups will increment by one to indicate that the index operation had been used. With singleton_lookup_count, for every row that uses the key lookup operation, the value in this column will increase by one.

For instance, running the code in Listing 3-6 will result in a key lookup. This can be validated by examining the execution plan, shown in Figure 3-10. The statistics from this were discussed previously and shown in Figure 3-16. The new information to look at can be investigated by running the T-SQL statement in Listing 3-19. In the results, you can see that instead of there being a value of 1 in singleton_lookup_count, the value is 243. This is an important distinct for this column. Rather than knowing that key lookups have occurred, this statistics provides information on the scope of the lookups. One could consider that if the number singleton lookups to range scans were high that there may be other indexing alternatives to consider.

Listing 3-19. Query for singleton_lookup_count from sys.dm_db_index_operational_stats

```
SELECT OBJECT_NAME(ios.object_id) AS table_name
      ,i.name AS index_name
      ,ios.singleton_lookup_count
FROM sys.dm_db_index_operational_stats(DB_ID(),OBJECT_ID('Sales.SalesOrderDetail'),NULL,NULL) ios
    INNER JOIN sys.indexes i
      ON i.object_id = ios.object_id
        AND i.index_id = ios.index_id
ORDER BY ios. singleton_lookup_count DESC
```

	table_name	index_name	singleton_lookup_count
1	SalesOrderDetail	PK_SalesOrderDetail_SalesOrderID_SalesOrderDet...	243
2	SalesOrderDetail	AK_SalesOrderDetail_rowguid	0
3	SalesOrderDetail	IX_SalesOrderDetail_ProductID	0

Figure 3-16. *Query results for singleton_lookup_count*

Forwarded Fetch

The last column of statistics collected on SELECT activity is forwarded_fetch_count. As discussed in Chapter 2, forwarded records occur in heaps when a record increases in size and can no longer fit on the page that it is currently on. The column forwarded_fetch_count increases by one every time a record forward operation occurs.

To demonstrate, the code in Listing 3-20 builds a table with a heap and populates it with some values. Then an UPDATE statement increases the size of every third row. The size of the new row will exceed the available space on the page, resulting in a forward record.

Listing 3-20. T-SQL Script for Forward Records

```
CREATE TABLE dbo.ForwardedRecords
    (
    ID INT IDENTITY(1,1)
    ,VALUE VARCHAR(8000)
    );

INSERT INTO dbo.ForwardedRecords (VALUE)
SELECT REPLICATE(type, 500)
FROM sys.objects;

UPDATE dbo.ForwardedRecords
SET VALUE = REPLICATE(VALUE, 16)
WHERE ID%3 = 1;
```

Once the script is completed, the sys.dm_db_index_operational_stats script in Listing 3-21 can be used to view the number of times that forwarded records have been fetched. In this case, the 193 records that were forwarded resulted in a forwarded_fetch_count of 193, shown in Figure 3-17. This column is useful when looking into the performance counter Forwarded Records/sec. Reviewing this column will help identify which heap is leading to the counter activity, providing a focus on the exact table to investigate.

Listing 3-21. Query for forwarded_fetch_count from sys.dm_db_index_operational_stats

```
SELECT OBJECT_NAME(ios.object_id) AS table_name
    ,i.name AS index_name
    ,ios.forwarded_fetch_count
FROM sys.dm_db_index_operational_stats(DB_ID(),OBJECT_ID('dbo.ForwardedRecords'),NULL,NULL) ios
    INNER JOIN sys.indexes i
        ON i.object_id = ios.object_id
            AND i.index_id = ios.index_id
ORDER BY ios.forwarded_fetch_count DESC
```

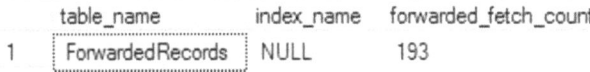

	table_name	index_name	forwarded_fetch_count
1	ForwardedRecords	NULL	193

Figure 3-17. *Query result for forwarded_fetch_count*

Locking Contention

As data is used within SQL Server databases, it is locked in order to provide consistency both in the data that users are requesting and preventing others from receiving incorrect results. At times, locking for one user can interfere with another user. In order to best monitor locking, sys.dm_db_index_operational_stats provides columns that detail the counts on locks and time spent waiting for locks to occur. A list of the columns in this group of columns is found in Table 3-13. There are three type of locks that are tracked in sys.dm_db_index_operational_stats to provide insight into locking contention: row locks, page locks, and index lock promotion.

Table 3-13. *Index Contention Columns in sys.dm_db_index_operational_stats*

Column Name	Data Type	Description
row_lock_count	bigint	Cumulative number of row locks requested
row_lock_wait_count	bigint	Cumulative number of times the database engine waited on a row lock
row_lock_wait_in_ms	bigint	Total number of milliseconds the database engine waited on a row lock
page_lock_count	bigint	Cumulative number of page locks requested
page_lock_wait_count	bigint	Cumulative number of times the database engine waited on a page lock
page_lock_wait_in_ms	bigint	Total number of milliseconds the database engine waited on a page lock
index_lock_promotion_attempt_count	bigint	Cumulative number of times the database engine tried to escalate locks
index_lock_promotion_count	bigint	Cumulative number of times the database engine escalated locks

Row Lock

The first set of columns are the row lock columns. These columns include row_lock_count, row_lock_wait_count, and row_lock_wait_in_ms. Through these columns you are able to measure the number of locks that occur on a row and then whether or not there was any contention when acquiring the row lock. Row lock contention can often be observed by its effect on transaction performance through blocking and deadlocking.

To demonstrate how this information is collected, execute the code in Listing 3-22. In this script, rows from the Sales.SalesOrderDetail tables are retrieved based on ProductID. In the AdventureWorks database, the query retrieves 44 rows.

Listing 3-22. T-SQL Script to Generate Row Locks

```
USE AdventureWorks2012
GO

SELECT SalesOrderID
  ,SalesOrderDetailID
  ,CarrierTrackingNumber
  ,OrderQty
FROM Sales.SalesOrderDetail
WHERE ProductID = 710
```

To observe the row locks that were acquired by the query, use the row lock columns in the query provided in Listing 3-23. In these results, you see that for each row that was returned by the query against Sales.SalesOrderDetail, there is one lock included in the results of sys.dm_db_index_operational_stats, shown in Figure 3-18. As a result, there were 44 row locks placed on the index IX_SalesOrderDetail_ProductID.

One thing to note: there is no information returned for the row_lock_wait_count and row_lock_wait_in_ms columns. This is because the script was not blocked by any other query. Had the query in Listing 3-2 been blocked by another transaction, then the values in these columns would have incremented.

Listing 3-23. Query for Row Locks in sys.dm_db_index_operational_stats

```
USE AdventureWorks2012
GO

SELECT OBJECT_NAME(ios.object_id) AS table_name
        ,i.name AS index_name
        ,ios.row_lock_count
        ,ios.row_lock_wait_count
        ,ios.row_lock_wait_in_ms
FROM sys.dm_db_index_operational_stats(DB_ID(),OBJECT_ID('Sales.SalesOrderDetail'),NULL,NULL) ios
    INNER JOIN sys.indexes i
      ON i.object_id = ios.object_id
        AND i.index_id = ios.index_id
ORDER BY ios.range_scan_count DESC
```

	table_name	index_name	row_lock_count	row_lock_wait_count	row_lock_wait_in_ms
1	SalesOrderDetail	IX_SalesOrderDetail_ProductID	44	0	0
2	SalesOrderDetail	PK_SalesOrderDetail_SalesOrderID_SalesOrderDet...	0	0	0
3	SalesOrderDetail	AK_SalesOrderDetail_rowguid	0	0	0

Figure 3-18. Query results for row locks

Page Lock

The next set of columns are the page lock columns. The columns in this group have similar characteristics to the row lock columns, with the exception that they are scoped at the page level instead of the row level. For every page that relates to an accessed row, a page lock is acquired. These columns are page_lock_count, page _lock_ wait_count, and page _lock_wait_in_ms. When monitoring for locking contention on an index, it is important to look at both the page and row levels to identify whether the contention is on the individual rows being accessed or possibly different rows accessed on the same pages.

To review the differences, let's continue with the query from Listing 3-22 but retrieve the page lock statistics that were collected in sys.dm_db_index_operational_stats for the query. This information is available using the script in Listing 3-24. The results this time are a bit different that those for the row locks. For the page locks, see Figure 3-19; there are only two page locks on the index IX_SalesOrderDetail_ProductID. Along with that, there are 44 page locks on PK_SalesOrderDetail_SalesOrderID_SalesOrderDetailID, which did not encounter any row locks.

Listing 3-24. Query for Page Locks in sys.dm_db_index_operational_stats

```
USE AdventureWorks2012
GO

SELECT OBJECT_NAME(ios.object_id) AS table_name
        ,i.name AS index_name
        ,ios.page_lock_count
        ,ios.page_lock_wait_count
        ,ios.page_lock_wait_in_ms
FROM sys.dm_db_index_operational_stats(DB_ID(),OBJECT_ID('Sales.SalesOrderDetail'),NULL,NULL) ios
    INNER JOIN sys.indexes i
        ON i.object_id = ios.object_id
            AND i.index_id = ios.index_id
ORDER BY ios.range_scan_count DESC
```

	table_name	index_name	page_lock_count	page_lock_wait_count	page_lock_wait_in_ms
1	SalesOrderDetail	IX_SalesOrderDetail_ProductID	2	0	0
2	SalesOrderDetail	PK_SalesOrderDetail_SalesOrderID_SalesOrderDet...	44	0	0
3	SalesOrderDetail	AK_SalesOrderDetail_rowguid	0	0	0

Figure 3-19. *Query results for page locks*

The statistics for the locking behavior may not make sense initially, until you consider the activity that occurred when the query (from Listing 3-22) executed. When query executed, it utilized an index seek and a key lookup (see the execution plan in Figure 3-20). The index seek on IX_SalesOrderDetail_ProductID accounts for the two page locks and the 44 row locks. There were 44 rows that matched the predicate for the query and they spanned two pages. The 44 page locks on PK_SalesOrderDetail_SalesOrderID_SalesOrderDetailID are the result of the key lookup operations that occurred for all of the rows from IX_SalesOrderDetail_ProductID. Together the row and page lock columns help describe the activity that occurred.

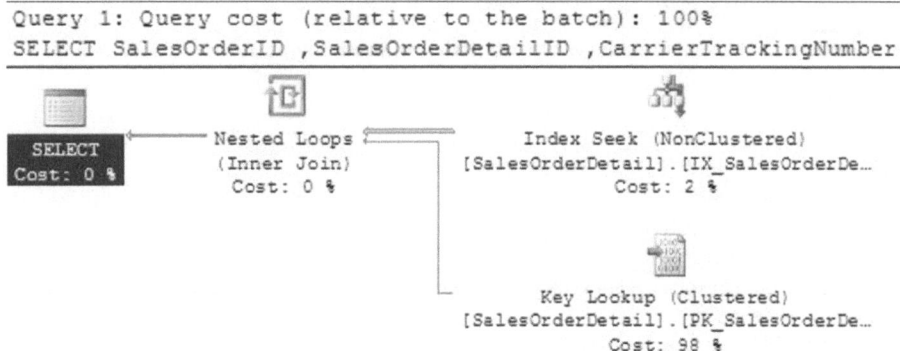

Figure 3-20. *Query results for page locks*

While row and page locking is useful for identifying when contention exists, there is one piece about locking that it does not provide. There is no information collected in the DMO about the types of locks that are being placed. All of the locks could be shared locks or they could also be exclusive locks. The lock wait count provides scope around the frequency of incompatible locks on the tables and the duration of those locks, but the locks themselves are not identified.

Lock Escalation

The last piece with locking contention to pay attention to is the amount of lock escalation that is occurring in the database. When the amount of locks acquired for an transaction exceeds the locking threshold on a SQL Server instance, the locks will escalate to the next higher level of locking. This escalation can happen at the page, partition, and table levels. There are a number of reasons for escalating locks on a database. One reason is that locks require memory, so the more locks there are, the more memory is required and the more resources are needed to manage locks. Another reason is that many individual low-level locks open the opportunity for blocking to escalate into deadlocking. For these reasons, it is important to pay attention to lock escalations.

To help provide an understanding of lock escalation, let's use a modification of the demo query that was used previously in this section. Instead of selecting 44 rows, though, you'll update all of the rows where ProductID is less than or equal to 712 (see Listing 3-25). The update will just change ProductID to its current value so as not to permanently change the data in AdventureWorks2012.

Listing 3-25. T-SQL Script to Generate Lock Promotion

```
USE AdventureWorks2012
GO

UPDATE Sales.SalesOrderDetail
SET ProductID = ProductID
WHERE ProductID <= 712
```

Now with the example script execution, you'll need to review the statistics in sys.dm_db_index_operational_stats to see if there were any lock escalations by using the script in Listing 3-26. As the output from the script shows (Figure 3-21), the column index_lock_promotion_attempt_count recorded four events for PK_SalesOrderDetail_SalesOrderID_SalesOrderDetailID and IX_SalesOrderDetail_ProductID. This means that there were four opportunities for lock escalation that were triggered. Looking at the column index_lock_promotion_count, there was one lock escalation on IX_SalesOrderDetail_ProductID. Translating the results into less technical terms, for the two indexes there were four times when SQL Server considered whether a lock escalation was appropriate for the query. At the fourth check on IX_SalesOrderDetail_ProductID, SQL Server determined that a lock escalation was needed and the lock was escalated.

Listing 3-26. Query for Lock Escalation in sys.dm_db_index_operational_stats

```
USE AdventureWorks2012
GO

SELECT OBJECT_NAME(ios.object_id) AS table_name
        ,i.name AS index_name
        ,ios.index_lock_promotion_attempt_count
        ,ios.index_lock_promotion_count
FROM sys.dm_db_index_operational_stats(DB_ID(),OBJECT_ID('Sales.SalesOrderDetail'),NULL,NULL) ios
    INNER JOIN sys.indexes i
        ON i.object_id = ios.object_id
            AND i.index_id = ios.index_id
ORDER BY ios.range_scan_count DESC
```

	table_name	index_name	index_lock_promotion_attempt_count	index_lock_promotion_count
1	SalesOrderDetail	PK_SalesOrderDetail_SalesOrderID_SalesOrderDet...	4	0
2	SalesOrderDetail	IX_SalesOrderDetail_ProductID	4	1
3	SalesOrderDetail	AK_SalesOrderDetail_rowguid	0	0

Figure 3-21. *Query results for lock escalation*

Monitoring lock escalation goes hand in hand with monitoring row and page locks. When row and page lock contention increases, either through increased frequency or duration of lock waits, evaluating lock escalation can help identify the number of times SQL Server considers escalating locks and when those locks have been escalated. In some cases where tables are improperly indexed, locks can escalate more frequently and lead to increased blocking and potentially deadlocking.

Latch Contention

Locking isn't the only type of contention that indexes can encounter. In addition to locking, there is latch contention. Latches are short, light-weight data synchronization objects. From a very high level, latches provide controls on memory objects while activities are executing. One example of a latch is when data is transferred from disk to memory. If there are disk bottlenecks while this occurs, latch waits will accumulate while the disk transfer completes. The value in this information is that when latch waits are occurring, these columns (shown in Table 3-14) provide a mechanism to track the waits down to specific indexes, thus allowing you to focus consider where indexes are stored as part of index management.

Table 3-14. Latch Activity Columns in sys.dm_db_index_operational_stats

Column Name	Data Type	Description
page_latch_wait_count	bigint	Cumulative number of times the database engine waited because of latch contention
page_latch_wait_in_ms	bigint	Cumulative number of milliseconds the database engine waited because of latch contention
page_io_latch_wait_count	bigint	Cumulative number of times the database engine waited on an I/O page latch
page_io_latch_wait_in_ms	bigint	Cumulative number of milliseconds the database engine waited on a page I/O latch
tree_page_latch_wait_count	bigint	Subset of page_latch_wait_count that includes only the upper-level B-tree pages. Always 0 for a heap.
tree_page_latch_wait_in_ms	bigint	Subset of page_latch_wait_in_ms that includes only the upper-level B-tree pages. Always 0 for a heap.
tree_page_io_latch_wait_count	bigint	Subset of page_io_latch_wait_count that includes only the upper-level B-tree pages. Always 0 for a heap.
tree_page_io_latch_wait_in_ms	bigint	Subset of page_io_latch_wait_in_ms that includes only the upper-level B-tree pages. Always 0 for a heap.

Page I/O Latch

When it comes to page I/O latches, two sets of data is collected: page level latching and tree page latching. Page level latching occurs when data pages at the leaf levels of an index, the data pages, need to be retrieved (as opposed to tree page latching, which happens at all of the other levels of the index). Both of these statistics are measure the number of latches created while moving data into the buffer and any time related to delays. Whenever time is accumulated in page_io_latch_wait_in_ms or tree_page_io_latch_wait_in_ms, it correlates to increases in wait times for the PAGEIOLATCH_* wait types.

To better understand how page I/O latches occur and the statistics you can collect, you'll review an example that will cause these waits to occur. In this demonstration, you'll return all of the data from Sales. SalesOrderDetail, Sales.SalesOrderHeader, and Production.Product via the script in Listing 3-27. Before executing the script, the buffer cache will be purged to force SQL Server to have to retrieve the data for the pages from disk. Be sure to only use this script on a non-production server where clearing the buffer cache will not impact other processes.

Listing 3-27. T-SQL Script to Generate Page I/O Latch

```
USE AdventureWorks2012
GO

DBCC DROPCLEANBUFFERS
GO

SELECT *
FROM Sales.SalesOrderDetail sod
INNER JOIN Sales.SalesOrderHeader soh ON sod.SalesOrderID = soh.SalesOrderID
INNER JOIN Production.Product p ON sod.ProductID = p.ProductID
GO
```

When the query completes, a number of page I/O latches will have occurred while populating the pages for the tables and indexes into the buffer cache. To review the page I/O latches, query against sys.dm_db_index_operational_stats on the page I/O latch columns using the script in Listing 3-28. The results, shown in Figure 3-22, indicate that there were page I/O latches issues on all three of the tables in the example query, including four milliseconds of waits incurred on Sales.SalesOrderDetail.

Listing 3-28. Query for Page I/O Latch Statistics in sys.dm_db_index_operational_stats

```
SELECT OBJECT_SCHEMA_NAME(ios.object_id) + '.' + OBJECT_NAME(ios.object_id) as table_name
,i.name as index_name
,page_io_latch_wait_count
,page_io_latch_wait_in_ms
,CAST(1. * page_io_latch_wait_in_ms
        / NULLIF(page_io_latch_wait_count ,0) AS decimal(12,2)) AS page_io_avg_lock_wait_ms
FROM sys.dm_db_index_operational_stats (DB_ID(), NULL, NULL, NULL) ios
INNER JOIN sys.indexes i ON i.object_id = ios.object_id AND i.index_id = ios.index_id
WHERE i.object_id = OBJECT_ID('Sales.SalesOrderHeader')
OR i.object_id = OBJECT_ID('Sales.SalesOrderDetail')
OR i.object_id = OBJECT_ID('Production.Product')
ORDER BY 5 DESC
```

	table_name	index_name	page_io_latch_wait_count	page_io_latch_wait_in_ms	page_io_avg_lock_wait_ms
1	Sales.SalesOrderDetail	PK_SalesOrderDetail_SalesOrderID_SalesOrderDet...	4	4	1.00
2	Sales.SalesOrderHeader	PK_SalesOrderHeader_SalesOrderID	3	1	0.33
3	Production.Product	PK_Product_ProductID	3	0	0.00
4	Production.Product	AK_Product_ProductNumber	0	0	NULL
5	Production.Product	AK_Product_Name	0	0	NULL
6	Production.Product	AK_Product_rowguid	0	0	NULL
7	Sales.SalesOrderHeader	AK_SalesOrderHeader_rowguid	0	0	NULL
8	Sales.SalesOrderHeader	AK_SalesOrderHeader_SalesOrderNumber	0	0	NULL
9	Sales.SalesOrderHeader	IX_SalesOrderHeader_CustomerID	0	0	NULL
10	Sales.SalesOrderHeader	IX_SalesOrderHeader_SalesPersonID	0	0	NULL
11	Sales.SalesOrderHeader	IX_SalesSalesOrderHeader_OrderDate	0	0	NULL
12	Sales.SalesOrderDetail	AK_SalesOrderDetail_rowguid	0	0	NULL
13	Sales.SalesOrderDetail	IX_SalesOrderDetail_ProductID	0	0	NULL

Figure 3-22. Query results for page I/O latch

Page Latch

The other kind of latching related to indexes that can occur in databases is page latching. Page latching covers any latching that occurs on non-data pages. Page latches includes allocation of GAM and SGAM pages and DBCC and backup activities. As pages are allocated by different resource, contention can occur and monitoring page latches can uncover this activity.

When it comes to an index, one common scenario in which page latches can occur is when a "hotspot" develops on an index due to frequent inserts and or page allocations. To demonstrate this scenario, you'll create the table dbo.PageLatchDemo in Listing 3-29. Next, using your preferred load generator tool, execute the code in Listing 3-30 continuously and a few simultaneous sessions. To generate the load for this example, we had five sessions with 500 total executions. Through this example, hundreds of rows will be inserted quickly into the same series of page and numerous page allocations made. Since these inserts will be so close, a "hotspot" will be created, which will lead to page latch contention.

Listing 3-29. T-SQL Script to Generate Page Latch Scenario

```
USE AdventureWorks2012
GO

IF OBJECT_ID('dbo.PageLatchDemo') IS NOT NULL
    DROP TABLE dbo.PageLatchDemo
GO

CREATE TABLE dbo.PageLatchDemo
(
PageLatchDemoID INT IDENTITY (1,1)
,FillerData bit
,CONSTRAINT PK_PageLatchDemo_PageLatchDemoID PRIMARY KEY CLUSTERED (PageLatchDemoID)
)
GO
```

Listing 3-30. T-SQL Script to Generate Page Latch Load

```
INSERT INTO dbo.PageLatchDemo
 (FillerData)
SELECT t.object_id % 2
FROM sys.tables t
```

To verify that the page latch contention did occur, use the script provided in Listing 3-31. The results, provided in Figure 3-23, show that there were numerous page latches and delays associated with them. In this example, the delayed per page latch was only about four milliseconds. In more critical situations, these values will be much higher and will help you identify when the manner in which the structures of an index are interfering with access or writing data to an index.

Listing 3-31. Query for Page Latch Statistics in sys.dm_db_index_operational_stats

```
SELECT OBJECT_SCHEMA_NAME(ios.object_id) + '.' + OBJECT_NAME(ios.object_id) as table_name
,i.name as index_name
,page_latch_wait_count
,page_latch_wait_in_ms
,CAST(100. * page_latch_wait_in_ms
    / NULLIF(page_latch_wait_count ,0) AS decimal(12,2)) AS page_avg_lock_wait_ms
```

```
FROM sys.dm_db_index_operational_stats (DB_ID(), NULL, NULL, NULL) ios
INNER JOIN sys.indexes i ON i.object_id = ios.object_id AND i.index_id = ios.index_id
WHERE i.object_id = OBJECT_ID('dbo.PageLatchDemo')
OR i.object_id = OBJECT_ID('dbo.PageLatchDemo')
```

	table_name	index_name	page_latch_wait_count	page_latch_wait_in_ms	page_avg_lock_wait_ms
1	dbo.PageLatchDemo	PK_PageLatchDemo_PageLatchDemoID	1320	50	3.79

Figure 3-23. *Query results for page latch*

■ **Note**   Page I/O and page latch contention are highly dependent on hardware. Your results for the demonstration queries in this section will not identically match the results shown.

Page Allocation Cycle

As a result of the DML activity, leaf and non-leaf pages are allocated or deallocated from indexes from time to time. Monitoring page allocations is an important part of monitoring an index (see Table 3-15 for options). Through this monitoring, it is possible to get a handle on how an index is "breathing" between maintenance windows. This breathing activity is the relationship between pages allocated to indexes through inserts and page-splits and then the removal, or merging, of pages through deletes. By monitoring this activity you can better maintain your indexes and get an idea of when it would be useful to increase index FILLFACTOR.

Table 3-15. *Page Allocation Cycle Columns in sys.dm_db_index_operational_stats*

Column Name	Data Type	Description
leaf_allocation_count	bigint	Cumulative count of leaf-level page allocations in the index or heap
nonleaf_allocation_count	bigint	Cumulative count of page allocations caused by page splits above the leaf level
leaf_page_merge_count	bigint	Cumulative count of page merges at the leaf level
nonleaf_page_merge_count	bigint	Cumulative count of page merges above the leaf level

As an example of how page allocation occurs on a table, execute the script in Listing 3-32. In this script, the table dbo.AllocationCycle is created. Afterward, 100,000 rows are inserted into the table. Since this is a new table, there is no contention on page allocations and data is added in an orderly fashion. At this point, pages have been allocated to the table and the allocations relate specifically to these inserts.

Listing 3-32. T-SQL Script to Generate Page Allocations

```
USE AdventureWorks2012 ;
GO

IF OBJECT_ID('dbo.AllocationCycle') IS NOT NULL
    DROP TABLE dbo.AllocationCycle ;
GO
```

```
CREATE TABLE dbo.AllocationCycle
(
ID INT
,FillerData VARCHAR(1000)
,CreateDate DATETIME
,CONSTRAINT PK_AllocationCycle PRIMARY KEY CLUSTERED (ID)
) ;
WITH lo AS (
  SELECT 0 AS C UNION ALL SELECT 0),
  l1 AS (SELECT 0 AS C FROM lo AS A CROSS JOIN lo AS B),
  l2 AS (SELECT 0 AS C FROM l1 AS A CROSS JOIN l1 AS B),
  l3 AS (SELECT 0 AS C FROM l2 AS A CROSS JOIN l2 AS B),
  l4 AS (SELECT 0 AS C FROM l3 AS A CROSS JOIN l3 AS B),
  l5 AS (SELECT 0.AS C FROM l4 AS A CROSS JOIN l4 AS B),
  nums AS (SELECT ROW_NUMBER() OVER (ORDER BY (SELECT NULL)) AS n FROM l5)
INSERT INTO dbo.AllocationCycle
SELECT TOP (100000) n, NEWID(), GETDATE()
FROM nums
ORDER BY n ;
```

To verify the allocations, you can check the leaf and non-leaf allocation columns leaf_allocation_count and nonleaf_allocation_count from sys.dm_db_index_operational_stats. Using the script in Listing 3-33, you see that there are 758 allocations that the leaf level and 3 at the non-leaf level (see Figure 3-24). This is an important point to remember whenever using these columns: a portion of the pages allocated can be insert related.

Listing 3-33. Query for Page Latch Statistics in sys.dm_db_index_operational_stats

```
SELECT OBJECT_SCHEMA_NAME(ios.object_id) + '.' + OBJECT_NAME(ios.object_id) as table_name
  ,i.name as index_name
  ,ios.leaf_allocation_count
  ,ios.nonleaf_allocation_count
  ,ios.leaf_page_merge_count
  ,ios.nonleaf_page_merge_count
FROM sys.dm_db_index_operational_stats(DB_ID(), OBJECT_ID('dbo.AllocationCycle'), NULL,NULL) ios
  INNER JOIN sys.indexes i ON i.object_id = ios.object_id AND i.index_id = ios.index_id
```

	table_name	index_name	leaf_allocation_count	nonleaf_allocation_count	leaf_page_merge_count	nonleaf_page_merge_count
1	dbo.AllocationCycle	PK_AllocationCycle	758	3	0	0

Figure 3-24. *Query results for page latch*

At the start of this section, there was a reference to using page allocations to monitor for page splits and identify where modifications to fillfactor can be useful. To understand this, you first need to generate page splits on the dbo.AllocationCycle table. You can do so using the script in Listing 3-34. This script increases the length of the FillerData column on every third row to 1,000 characters.

Listing 3-34. T-SQL Script to Increase Page Allocations

```
USE AdventureWorks2012 ;
GO

UPDATE dbo.AllocationCycle
SET    FillerData = REPLICATE('x',1000)
WHERE  ID % 3 = 1 ;
```

Once the data is modified, the results from executing the sys.dm_db_index_operational_stats query in Listing 3-33 change drastically. With the size of the rows expanding, the number of pages allocated jumps up to 9,849 with a total of 35 non-leaf pages (Figure 3-25). Since the order of the rows hasn't changed, this activity is related to page split from expanding the sizes of the rows. By monitoring these statistics, indexes affected by this pattern of activity can be identified.

	table_name	index_name	leaf_allocation_count	nonleaf_allocation_count	leaf_page_merge_count	nonleaf_page_merge_count
1	dbo.AllocationCycle	PK_AllocationCycle	9849	35	0	0

Figure 3-25. Query results for page latch

Compression

While not the most exciting set of columns, there are two columns in sys.dm_db_index_operational_stats that are used for monitoring compression. These columns, listed in Table 3-16, count the number of attempts that have been made at compressing a page and then the number of successful attempts in doing so. The primary value in these columns is providing feedback on PAGE level compression. Failures can lead to decisions to remove compression as it is usually not practical to have compression enabled when there is a high rate of failure with compression.

Table 3-16. Compression Columns in sys.dm_db_index_operational_stats

Column Name	Data Type	Description
page_compression_attempt_count	bigint	Number of pages that were evaluated for PAGE level compression for specific partitions of a table, index, or indexed view. Includes pages that were not compressed because significant savings could not be achieved.
page_compression_success_count	bigint	Number of data pages that were compressed by using PAGE compression for specific partitions of a table, index, or indexed view.

Page compression can fail when the cost to compress the data exceeds the value in uncompressing that data later. This is typically found in data that has very low patterns of repeating data, such as images. When image data is compressed, it often does not receive sufficient benefit from the compression and SQL Server will not store the page as a compressed page. To demonstrate this, execute the code in Listing 3-35, which creates a table with page compression enabled and inserts a number of images into it.

Listing 3-35. T-SQL Script to Generate Page Latch Scenario

```
USE AdventureWorks2012
GO

IF OBJECT_ID('dbo.PageCompression') IS NOT NULL
    DROP TABLE dbo.PageCompression
GO

CREATE TABLE dbo.PageCompression(
        ProductPhotoID int NOT NULL,
        ThumbNailPhoto varbinary(max) NULL,
        LargePhoto varbinary(max) NULL,
  CONSTRAINT PK_PageCompression PRIMARY KEY CLUSTERED (ProductPhotoID))
  WITH (DATA_COMPRESSION = PAGE);

INSERT INTO dbo.PageCompression
SELECT ProductPhotoID
  ,ThumbNailPhoto
  ,LargePhoto
FROM Production.ProductPhoto
```

The insert into the table doesn't fail, but are all of the pages compressed? To find out, execute the script in Listing 3-36; it returns the page_compression_attempt_count and page_compression_success_count columns. As the results show (Figure 3-26), seven pages were successfully compressed but another 46 pages failed to compress. With this ratio of success-to-failures for page compression, it is easy to see that the value of page compression on the clustered index on dbo.PageCompression is not very high.

Listing 3-36. Query for Compression in sys.dm_db_index_operational_stats

```
SELECT OBJECT_SCHEMA_NAME(ios.object_id) + '.' + OBJECT_NAME(ios.object_id) as table_name
,i.name as index_name
,page_compression_attempt_count
,page_compression_success_count
FROM sys.dm_db_index_operational_stats (DB_ID(), OBJECT_ID('dbo.PageCompression'), NULL, NULL) ios
  INNER JOIN sys.indexes i ON i.object_id = ios.object_id AND i.index_id = ios.index_id
```

	table_name	index_name	page_compression_attempt_count	page_compression_success_count
1	dbo.PageCompression	PK_PageCompression	46	7

Figure 3-26. Query results for compression

LOB Access

The last group of columns in sys.dm_db_index_operational_stats pertains to large objects (LOB). They provide information on the number of pages fetched and the size of those pages. Also, there are columns that measure the amount of LOB data that is pushed off and pulled into rows. All of these columns, and others in this group, are listed in Table 3-17.

The LOB access columns can be useful in determining the volume of large object activity and when data may be moving from large object to in-row overflow storage. This is important when you are seeing performance issues related to retrieving or updating LOB data. For instance, the column lob_fetch_in_bytes measures the bytes from LOB columns retrieved by the SQL Server for the index.

Table 3-17. *LOB Access Columns in sys.dm_db_index_operational_stats*

Column Name	Data Type	Description
lob_fetch_in_pages	bigint	Cumulative count of LOB pages retrieved from the LOB_DATA allocation unit. These pages contain data that is stored in columns of type text, ntext, image, varchar(max), nvarchar(max), varbinary(max), and xml. For more information, see Data Types (Transact-SQL). For more information about allocation units, see Table and Index Organization.
lob_fetch_in_bytes	bigint	Cumulative count of LOB data bytes retrieved
lob_orphan_create_count	bigint	Cumulative count of orphan LOB values created for bulk operations
lob_orphan_insert_count	bigint	Cumulative count of orphan LOB values inserted during bulk operations
row_overflow_fetch_in_pages	bigint	Cumulative count of row-overflow data pages retrieved from the ROW_OVERFLOW_DATA allocation unit.
row_overflow_fetch_in_bytes	bigint	Cumulative count of row-overflow data bytes retrieved
column_value_push_off_row_count	bigint	Cumulative count of column values for LOB data and row-overflow data that is pushed off-row to make an inserted or updated row fit within a page.
column_value_pull_in_row_count	bigint	Cumulative count of column values for LOB data and row-overflow data that is pulled in-row. This occurs when an update operation frees up space in a record and provides an opportunity to pull in one or more off-row values from the LOB_DATA or ROW_OVERFLOW_DATA allocation units to the IN_ROW_DATA allocation unit. For more information about allocation units, see Table and Index Organization.

To demonstrate some LOB activity, run the script in Listing 3-37. This script doesn't represent all of the possible activity, but it does cover the basics. At the start of the script, the table dbo.LOBAccess is created with the column LOBValue, which uses a large object data type. The first operation against the table inserts ten rows that are narrow enough that the LOBValue values can be stored on the data page with the row. The second operation increases the size of the LOBValue column forcing it to expand outside the 8K max for a data row. The final operation retrieves all of the rows from the table.

Listing 3-37. T-SQL Script to Generate LOB Scenario

```
IF OBJECT_ID('dbo.LOBAccess') IS NOT NULL
    DROP TABLE dbo.LOBAccess
GO

CREATE TABLE dbo.LOBAccess
  (
  ID INT IDENTITY(1,1) PRIMARY KEY CLUSTERED
  ,LOBValue VARCHAR(MAX)
```

```
 ,FillerData CHAR(2000) DEFAULT(REPLICATE('X',2000))
 ,FillerDate DATETIME DEFAULT(GETDATE())
 )

INSERT INTO dbo.LOBAccess (LOBValue)
SELECT TOP 10 'Short Value'
FROM Production.ProductPhoto

UPDATE dbo.LOBAccess
SET LOBValue = REPLICATE('Long Value',8000)

SELECT * FROM dbo.LOBAccess
```

Using the LOB access columns listed in Table 3-17, you can observe what happens under the covers with the script in Listing 3-38. As the output in Figure 3-27 shows, the column column_value_push_off_row_count tracked ten row operations on the index where the row moved in-row data off into large object storage. The operation coincided with the update that increased the length of the rows. The other two statistics that were accumulated, lob_fetch_in_pages and lob_fetch_in_bytes, detail the amount of pages and the size of the data retrieved during the SELECT statement. As these statistics show, the LOB access statistics provide granular tracking of LOB activity.

Listing 3-38. Query for LOB Statistics in sys.dm_db_index_operational_stats

```
SELECT OBJECT_SCHEMA_NAME(ios.object_id) + '.' + OBJECT_NAME(ios.object_id) as table_name
  ,i.name as index_name
  ,lob_fetch_in_pages
  ,lob_fetch_in_bytes
  ,lob_orphan_create_count
  ,lob_orphan_insert_count
  ,row_overflow_fetch_in_pages
  ,row_overflow_fetch_in_bytes
  ,column_value_push_off_row_count
  ,column_value_pull_in_row_count
FROM sys.dm_db_index_operational_stats (DB_ID(), OBJECT_ID('dbo.LOBAccess'), NULL, NULL) ios
INNER JOIN sys.indexes i ON i.object_id = ios.object_id AND i.index_id = ios.index_id
```

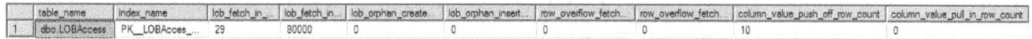

	table_name	index_name	lob_fetch_in...	lob_fetch_in...	lob_orphan_create...	lob_orphan_insert...	row_overflow_fetch...	row_overflow_fetch...	column_value_push_off_row_count	column_value_pull_in_row_count
1	dbo.LOBAccess	PK__LOBAcces_...	29	80000	0	0	0	0	10	0

Figure 3-27. *Query results for LOB statistics*

Index Operational Stats Summary

This section discussed the statistics available in the DMO sys.dm_db_index_operational_stats. While it isn't a DMO that is widely used, it does provide a lot of low level detail regarding indexes that can be leveraged to dig deep into how indexes are behaving. From the columns on DML and SELECT activity to locking contention to compression, the columns in this DMO provide a wealth of information.

Physical Statistics

The last area of statistics that SQL Server collects is the index physical stats. These statistics report the information about the current structure of the index along with the physical effect of insert, update, and delete operations on indexes. These statistics are collected in the DMO sys.dm_db_index_physical_stats.

Just like `sys.dm_db_index_operational_stats`, `sys.dm_db_index_physical_stats` is a dynamic management function (DMF). To use the DMF a number of parameters need to be supplied when it is used. The parameters for the DMF are detailed in Listing 3-39.

Listing 3-39. Parameters for sys.dm_db_index_physical_stats

```
sys.dm_db_index_physical_stats (
  { database_id | NULL | 0 | DEFAULT }
, { object_id | NULL | 0 | DEFAULT }
, { index_id | NULL | 0 | -1 | DEFAULT }
, { partition_number | NULL | 0 | DEFAULT }
, { mode | NULL | DEFAULT }
)
```

The mode parameter for `sys.dm_db_index_physical_stats` accepts one of five values: DEFAULT, NULL, LIMITED, SAMPLED, or DETAILED. DEFAULT, NULL, and LIMITED are in effect the same value and will be described together. The parameters are listed in Table 3-18.

■ **Note**   The DMF `sys.dm_db_index_physical_stats` can accept the use of the Transact SQL functions `DB_ID()` and `OBJECT_ID()`. These functions can be used for the parameters `database_id` and `object_id`, respectively.

Table 3-18. *Parameters for sys.dm_db_index_physical_stats*

Parameter Name	Description
LIMITED	The fastest mode that scans the smallest number of pages. For an index, only the parent-level pages of the B-tree are scanned. In a heap, only the associated PFS and IAM pages are examined.
SAMPLED	This mode returns statistics based on a 1 percent sample of all the pages in the index or heap. If the index or heap has fewer than 10,000 pages, DETAILED mode is used instead of SAMPLED.
DETAILED	This mode scans all pages, both leaf and non-leaf, of an index and returns all statistics.

When executed, there are three areas of information that are reported from the DMF: header columns, row statistics, and fragmentation statistics. One word of caution: this DMF gathers the information that it reports as it is executed. If your system is heavily used, this DMF can interfere with production workloads.

Header Columns

The first set of columns returned from `sys.dm_db_index_physical_stats` are the header columns. These columns provide metadata and descriptive information around the types of information that are included in that row of the results. The header columns for this are listed in Table 3-19. The most important information to pay attention to when looking at the header columns are the `alloc_unit_type_desc` and `index_level`. These two columns provide information on what type of data is being reported on and where in the index the statistics are originating from.

Table 3-19. Header Columns for sys.dm_db_index_physical_stats

Column Name	Data Type	Description
database_id	smallint	Database ID of the table or view
object_id	int	Object ID of the table or view that the index is on
index_id	int	Index ID of an index
partition_number	int	1-based partition number within the owning object: a table, view, or index.
index_type_desc	nvarchar(60)	Description of the index type
alloc_unit_type_desc	nvarchar(60)	Description of the allocation unit type
index_depth	tinyint	Number of index levels
index_level	tinyint	Current level of the index

Row Statistics

The second group of columns in sys.dm_db_index_physical_stats is the Row Statistics columns. These columns provide statistics on the rows contained in the index, shown in Table 3-20. From the number of pages in the index to the record count, these columns provide some general statistics along these lines. There are a few items of interest in these columns that can be quite useful.

Table 3-20. Row Statistics Columns for sys.dm_db_index_physical_stats

Column Name	Data Type	Description
page_count	bigint	Total number of index or data pages
record_count	bigint	Total number of records
ghost_record_count	bigint	Number of ghost records ready for removal by the ghost cleanup task in the allocation unit
version_ghost_record_count	bigint	Number of ghost records retained by an outstanding snapshot isolation transaction in an allocation unit
min_record_size_in_bytes	int	Minimum record size in bytes
max_record_size_in_bytes	int	Maximum record size in bytes
avg_record_size_in_bytes	float	Average record size in bytes
forwarded_record_count	bigint	Number of records in a heap that have forward pointers to another data location
compressed_page_count	bigint	The number of compressed pages

The first items of interest are the columns ghost_record_count and version_ghost_record_count. These columns provide a breakdown of the ghost_record_count found in sys.dm_db_index_operational_stats.

The next column to check is forwarded_record_count. This column provides an accounting to the number of forwarded records in a heap. This was discussed some in sys.dm_db_index_operational_stats with the forwarded_fetch_count column. In that DMF, the count was due to the number of times that forwarded records were accessed. In sys.dm_db_index_operational_stats, the count refers to the number of forwarded records that exist within the table.

The last column to look at is compressed _page_count. The compressed page count provides a count of all of the pages in an index that have been compressed. This helps provide a measure of value in having pages compressed by PAGE level compression.

Fragmentation Statistics

The last group of statistics in the DMF are the fragmentation statistics. For the most part, fragmentation is what most frequently turns people to looking at sys.dm_db_index_physical_stats. Fragmentation occurs in indexes when rows are inserted or modified in an index where the row no longer fits on the page where the index should be placed. When this happens, the page is split to move half of the page to another page. Since there usually isn't a contiguous page available after the page that has been split, the page gets moved to an available free page. This results in gaps in an index where pages are expected to be continuous, preventing SQL Server from completing sequential reads while reading an index on disk.

There are four columns, shown in Table 3-21, that provide the information needed to analyze the state of fragmentation within an index. Each of these helps provide a view on the extent of the fragmentation and assists in determining how to resolve or mitigate the fragmentation.

Table 3-21. Fragmentation Statistics Columns for sys.dm_db_index_physical_stats

Column Name	Data Type	Description
avg_fragmentation_in_percent	float	Logical fragmentation for indexes or extent fragmentation for heaps in the IN_ROW_DATA allocation unit.
fragment_count	bigint	Number of fragments in the leaf level of an IN_ROW_DATA allocation unit
avg_fragment_size_in_pages	float	Average number of pages in one fragment in the leaf level of an IN_ROW_DATA allocation unit
avg_page_space_used_in_percent	float	Average percentage of available data storage space used in all pages

The first fragment column is the avg_fragmentation_in_percent. This column provides a percent count of the amount of fragmentation in an index. As fragmentation increases, SQL Server will likely see an increase in the amount of physical I/Os required to retrieve data from database. Using this column, you can build a maintenance plan to mitigate fragmentation by either rebuilding or reorganizing the index. The general guideline is to reorganize indexes with less than 30 percent fragmentation and to rebuild indexes with more than 30 percent fragmentation.

The next column, fragment_count, provides a count of all of the fragments in an index. For each fragment created in an index, this column will summarize a count of those pages.

The third column is `avg_fragment_size_in_pages`. This column represents that average number of page that is in each fragment. The higher this value is and closer it is to `page_count`, the less I/O that SQL Server requires to read the data.

The last column is `avg_page_space_used_in_percent`. This column provides information on the amount of space available on pages. An index with little DML activity should be as close to 100 percent as possible. If there are no updates expected on an index, the goal should be to have the index as compacted as possible.

Index Physical Stats Summary

The primary purpose in looking at `sys.dm_db_index_physical_stats` is to help guide index maintenance. Through this DMF, statistics at every level of an index can be analyzed. Through this the appropriate amount of maintenance for each level of an index can be identified. Whether the need is to defragment the index, modify the fill factor, or pad the index, the information in `sys.dm_db_index_physical_stats` can help guide this activity.

Summary

In this chapter, you looked at the statistical information available in SQL Server on indexes. From statistics on cardinality to the physical layout of an index, you learned what information is available and how to retrieve it. For the most part, this information is the tip of the iceberg. In upcoming chapters, you'll leverage this information by looking at the statistics that have been captured and leveraging them to improve your ability to index your database.

CHAPTER 4

■ ■ ■

XML, Spatial, and Full-Text Indexing

The last couple chapters focused on indexing what is commonly referred to as structured data, where there is common schema and organization around the data and its storage. In this chapter, the indexing focus shifts to unstructured data. With both structured and unstructured data, the task of indexing is to gain optimal efficiency for retrieving and manipulating data, but the data types that represent these different types of data have differences in how they are stored in the database. These differences dictate how and why indexing is implemented. SQL Server has specialized data types and features that implement indexing for enhancing the efficiency of unstructured data and its features. The data types covered in this chapter include XML and spatial data. The chapter also covers the full-text search feature, and how we implement and consider indexing for this fully-integrated feature of SQL Server.

XML Indexing

Extensible Markup Language (XML) was introduced into information technology around 1998 and was accepted widely. XML data had been stored in databases for years but was stored in SQL Server as text values over a true XML-capable data type. The XML data type, introduced in SQL Server 2005, was a long-awaited enhancement that extended the capabilities of SQL Server to this method of passing and storing information. With the acceptance of XML, the use and size of the total XML content in singular forms or groupings of elements grew.

Benefits

The introduction of the XML data type allowed for the full capability of XML storage in a database. This included the ability to retrieve XML contents based on queries written against the XML itself. Although the XML data type sounds like a perfect fit for every instance of XML, some considerations should be taken when designing a column in SQL Server that will be storing XML. One of the most critical is that the XML content should be well formed. This ensures that the XML data type and features that are provided to utilize the data more efficiently are used to their full advantage. XML columns are stored as binary large objects, more commonly known as BLOB. This storage means that runtime querying of the content is resource-intensive and very slow in most cases. With any task that involves data retrieval, efficiency of that retrieval is of concern. In SQL Server, indexing is paramount to how efficient or non-efficient this can be. No indexing (also known as HEAP) or too many indexes will affect any data manipulation task. The XML data type also falls into this requirement. XML indexing is unique compared to the other indexing methods in SQL Server.

Categories

XML indexing consists of two categories: primary and secondary indexes. These two indexes types provide an indexing relationship within the XML documents similar to the relationship between clustered and non-clustered indexes. When implementing XML indexes, there are some basic rules that apply to each.

- Primary XML indexes include paths, tags, and values of the XML content.

- Primary XML indexes cannot exist without a clustered index on the primary key of the table that the XML column is in. This clustered index is required for partitioning the table, and the XML index can use the same partitioning scheme and functioning.

- A secondary XML index extends the primary index including paths, values, and properties.

- A secondary XML index cannot exist without a primary XML index.

Creating an XML Index

As mentioned, the XML data type should be used with well-formed XML. In order to show this in more detail, let's use a fictitious system that provides communications between cash registers and a database server. The checkout system uses XML that is built for each complete sale and then passed to SQL Server to be stored for later analysis of coupon usage trends. The XML information is received by SQL Server and is then processed and inserted into a database named AdventureWorks and table named XMLTable. The XMLTable definition will be shown later in this section. Before creating the table, rules must be set based on the XML data that will be inserted into the table. Listing 4-1 shows an example based on XML captured by this grocery checkout system.

Listing 4-1. An Example of Well-formed XML

```
<CheckoutItem>
 <TotalSales>
  <Product ProdID="937" ProdName="Wonder bread">
   <ItemSale>
    <NetPrice>1.32</NetPrice>
    <CouponPrice>.97</CouponPrice>
   </ItemSale>
  </Product>
  <Product ProdID="468" ProdName="JIFF Peanut Butter">
   <ItemSale>
    <NetPrice>2.99</NetPrice>
    <CouponPrice>.40</CouponPrice>
   </ItemSale>
  </Product>
 </TotalSales>
</CheckoutItem>
```

As mentioned, well-formed XML is ideal for taking advantage of SQL Server's full abilities. To achieve well-formedness, the XML must follow a set of basic rules and standards involving consistency in opening tags and closing each tag, prevention of special characters that are utilized by XML processing (such as < and >), and consistency in creating XML data that follows a root encapsulating tag with parent-child relating tags under the root tag.

As with well-formed XML, typed XML can take better advantage of the Optimizer than untyped XML. To create typed XML, a schema collection must first be created. In Listing 4-2, a schema collection has been written for the XML data shown in Listing 4-1. The CREATE SCHEMA COLLECTION command is used to save the schema collection for use in validating the well-formed state of the XML data that is being processed.

Listing 4-2. CREATE SCHEMA COLLECTION Used to Create Typed XML

```
CREATE XML SCHEMA COLLECTION CheckoutCouponSchema AS '
<schema xmlns="http://www.w3.org/2001/XMLSchema">
 <element name="CheckoutItem">
  <complexType>
   <sequence>
    <element name="TotalSales" minOccurs="0">
     <complexType>
      <sequence>
       <element name="Product" minOccurs="1" maxOccurs="unbounded">
        <complexType>
         <sequence>
       <element name="ItemSale" minOccurs="1" maxOccurs="unbounded">
       <complexType>
        <sequence>
         <element name="NetPrice" type="string" />
         <element name="CouponPrice" type="string" />
        </sequence>
       </complexType>
      </element>
      </sequence>
      <attribute name="ProdID" type="string" use="required" />
      <attribute name="ProdName" type="string" use="required" />
        </complexType>
      </element>
      </sequence>
     </complexType>
    </element>
   </sequence>
   <attribute name="date" type="string" use="required" />
  </complexType>
 </element>
</schema>'
GO
```

With the schema collection created in Listing 4-2, the table XMLTable can now be created. The schema collection is assigned to the XML column that will validate for any XML data that is inserted into the column. This combination of the schema collection and the XML data type on the column will only allow well-formed XML, or XML that follows the rules set by the schema collection, to be inserted into the column. Listing 4-3 shows the CREATE TABLE statement.

Listing 4-3. Creating a Table and Specifying a Schema Collection on XML Columns

```
CREATE TABLE [dbo].[XMLTable](
        [XMLValue] [xml](CONTENT [dbo].[CheckoutCouponSchema]) NULL,
        [TransID] [bigint] IDENTITY(1,1) NOT NULL,
PRIMARY KEY CLUSTERED
(
    [TransID] ASC
))
```

Listing 4-3 includes a primary key on TransID. This primary key is the clustered index for XMLTable. The importance of the existence of a clustered index and primary key will be shown later when creating other indexes on the XML data.

With the table and schema collection created, the XML information shown in Listing 4-1 can be inserted into the table. The script in Listing 4-4 provides an example of inserting the XML value into XMLTable.

Listing 4-4. Inserting XML into a SQL Server Table and XML Column

```
DECLARE @XML XML
SET @XML = '<CheckoutItem date="2/2/2010">
 <TotalSales>
  <Product ProdID="937" ProdName="Wonder bread">
   <ItemSale>
    <NetPrice>1.32</NetPrice>
    <CouponPrice>.97</CouponPrice>
   </ItemSale>
  </Product>
  <Product ProdID="468" ProdName="JIFF Peanut Butter">
   <ItemSale>
    <NetPrice>2.99</NetPrice>
    <CouponPrice>.40</CouponPrice>
   </ItemSale>
  </Product>
 </TotalSales>
</CheckoutItem>'

INSERT INTO XMLTable VALUES (@XML)
```

To query this data, there are distinct XML data type methods built into SQL Server that can be used. These include `query()`, `value()`, `exist()`, `modify()`, and `nodes()`. For example, here is a query using the `query()` method to retrieve a full XML representation of the `TotalSales`:

```
SELECT XMLValue.query('/CheckoutItem/TotalSales') AS Results FROM XMLTable
```

Figure 4-1 shows the result from executing this query.

Figure 4-1. *An XML query using query() and its result*

This query approach is efficient with a very small amount of data in the table. However, in real life, tables can become quite large, surpassing the point in which scanning through multiple XML documents is efficient. For instance, imagine if a Point of Sale system stored receipt information in XML documents for each sale. With this kind of data volume, performance would begin to suffer quickly. So let's look to indexing in order to retrieve the data as efficiently as possible.

To create either a primary or secondary index on an XML column, the `CREATE INDEX` syntax is used. This can be found in Chapter 1. In order to create a secondary index, a primary index must first be created or be pre-existing on the table. The basic syntax for creating a primary index is

```
CREATE PRIMARY XML INDEX IDX_PRIMARY on XMLTable (XMLValue)
GO
```

and the essential syntax for creating a secondary index is

```
CREATE XML INDEX IDX_SEC_PATHS ON XMLTable (XMLValue)
USING XML INDEX IDX_PRIMARY
FOR VALUE
GO
```

■ **Caution**   If you create and then drop a primary XML index, any secondary XML indexes will also be dropped, as they are dependent on the primary. No warning will be shown for this action.

The primary XML index essentially is a shredded version of the XML content that is stored in the XML column. As with all indexes, the data management view `sys.dm_db_index_physical_stats` can be used to review the index in detail. Reviewing the data returned by a query against the view shows a distinct difference in the size of the index vs. the clustered index. This size difference is important to take into account as XML indexing will take approximately three to four times the space of the column itself. This is due to the nature of XML indexes and how the contents of the XML are shredded into a table format.

The following is a query against `sys.dm_db_index_physical_stats`. Figure 4-2 shows the results.

```
SELECT index_type_desc,fragment_count,avg_page_space_used_in_percent,record_count
FROM sys.dm_db_index_physical_stats(DB_ID(N'AdventureWorks'),
    OBJECT_ID(N'XMLTable'), NULL, NULL , 'DETAILED');
```

	index_type_desc	fragment_count	avg_page_space_used_in_percent	record_count
1	CLUSTERED INDEX	1	4.54657771188535	1
2	PRIMARY XML INDEX	1	14.801087225105	19
3	XML INDEX	1	9.97034840622683	19

Figure 4-2. *sys.dm_db_index_physical_stats query results showing space utilization of indexes*

Although `sys.dm_db_index_physical_stats` is beneficial for finding information needed to maintain all indexes, including XML indexes, there is a system view specifically for XML indexing named `sys.xml_indexes`. This system view shows all the options that have been applied to an XML index. Information returned by the view can be useful in further maintaining an index, by knowing the type and other options set. This view is inherited from `sys.indexes` and returns the same columns and information as `sys.indexes`. The following additional columns also exist:

- `using_xml_index_id`: The parent index to a secondary index. As discussed, secondary indexes require a primary index to exist before creation. This column will be NULL for primary XML indexes and only used for secondary indexes.

- `secondary_type`: A flag specifying the type upon which a secondary index is based. Each secondary index is based on a specific type (V = VALUE, P = PATH, R= PROPERTY). For primary XML indexes, this column is NULL.

- `secondary_type_desc`: A description of the secondary index type. The values for the description map to those described in the `secondary_type` column.

Effects on Execution Plans

Until now we have discussed a basic overview of the primary and secondary XML indexes. Now let's look at the effect XML indexes can have on execution plans. We'll begin with an example.

In the previous example of the grocery store system, coupon data was collected for use in analysis of sales This data may prove useful in a later query for the use of coupons that save customers money on a specific product. Let's say that the sales team wants to look into JIF peanut butter coupon usage. To do this, the developer writing a query to retrieve this data could use the .value and .exist methods, as shown in Listing 4-5.

Listing 4-5. Querying XML Data with the exist() Method

```
SELECT
XMLValue.value('(/CheckoutItem/TotalSales/Product/ItemSale/NetPrice)[1]','varchar(max)')
 AS [Net Price],
XMLValue.value('(/CheckoutItem/TotalSales/Product/ItemSale/CouponPrice)[1]','varchar(max)')
  AS [Coupon Savings]
FROM XMLTable
WHERE
  XMLValue.exist('//TotalSales/Product/@ProdID[.="468"]') = 1
```

This query returns all the XML content for NetPrice and the coupon savings the customer had in CouponPrice. Looking at the execution plan, without a primary index this query would show many problems and normal operations that would need to be performed on the XML column.

As shown in Figure 4-3, extremely high-cost operations are occurring. The first operation that is significant is the Table Valued function based on an XML Reader with XPath Filter; the second is another Table Valued function with XML Reader.

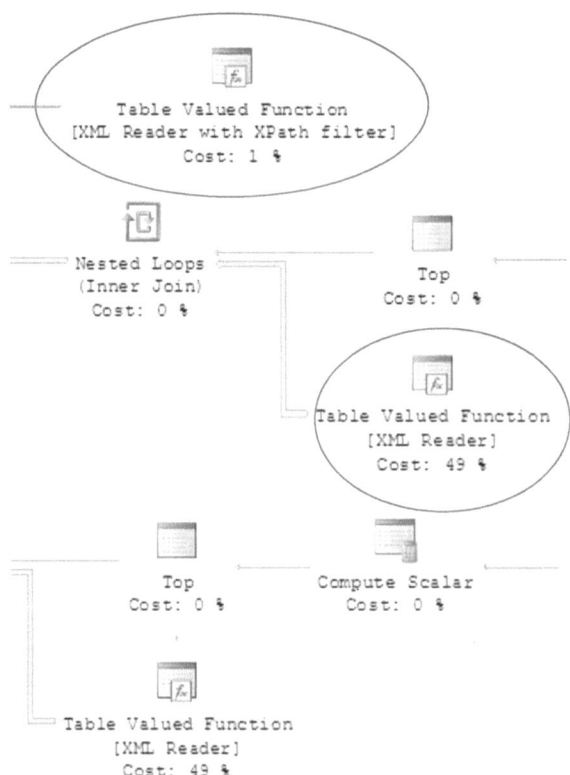

Figure 4-3. Execution plans results from query utilizing the exists() method

The execution plan in Figure 4-3 shows the XML content being shredded by Table Valued function operations, which are extremely slow and resource intensive processes overall. Creating a primary XML index on XMLValue in XMLTable will greatly benefit this query, as it will provide a representation of @prodID and allow the optimizer to perform an index seek.

Effects from a Primary Index

You can create a primary XML index with the following syntax:

```
CREATE PRIMARY XML INDEX IDX_PRIMARY on XMLTable (XMLValue)
GO
```

Now rerun the estimated execution plan to show the changes made because of the use of the primary index. You can see that the execution plan takes on an extremely different pattern, as shown in Figure 4-4. This pattern revolves around the use of the primaryXML index you created as an XMLindex. This indexing change will dramatically decrease the total duration of the query itself.

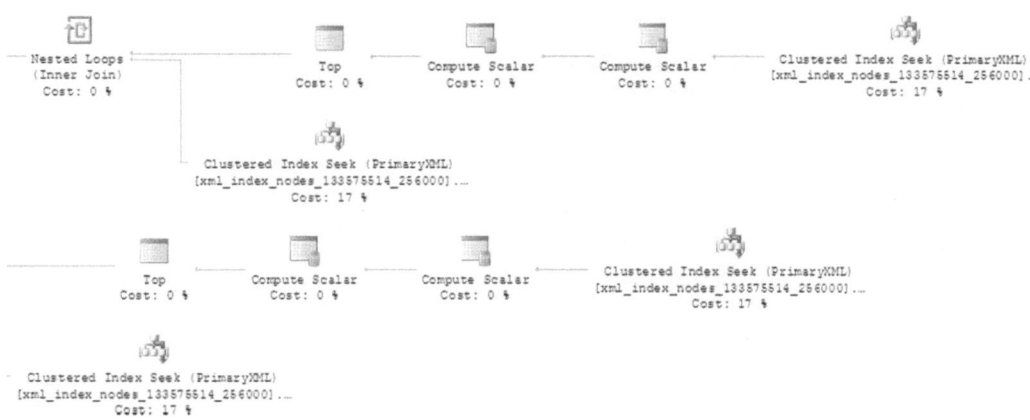

Figure 4-4. *Execution plans generated after the creation of a primary index*

Effects from a Secondary Index

In the last section, you used a primary XML index to improve three basic queries. There will be times, though, when greater improvement is desired. In these cases, secondary XML indexes can be an option. In the next set of examples, you will look at how a secondary index will improve the performance of the queries on the sample table and XML column. As mentioned, a secondary index consists of a path, value, and property. The path is typically helpful for looking directly at the paths in the content without the use of wildcards. To create a secondary XML index on PATH, the following statement is used:

```
CREATE XML INDEX IDX_SEC_PATH ON XMLTable (XMLValue)
USING XML INDEX IDX_PRIMARY
FOR PATH
GO
```

The benefit is shown in Figure 4-5, which is the result of the following query using the exists() method as a search for a specifc ProdName attribute:

```
SELECT
    XMLValue
FROM
  XMLTable
WHERE
    XMLValue.exist('(CheckoutItem[@date="2/2/2010"])[1]') = 1
```

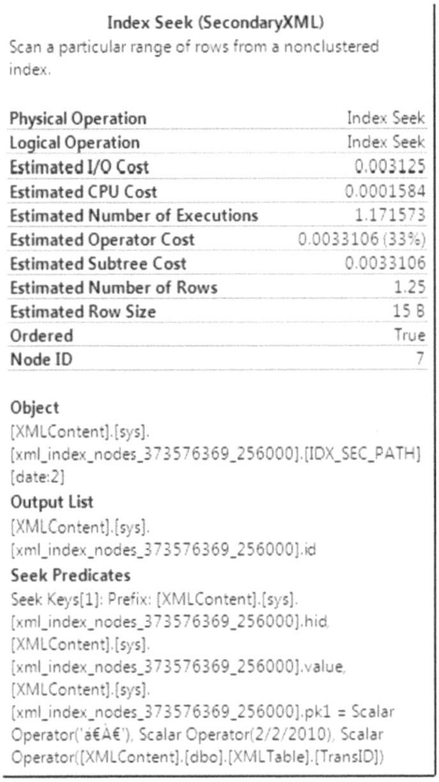

Index Seek (SecondaryXML)

Scan a particular range of rows from a nonclustered index.

Physical Operation	Index Seek
Logical Operation	Index Seek
Estimated I/O Cost	0.003125
Estimated CPU Cost	0.0001584
Estimated Number of Executions	1.171573
Estimated Operator Cost	0.0033106 (33%)
Estimated Subtree Cost	0.0033106
Estimated Number of Rows	1.25
Estimated Row Size	15 B
Ordered	True
Node ID	7

Object
[XMLContent].[sys].
[xml_index_nodes_373576369_256000].[IDX_SEC_PATH]
[date:2]
Output List
[XMLContent].[sys].
[xml_index_nodes_373576369_256000].id
Seek Predicates
Seek Keys[1]: Prefix: [XMLContent].[sys].
[xml_index_nodes_373576369_256000].hid,
[XMLContent].[sys].
[xml_index_nodes_373576369_256000].value,
[XMLContent].[sys].
[xml_index_nodes_373576369_256000].pk1 = Scalar
Operator('a€A€'), Scalar Operator(2/2/2010), Scalar
Operator([XMLContent].[dbo].[XMLTable].[TransID])

Figure 4-5. *Detailed view of the index seek operation*

Let's take a closer look at the same query in terms of XMLindexing. The query could benefit from a VALUE secondary index as well. This is due to the predicate searching for the date 2/2/2010. You can show the change in how the optimizer decides to use a VALUE secondary index over the already created PATH index. First, create another secondary index with type VALUE.

```
CREATE XML INDEX IDX_SEC_VALUE ON XMLTable (XMLValue)
USING XML INDEX IDX_PRIMARY
FOR VALUE
GO
```

As shown in Figure 4-6, the IDX_SEC_VALUE index has taken over the IDX_SEC_PATH index for the same secondaryXML operation.

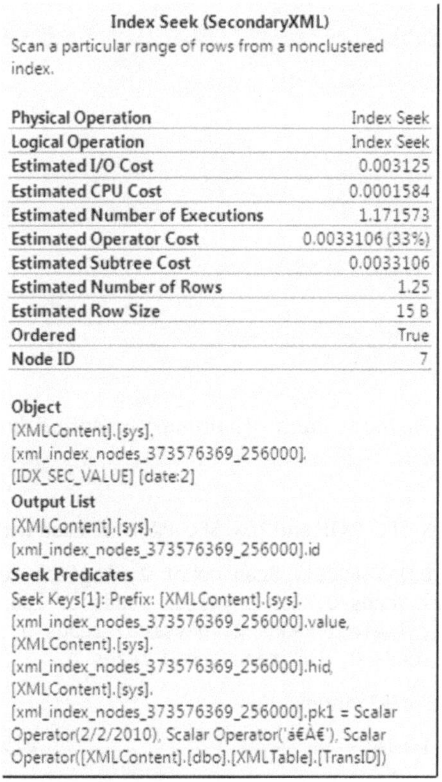

Index Seek (SecondaryXML)

Scan a particular range of rows from a nonclustered index.

Physical Operation	Index Seek
Logical Operation	Index Seek
Estimated I/O Cost	0.003125
Estimated CPU Cost	0.0001584
Estimated Number of Executions	1.171573
Estimated Operator Cost	0.0033106 (33%)
Estimated Subtree Cost	0.0033106
Estimated Number of Rows	1.25
Estimated Row Size	15 B
Ordered	True
Node ID	7

Object
[XMLContent].[sys].
[xml_index_nodes_373576369_256000].
[IDX_SEC_VALUE] [date:2]
Output List
[XMLContent].[sys].
[xml_index_nodes_373576369_256000].id
Seek Predicates
Seek Keys[1]: Prefix: [XMLContent].[sys].
[xml_index_nodes_373576369_256000].value,
[XMLContent].[sys].
[xml_index_nodes_373576369_256000].hid,
[XMLContent].[sys].
[xml_index_nodes_373576369_256000].pk1 = Scalar
Operator(2/2/2010), Scalar Operator('ä€Ä€'), Scalar
Operator([XMLContent].[dbo].[XMLTable].[TransID])

Figure 4-6. Detailed view of the index seek on a VALUE secondary index

Let's take things further now and show just how different secondary index types have an effect on the same query based on the index type that is created. In all, this query would be optimized under a primary XML index and a secondary value-based index. However, if all three secondary indexes are created, the query will utilize the property and path indexes over either the primary or VALUE secondary indexes. This may not be ideal given storage and overall execution times. For example, if a primary index alone can be used and optimal execution times can be met, then a secondary index may not be beneficial. The same situation exists if the correct secondary index is created and optimal execution times are achieved. Creating more secondary indexes would affect the overall performance of other operations on the table such as INSERT, UPDATE, and DELETE.

To illustrate, create the third secondary index type of PROPERTY.

```
CREATE XML INDEX IDX_SEC_PROP ON XMLTable (XMLValue)
USING XML INDEX IDX_PRIMARY
FOR PROPERTY
GO
```

Running the query with all three secondary indexes produces the plan in Figure 4-7.

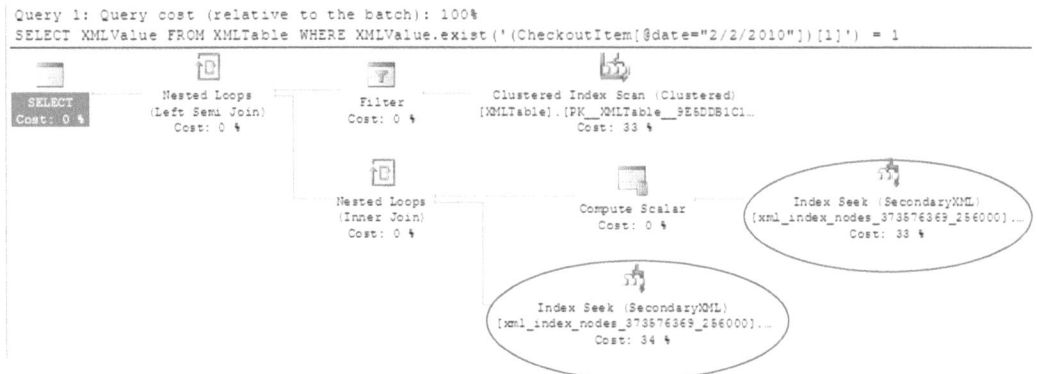

```
Query 1: Query cost (relative to the batch): 100%
SELECT XMLValue FROM XMLTable WHERE XMLValue.exist('(CheckoutItem[@date="2/2/2010"])[1]') = 1
```

Figure 4-7. *Execution plan results from the existance of a primary index and three secondary indexes*

Both the secondary indexes IDX_SEC_PATH and IDX_SEC_PROP are used with the following statistics:

```
Table 'xml_index_nodes_1687013091_256000'. Scan count 2, logical reads 4, physical reads 0,
read-ahead reads 0, lob logical reads 0, lob physical reads 0, lob read-ahead reads 0.
Table 'XMLTable'. Scan count 1, logical reads 2, physical reads 0, read-ahead reads 0, lob
logical reads 0, lob physical reads 0, lob read-ahead reads 0.
```

Now drop both the PATH and PROPERTY indexes.

```
DROP INDEX IDX_SEC_PATH ON XMLTable
GO
DROP INDEX IDX_SEC_PROP ON XMLTable
GO
```

Then execute the query again. The resulting statistics from the primary index and value secondary index used in the execution plan are

```
Table 'xml_index_nodes_1687013091_256000'. Scan count 1, logical reads 4, physical reads 0,
read-ahead reads 0, lob logical reads 0, lob physical reads 0, lob read-ahead reads 0.
Table 'XMLTable'. Scan count 1, logical reads 2, physical reads 0, read-ahead reads 0, lob
logical reads 0, lob physical reads 0, lob read-ahead reads 0.
```

This is an example of a comparable execution utilizing different secondary indexes, with a slight advantage over the use of the primary XML index combined with secondary value index in the number of scans performed. The result from this one query and different utilization of the secondary indexes shows there is value in knowing how each will possibly benefit querying the XML content. This, as well as the storage needs of each secondary index, will weigh on if either is created. Follow the basic rules of PATH being utilized for knowing the path in which the query requires, PROPERTY for searching proeprty values and PATH possibly being unknown, and VALUE based on exact value searches in queries.

Secondary indexes provide a lot of benefit when there are multiple unique values in the XML content. In many cases cases, though, a primary XML index will be sufficient. There are a number of other things to keep in mind when building secondary XML indexes. First, creating XML indexes takes a large amount of storage. Also, think about nodes and paths to indexes based on queries that will be encountered in the system. Strive to strike a balance between hardware resources, storage, index usefulness, amount of indexes created, and the number of times an index may actually be needed when building XML indexes.

Spatial Data Indexing

Spatial data storage was introduced in SQL Server 2008, advancing the storage capabilities of SQL Server into the spatial realm. Before these enhancements, spatial data was often stored as string values that required cumbersome conversions. As part of the spatial data support, SQL Server introduced the geometry and geography data types. These types support planar and geodetic data, respectively. Planar data is composed of lines, points, and polygons on a 2-D plane, while geodetic is composed of the same but on a geodetic ellipsoid. In simple terms, you can look at these two data types with geometry as a flat map representation and geography encompassing a round map aspect.

Spatial data indexes are unique in how they are created and interpreted. Each index is made of cells in a specific grid. These grids can be up to 16X16 and as small as 4X4 area of coverage. Each grid contains cells, which contain values, or in loose terms, objects making up the spatial data. There is a distinct difference between the geography and geometry data types in this type of indexing. Geography data types do not use a bounding box while a geometry data type must use a bounding box, given the dimensional concept.

How Spatial Data Is Indexed

Figure 4-8 shows how a geometry index is made up of four layers. Each of these layers consists of the grid and then cells that make the index. This layering and grid hierarchy, called decomposing, is created when the index is created.

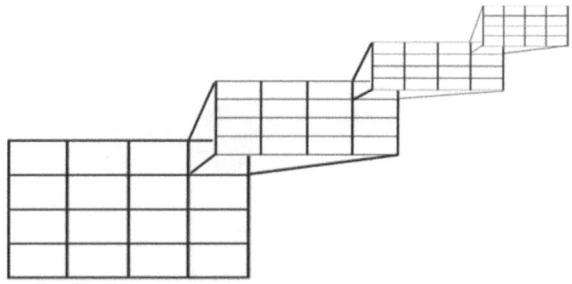

Figure 4-8. *Grid storage representation of the geometry index storage and cells*

As many as four billion cells are possible, as shown in Figure 4-8. This is important when creating the index and determining what density to use at creation. Each layer or level can have a specified density. There are three levels of density (Low = 4X4, Medium = 8X8, and High = 16X16). If the density is omitted at the time an index is created, the default is Medium. Manipulating the density is most commonly useful for tuning the actual space of the index itself. All layers may not be required at a high density. Save space by not using more density than you need.

The next step in the indexing process that SQL Server performs is tessellation. *Tessellation* is the process that places or fits the objects into the grid hierarchy starting at layer 1. This process may only require the first layer of the grid, but can require all four depending on the objects involved. Tessellation is essentially taking all the data from the spatial column and placing it onto the grids in cells while retaining each cell that is touched. The index then knows exactly how to go back to find the cells in each grid when a request is evaluated.

So far, we've gone over how the the cells in a grid are filled and how the overall tessellation process is achieved. Having the cells in a grid storage and tessellation process, however, doesn't sit well in theory because there are openings for the cells to be misused or not used efficiently based on an extreme amount of touched cells to retain. With the geometry data type and indexes created on it, the bounding box is required because SQL Server needs a finite space. Creating such a box is done by using coordinates xmin, ymax and xmin, ymax. The result can be visualized as a square having the x-coordinate and the y-coordinate of the lower left corner and the x-coordinate and y-coordinate of the upper right corner. What is most critical when determining the bounding box with an index on a geometry data type is to ensure that all the objects are within the bounding box. An index will only be effective for the objects, or shapes, within the bounding box. Not containing objects within a bounding box could severely impact performance and cause *mistuning* in spatial queries.

Furthermore, in order to retain the ability to use an index efficiently in the tessellation process, rules are applied. These rules are as follows:

> **Covering Rule:** The covering rule is the most basic rule applied in tessellation. Not to be confused with the common term of *covering index*, this rule states that any cell that is completely covered is not recorded. You can imagine the amount of processing and recorded data that this process saves.

> **Cells-Per-Object Rule:** The cells-per-object rule is a more in-depth rule that applies to the number of cells that can be counted for a specific object. In Figure 4-9, the circle shown is tessellated to the fourth layer due to a cells-per-object default of 16 in SQL Server 2008 R2 and a default of 8 in SQL Server 2012. If the circle did cover 16 cells at the second layer, tessellation would not continue through. This tuning of the cells per object can enhance the accuracy of an index. Tuning this value based on the data stored can be very effective. Given the importance of the cells-per-object rule, the setting is exposed in sys.spatial_index_tessellations. We will review this setting later in this chapter.

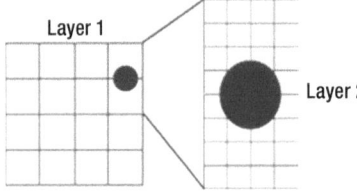

Figure 4-9. *Visual representation of an object and how many cells the object covers within the grid layers*

> **Deepest Cell Rule**. The last rule of the tessellation process is the deepest cell rule. As discussed, each layer of grids, and the cells within them, are referenced in each deeper layer. So in Figure 4-9, cell 4 is in the same location on layer 1, 2, 3, and 4. This means only the deepest layer is needed to completely refer back to any other layers effectively. This rule cannot be broken and is built into the Optimizer's processing of retrieving the data from the index.

With the geography type, there is the added challenge of projecting the form in a flattened representation through the tessellation process. This process first divides the geography grid into two hemispheres. Each hemishpere is projected onto the facets of a quadrilateral pyramid and flattened, and then the two are joined into a non-Euclidean plane. Once this process is complete, the plane is decomposed into the aforementioned grid hierachy.

Creating Spatial Indexes

The Create Spatial Index statement has most of the same options of a normal clustered or nonclustered index. However, there are specific options that are also required for this unique index. These options are listed in Table 4-1.

Table 4-1. Spatial Index Options

Option Name	Description
USING	The USING clause specifies the spatial data type. This will be GEOMETRY_GRID or GEOGRAPHY_GRID and cannot be NULL.
WITH GEOMETRY_GRID, GEOGRAPHY_GRID	The WITH options includes the setting of the tessellation schema for either the GEOMETRY_GRID or GEOGRAPHY_GRID based on the column data type.
BOUNDING_BOX	The BOUNDING_BOX is used in the geometry data type in order to define the bounding box of the cells. This option does not have defaults and must be specified when creating indexes on the geometry data type. The CREATE SPATIAL INDEX IDX_CITY_GEOM (discussed later in this section) shows the syntax for this option. Setting the BOUNDING_BOX is done by setting the xmin, ymin, xmax, and ymax coordinates, like so: BOUNDING_BOX = (XMIN = xmin, YMIN = ymin, XMAX = xmax, YMAX = ymax).
GRIDS	The GRIDS option is used for altering the density of each grid layer. All layer defaults are Medium density but can be altered to Low or High to further tune spatial indexes and density settings.

Take the follwing CREATE TABLE statement:

```
CREATE TABLE CITY_MAPS (ID BIGINT PRIMARY KEY IDENTITY(1,1),
  CITYNAME NVARCHAR(150), CITY_GEOM GEOMETRY);
GO
```

This table will consist of the primary key, city name, and then a geometry column that holds map data for the city itself. The city's density may affect tuning the cell-per-object rule in tessellation as well as the density of each layer in the grid hiearchy.

To index the CITY_GEOM column, the following CREATE statement would be used with a grid-layer density of Low for the first two layers and then Medium and High for third and fourth layers. This density change allows for tuning the object in the index and the covering cells as the layers go deeper in the grid. The cell-per-object setting is 24 maximum cells an object can cover. The bounding box coordinates are also set.

```
CREATE SPATIAL INDEX IDX_CITY_GEOM
  ON CITY_MAPS (CITY_GEOM)
  USING GEOMETRY_GRID
  WITH (
    BOUNDING_BOX = ( xmin=-50, ymin=-50, xmax=500, ymax=500 ),
    GRIDS = (LOW, LOW, MEDIUM, HIGH),
    CELLS_PER_OBJECT = 24,
    PAD_INDEX = ON );
```

To utilize and test the index created, a DBA will need to review the estimated and actual execution plans. In the case of spatial data, reviewing the actual results that a query will yield is also beneficial. SQL Server Management Studio has a built-in spatial data viewer that can be used for reviewing spatial data.

Listing 4-6 creates a table that can benefit from spatial indexing. The table is created to store ZIP codes and other data from the U.S. Census Bureau. This table will be created in the AdventureWorks database.

Listing 4-6. Creating a Database to Hold Geometry-related Data

```
CREATE TABLE [dbo].[AREAZIP](
    [ident] [int] IDENTITY(1,1) NOT NULL,
    [AREA] [real] NULL,
    [PERIMETER] [real] NULL,
    [ZT55_D00_] [bigint] NULL,
    [ZT55_D00_I] [bigint] NULL,
    [ZCTA] [nvarchar](255) NULL,
    [NAME] [nvarchar](255) NULL,
    [LSAD] [nvarchar](255) NULL,
    [LSAD_TRANS] [nvarchar](255) NULL,
    [geom] [geometry] NULL,
 CONSTRAINT [PK_AREAZIP] PRIMARY KEY CLUSTERED
(
    [ident] ASC
)WITH (PAD_INDEX = OFF, STATISTICS_NORECOMPUTE = OFF, IGNORE_DUP_KEY = OFF, ALLOW_ROW_LOCKS =
ON, ALLOW_PAGE_LOCKS = ON) ON [PRIMARY]
) ON [PRIMARY]
```

The geom column will store the geometry data. This column will be used to query the data from SQL Server Management Studio to show the imaging that can be done from other applications.

■ **Note**   To import data from the U.S Census Bureau, go to `www.census.gov/geo/www/cob/z52000.html` and download any of the Shapefiles from that page. This data can be loaded directly into SQL Server using a tool that can read and load the data into table(s). Shapefile Uploader for SQL Server 2008 by SQL Server MVP Morten Nielsen is one such tool that can accomplish the task; go to `www.sharpgis.net/page/Shape2SQL.aspx`. Shape2SQL requires some changes that are outlined on the tools documentation on the web site to provide SQL Server 2012 import functionality. Please follow the web site path to configure the tool.

Utilizing Shape2SQL and the Shapefile `zt55_d00.shp` from the census web site, load the data into database created in Listing 4-6. Figure 4-10 shows the Shape2SQL application. You can see that the option to create a spatial index is unchecked. You'll also see that the data is directed to the table created in Listing 4-6.

Reviewing the actual data from a query of a geometry data type column is not useful in the normal grid and tabular resultset from within SSMS. In order to take advantage of the spatial data features, using the Spatial Results tab in SSMS is much more effective. Given the table from Listing 4-6, a simple SELECT on the column geom can be executed and the results of the select statement will automatically generate the Spatial Results tab. For example, this query

```
SELECT geom FROM AREAZIP
```

will result in an image generated of the state of Wisconsin, coding each ZIP code area in a different color. Click the Spatial Results tab in the result window of SSMS to reveal the image generated by the query. You should see something like that in Figure 4-11.

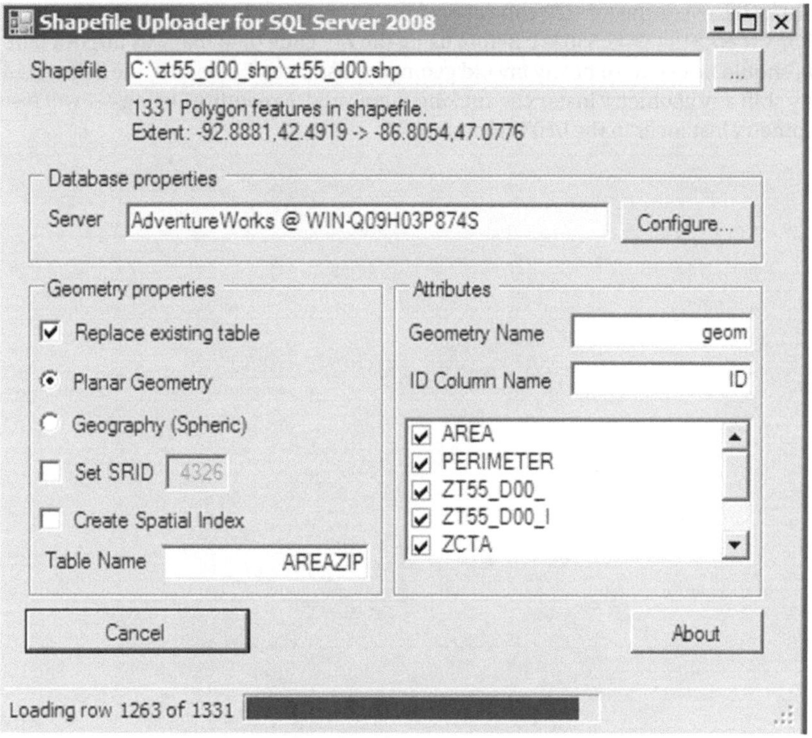

Figure 4-10. *Shape2SQL importing census ZIP code data*

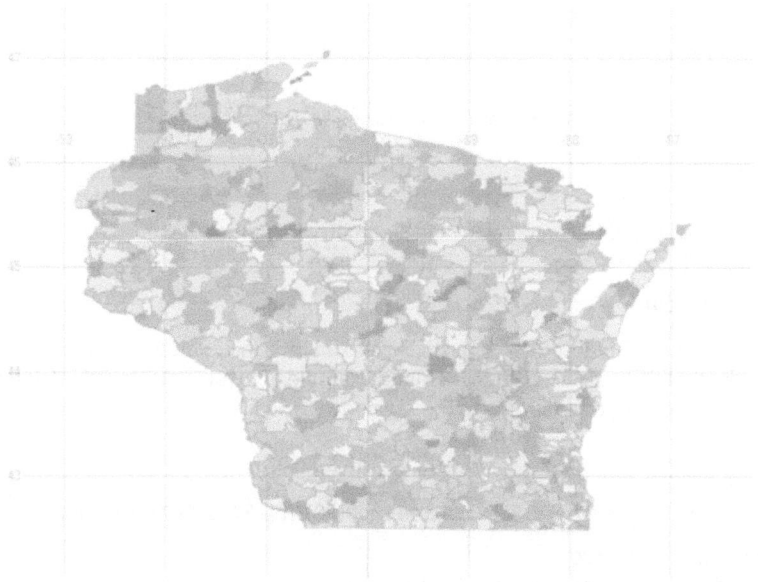

Figure 4-11. *Output from spatial query against ZIP code data*

In Figure 4-12, you can see the ten ZIP code areas from a specific point. In this case, the point is coded as ZIP code 53158, or POINT(-87.819473 42.55022). Before using the ZIP code data that was imported from the census web site, the data should be cleansed of any invalid geometry instances. To do this, the MakeValid() method can be used to slightly shift any geometry instances, making them valid. Executing Listing 4-7 will result in an update to any invalid geometry instances in the GEOM column.

Figure 4-12. *Narrowing the results of the ZIP code data using STDistance()*

Listing 4-7. Using MakeValid() to Correct any Invalid Geometry Instances

```
UPDATE AREAZIP
SET GEOM = GEOM.MakeValid()
```

The MakeValid() method should be used sparingly, and all invalid geometry instances that are found should be reviewed in a production setting. See Listing 4-8 for an example of invoking the method; it returns the ten ZIP codes closest to the given point corresponding to the ZIP code 53158.

Listing 4-8. Query for the Top Ten Closest ZIP Codes to a Given Point

```
Declare @point geometry = geometry::STGeomFromText('POINT(-87.819473 42.55022)', 0)

SELECT TOP 10 geom FROM zt55_d00
WHERE geom.MakeValid().STDistance(@point) IS NOT NULL AND geom.MakeValid().STDistance(@point) < 1
ORDER BY geom.MakeValid().STDistance(@point);
```

The query from Listing 4-8 creates execution plan shown in Figure 4-13.

Figure 4-13. Execution plan generated from STDistance() without indexing

If the spatial results tab is reviewed, the southeastern corner of Wisconsin containing the ten ZIP code areas will look like Figure 4-12. However, the query's execution plan shown in Figure 4-13 is less than ideal, with an index scan on the clustered index created from the primary key. With the use of the STDistance predicate, the query is a candidate for using an index on the geometry column, so an index should be added.

Supporting Methods with Indexes

With geometry and geography data types, only certain methods are supported with the use of indexes. The STDistance() method will support indexing, as shown in Figure 4-12. Before diving deeply into indexing the query (also from Figure 4-13), the methods that do support indexing should be pointed out. These methods have rules in how respective predicates are written. The following is a list of supported methods for the geometry type:

- geometry1.STContains(geometry2) = 1
- geometry1.STDistance(geometry2) < number
- geometry1.STDistance(geometry2) <= number
- geometry1.STEquals(geometry2) = 1
- geometry1.STIntersects(geometry2) = 1
- geometry1.STOverlaps(geometry2) = 1
- geometry1.STTouches(geometry2) = 1
- geometry1.STWithin(geometry2) = 1

And the following are the supported methods for the geography type:

- geography1.STIntersects(geography2) = 1
- geography1.STEquals(geography2) = 1
- geography1.STDistance(geography2) < number
- geography1.STDistance(geography2) <= number

For both geometry and geography, in order to return any result that is not null, the first parameter and second parameter must have the same spatial reference identifier (SRID), which is a spatial reference system based on a specific ellipsoid used to flatten or round the earth.

Recall that the query used in Figure 4-13 to return the southeastern corner of Wisconsin and the ten ZIP code areas uses the STDistance() method in the expression STDistance(@point) < 1. Based on the methods supported and analyzing the options and CREATE syntax for spatial indexing, the INDEX CREATE statement shown in Listing 4-9 could be utilized in an attempt to optimize the query.

Listing 4-9. Create Statement for a Spatial Index

```
CREATE SPATIAL INDEX IDX_WIZIP_GEOM ON [dbo].[AREAZIP]
(
    [geom]
)USING GEOMETRY_GRID
WITH (
BOUNDING_BOX =(-91.513079, -87.496494, 36.970298, 36.970298), GRIDS =(LEVEL_1 = LOW,LEVEL_2 =
MEDIUM,LEVEL_3 = MEDIUM,LEVEL_4 = HIGH),
CELLS_PER_OBJECT = 16, PAD_INDEX = OFF, SORT_IN_TEMPDB = OFF, DROP_EXISTING = OFF, ALLOW_ROW_
LOCKS = ON, ALLOW_PAGE_LOCKS = ON) ON [PRIMARY]
GO
```

Executing the query in Listing 4-9 results in the much different execution plan, shown in Figure 4-14. It results in a shorter duration when executing and returning the results, plus spatial results. The largest difference in the execution plan is the use of the index IDX_WINZIP_GEOM.

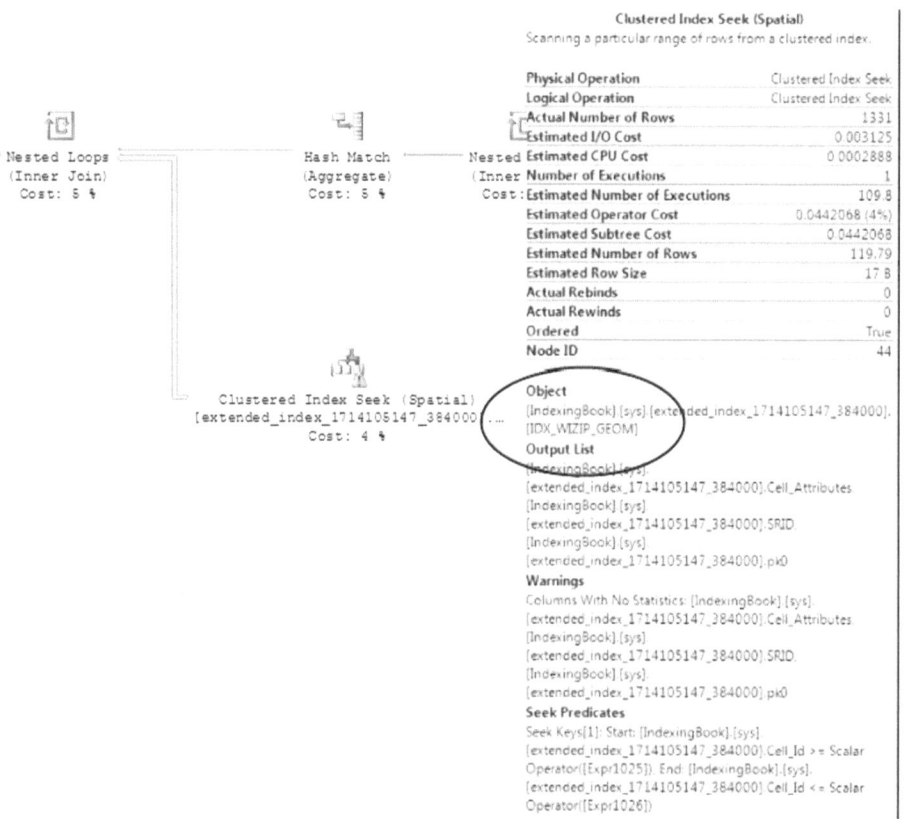

Figure 4-14. *Optimized details of a tuned execution plan using spatial data*

You can see an overall improvement and more optimal execution plan from the creation of the spatial index. The index and optimal execution plan is good, but validating the actual improvement by checking the overall duration in execution time should not be skipped. By turning Show Client Statistics on in SSMS, an overall review of the execution of the statement can be retrieved. In the case of the query that searches for the southeastern corner of Wisconsin and the area code coverages, the client statistics results with the index in place returned 559 milliseconds. Dropping the index and executing the same query returns 1279 milliseconds for total execution time. This test is an extremely basic, but solid, foundation upon which you can begin to form a strategy for indexing existing spatial data to improve overall performance.

Understanding Statistics, Properties, and Information

Indexes in general have many data management views and functions that make the administration of the indexes much easier and more efficient than manual statistics gathering.With spatial indexes, there are additional catalog views that are added to assist in the unique settings and administration of them. In addition to the views, there are also some built-in procedures that you can invoke to get information about spatial indexes.

The Views

There are two catalog views: sys.spatial_index and sys.spatial_index_tessellation. The sys.spatial_index view provides the type and tessellation scheme as well as basic information about each spatial index. The spatial_index_type column returned by sys.spatial_index returns a 1 for geometry indexes and a 2 for geography indexes. The following is an example query against the view, and Figure 4-15 shows the results.

```
SELECT
        [name],
        type_desc,
        spatial_index_type,
        spatial_index_type_desc,
        tessellation_scheme
FROM sys.spatial_indexes
```

	name	type_desc	spatial_index_type	spatial_index_type_desc	tessellation_scheme
1	IDX_WIZIP_GEOM	SPATIAL	1	GEOMETRY	GEOMETRY_GRID

Figure 4-15. Querying sys.spatial_indexes and results showing IDX_WIZIP_GEOM index

Now query the sys.spatial_index_tessellation view to see the parameters of the index and the tessellation scheme. The following is the query, and Figure 4-16 shows the results.

```
SELECT
        tessellation_scheme,
        bounding_box_xmax,
        bounding_box_xmin,
        bounding_box_ymax,
        bounding_box_ymin,
        level_1_grid_desc,
        level_2_grid_desc,
        level_3_grid_desc,
        level_4_grid_desc,
        cells_per_object
FROM sys.spatial_index_tessellations
```

	tessellation_scheme	bounding_box_xmax	bounding_box_xmin	bounding_box_ymax	bounding_box_ymin	level_1_c··
1	GEOMETRY_GRID	36.970298	-91.513079	36.970298	-87.496494	LOW

Figure 4-16. *Querying sys.spatial_index_tessellations and partial results*

Both of these catalog views can be joined on the `object_id` to become extremely useful for tuning and maintenance tasks. At times, it may prove effective to manipulate and recreate indexes as needed when the spatial data dictates.

The Procedures

As well as the additional catalog views, four other procedures have been provided internally for further analysis of the spatial indexes. These procedures return a complete listing of properties that are set on the indexes. The four procedures and their parameters are as follows:

```
sp_help_spatial_geometry_index [ @tabname =] 'tabname'
   [ , [ @indexname = ] 'indexname' ]
   [ , [ @verboseoutput = ] 'verboseoutput'
   [ , [ @query_sample = ] 'query_sample']

sp_help_spatial_geometry_index_xml [ @tabname =] 'tabname'
   [ , [ @indexname = ] 'indexname' ]
   [ , [ @verboseoutput = ]'{ 0 | 1 }]
   [ , [ @query_sample = ] 'query_sample' ]
   [ ,.[ @xml_output = ] 'xml_output' ]

sp_help_spatial_geography_index [ @tabname =] 'tabname'
   [ , [ @indexname = ] 'indexname' ]
   [ , [ @verboseoutput = ] 'verboseoutput' ]
   [ , [ @query_sample = ] 'query_sample' ]

sp_help_spatial_geography_index_xml [ @tabname =] 'tabname'
   [ , [ @indexname = ] 'indexname' ]
   [ , [ @verboseoutput = ] 'verboseoutput' ]
   [ , [ @query_sample = ] 'query_sample' ]
   [ ,.[ @xml_output = ] 'xml_output' ]
```

The following is an example showing how to execute these stored procedures. The example returns information about the geometry index `IDX_WIZIP_GEOM` created earlier in Listing 4-9. Figure 4-17 shows the results.

```
DECLARE @Sample GEOMETRY
  = 'POLYGON((-90.0 -180.0, -90.0 180.0, 90.0 180.0, 90.0 -180.0, -90.0 -180.0))';
EXEC sp_help_spatial_geometry_index 'dbo.AREAZIP', 'IDX_WIZIP_GEOM', 0, @Sample;
```

	propname	propvalue
1	Total_Number_Of_ObjectCells_In_Level0_For_QuerySample	1
2	Total_Number_Of_ObjectCells_In_Level0_In_Index	1331
3	Total_Number_Of_ObjectCells_In_Level1_For_QuerySample	60
4	Total_Number_Of_ObjectCells_In_Level2_For_QuerySample	960
5	Total_Number_Of_Interior_ObjectCells_In_Level1_For_QuerySample	56
6	Total_Number_Of_Interior_ObjectCells_In_Level2_For_QuerySample	896
7	Total_Number_Of_Intersecting_ObjectCells_In_Level1_For_QuerySample	4
8	Total_Number_Of_Intersecting_ObjectCells_In_Level2_For_QuerySample	64
9	Total_Number_Of_Border_ObjectCells_In_Level0_For_QuerySample	1
10	Total_Number_Of_Border_ObjectCells_In_Level0_In_Index	1331
11	Number_Of_Rows_Selected_By_Primary_Filter	1331
12	Number_Of_Rows_Selected_By_Internal_Filter	0
13	Number_Of_Times_Secondary_Filter_Is_Called	1331
14	Number_Of_Rows_Output	776
15	Percentage_Of_Rows_NotSelected_By_Primary_Filter	0
16	Percentage_Of_Primary_Filter_Rows_Selected_By_Internal_Filter	0
17	Internal_Filter_Efficiency	0
18	Primary_Filter_Efficiency	58.3020285499624

Figure 4-17. sp_help_spatial_geometry_index example and results (results may vary)

Restrictions on Spatial Indexes

Spatial indexes provide some unique features and restrictions. The following is a comprehensive listing of restrictions for spatial indexing:

- spatial index can be created only on a column of type geometry or geography.

- Spatial indexes can be defined only on a table that has a primary key. The maximum number of primary key columns on the table is 15.

- The maximum size of index key records is 895 bytes. Larger sizes raise an error.

- The use of Database Tuning Advisor is not supported.

- You cannot perform an online rebuild of a spatial index.

- Spatial indexes cannot be specified on indexed views.

- You can only create up to 249 spatial indexes on any of the spatial columns in a supported table. Creating more than one spatial index on the same spatial column can be useful, for example, to index different tessellation parameters in a single column.

- You can create only one spatial index at a time.

- An index build of a spatial cannot make use of available process parallelism.

Indexing of spatial data is a complicated form of data storage and manipulation. This review has covered the main points in how spacial data is processed and stored to help in managing and reviewing an implementation of the spatial data types in databases.

Full-Text Indexing

Full-text search indexing is another indexing feature in SQL Server, outside the normal indexing methods and objects. This section will provide a brief description of the full-text search architecture, storage, and indexing for optimal performance.

Full-text search (FTS) allows the storage of large amounts of text-based content. This content can include a number of document types including formats like Word document (.doc) files. This storage is then in BLOB columns instead of plain text data. The abilitiy to search and store content of unstructured nature provides a number of opportunities in a database management system.

Document retention is one such opportunity; it allows the storing of documents for vast lengths of time at a much lower cost. The search abilities then allow for querying this content for all types of needs. Imagine a shipping company that creates thousands of shipping documents from a template created in plain text. Those documents create a massive initiative for retention purposes to ensure shipments can be tracked for later needs. Storage warehouse rooms cost money to maintain. When the task of researching a specific shipment arises, the hours taken for that task are significant.

Now imagine this shipping company using the FTS feature and an indexing structure. The documents are scanned with systems that read the text into a system that later inserts this data into a SQL Server database. This allows for a full-text search of specific account numbers, shipping invoices, and any distinct text in the documents that is later needed for review. An index just like an index in a book can be created, making it even quicker tofind specific documents . Going further, FTS lets you search for specific content in the documents themselves. If a request comes in to find all shipping documents that were sent by a specific freight company on a specific trailer, the FTS capabilities allow the information to be retrieved in a fraction of the time as compared to a manual process.

Creating a Full-Text Example

Now that you unserstand the concept of FTS, let's look at the indexing strategy. Full-text indexes are essentially the backbone of searching and querying the data. This data can be a number of data types including char, varchar, nchar, nvarchar, text, ntext, image, xml, varbinary, and varbinary(max). Utilizing varchar(max) on most 64-bit based systems has been known to outperform most data types in latest tests by the CAT team as described in "Best Practices for Integrated Full Text Search (iFTS) in SQL 2008" (http://blogs.msdn.com/b/sqlcat/archive/2008/11/06/best-practices-for-integrated-full-text-search-ifts-in-sql-2008.aspx). This is, in part, due to data types like char using a direct parsing mechanism and the others using specialized processing. 64-bit systems and FTS tend to outperform 32-bit systems due to the memory-intense use of the FTS process itself. When 32-bit systems are in use, the memory consumption should be configured and monitored carefully. This is partly why FTS on larger installations are utilized on designated hardware and databases. This allows the database administrator to maintain a system for FTS specifically.

For the remainder of this section on full-text search indexing, the contents of the whitepaper "High Availability with SQL Server 2008" by Paul S. Randal has been inserted into the the sample table using the script in Listing 4-10. The document will be used to demonstrate full-text indexing. The document can be found in Books Online or downloaded from http://msdn.microsoft.com/en-us/library/ee523927.aspx.

Using AdventureWorks, a table can be prepared that will be used for full-text searching. Using the varbinary(max) data type allows the import of most document types and images. In Listing 4-10, the CREATE TABLE and INSERT statements prepare the objects needed to create a full-text search index.

Listing 4-10. Table and INSERT Statements Used with Full-Text Search

```
CREATE TABLE SQLServerDocuments (ID INT IDENTITY(1,1) PRIMARY KEY, DocType VARCHAR(6), DOC
VARBINARY(MAX))
GO
DECLARE @worddoc VARBINARY(MAX)
SELECT @worddoc = CAST(bulkcolumn AS VARBINARY(MAX))
FROM OPENROWSET( BULK 'C:\High Availability with SQL Server 2008.doc', SINGLE_BLOB ) AS x
```

```
INSERT INTO SQLServerDocuments (DocType,DOC)
VALUES ('doc',@worddoc)
GO
```

Creating a Full-Text Catalog

When creating a FTS Index, a full-text catalog must first be created. Prior to SQL Server 2008 and SQL Server 2012, this catalog was a physical object and was optimized by designating a specific file group for the catalog. In SQL Server 2008 and SQL Server 2012, the catalog is now contained in the database as a definition. The catalog itself is now a virtual object and greatly enhances the performance by elimating I/O bottlenecks. A catalog contains all the properties that are searchable.

The catalog is the link to the full-text index. To create a new full-text catalog, use the CREATE FULLTEXT CATALOG syntax shown in Listing 4-11.

Listing 4-11. The Create Full-Text Catalog Syntax

```
CREATE FULLTEXT CATALOG <catalog name>
WITH <catalog specific options>
AS DEFAULT
AUTHORIZATION <the owners name - ownership>
ACCENT_SENSITIVITY = <ON|OFF>
```

The first option that should be considered in the creation of a catalog is the AS DEFAULT setting. Commonly, full-text indexes are created without thought of the catalog they should be applied to. If the catalog is omitted in the index creation, the catalog that has been set as default will be used.

Authorization and accent sensitivity are specific in the CREATE command. When omitting the authorization option, ownership will fall under dbo. This is the same for most objects in SQL Server when ownership is not declared. It is recommended to assign ownership for managing security and grouping objects under the proper areas. When specifying a user for ownership, you must specify a user name matching one of the following:

- The name of the user running the statement.

- The name of a user that the user executing the command has impersonate permissions for.

- The user executing the command must be the database owner or system administrator.

Accent sensitivity dictates whether the catalog will be accent sensitive or insensitive. Be sure to research if accent sensitivity should be on or off prior to the creation of the catalog. If this option is changed, the full-text indexes on the catalog must be rebuilt.

Execute the following statement to create a catalog as the default to be used with the whitepaper inserted into the table created in Listing 4-10:

```
CREATE FULLTEXT CATALOG WhitePaperCatalog AS DEFAULT
```

Creating a Full-Text Index

With the catalog created and the decision made for how you want to handle it, now some decisions and restrictions need to be applied to the creation of the full-text index. The most critical of these decisions is the requirement of a key index.

Syntax

The full-text index can be created using the syntax in Listing 4-12. Table 4-2 describes the different options available.

Table 4-2. *Full-Text Index Options*

Option Name	Description
TYPE COLUMN	Specifies the name of the column that holds the document type for documents loaded in BLOB types, such as .doc, .pdf, and .xls. This option is only used for varbinary, varbinary(max), and image data types. If this option is specified on any other data type, the CREATE FULLTEXT INDEX statement will throw an error.
LANGUAGE	Alters the default language that is used for the index with the following variations and options: • Language can be specified as string, integer, or hexadecimal. • If language is specified, the language is used when a query is run using the index. • When language is specified as a string value, the syslanguages system table must correspond to the language. • If a double-byte value is used, it is converted to hexadecimal at creation time. • Word breakers and stemmers for the specific language must be enabled or a SQL Server error will be generated. • Non-BLOB and non-XML columns containing multiple languages should follow the 0x0 neutral language setting. • For BLOB and XML types, language types in the documents themselves will be used. Example: a Word document with a language type of Russian or LCID 1049 will force the same setting in the index. Use sys.fulltext_languages to review all the language types and LCID codings available.
KEY INDEX	Every full-text index requires an adjoining unique, single-key, non-null column to be designated. Specify the column in the same table using this option.
FULLTEXT_ CATALOG_NAME	If the full-text index is not to be created using the default catalog, specify the catalog name using this option.
CHANGE_TRACKING	Determines how and when an index is populated. Options are MANUAL, AUTO, and OFF [NO_ POPULATION]. MANUAL setting requires ALTER FULLTEXT INDEX … START UPDATE POPULATION to be executed before the index is populated. AUTO setting populates the index at creation time and automatically updates based on changes that are made ongoing. This is the default setting if CHANGE_TRACKING is omitted in the CREATE statement. OFF [NO_POPULATION] is used to completely turn population off for the index and SQL Server will not retain a list of changes. The index is populated upon creation one time unless the NO_POPULATION is specified.
STOPLIST	Specifies a StopList that will essentially stop certain words from being indexed. OFF, SYSTEM, and a custom StopList are available options. OFF setting will not use a StopList and will have more overhead on performance of population of the index. SYSTEM is the default StopList created already. User-created StopList is a StopList that was created that can be used in association with an index.

Listing 4-12. Create Full-Text Index Syntax

```
CREATE FULLTEXT INDEX ON <table name>
(<column name>)
KEY INDEX <index name [must be specified]>
ON <catalog filegroup>
WITH <index options>
CHANGE_TRACKING = <Manual | Auto | Off>
STOPLIST = <default system or specifed stoplist name>
```

In most other `CREATE INDEX` statements, the basic syntax and options are alike with slight modifications. With the FTS index creation, you can see there is a completely different set of options and considerations. The initial `CREATE FULLTEXT INDEX` is the same as any `CREATE INDEX` with the given table required and then column to index. After this start to writing the statement, other options must be considered not typical to normal index creations.

Key Indexes

Chosing the key index can be a straightforward choice given the restrictions of the key index being unique, single-key, and non-nullable column. A primary key will commonly work well for this, like the primary key seen in Listing 4-10 on the `SQLServerDocuments` table. However, thought should be given to the size of the key itself. Ideally, a 4-byte key is recommended and documented as optimal to reduce overhead on I/O and CPU resource consumption. Recall that one of the restrictions of the unique key is that it cannot exceed 900 bytes. If this maxiumum restriction is met, the population will fail. Resolving the problem could force a new index and alteration of the table itself to occur. This could be costly downtime for tables that are in a high use situation.

Population

Change tracking in full-text indexing should be weighed heavily when creating full-text indexes. The default setting of AUTO may have overhead that can affect the performance negatively if the contents change frequently. For example, a system that is storing shipping invoices that never change and are only inserted once a month would not likely benefit from AUTO being set. A MANUAL population would most likely be better run at a given time by using the SQL Server Agent based on the loading of the contents in the table. Although not common, some systems are static and loaded only one time. This would be an ideal situation for using the OFF setting, with the initial population only being performed at that time.

The last option for population is incremental population. It is an alternative to manual population. Incremental population is the same concept as an incremental update to data. As you run through the data and changes are made, they are tracked. Think of merge replication as a comparison. Merge replication retains changes by the use of triggers and insert/update/delete tracking rows into merge system tables. At a given point in time, a DBA can set a synchronization schedule to process those changes and replicate them to the susbcribers. This is the same way incremental population functions. By using a `timestamp` column in the table, the changes are tracked. Only those that are found needing a change are processed. This does mean the requirement for a timestamp column on the table must be met in order to perform incremental populations. For data that has an extreme amount of change, this may not be ideal. However, for data that changes randomly and seldomly, incremental population may be suited for the installation.

StopLists

StopLists are extremely useful in managing what not to populate. This can improve the population performance by bypassing what are known as *noise words*. As an example, consider the sentence "A dog chewed through the fiber going to the SAN causing the Disaster and Recovery plans to be used for the SQL Server instance." In this sentence you would most likely want *fiber*, *SAN*, *Disaster*, *Recovery* and *SQL* or *Server* indexed. The *A, the, to* and *be* words would not be ideal. These are considered noise words and are not part of the population process. As you can imagine, the use of StopList can be extremely helpful in the overall population performance and parsing of the content. Use of the StopList can be specific to languages as well. For example, *la* in French would be specified over *the* in English.

In order to create a custom StopList, use the `CREATE FULLTEXT STOPLIST` statement. The system default StopList can be used to pre-generate all the noise words already identified as such. For the Whitepaper example, the name of the StopList would be `WhitePaperStopList`.

```
CREATE FULLTEXT STOPLIST WhitePaperStopList FROM SYSTEM STOPLIST;
```

To view the StopList, use the system views `sys.fulltext_stoplists` and `sys.fulltext_stopwords`. The `sys.fulltext_stoplists` view will hold metadata related to the stoplists that are created on the SQL Server instance. Determine the stoplist_id to join to the `sys.fulltext_stopwords` to show a complete listing of the words. Alone, this StopList is no better than the system default StopList. To add words to the StopList, use the `ALTER FULLTEXT STOPLIST` statement.

```
ALTER FULLTEXT STOPLIST WhitePaperStopList ADD 'Downtime' LANGUAGE 1033;
```

To review the StopList words, run the query shown in Listing 4-13.

Listing 4-13. Using sys.fulltext_stoplists to Review StopList Words

```
SELECT
        lists.stoplist_id,
        [name],
        stopword
FROM
sys.fulltext_stoplists lists
JOIN sys.fulltext_stopwords words on lists.stoplist_id = words.stoplist_id
WHERE words.[language] = 'English'
ORDER BY lists.[name]
```

Looking at the query results in Figure 4-18. You can see the word *Downtime* has been successfully added.

	stoplist_id	name	stopword
13	5	WhitePaperStopList	B
14	5	WhitePaperStopList	C
15	5	WhitePaperStopList	D
16	5	WhitePaperStopList	Downtime
17	5	WhitePaperStopList	E
18	5	WhitePaperStopList	F
19	5	WhitePaperStopList	G
20	5	WhitePaperStopList	H
21	5	WhitePaperStopList	I
22	5	WhitePaperStopList	J

Figure 4-18. Query results of a StopList

With the catalog, StopList, and key index availability within the primary key ID in the table created in Listing 4-10, a full-text index can be created on the DOC column in the same table from Listing 4-10. To create a full-text index, the `CREATE FULLTEXT INDEX` statement is used. (see Listing 4-14).

Listing 4-14. CREATE FULL TEXT INDEX Statement

```
CREATE FULLTEXT INDEX ON dbo.
SQLServerDocuments
    (
    DOC
    TYPE COLUMN DocType
    )
  KEY INDEX [PK__SQLServe__3214EC2769F9A9EA]
  ON WhitePaperCatalog
  WITH STOPLIST = WhitePaperStopList;
GO
```

Once the index is created, population will begin since there was no option added for CHANGE_TRACKING. The default AUTO setting takes effect. To query the content of the `Whitepaper` table and `Contents` column, you can run a `CONTAINS` statement to return a specific word. Listing 4-15 shows an example of such a statement.

Listing 4-15. Using <u>CONTAINS</u> to Query for a Specific Word

```
SELECT
    DOC, DocType
FROM SQLServerDocuments
WHERE CONTAINS(DOC, 'replication')
```

Figure 4-19 shows the execution plan from the query.

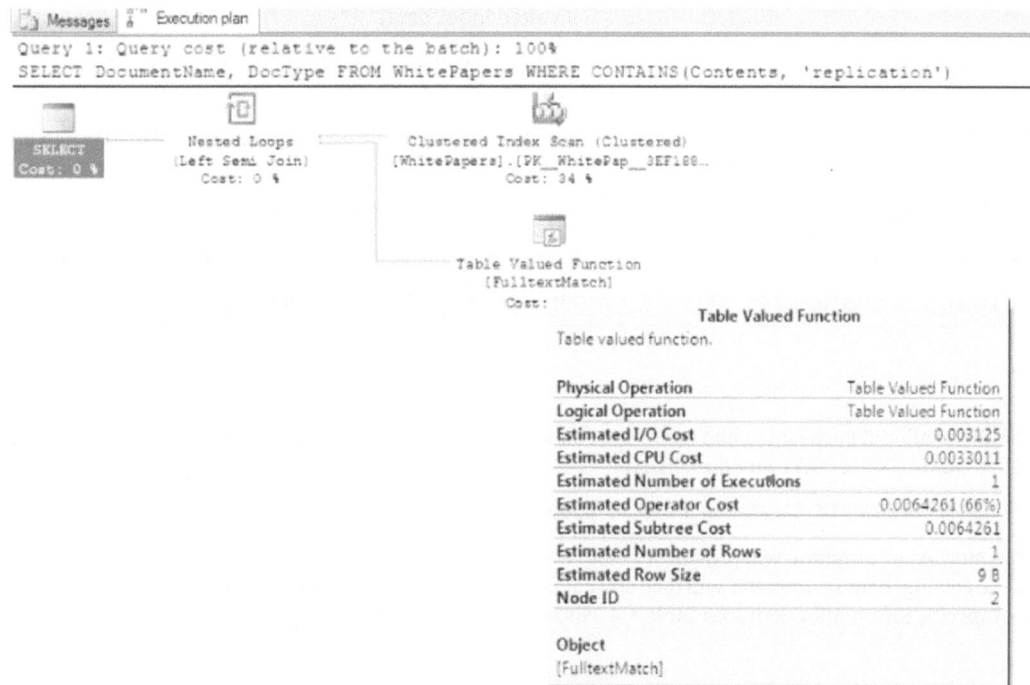

Figure 4-19. *Execution plan of CONTAINS and FTS Index usage*

By searching by means of `CONTAINS(Contents,'replication')`, the execution plan in Figure 4-19 shows the operation on `FulltextMatch`. It also returns the Whitepaper, High Availability with SQL Server 2008 with document type of `.doc` as a match for this word search.

Full-Text Search Index Catalog Views and Properties

SQL Server provides a wealth of information about indexes in general. Performance, configurations, usage, and storage are just a few. As with normal index objects, full-text indexes require the same attention and detail to maintenance and options set to ensure they consistently benefit the overall performance rather than hinder it. Each object that assists in gathering information has a specific task in mind or object that it is directly reviewed.

Table 4-3 describes the catalog views available to full-text search.

Table 4-3. *Full-Text Catalog Views*

Catalog View Name	Description
sys.fulltext_catalogs	Listing of all full-text catalogs and high level properties.
sys.fulltext_document_types	Returns a complete list of document types that are available for indexing. Each of these document types will be registered on the instance of SQL Server.
sys.fulltext_index_columns	Listing of all columns that are indexed.
sys.fulltext_index_fragments	Lists all details of the full-text index fragments (storage of the inverted index data).
sys.fulltext_indexes	Listing of every full-text index and properties set on the indexes.
sys.fulltext_languages	Listing of all the available languages on the instance to full-text indexing.
sys.fulltext_stoplists	Listing of every StopList created.
sys.fulltext_stopwords	Complete listing of all StopWords in the database executed in.
sys.fulltext_system_stopwords	Listing of the preloaded system StopWords.

For informational purposes, while reviewing catalogs, properties, and status results for population, invoke the `FULLTEXTCATALOGPROPERTY` function, like so:

```
FULLTEXTCATALOGPROPERTY ('catalog_name' ,'property')
```

The returned information will provide a wealth of detail on the state of the catalog including population status. The catalog_name parameter will take any catalog created and then a listing of properties can be utilized to return specific information required.Table 4-4 lists the properties you can pass.

Table 4-4. Full-Text Catalog Properties

Property Name	Description
AccentSensitivity	Catalog current accent sensitivity setting. Returns 0, insensitive and 1, sensitive.
IndexSize	Logical size in MB of the catalog.
ItemCount	The total items that have been indexed in the catalog
LogSize	Backward capability property. Returns 0.
MergeStatus	Returns 0 if no master merge is in progress and 1 if a master merge is in progress.
PopulateCompletionAge	The elapsed time since index population, in seconds, measured since 01/01/1990 00:00:00 and will always return 0 if the population has not run yet.
PopulateStatus	PopulateStatus can return nine different values. 0 = Idle 1 = Full population in progress 2 = Paused 3 = The population has been throttled. 4 = The population is in recovering. 5 = The status is shutdown. 6 = Incremental population in currently in progress. 7 = The status is currently building an index. 8 = The disk is full. 9 = Change tracking
UniqueKeyCount	Number of individual full-text index keys in the catalog
ImportStatus	Returns 0 is when the full-text catalog is not being imported and 1 is when it is being imported

For example, to show the population status of the WhitePaperCatalog catalog used earlier, the statement in Listing 4-16 can be used.

Listing 4-16. FULLTEXTCATALOGPROPERTY to Return Population Status of a Catalog

```
SELECT FULLTEXTCATALOGPROPERTY('WhitePaperCatalog','PopulateStatus')
```

Catalogs and the referencing indexes can be reviewed by executing sys.fulltext_index_catalog_usages. This catalog view returns all the indexes that have been referenced from it, as shown in Listing 4-17.

Listing 4-17. Utilizing sys.fulltext_index_catalog_usages

```
SELECT
    OBJECT_NAME(object_id) [Object Name],
    index_id,
    fulltext_catalog_id
FROM sys.fulltext_index_catalog_usages
```

For detailed information on all catalogs and settings currently applied to them, query sys.fulltext_catalogs. This catalog view is helpful in determing the default catalog and properties status indicators, like the is_importing that shows if the catalog is in the process of being imported.

For a detailed review of the full-text indexes in the database, the sys.fulltext_indexes can be utilized along with joining catalog views to create a more meaningful result set. Important information from this catalog view consists of the full-text catalog name and properties; change tracking property, crawl type, and state; and the StopList set to be used.

The query in Listing 4-18 returns an information result set of all indexes including catalog and StopList information for the index.

Listing 4-18. Using all the Catalog Views for Full-Text Index Information

```
SELECT
        idx.is_enabled,
        idx.change_tracking_state,
        idx.crawl_type_desc,
        idx.crawl_end_date [Last Crawl],
        cat.[name],
        CASE WHEN cat.is_accent_sensitivity_on = 0 THEN 'Accent InSensitive'
             WHEN cat.is_accent_sensitivity_on = 1 THEN 'Accent Sensitive'
        END [Accent Sensitivity],
        lists.[name],
        lists.modify_date [Last Modified Date of StopList]
FROM sys.fulltext_indexes idx
JOIN sys.fulltext_catalogs cat on idx.fulltext_catalog_id = cat.fulltext_catalog_id
JOIN sys.fulltext_stoplists lists on idx.stoplist_id = lists.stoplist_id
```

Summary

This chapter covered the need to be able to search and index the unstructured data that can now be stored within SQL Server. Three areas of unstructured data were covered in this chapter: XML indexes, spatial indexes, and full-text indexing. XML indexes provide developers and database administrators with the options to improve the performance of searches through XML documents. This benefits queries both from the aspect of filtering data in XML documents and retrieving the data for display. With spatial indexes, you now have the ability to quickly determine whether points lie within regions or whether regions overlap other regions. Instead of having to fully render each spatial artifact, spatial indexes allow queries to quickly calculate the results of the spatial function. Lastly, with full-text indexing, you can use examine not only the contents of a column but also the contents of a file within a column, allowing applications to much better identify documents and other artifacts that match contextually with the requests being submitted. Much information regarding these three types of indexes was covered in this chapter. While each of these topics could easily consume an entire book, the aim here was to provide an overview of how and when to utilize these types of indexes in your environments.

CHAPTER 5

■ ■ ■

Index Myths and Best Practices

In the past few chapters, we've defined indexes and looked at how they are structured. In the upcoming chapters, we'll be looking at strategies to build indexes and ensure that they behave as expected. In this chapter we'll be dispelling some common myths and building the foundation for how to create indexes.

Myths result in an unnecessary burden when attempting to build an index. Knowing the myths associated with indexes can prevent you from using indexing strategies that will be counterproductive. The indexing myths discussed in this chapter include:

- Databases don't need indexes.

- Primary keys are always clustered.

- Online index operations don't block.

- Any column can be filtered in multicolumn indexes.

- Clustered indexes store records in physical order.

- Fill factor is applied to indexes during inserts.

- Every table should have a heap/clustered index.

When reviewing myths, it's also a good idea to take a look at best practices. Best practices are like myths in many ways, in the sense that they are commonly held beliefs. The primary difference is that best practices stand up to scrutiny and are useful recommendations when building indexes. This chapter will examine the following best practices:

- Use clustered indexes on primary keys by default.

- Balance index count.

- Database level fill factor.

- Index level fill factor.

- Indexing foreign key columns.

- Index to your environment.

Index Myths

One of the problems that people encounter when building databases and indexes, is dealing with myths. Indexing myths originate from many different places. Some come from previous versions of SQL Server and its tools and/or are based on former functionality. Others come from the advice of others, based on conditions in a specific database that don't match those of other databases.

The trouble with indexing myths is that they cloud the water of indexing strategies. In situations where an index can be built to resolve a serious performance issue, a myth can sometimes prevent the approach from being considered. Throughout the next few sections, we'll look at a number of myths regarding indexing and do our best to dispel them.

Myth 1: Databases Don't Need Indexes

Usually, when developers are building applications, one or more databases are created to store data for the application. In many development processes, the focus is on adding new features with the mantra "performance will work itself out." An unfortunate result is that there are many databases that get developed and deployed without indexes being built due to the belief that they aren't needed.

Along with this, there are some who believe their databases are somehow unique from other databases. The reasons that are heard from time to time include some of the following:

- "It's a small database that won't get much data."

- "It's just a proof of concept and won't be around for very long."

- "It's not a very important application, performance isn't important."

- "The whole database already fits into memory; indexes will just make it require more memory."

Each of these reasons is easy to break down. In today's world of big data, even databases that are expected to be small can start growing quickly as they are adopted. Besides that, small in terms of a database, is definitely in the eye of the beholder. Any proof of concept or unimportant database and application wouldn't have been created if there weren't a need and someone wasn't interested in expending resources for the features. Those same people likely expect that the features they asked for will perform as expected. Lastly, fitting a database into memory doesn't mean it will be fast. As was discussed in previous chapters, indexes provide an alternative access path to data, with the aim of decreasing the number of pages required to access the data. Without these alternative routes, data access will likely require reading every page of a table.

These reasons may not be the ones you hear concerning your databases, but they will likely be similar. As easily as these were broken down, the reasons you encounter can be broken down as well. The general idea surrounding this myth is that indexes don't help the database perform better. One of the strongest ways to break apart this myth is by demonstrating the benefits of indexing against a given scenario.

To demonstrate, let's look at the code in Listing 5-1. In this code sample, the table MythOne is created. Next, you will find a query similar to one in almost any application. In the output from the query, in Listing 5-2, the query generated 1,494 reads.

Listing 5-1. Table with No Index

```
SELECT * INTO MythOne
FROM Sales.SalesOrderDetail
GO

SET STATISTICS IO ON
SET NOCOUNT ON
GO

SELECT SalesOrderID, SalesOrderDetailID, CarrierTrackingNumber, OrderQty, ProductID,
SpecialOfferID, UnitPrice, UnitPriceDiscount, LineTotal
FROM MythOne
WHERE CarrierTrackingNumber = '4911-403C-98'
GO

SET STATISTICS IO OFF
GO
```

Listing 5-2. I/O Statistics for Table with No Index

```
Table 'MythOne'. Scan count 1, logical reads 1494, physical reads 0, read-ahead reads 0, lob
logical reads 0, lob physical reads 0, lob read-ahead reads 0.
```

It could be argued that 1,494 isn't a lot of input/output (I/O). This might be true given the sizes of some of the databases and the amount of data in today's world. But the I/O of a query shouldn't be compared to the performance of the rest of the world; it needs to be compared to its potential I/O, the needs of the application, and the platform in which it is deployed.

Improving the query from the last demonstration can be as simple as adding an index on the table on the CarrierTrackingNumber column. To see the effect of adding an index to MythOne, execute the code in Listing 5-3. With the index created, the reads for the query were reduced from 1,464 to 15 reads, shown in Listing 5-4. With just a single index, the I/O for the query was reduced by nearly two orders of magnitude. Suffice it to say, an index in this situation provides a significant amount of value.

Listing 5-3. Adding an Index to MythOne

```
CREATE INDEX IX_CarrierTrackingNumber ON MythOne (CarrierTrackingNumber)
GO

SET STATISTICS IO ON
SET NOCOUNT ON
GO

SELECT SalesOrderID, SalesOrderDetailID, CarrierTrackingNumber, OrderQty, ProductID,
SpecialOfferID, UnitPrice, UnitPriceDiscount, LineTotal
FROM MythOne
WHERE CarrierTrackingNumber = '4911-403C-98'
GO

SET STATISTICS IO OFF
GO
```

Listing 5-4. I/O Statistics for Table with an Index

```
Table 'MythOne'. Scan count 1, logical reads 15, physical reads 0, read-ahead reads 0,
lob logical reads 0, lob physical reads 0, lob read-ahead reads 0.
```

We've show in these examples that indexes do provide a benefit. If you encounter a situation where there is angst for building indexes on a database, try to break down the real reason for the pushback, and provide an example similar to the one presented in this section. In Chapter 8 we'll discuss approaches that can be used to determine what indexes to create in a database.

Myth 2: Primary Keys Are Always Clustered

The next myth that is quite prevalent is the idea that primary keys are always clustered. While this is true in many cases, you cannot assume that all PRIMARY KEYS are also CLUSTERED indexes. Earlier in this book, we discussed how a table can have only a single clustered index on it. If a PRIMARY KEY is created after the CLUSTERED index is built, then the PRIMARY KEY will be created as a NONCLUSTRED index.

To illustrate the indexing behavior of primary keys, we'll use another demonstration that includes building two tables. On the first table, named dbo.MythTwo1, we'll build the table and then create a PRIMARY KEY on the RowID column. For the second table, named dbo.MythTwo2, after the table is created, the script will build a CLUSTERED index before creating the PRIMARY KEY. The code for this is included in Listing 5-5.

Listing 5-5. Two Ways to Create PRIMARY KEYS

```
CREATE TABLE dbo.MythTwo1
  (
  RowID int NOT NULL
  ,Column1 nvarchar(128)
  ,Column2 nvarchar(128)
  )

ALTER TABLE dbo.MythTwo1
ADD CONSTRAINT PK_MythTwo1 PRIMARY KEY (RowID)

GO
CREATE TABLE dbo.MythTwo2
  (
  RowID int NOT NULL
  ,Column1 nvarchar(128)
  ,Column2 nvarchar(128)
  )

CREATE CLUSTERED INDEX CL_MythTwo2 ON dbo.MythTwo2 (RowID)

ALTER TABLE dbo.MythTwo2
ADD CONSTRAINT PK_MythTwo2 PRIMARY KEY (RowID)
GO
SELECT OBJECT_NAME(object_id) AS table_name
  ,name
  ,index_id
  ,type
  ,type_desc
  ,is_unique
  ,is_primary_key
FROM sys.indexes
WHERE object_id IN (OBJECT_ID('dbo.MythTwo1'),OBJECT_ID('dbo.MythTwo2'))
```

After running the code segment, the final query will return results like those shown in Figure 5-1. This figure shows that PK_MythTwo1, which is the PRIMARY KEY on the first table, was created as a CLUSTERED index. Then on the second table, PK_MythTwo2 was created as a NONCLUSTERED index.

	table_name	name	index_id	type	type_desc	is_unique	is_primary_key
1	MythTwo1	PK_MythTwo1	1	1	CLUSTERED	1	1
2	MythTwo2	CL_MythTwo2	1	1	CLUSTERED	0	0
3	MythTwo2	PK_MythTwo2	2	2	NONCLUSTERED	1	1

Figure 5-1. *Primary key sys.indexes output*

The behavior discussed in this section is important to remember when building primary keys and clustered indexes. If you have a situation where they need to be separated, the PRIMARY KEY will need to be defined after the CLUSTERED index.

Myth 3: Online Index Operations Don't Block

One of the advantages of SQL Server Enterprise and Data Center editions is the ability to build indexes online. During an online index build, the table on which the index is being created will still be available for queries and data modifications. This feature can be extremely useful when a database needs to be accessed and maintenance windows are short to nonexistent.

A common myth with online index rebuilds, is that they don't cause any blocking. Of course, like many myths, this one is false. When using an online index operation, there is an intent shared lock held on the table for the main portion of the build. At the finish, either a shared lock, for nonclustered index, or a schema modification lock, for a clustered index, is held for a short time while the operation moves in the updated index. This differs from an offline index build where the shared or schema modification lock is held for the duration of the index build.

Of course, you will want to see this in action, so you can do this by entering the code in Listing 5-6. In the script, the table dbo.MythThree is built and populated with one million records. Next in the script, there are two nonclustered indexes built on the table. The first index is created using the ONLINE option. Then the second index is created; it does not use that functionality.

■ **Note** The demos in this section rely on SQL Server Enterprise or Developer Edition.

Listing 5-6. Online Index to Build Myth Script

```
CREATE TABLE dbo.MythThree
    (
    RowID int NOT NULL
    ,Column1 uniqueidentifier
    );
WITH L1(z) AS (SELECT 0 UNION ALL SELECT 0)
, L2(z) AS (SELECT 0 FROM L1 a CROSS JOIN L1 b)
, L3(z) AS (SELECT 0 FROM L2 a CROSS JOIN L2 b)
, L4(z) AS (SELECT 0 FROM L3 a CROSS JOIN L3 b)
, L5(z) AS (SELECT 0 FROM L4 a CROSS JOIN L4 b)
, L6(z) AS (SELECT TOP 10000000 0 FROM L5 a CROSS JOIN L5 b)
INSERT INTO dbo.MythThree
SELECT ROW_NUMBER() OVER (ORDER BY z) AS RowID, NEWID()
FROM L6;
GO

CREATE INDEX IX_MythThree_ONLINE ON MythThree (Column1) WITH (ONLINE = ON);
GO

CREATE INDEX IX_MythThree ON MythThree (Column1);
GO
```

The information that will be of use when these indexes are built will be the lock_acquired and lock_released events. To monitor those events in this scenario, it is recommended that you use the extended events feature set. SQL Server 2012 includes a number of improvements to extended events, including the ability to watch live data. Although using extended events is not the focus of this book, a session for monitoring is included in Listing 5-7 to get you started. That session is scoped to filter on session_id 66. You would need to change the session number to match an active session in your environment. After the extended event session is running, you can use the live view to monitor the locks as they occur.

■ **Note**   SQL Server 2012 includes a number of improvements to the extended events platform. One of the significant improvements is a graphical interface that can be used to build and edit extended event sessions. A live viewer feature also allows for monitoring extended event sessions while they collect session data.

Listing 5-7. Extended Event Session for Lock Acquired and Released

```
CREATE EVENT SESSION [MythThree] ON SERVER
ADD EVENT sqlserver.lock_acquired(SET collect_database_name=(1)
    WHERE ([sqlserver].[session_id]=(66))),
ADD EVENT sqlserver.lock_released(
    WHERE ([sqlserver].[session_id]=(66)))
ADD TARGET package0.ring_buffer
GO
```

In the example from Listing 5-6, creating the index with the ONLINE option will cause the lock acquired and released events shown in Figure 5-2. In the output, the SCH_S (Schema_Shared) lock is held from the beginning of the build to the end. The S (Shared) locks are held only for a few milliseconds at the beginning and ending of the index build. For the time between the S locks, the indexes are fully available and ready for use.

By default, only the name and timestamp appear in the live viewer. The live viewer allows for customizing the columns that are displayed. In Figure 5-2 columns have been added to the defaults of name and timestamp. To add additional columns, right-click a column header and select Choose columns.

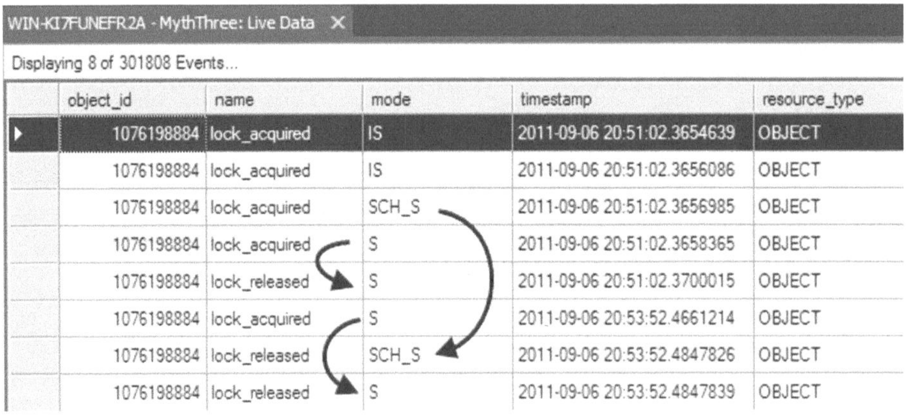

Figure 5-2. Index create with ONLINE option

With the default index creation, which does not use the ONLINE option, S locks are held for the entirety of the index build. Shown in Figure 5-3, the S lock is taken before the SCH_S lock and isn't released until after the index is build. The result is that the index is unavailable during the index build.

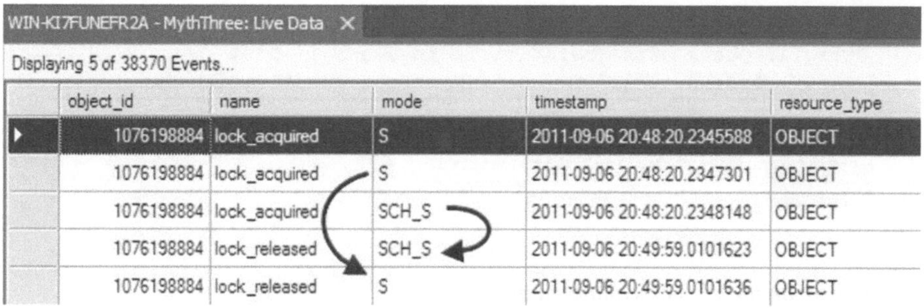

Figure 5-3. *Index create without Online option*

Myth 4: Any Column Can Be Filtered In Multicolumn Indexes

The next common myth with indexes is that regardless of the position of the column in an index, the index can be used to filter for the column. As with the other myths discussed so far in this chapter, this one is also incorrect. An index does not need to use all of the columns in a table. It does, however, need to start with the left-most column in an index and use the columns from left to right, in order. This is why the order of the columns in an index is so important.

To demonstrate this myth, we'll run through a few examples, shown in Listing 5-8. In the script, a table is created based on Sales.SalesOrderHeader with a primary key on SalesOrderID. To test the myth on searching all columns through multicolumn indexes, an index with the columns OrderDate, DueDate, and ShipDate is created.

Listing 5-8. Multicolumn Index Myth

```
SELECT SalesOrderID, OrderDate, DueDate, ShipDate
INTO dbo.MythFour
FROM Sales.SalesOrderHeader;

ALTER TABLE dbo.MythFour
ADD CONSTRAINT PK_MythFour PRIMARY KEY CLUSTERED (SalesOrderID);

CREATE NONCLUSTERED INDEX IX_MythFour ON dbo.MythFour (OrderDate, DueDate, ShipDate);
```

With the test objects in place, the next thing to check is the behavior of the queries against the table that could potentially use the nonclustered index. First, we'll run a query that uses the left-most column in the index. The code for this is given in Listing 5-9. As shown in Figure 5-4, by filtering on the left-most column, the query uses a seek operation on IX_MythFour.

Listing 5-9. Query Using Left-most Column in Index

```
SELECT OrderDate FROM dbo.MythFour
WHERE OrderDate = '2001-07-17 00:00:00.000'
```

Next we'll look at what happens when querying from the other side of the index key columns. In Listing 5-10, the query filters the results on the right-most column of the index. The execution plan for this query, shown in Figure 5-5, uses a scan operation on IX_MythFour. Instead of being able to go directly to the records that match the OrderDate, the query needs to check all records to determine which match the filter. While the index is used, it isn't able to actually filter the rows.

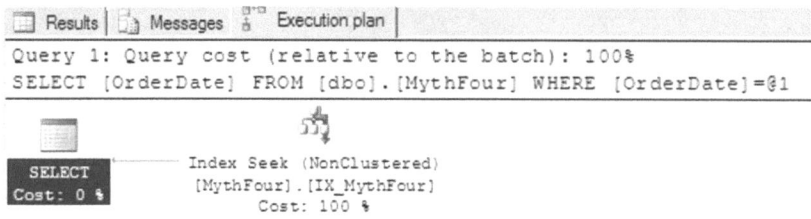

Figure 5-4. *Execution plan for left-most column in index*

Listing 5-10. Query Using Right-most Column in Index

```
SELECT ShipDate FROM dbo.MythFour
WHERE ShipDate = '2001-07-17 00:00:00.000'
```

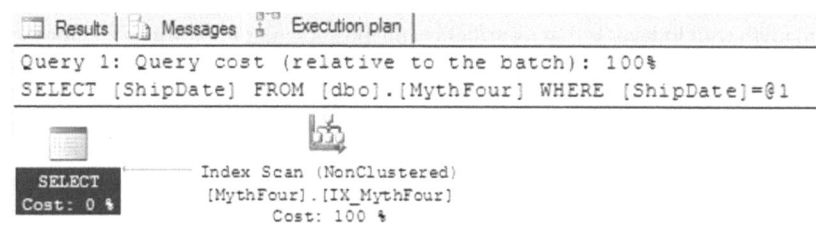

Figure 5-5. *Execution plan for right-most column in index*

At this point, you've seen that the left-most column can be used for filtering and that filtering on the right-most column can use the index, but cannot use it optimally with a seek operation. The last validation is to check the behavior of columns in an index that are not on the left or right side of the index. In Listing 5-11, a query is included that uses the middle column in the index IX_MythFour. As with any execution plan, the execution plan for the middle column query, shown in Figure 5-6, uses the index but also uses a scan operation. The query is able to use the index but not in an optimal fashion.

Listing 5-11. Query Using Middle Column in Index

```
SELECT DueDate FROM dbo.MythFour
WHERE DueDate = '2001-07-17 00:00:00.000'
```

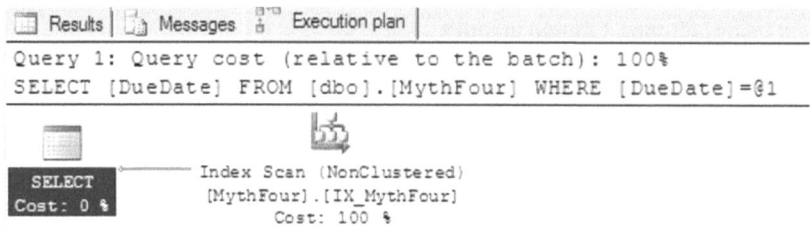

Figure 5-6. *Execution plan for middle column in index*

The myth of how columns in a multicolumn index can be used is one that can sometimes be confusing. As the examples showed, queries can use the index regardless of which columns of the index are being filtered. The key is to effectively use the index. To accomplish this goal, filtering must start on the left-most column of the index.

Myth 5: Clustered Indexes Store Records in Physical Order

One of the more pervasive myths commonly held is the idea that a clustered index stores the records in a table in their physical order when on disk. This myth seems to be primarily driven by confusion between what is stored on a page and where records are stored on those pages. As was discussed in Chapter 2, there is a difference between data pages and records. As a refresher, we'll look at a simple demonstration that dispels this myth.

To begin this example, execute the code in Listing 5-12. The code in the example will create a table named dbo.MythFive. Then it will add three records to the table. The last part of the script will output, through the DBCC IND command, the page location for the table. In this example, the page with the records inserted into dbo.MythFive is on page 14107, shown in Figure 5-7.

Listing 5-12. Create and Populate Myth Five Table

```
CREATE TABLE dbo.MythFive
(
RowID int PRIMARY KEY CLUSTERED
,TestValue varchar(20) NOT NULL
);

INSERT INTO dbo.MythFive (RowID, TestValue) VALUES (1, 'FirstRecordAdded');
INSERT INTO dbo.MythFive (RowID, TestValue) VALUES (3, 'SecondRecordAdded');
INSERT INTO dbo.MythFive (RowID, TestValue) VALUES (2, 'ThirdRecordAdded');
GO

DBCC IND ('AdventureWorks2008R2', 'dbo.MythFive', 1);
GO
```

	PageFID	PagePID	IAMFID	IAMPID	ObjectID	IndexID	PartitionNumber	PartitionID	iam_chain_type	PageType	IndexLevel	NextPageFID	NextPagePID	PrevPageFID	PrevPagePID
1	1	140108	NULL	NULL	1284199625	1	1	72057594067288064	In-row data	10	NULL	0	0	0	0
2	1	140107	1	140108	1284199625	1	1	72057594067288064	In-row data	1	0	0	0	0	0

Figure 5-7. DBCC IND output

The evidence to dispel this myth can be uncovered with the DBCC PAGE command. To do this, use the PagePID identified in Listing 5-12 with PageType equal to one. Since there are only two pages for this table, the first data page is where the data will be located. (For more information on DBCC commands, see Chapter 2.)

For this example, the T-SQL required to look at the data in the table is shown in Listing 5-13. This command outputs a lot of information that includes some header information that isn't useful in this example. The portion that we need is at the end, with the memory dump of the page, as shown in Figure 5-8. In the memory dump, the records are shown in the order in which they are placed on the page. As the dump shows from reading the far right column, the records are in the order in which they are added to the table, not the order that they will appear in the clustered index.

Listing 5-13. Create and Populate Myth Five Table

```
DBCC TRACEON (3604);
GO

DBCC PAGE (AdventureWorks, 1, 140107, 2);
GO
```

```
Memory Dump @0x00000000439AA000

00000000439AA000:   01010000 00000001 00000000 00000800 00000000 †....................
00000000439AA014:   00000300 01020000 3c1fbe00 4b230200 01000000 †........<.K.K#......
00000000439AA028:   27020000 96020000 02000000 00000000 00000000 †'..................
00000000439AA03C:   00000000 01000000 00000000 00000000 00000000 †....................
00000000439AA050:   00000000 00000000 00000000 00000000 30000800 †................0...
00000000439AA064:   01000000 02000001 001f0046 69727374 5265636f †...........FirstReco
00000000439AA078:   72644164 64656430 00080003 00000002 00000100 †rdAdded0............
00000000439AA08C:   20005365 636f6e64 5265636f 72644164 64656430 † .SecondRecordAdded0
00000000439AA0A0:   00080002 00000002 00000100 1f005468 69726452 †..............ThirdR
00000000439AA0B4:   65636f72 64416464 65640000 381f0000 00000000 †ecordAdded..8.......
00000000439AA0C8:   00000000 00000000 00000000 00000000 00000000 †....................
00000000439AA0DC:   00000000 00000000 00000000 00000000 00000000 †....................
00000000439AA0F0:   00000000 00000000 00000000 00000000 00000000 †....................
```

Figure 5-8. *Page contents portion of DBCC PAGE output*

Based on this evidence, it is easy to discern that clustered indexes do not store records in the physical order of the index. If this example were expanded, you would be able to see that the pages are in physical order, but the rows on the pages are not.

Myth 6: Fill Factor Is Applied to Indexes During Inserts

When the fill factor is set on an index, it is applied to the index when the index is built, rebuilt, or reorganized. Unfortunately, with this myth many people believe that fill factor is applied when records are inserted into a table. In this section, we'll investigate this myth and show that it is not correct.

To begin pulling this myth apart, let's look at what most people believe. In the myth, the thought is that if a fill factor has been specified when rows are added to a table, the fill factor is used during the inserts. To dispel this portion of the myth, execute the code in Listing 5-14. In this script, the table dbo.MythSix is created with a clustered index with a 50 percent fill factor. That means that 50 percent of every page in the index should be left empty. With the table built, we'll insert records into the table. Finally, we'll check the average amount of space available on each page through the sys.dm_db_index_physical_stats DMV. Looking at the results of the script, included in Figure 5-9, the index is using 95 percent of every page versus the 50 percent that was specified in the creation of the clustered index.

Listing 5-14. Create and Populate Myth Six Table

```
CREATE TABLE dbo.MythSix
    (
    RowID int NOT NULL
    ,Column1 varchar(500)
    );

ALTER TABLE dbo.MythSix ADD CONSTRAINT
    PK_MythSix PRIMARY KEY CLUSTERED (RowID) WITH(FILLFACTOR = 50);

WITH L1(z) AS (SELECT 0 UNION ALL SELECT 0)
, L2(z) AS (SELECT 0 FROM L1 a CROSS JOIN L1 b)
, L3(z) AS (SELECT 0 FROM L2 a CROSS JOIN L2 b)
, L4(z) AS (SELECT 0 FROM L3 a CROSS JOIN L3 b)
, L5(z) AS (SELECT 0 FROM L4 a CROSS JOIN L4 b)
, L6(z) AS (SELECT TOP 1000 0 FROM L5 a CROSS JOIN L5 b)
INSERT INTO dbo.MythSix
```

```
SELECT ROW_NUMBER() OVER (ORDER BY z) AS RowID, REPLICATE('X', 500)
FROM L6

SELECT object_id, index_id, avg_page_space_used_in_percent
FROM sys.dm_db_index_physical_stats(DB_ID(),OBJECT_ID('dbo.MythSix'),NULL,NULL,'DETAILED')
WHERE index_level = 0
```

	object_id	index_id	avg_page_space_used_in_percent
1	1812201506	1	95.3103286384976

Figure 5-9. *Fill factor myth on inserts*

Sometimes when this myth is dispelled, the belief is reversed and it is believed that fill factor is broken or doesn't work. This is also incorrect. Fill factor isn't applied to indexes during data modifications. As stated previously, it is applied when the index is rebuilt, reorganized, or created. To demonstrate this, you can rebuild the clustered index on dbo.MythSix with the script included in Listing 5-15.

Listing 5-15. Rebuild Clustered Index on Myth Six Table

```
ALTER INDEX PK_MythSix ON dbo.MythSix REBUILD

SELECT object_id, index_id, avg_page_space_used_in_percent
FROM sys.dm_db_index_physical_stats(DB_ID(),OBJECT_ID('dbo.MythSix'),NULL,NULL,'DETAILED')
WHERE index_level = 0
```

After the clustered index is rebuilt, the index will have the specified fill factor, or very close to the value specified, as shown in Figure 5-10. The average space used on the table, after the rebuild, changed from 95 to 51 percent. This change is in alignment with the fill factor that was specified for the index.

	object_id	index_id	avg_page_space_used_in_percent
1	1812201506	1	51.0748702742772

Figure 5-10. *Fill factor myth after index rebuild*

When it comes to fill factor, there are a number of myths surrounding the index property. The key to understanding fill factor is to remember when and how it is applied. It isn't a property enforced on an index as it is used. It is, instead, a property used to distribute data within an index when it is created or rebuilt.

Myth 7: Every Table Should Have a Heap/Clustered Index

The last myth to consider is twofold. On the one hand, some people will recommend you should build all of your tables with heaps. On the other hand, others will recommend that you create clustered indexes on all of your tables. The trouble is that this viewpoint will exclude considering the benefits that each of the structures can offer on a table. The viewpoint makes a religious-styled argument for or against ways to store data in your databases without any consideration for the actual data that is being stored and how it is being used.

Some of the arguments against the use of clustered indexes are:

- Fragmentation negatively impacts performance through additional I/O.

- The modification of a single record can impact multiple records in the clustered index when a page split is triggered.

- Excessive key lookups will negatively impact performance through additional I/O.

Of course, there are some arguments against using heaps:

- Excessive forwarded records negatively impact performance through additional I/O.

- There are no direct methods to maintain heaps by removing forwarded records.

- Nonclustered indexes are required for any sorted data access.

The negative impacts associated with either clustered indexes or heaps aren't the only things to consider when deciding between one or the other. Each has circumstances where they will outperform the other.

For instance, clustered indexes perform best in the following circumstances:

- The key on the table is a unique, ever increasing key value.

- The table has a key column that has a high degree of uniqueness.

- Ranges of data in table will be accessed via queries.

On the other hand, heaps are ideal for some of the following situations:

- When records in the table will be inserted and deleted at a high rate.

- When key values will change frequently, which in turn would change the position of the record in an index.

- When you are inserting copious amounts of records into a staging table.

- When the primary key is a nonascending value, such as a unique identifier.

Although this section doesn't include a demonstration of why this myth is false, it is important to remember that both heaps and clustered indexes are available and should be used appropriately. Knowing which type of index to choose is a matter of testing, not a matter of doctrine.

A good resource to consider for those in the "cluster everything camp" is the Fast Track Data Warehouse 2.0 Architecture whitepaper (`http://msdn.microsoft.com/en-us/library/dd459178(v=sql.100).aspx`). The whitepaper addresses some significant performance improvements that can be found with heaps and also the point in which these improvements dissipate.

Index Best Practices

Similar to myths are the indexing best practices. A best practice should be considered the default recommendations that can be applied when there isn't enough information available to validate proceeding in another direction. Best practices are not the only option and are just a place to start from when working with any technology.

When using a best practice provided from someone else, such as those appearing in this chapter, it is important to check them out for yourself first. Always take them "with a grain of salt." You can trust that best practices will steer you in the correct direction, but you need to verify that it is appropriate to follow the practice.

Given the preceding precautions, there are a number of best practices that can be considered when working with indexes. This section will review these best practices and discuss what they are and what they mean.

Use Clustered Indexes on Primary Keys by Default

The first best practice is to use clustered indexes on primary keys by default. This may seem to run contrary to the seventh myth presented in the previous section. Myth 7 discussed whether to choose clustered indexes or heaps as a matter of doctrine. Whether the database was built with one or the other, the myth would have you believe that if your table design doesn't match the myth, it should be changed regardless of the situation. This best practice recommends using clustered indexes on primary keys as a starting point.

By clustering the primary key of a table by default, there is an increased likelihood that the indexing choice will be appropriate for the table. As stated earlier in this chapter, clustered indexes control how the data in a table is stored. Many primary keys, possibly most, are built on a column that utilizes the identity property that increments as each new record is added to the table. Choosing a clustered index for the primary key will provide the most efficient method to access the data.

Balance Index Count

As previously discussed in this book, indexes are extremely useful for improving the performance when accessing information in a record. Unfortunately, indexes are not without costs. The costs to having indexes go beyond just space within your database. When you build an index you need to consider some of the following:

- How frequently will records be inserted or deleted?

- How frequently will the key columns be updated?

- How often will the index be used?

- What processes does the index support?

- How many other indexes are on the table?

These are just some of the first considerations that need to be accounted for when building indexes. After the index is built, how much time will be spent updating and maintain the index? Will you modify the index more frequently than the index is used to return results for queries?

The trouble with balancing the index count on a table is that there is no precise number that can be recommended. Deciding on the number of indexes that it makes sense to have on an index is a per table decision. You don't want too few, which may result in excessive scans of the clustered index or heap to return results. Also, the table shouldn't have too many indexes, where more time is being spent keeping the index current than returning results. As a rule of thumb, if a table has more than ten indexes on it in a transactional system, it will be increasingly likely that there are too many indexes on the table.

Fill Factor

Fill factor controls the amount of free space left on the data pages of an index after an index is built or defragmented. This free space is made available to allow for records on the page to expand with the risk that the change in record size may result in a page split. This is an extremely useful property of indexes to use for index maintenance. Modifying the fill factor can mitigate the risk of fragmentation. A more thorough discussion of fill factor is presented in Chapter 6. For the purposes of best practices, we are concerned with the ability to set the fill factor at the database and index levels.

Database Level Fill Factor

As already mentioned, one of the properties of SQL Server is the option to set a default fill factor for indexes. This setting is a SQL Server-wide setting and can be altered in the properties of SQL Server on the Database Properties page. By default, this value is set to zero, which equates to 100. Do not modify the default fill factor to anything other than 100. Doing so will change the fill factor for every index in the database to the new value; which will add the specified amount of free space to all indexes the next time indexes are created, rebuilt, or reorganized.

On the surface this may seem like a good idea, but this will blindly increase the size of all indexes by the specified amount. The increased size of the indexes will require more I/O to perform the same work as before the change. For many indexes, making this change would result in a needless waste of resources.

Index Level Fill Factor

At the index level, you should modify the fill factor for indexes that are frequently becoming heavily fragmented. Decreasing the fill factor will increase the amount of free space in the index and provide additional space to compensate for the changes in record length that is leading to fragmentation. Managing fill factor at the index level is appropriate since it provides the ability to tune the index precisely to the needs of the database.

Indexing Foreign Key Columns

When a foreign key is created on a table, the foreign key column in the table should be indexed. This is necessary to assist the foreign key in determining which records in the parent table are constrained to each record in the referenced table. This is important when changes are being made against the referenced table. The changes in the referenced table may need to check all of the rows that match the record in the parent table. If an index does not exist, then a scan of the column will occur. On a large parent table, this could result in a significant amount of I/O and potentially some concurrency issues.

An example of this issue would be a state and address table. There would likely be thousands or millions of records in the address table and maybe a hundred records in the state table. The address table would include a column that is referenced by the state table. Consider if one of the records in the state table needed to be deleted. If there wasn't an index on the foreign key column in the address table, then how would the address table identify the rows that would be affected by deleting the state record? Without an index, SQL Server would have to check every record in the address table. If the column is indexed, SQL Server would be able to perform a range scan across the records that match to the value being deleted from the state table.

By indexing your foreign key columns, performance issues, such as the one described in this section, can be avoided. The best practice with foreign keys is to index their columns. More details on this best practice and a code example are included in Chapter 8.

Index to Your Environment

The indexing that exists today will likely not be the indexing that will be needed in databases in the future. For this reason, the last best practice is to continuously review, analyze, and implement changes to the indexes in your environment. Realize that regardless of how similar two databases are, if the data in the databases is not the same, then the indexing for the two databases may also be different. For an expanded conversation on managing indexes, see Chapter 10.

Summary

This chapter looked at some myths surrounding indexes as well as some best practices. For both areas, we investigated what some commonly held beliefs are and presented some details around each of them.

With the myths, we looked at a number of ideas that are generally believed about indexes that are in fact not true. The myths covered clustered indexes, fill factor, the column makeup of indexes, and more. The key to how to view anything that is believed about indexes that may be a myth is to take it upon yourself to test them.

We also looked at best practices. The best practices provided in the chapter should be the basis on which indexes for your databases can be built. We defined what a best practice is and what it is not. Then we discussed a number of best practices that can be considered when indexing your databases.

CHAPTER 6

Index Maintenance

Like anything in life, indexes require maintenance. Over time, the performance benefits of indexes can wane or, through data modifications, their sizes and the underlying statistics can bloat. To prevent these issues, indexes must be maintained. If you do so, your database will remain lean, mean, querying machines.

When it comes to maintenance, there are two areas to consider: index fragmentation and statistics. Each plays a key role in maintaining a properly indexed and well performing database.

This chapter explains both of these areas. You'll learn about issues that arise from not maintaining indexes and review strategies for implementing a maintenance process. To illustrate how fragmentation occurs, there will be a number of simple demos. The statistics conversation will expand on the items discussed in Chapter 3 and layout how to update statistics to keep them accurate.

Index Fragmentation

The primary maintenance issue that can lead to a degradation of index performance is index fragmentation. Fragmentation happens when the pages in an index are no longer physically sequential. There are a few events in SQL Server that can lead to this. These events are

- INSERT operations
- UPDATE operations
- DELETE operations
- DBCC SHRINKDATABASE operations

As you can see, except for selecting data out of the database, pretty much everything that you can do to an index can lead to fragmentation. Unless your database is read-only, you must pay attention to fragmentation and address it in an index before it becomes an issue.

Fragmentation Operations

The best way to understand fragmentation is to see it in action. In Chapter 3, you looked at the information returned by the Dynamic Management Object (DMO) sys.dm_index_physical_stats. In this section, you'll review a number of scripts that cause fragmentation and then use the DMO to investigate the amount of fragmentation that has occurred.

As mentioned, fragmentation occurs when physical pages within an index are not sequential. When an insert occurs and the new row is not placed at the beginning or ending of the pages for the index, the new row will be placed on a page that already has other rows on it. If there is not enough room on the page for the new row, then the page will split—leading to fragmentation of the index. Fragmentation is the physical result of page splits in the index.

Insert Operations

The first operation that can lead to index fragmentation is an INSERT operation. This isn't usually considered the most likely operation to result in fragmentation, but there are database design patterns that can lead to fragmentation. There are two areas in which INSERT operations can lead to fragmentation: on clustered and non-clustered indexes.

The most common pattern for designing clustered indexes is to place the index on a single column with a value that is ever increasing. This is often done using an int data type and the IDENTITY property. When this pattern is followed, the chances of fragmentation occurring during inserts are relatively rare. Unfortunately, this isn't the only clustered index pattern that exists and the others can often cause fragmentation. For example, using business keys or uniqueidentifier data type values often causes fragmentation.

Clustered indexes that use uniqueidentifier data type values often use the NEWID() function to generate a random, unique value to serve as the clustering key. This value is unique, but not ever increasing. The most recent value generated may or may not be after the previous value. Because of this, when a new row is inserted into the clustered index, it is most likely to be placed between a number of other rows already in the index. And, as mentioned, if there isn't enough room in the index, fragmentation will occur.

To demonstrate fragmentation caused by the use of uniqueidentifier data type values, try the code in Listing 6-1. This code creates a table named dbo.UsingUniqueidentifier. It is populated with rows from sys.columns and then a clustered index is added. At this point, all of the pages in the indexes are physically sequential. Run the code in Listing 6-2 to view the results shown in Figure 6-1; these results show that the average fragmentation for the index is 0.00 percent.

Listing 6-1. Populate Uniqueidentifier Table

```
IF OBJECT_ID('dbo.UsingUniqueidentifier') IS NOT NULL
    DROP TABLE dbo.UsingUniqueidentifier;

CREATE TABLE dbo.UsingUniqueidentifier
(
RowID uniqueidentifier CONSTRAINT DF_GUIDValue DEFAULT NEWID()
,Name sysname
,JunkValue varchar(2000)
);

INSERT INTO dbo.UsingUniqueidentifier (Name, JunkValue)
SELECT name, REPLICATE('X', 2000)
FROM sys.columns

CREATE CLUSTERED INDEX CLUS_UsingUniqueidentifier ON dbo.UsingUniqueidentifier(RowID);
```

Listing 6-2. View INSERT Index Fragmentation

```
SELECT index_type_desc
  ,index_depth
  ,index_level
  ,page_count
  ,record_count
  ,CAST(avg_fragmentation_in_percent as DECIMAL(6,2)) as avg_fragmentation_in_percent
  ,fragment_count
  ,avg_fragment_size_in_pages
  ,CAST(avg_page_space_used_in_percent as DECIMAL(6,2)) as avg_page_space_used_in_percent
FROM sys.dm_db_index_physical_stats(DB_ID(),OBJECT_ID('dbo.UsingUniqueidentifier'),
NULL,NULL,'DETAILED')
```

	index_type_desc	index_depth	index_level	page_count	record_count	avg_fragmentation_in_percent	fragment_count	avg_fragment_size_in_pages	avg_page_space_used_in_percent
1	CLUSTERED INDEX	2	0	233	697	0.00	1	233	75.66
2	CLUSTERED INDEX	2	1	1	233	0.00	1	1	80.58

Figure 6-1. *Starting fragmentation results (results may vary)*

With the table built with a clustered index based on uniqueidentifier data types, you are now ready to perform an INSERT into the table to see the effect that the insert has on the index. To demonstrate, insert all of the rows in sys.objects into dbo.UsingUniqueidentifier using the code in Listing 6-3. After the insert, you can review the fragmentation of the index in the results, using Listing 6-2 again. Your results should be similar to those shown in Figure 6-2, which shows fragmentation in the clustered index of over 40 percent after adding just 78 rows to the table.

Listing 6-3. INSERT into Uniqueidentifier Table

```
INSERT INTO dbo.UsingUniqueidentifier (Name, JunkValue)
SELECT name, REPLICATE('X', 2000)
FROM sys.objects
```

As this code sample demonstrated, clustered indexes that are based on values that are not ever increasing will likely result in fragmentation. The best example of this type of behavior is through the use of uniqueidentifiers. This can also happen when the clustering key is a computed value or based on a business key. When looking at business keys, if a random purchase order is assigned to an order, then that value will likely behave similar to a uniqueidentifier data type value.

	index_type_desc	index_depth	index_level	page_count	record_count	avg_fragmentation_in_percent	fragment_count	avg_fragment_size_in_pages	avg_page_space_used_in_percent
1	CLUSTERED INDEX	3	0	301	775	43.52	133	2.26315789473684	65.16
2	CLUSTERED INDEX	3	1	2	301	0.00	2	1	52.04
3	CLUSTERED INDEX	3	2	1	2	0.00	1	1	0.67

Figure 6-2. *Post-INSERT fragmentation results (percentage results may vary)*

The other way in which INSERT operations can affect fragmentation is on the non-clustered indexes. While the clustered index values may be ever-increasing values, the values for the columns in the non-clustered index won't necessarily have that same quality. A good example of this is when indexing the name of a product in a non-clustered index. The next record inserted into the table may start with the letter M and will need to be placed near the middle of the non-clustered index. If there isn't room at that location, a page split will occur and fragmentation will result.

To demonstrate this behavior, add a non-clustered index to the table dbo.UsingUniqueidentifier that you have been using in the previous demonstrations. The schema for the new index is in Listing 6-4. Before inserting more records to see the effect of inserting into a non-clustered index, run Listing 6-2 again. Your results should be similar to those in Figure 6-3.

Listing 6-4. Create Non-Clustered Index

```
CREATE NONCLUSTERED INDEX IX_Name ON dbo.UsingUniqueidentifier(Name) INCLUDE (JunkValue);
```

	index_type_desc	index_depth	index_level	page_count	record_count	avg_fragmentation_in_percent	fragment_count	avg_fragment_size_in_pages	avg_page_space_used_in_percent
1	CLUSTERED INDEX	3	0	301	775	43.52	133	2.26315789473684	65.16
2	CLUSTERED INDEX	3	1	2	301	0.00	2	1	52.04
3	CLUSTERED INDEX	3	2	1	2	0.00	1	1	0.67
4	NONCLUSTERED INDEX	3	0	259	775	0.00	3	86.3333333333333	75.61
5	NONCLUSTERED INDEX	3	1	2	259	0.00	1	2	76.91
6	NONCLUSTERED INDEX	3	2	1	2	0.00	1	1	1.19

Figure 6-3. *Post-INSERT fragmentation results*

At this point, you need to insert more records into dbo.UsingUniqueidentifier. Use Listing 6-3 again to insert another 78 records into the table, then Listing 6-4 to view the state of fragmentation in the non-clustered index. With this complete, your non-clustered index has gone from no fragmentation to over 25 percent fragmentation, as shown in Figure 6-4.

	index_type_desc	index_depth	index_level	page_count	record_count	avg_fragmentation_in_percent	fragment_count	avg_fragment_size_in_pages	avg_page_space_used_in_percent
1	CLUSTERED INDEX	3	0	360	853	64.17	233	1.5450643776824	59.98
2	CLUSTERED INDEX	3	1	2	360	0.00	2	1	62.24
3	CLUSTERED INDEX	3	2	1	2	0.00	1	1	0.67
4	NONCLUSTERED INDEX	3	0	306	853	25.49	82	3.73170731707317	70.47
5	NONCLUSTERED INDEX	3	1	3	306	66.67	2	1.5	62.24
6	NONCLUSTERED INDEX	3	2	1	3	0.00	1	1	1.63

Figure 6-4. *Post-INSERT fragmentation results*

Whenever you perform INSERT operations, there will always be a way in which fragmentation can occur. This will happen on both clustered and non-clustered indexes.

Update Operations

Another operation that can lead to fragmentation is an UPDATE operation. There are two main ways in which an UPDATE operation will result in fragmentation. First, the data in the record no longer fits on the page in which it currently resides. Second, the key values for the index change and the index location for the new key value is not on the same page or doesn't fit on the page where the record is destined. In both of these cases, the page splits and fragmentation occurs.

To demonstrate how these situations lead to fragmentation, you'll first look at how increasing the size of a record in an update can lead to fragmentation. For this, you'll create a new table and insert a number of records into it. Then you'll add a clustered index to the table. The code for this is in Listing 6-6. Using the script from Listing 6-5 again, you can see that there is no fragmentation on the clustered index, as the results in Figure 6-5 show. One thing to pay attention to with these fragmentation results is that the average page space used is almost 90 percent. Due to this, any significant growth in record size will likely fill the available space on the pages.

Listing 6-5. View UPDATE Index Fragmentation

```
SELECT index_type_desc
  ,index_depth
  ,index_level
  ,page_count
  ,record_count
  ,CAST(avg_fragmentation_in_percent as DECIMAL(6,2)) as avg_fragmentation_in_percent
  ,fragment_count
  ,avg_fragment_size_in_pages
  ,CAST(avg_page_space_used_in_percent as DECIMAL(6,2)) as avg_page_space_used_in_percent
FROM sys.dm_db_index_physical_stats(DB_ID(),OBJECT_ID('dbo.UpdateOperations'),
NULL,NULL,'DETAILED')
```

Listing 6-6. CreateTable for UPDATE Operations

```
IF OBJECT_ID('dbo.UpdateOperations') IS NOT NULL
    DROP TABLE dbo.UpdateOperations;

CREATE TABLE dbo.UpdateOperations
(
```

```
RowID int IDENTITY(1,1)
,Name sysname
,JunkValue varchar(2000)
);

INSERT INTO dbo.UpdateOperations (Name, JunkValue)
SELECT name, REPLICATE('X', 1000)
FROM sys.columns
CREATE CLUSTERED INDEX CLUS_UsingUniqueidentifier ON dbo.UpdateOperations(RowID);
```

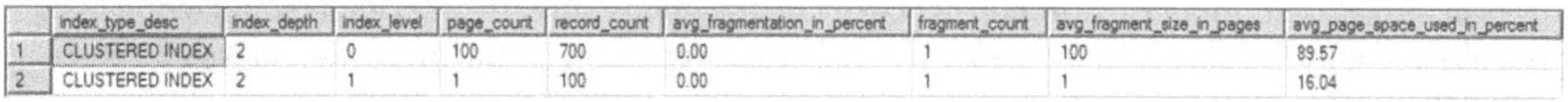

	index_type_desc	index_depth	index_level	page_count	record_count	avg_fragmentation_in_percent	fragment_count	avg_fragment_size_in_pages	avg_page_space_used_in_percent
1	CLUSTERED INDEX	2	0	100	700	0.00	1	100	89.57
2	CLUSTERED INDEX	2	1	1	100	0.00	1	1	16.04

Figure 6-5. *Initial UPDATE fragmentation results*

Now increase the size of some of the rows in the index. To accomplish this, execute the code in Listing 6-7. This code will update the JunkValue column for every five rows from a 1,000 to a 2,000 character value. Using Listing 6-2 to view current index fragmentation, you can see that, through the results in Figure 6-6, the clustered index is now over 99 percent fragmented and the average page space used has dropped to about 50 percent. As this code demonstrates, when a row increases in size during an UPDATE operation, there can be significant amounts of fragmentation.

Listing 6-7. Create Table for UPDATE Operations

```
UPDATE dbo.UpdateOperations
SET JunkValue = REPLICATE('X', 2000)
WHERE RowID % 5 = 1
```

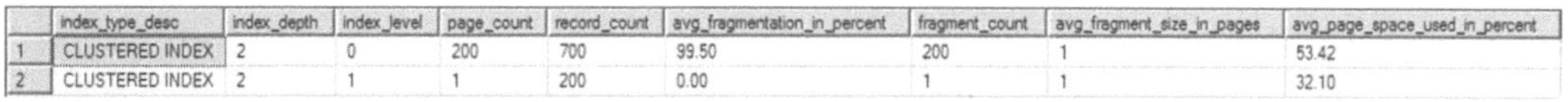

	index_type_desc	index_depth	index_level	page_count	record_count	avg_fragmentation_in_percent	fragment_count	avg_fragment_size_in_pages	avg_page_space_used_in_percent
1	CLUSTERED INDEX	2	0	200	700	99.50	200	1	53.42
2	CLUSTERED INDEX	2	1	200	0.00	1	1	32.10

Figure 6-6. *UPDATE fragmentation results after record length increase*

As mentioned, the second way in which an index can incur fragmentation is by changing the key values for the index. When the key values for an index change, the record may need to change its position in the index. For instance, if an index is built on the name of the product, then changing the name from "Acme Mop" to "XYZ Mop" will change where the product name will be placed in the sorting for the index. Changing the location of the record in the index may place the record on a different page, and if there isn't sufficient space on the new page, then a page split and fragmentation may occur.

To demonstrate this concept, execute Listing 6-8 and then use Listing 6-6 to obtain the results shown in Figure 6-7. You will see that for the new non-clustered index there is no fragmentation in the index.

■ **Note** If key values for a clustered index change often, that may indicate that the key values selected for the clustered index are inappropriate.

Listing 6-8. Create Non-clustered Index for UPDATE operations

```
CREATE NONCLUSTERED INDEX IX_Name ON dbo.UpdateOperations(Name) INCLUDE (JunkValue);
```

	index_type_desc	index_depth	index_level	page_count	record_count	avg_fragmentation_in_percent	fragment_count	avg_fragment_size_in_pages	avg_page_space_used_in_percent
1	CLUSTERED INDEX	2	0	200	700	99.50	200	1	53.42
2	CLUSTERED INDEX	2	1	1	200	0.00	1	1	32.10
3	NONCLUSTERED INDEX	2	0	122	700	0.00	1	122	87.37
4	NONCLUSTERED INDEX	2	1	1	122	0.00	1	1	46.87

Figure 6-7. *UPDATE fragmentation results after adding non-clustered index*

At this point, you need to modify some key values. Using Listing 6-9, perform UPDATE activity on the table and update one of every nine rows. To simulate changing of the key values, the UPDATE statement reverses the characters in the column. This small amount of activity is enough to cause a significant amount of fragmentation. As the results in Figure 6-8 illustrate, the non-clustered index went from no fragmentation to over 35 percent fragmentation.

One thing to note is that the fragmentation on the clustered index did not change with these updates. Not all updates will result in fragmentation; only those that move data around due to space being unavailable on the pages where the record is currently stored.

Listing 6-9. UPDATE Operation to Change Index Key Value

```
UPDATE dbo.UpdateOperations
SET Name = REVERSE(Name)
WHERE RowID % 9 = 1
```

	index_type_desc	index_depth	index_level	page_count	record_count	avg_fragmentation_in_percent	fragment_count	avg_fragment_size_in_pages	avg_page_space_used_in_percent
1	CLUSTERED INDEX	2	0	200	700	99.50	200	1	53.42
2	CLUSTERED INDEX	2	1	1	200	0.00	1	1	32.10
3	NONCLUSTERED INDEX	2	0	157	700	35.03	58	2.70689655172414	75.49
4	NONCLUSTERED INDEX	2	1	1	157	0.00	1	1	61.49

Figure 6-8. *UPDATE fragmentation results after changing index key values*

Delete Operations

The third operation that causes fragmentation is DELETE operations. Deletes are a bit different in the nature in which they create fragmentation within a database. Instead of relocating pages due to page splits, a delete can lead to pages being removed from an index. Gaps will then appear in the physical sequence of pages for the index. Since the pages are no longer physically sequential, they are considered fragmented—especially since once the pages are deallocated from the index, they can be reallocated to other indexes for a more traditional form of fragmentation.

To demonstrate this type of behavior, create a table, populate it with a number of records, and then add a clustered index. The script for these tasks is in Listing 6-11. Run the script followed by the script from Listing 6-10 to get the current fragmentation for the clustered index. Your results should match those in Figure 6-9. As you can see from the average fragmentation in percent column (avg_fragmentation_in_percent), there is no fragmentation currently in the index.

Listing 6-10. View DELETE Index Fragmentation

```
SELECT index_type_desc
   ,index_depth
   ,index_level
   ,page_count
   ,record_count
```

```
,CAST(avg_fragmentation_in_percent as DECIMAL(6,2)) as avg_fragmentation_in_percent
,fragment_count
,avg_fragment_size_in_pages
,CAST(avg_page_space_used_in_percent as DECIMAL(6,2)) as avg_page_space_used_in_percent
FROM sys.dm_db_index_physical_stats(DB_ID(),OBJECT_ID('dbo.DeleteOperations'),
NULL,NULL,'DETAILED')
```

Listing 6-11. Creating a Table for DELETE Operation

```
IF OBJECT_ID('dbo.DeleteOperations') IS NOT NULL
    DROP TABLE dbo.DeleteOperations;

CREATE TABLE dbo.DeleteOperations
(
RowID int IDENTITY(1,1)
,Name sysname
,JunkValue varchar(2000)
);

INSERT INTO dbo.DeleteOperations (Name, JunkValue)
SELECT name, REPLICATE('X', 1000)
FROM sys.columns

CREATE CLUSTERED INDEX CLUS_UsingUniqueidentifier ON dbo.DeleteOperations(RowID);
```

	index_type_desc	index_depth	index_level	page_count	record_count	avg_fragmentation_in_percent	fragment_count	avg_fragment_size_in_pages	avg_page_space_used_in_percent
1	CLUSTERED INDEX	2	0	101	703	0.00	1	101	89.06
2	CLUSTERED INDEX	2	1	1	101	0.00	1	1	16.20

Figure 6-9. *Fragmentation results before DELETE operation*

Now, to demonstrate fragmentation caused by DELETE operations, you'll delete every other fifty records in the table, using the code in Listing 6-12. As before, you'll use Listing 6-10 to view the state of fragmentation in the index. The results, shown in Figure 6-10, indicate that the DELETE operation resulted in about 12 percent fragmentation. With DELETE operations, the rate in which fragmentation usually occurs isn't too fast. Also, since the fragmentation is not the result of page splits, the order of the pages does not become logically out of order. Instead, there are gaps in the contiguous pages.

Listing 6-12. Performing DELETE Operation

```
DELETE dbo.DeleteOperations
WHERE RowID % 100 BETWEEN 1 AND 50
```

	index_type_desc	index_depth	index_level	page_count	record_count	avg_fragmentation_in_percent	fragment_count	avg_fragment_size_in_pages	avg_page_space_used_in_percent
1	CLUSTERED INDEX	2	0	57	350	12.28	8	7.125	78.81
2	CLUSTERED INDEX	2	1	1	57	0.00	1	1	9.13

Figure 6-10. *Fragmentation results after DELETE*

As a final note on DELETE operations, the fragmentation may not appear immediately after the DELETE operation. When records are deleted, they are first marked for deletion before the record itself is actually deleted. While it is marked for delete, the record is considered to be a ghost record. During this stage, the record is logically deleted but is physically still present in the index. At a future point, after the transaction has been committed and a CHECKPOINT has completed, the ghost cleanup process will physically remove the row. At this time, the fragmentation will show in the index.

Shrink Operations

The last type of operation that leads to fragmentation is when databases are shrunk. Databases can be shrunk using either DBCC SHRINKDATABASE or DBCC SHRINKFILE. These operations can be used to shrink the size of a database or its files. When they are used, the pages at the end of a data file are relocated towards the beginning of the data file. For their intended purpose, shrink operations can be effective tools.

Unfortunately, these shrink operations do not take into account the nature of the data pages that are being moved. To the shrink operation, a data page is a data page is a data page. The priority of the operation is that pages at the end of the data file find a place at the beginning of the data file. As discussed, when the pages of an index are not physically stored in order, the index is considered fragmented.

To demonstrate the fragmentation damage that a shrink operation can cause, you'll create a database and perform a shrink on it; the code appears in Listing 6-14. In this example, there are two tables: FirstTable and SecondTable. Some records will be inserted into each table. The inserts will alternate back and forth with three inserts into FirstTable and two inserts into SecondTable. Through these inserts, there will be alternating bands of pages allocated to the two tables. Next, SecondTable will be dropped, which will result in unallocated data pages between each of the bands of pages for FirstTable. Using Listing 6-13 again will show a small amount of fragmentation exists on FirstTable, shown in Figure 6-11.

Listing 6-13. View Index Fragmentation from Shrink

```
SELECT index_type_desc
    ,index_depth
    ,index_level
    ,page_count
    ,record_count
    ,CAST(avg_fragmentation_in_percent as DECIMAL(6,2)) as avg_fragmentation_in_percent
    ,fragment_count
    ,avg_fragment_size_in_pages
    ,CAST(avg_page_space_used_in_percent as DECIMAL(6,2)) as avg_page_space_used_in_percent
FROM sys.dm_db_index_physical_stats(DB_ID(),OBJECT_ID('dbo.FirstTable'),NULL,NULL,'DETAILED')
```

Listing 6-14. Shrink Operation Database Preparation

```
USE master
GO

DROP DATABASE Fragmentation
GO

CREATE DATABASE Fragmentation
GO

Use Fragmentation
GO

IF OBJECT_ID('dbo.FirstTable') IS NOT NULL
    DROP TABLE dbo.FirstTable;

CREATE TABLE dbo.FirstTable
(
RowID int IDENTITY(1,1)
,Name sysname
,JunkValue varchar(2000)
,CONSTRAINT PK_FirstTable PRIMARY KEY CLUSTERED (RowID)
);
```

```
INSERT INTO dbo.FirstTable (Name, JunkValue)
SELECT name, REPLICATE('X', 2000)
FROM sys.columns

IF OBJECT_ID('dbo.SecondTable') IS NOT NULL
    DROP TABLE dbo.SecondTable;

CREATE TABLE dbo.SecondTable
(
RowID int IDENTITY(1,1)
,Name sysname
,JunkValue varchar(2000)
,CONSTRAINT PK_SecondTable PRIMARY KEY CLUSTERED (RowID)
);
INSERT INTO dbo.SecondTable (Name, JunkValue)
SELECT name, REPLICATE('X', 2000)
FROM sys.columns
GO

INSERT INTO dbo.FirstTable (Name, JunkValue)
SELECT name, REPLICATE('X', 2000)
FROM sys.columns
GO

INSERT INTO dbo.SecondTable (Name, JunkValue)
SELECT name, REPLICATE('X', 2000)
FROM sys.columns
GO

INSERT INTO dbo.FirstTable (Name, JunkValue)
SELECT name, REPLICATE('X', 2000)
FROM sys.columns
GO

IF OBJECT_ID('dbo.SecondTable') IS NOT NULL
    DROP TABLE dbo.SecondTable;
GO
```

	index_type_desc	index_depth	index_level	page_count	record_count	avg_fragmentation_in_percent	fragment_count	avg_fragment_size_in_pages	avg_page_space_used_in_percent
1	CLUSTERED INDEX	3	0	699	2097	0.43	6	116.5	75.36
2	CLUSTERED INDEX	3	1	2	699	0.00	2	1	56.11
3	CLUSTERED INDEX	3	2	1	2	0.00	1	1	0.30

Figure 6-11. Fragmentation of FirstTable After Inserts

With the database prepared, the next step is to shrink the database, the purpose of which is to recover the space that SecondTable had been allocated and trim down the size of the database to only what is needed. To perform the shrink operation, use the code in Listing 6-15. When the SHRINKDATABASE operation completes, you can see in Figure 6-12 that running the code from Listing 6-13 causes the fragmentation for the index to increase from less that 1 percent fragmentation to over 30 percent fragmentation. This is a significant change in fragmentation on a database with just a single table. Consider the effect of a shrink operation on a database with hundreds or thousands of indexes.

Listing 6-15. Shrink Operation

```
DBCC SHRINKDATABASE (Fragmentation)
```

	index_type_desc	index_depth	index_level	page_count	record_count	avg_fragmentation_in_percent	fragment_count	avg_fragment_size_in_pages	avg_page_space_used_in_percent
1	CLUSTERED INDEX	3	0	699	2097	34.05	240	2.9125	75.36
2	CLUSTERED INDEX	3	1	2	699	0.00	2	1	56.11
3	CLUSTERED INDEX	3	2	1	2	0.00	1	1	0.30

Figure 6-12. *Fragmentation of FirstTable after shrink operation*

This has been a simple example of the damage in terms of fragmentation that a shrink operation can have on an index. As was evident even with this example, the shrink operation led to a significant amount of fragmentation. Most SQL Server database administrators will agree that shrink operations should be an extremely rare operation on any database. Many DBAs are also of the opinion that this operation should never be used on any database for any reason. The guideline that is most often recommended is to be extremely cautious when shrink database operations are performed. Also, don't get caught in a cycle of shrinking a database to recover space and causing fragmentation, then expanding the database through defragmenting the indexes. This is only a waste of time and resources that could be better spent on real performance and maintenance issues.

Fragmentation Issues

You've seen a number of ways in which indexes can become fragmented, but there hasn't been a discussion around why this is important. There are a couple important reasons why fragmentation within indexes can be a problem. These reasons are

- Index I/O

- Contiguous Reads

As the fragmentation of an index increases, each of these two areas affects the index's ability to perform well. In some worst-case scenarios, the level of fragmentation can be so severe that the query optimizer will stop using the index in query plans.

Index I/O

When it comes to I/O, this is an area of SQL Server where it is easy to have performance bottlenecks; likewise, there are a multitude of solutions to help mitigate the bottleneck. From the perspective of this chapter, we are concerned with the effect of fragmentation on I/O.

Since page splits are often the cause of fragmentation, they provide a good place to start investigating the effect of fragmentation on I/O. To review, when a page split occurs, half of the contents on the page are moved off of the page and onto another page. Generally speaking, if the original page was 100 percent full, then both pages will be about 50 percent full. In essence, it will take two I/Os to read from storage the same amount of information that required one I/O prior to the page split. This increase in I/Os will drive up reads and writes and thus can have a negative effect on performance.

To validate that effect of fragmentation on I/O, let's walk through another fragmentation example. This time you'll build a table, populate it with some data, and perform an update to generate page splits and fragmentation. The code in Listing 6-17 will perform these operations. The last portion of the script will query `sys.dm_db_partition_stats` to return the number of pages that have been reserved for the index. Execute the fragmentation script from Listing 6-16. You'll see the index at this point is over 99 percent fragmented and the results from Listing 6-14 show the index is using 209 pages. See Figure 6-13 for the results.

Listing 6-16. View Index Fragmentation for I/O Example

```
SELECT index_type_desc
  ,index_depth
  ,index_level
  ,page_count
  ,record_count
  ,CAST(avg_fragmentation_in_percent as DECIMAL(6,2)) as avg_fragmentation_in_percent
  ,fragment_count
  ,avg_fragment_size_in_pages
  ,CAST(avg_page_space_used_in_percent as DECIMAL(6,2)) as avg_page_space_used_in_percent
FROM sys.dm_db_index_physical_stats(DB_ID(),OBJECT_ID('dbo.IndexIO'),NULL,NULL,'DETAILED')
```

Listing 6-17. Script to Build Index I/O Example

```
IF OBJECT_ID('dbo.IndexIO') IS NOT NULL
    DROP TABLE dbo.IndexIO;

CREATE TABLE dbo.IndexIO
(
RowID int IDENTITY(1,1)
,Name sysname
,JunkValue varchar(2000)
);

INSERT INTO dbo.IndexIO (Name, JunkValue)
SELECT name, REPLICATE('X', 1000)
FROM sys.columns

CREATE CLUSTERED INDEX CLUS_IndexIO ON dbo.IndexIO(RowID);

UPDATE dbo.IndexIO
SET JunkValue = REPLICATE('X', 2000)
WHERE RowID % 5 = 1

SELECT i.name, ps.in_row_reserved_page_count
FROM sys.indexes i
INNER JOIN sys.dm_db_partition_stats ps ON i.object_id = ps.object_id AND i.index_id = ps.index_id
WHERE i.name = 'CLUS_IndexIO'

ALTER INDEX CLUS_IndexIO ON dbo.IndexIO REBUILD

SELECT i.name, ps.in_row_reserved_page_count
FROM sys.indexes i
INNER JOIN sys.dm_db_partition_stats ps ON i.object_id = ps.object_id AND i.index_id = ps.index_id
WHERE i.name = 'CLUS_IndexIO'
```

	name	in_row_reserved_page_count
1	CLUS_IndexIO	209

Figure 6-13. Fragmentation of FirstTable after shrink operation

But would removing the fragmentation from the index have a noticeable impact in the number of pages in the index? As the demo will demonstrate, reducing fragmentation does have an impact.

Continuing on, the next thing to do is to remove the fragmentation from the index. To accomplish this, execute the ALTER INDEX statement in Listing 6-18 to remove the fragmentation. In the rest of the chapter, we'll be discussing the mechanics of removing fragmentation from an index, so for the time being this statement won't be explained. The effect of this command is that all of the fragmentation has been removed from the index. The results from Listing 6-15 are in Figure 6-14. They show that the number of pages that the index is using dropped from 209 to 146. The effect of removing the fragmentation is an impressive reduction of almost 30 percent in pages in the index.

Listing 6-18. Script to Rebuild Index to Remove Fragmentation

```
ALTER INDEX CLUS_IndexIO ON dbo.IndexIO REBUILD

SELECT i.name, ps.in_row_reserved_page_count
FROM sys.indexes i
INNER JOIN sys.dm_db_partition_stats ps ON i.object_id = ps.object_id AND i.index_id = ps.index_id
WHERE i.name = 'CLUS_IndexIO'
```

	name	in_row_reserved_page_count
1	CLUS_IndexIO	146

Figure 6-14. *Page count resulting from rebuild operations*

This proves that fragmentation can have an effect on the number of pages in an index. The more pages in an index, the more reads are required to get the data you need. Reducing the count of pages can help with allowing SQL Server databases to process more data in the same number of reads or to improve the speed in which it reads the same information across fewer pages.

Contiguous Reads

The other negative effect that fragmentation can have on performance relates to contiguous reads. Within SQL Server, contiguous reads affects its ability to utilize read-ahead operations. Read-ahead allows SQL Server to request pages into memory that are going to be used in the immediate future. Rather than waiting for an I/O request to be generated for the page, SQL Server can read large blocks of pages into memory with the expectation that the data pages will be used by the query in the future.

Going back to indexes, we previously discussed how fragmentation within an index occurs as a result of breaks in the continuity of physical data pages in an index. Every time there is a break in the physical pages, I/O operations must change the place in which data is being read from the SQL Server. This is how fragmentation creates a hindrance in contiguous reads.

Defragmentation Options

SQL Server offers a number of ways in which fragmentation can be removed or mitigated within an index. Each of the methods has pros and cons associated with using it. In this section, we'll look at the options and the reasons for using each one.

Index Rebuild

The first method for removing fragmentation from an index is to rebuild the index. Rebuilding an index builds a new contiguous copy of the index. When the new index is complete, the existing index is dropped. Index rebuild operations are accomplished through either a CREATE INDEX or ALTER INDEX statement. Typically, indexes with more than 30 percent fragmentation are considered good candidates for index rebuilds. Note that 30 percent and lower levels of fragmentation in most databases will not show as large negative impact in performance. The usage of 30 percent is a good starting point, but each database and index usage should be reviewed and adjusted if performance shows more negative effects with less than 30 percent fragmentation of the index.

The chief benefit of performing an index rebuild is that the resulting new index has contiguous pages. When an index is highly fragmented, sometimes the best way to resolve the fragmentation is to simply start over with the index and rebuild. Another benefit of rebuilding an index is that the index options can modified during the rebuild. Lastly, for most indexes, the index can remain online while it is being rebuilt.

■ **Note**   Clustered indexes cannot be rebuilt online when they contain the following data types: image, ntext, text, varchar(max), nvarchar(max), varbinary(max), or XML. Also, online rebuilds are limited to SQL Server Data Center, Enterprise, Developer, and Evaluation editions.

The first option for rebuilding an index is to use the CREATE INDEX statement, shown in Listing 6-19. This is accomplished through the use of the DROP_EXISTING index option. There are a few reasons to choose the CREATE INDEX option instead of ALTER INDEX.

- The index definition needs to be changed, such as when the columns need to be added, removed, or their order needs to change.

- The index needs to be moved from one filegroup to another.

- The index partitioning needs to be modified.

Listing 6-19. Index Rebuild with CREATE INDEX

```
CREATE [ UNIQUE ] [ CLUSTERED | NONCLUSTERED ] INDEX index_name
    ON <object> ( column [ ASC | DESC ] [ ,...n ] )
    [ INCLUDE ( column_name [ ,...n ] ) ]
    [ WHERE <filter_predicate> ]
    [ WITH ( <relational_index_option> [ ,...n ] ) ]
    [ ON { partition_scheme_name ( column_name )
       | filegroup_name
       | default
       }
    ]
    [ FILESTREAM_ON { filestream_filegroup_name | partition_scheme_name | "NULL" } ]
[ ; ]
<relational_index_option> ::=
  DROP_EXISTING = { ON | OFF }
```

The other option is the ALTER INDEX statement, shown in Listing 6-20. This option utilizes the REBUILD option in the syntax. Conceptually, this accomplishes that same thing as the CREATE INDEX, but with the following benefits:

- More than one index can be rebuilt in a single statement.

- single partition of an index can be rebuilt.

Listing 6-20. Index Rebuild with ALTER INDEX

```
ALTER INDEX { index_name | ALL }
    ON <object>
    { REBUILD
      [ [PARTITION = ALL]
       [ WITH ( <rebuild_index_option> [ ,…n ] ) ]
      | [ PARTITION = partition_number
         [ WITH ( <single_partition_rebuild_index_option>
             [ ,…n ] )
        ]
      ]
    ]
```

The primary downside to index rebuilds is the amount of space that is required for the index during the rebuild operation. At a minimum, there should be 120 percent of the size of the current index available within the database for the rebuilt index. The reason for this is that the current index will not be dropped until after the rebuild is completed. For a short time, the index will exist twice in the database.

There are two ways to mitigate some of the space required for an index during a rebuild. First, the SORT_IN_TEMPDB index option can be used to reduce the amount of space needed for intermediate results. You will still need room in the database for two copies of the index, but the 20 percent buffer won't be necessary. The second way to mitigate space is to disable the index prior to the rebuild. Disabling an index drops all of the data pages from an index while retaining the index metadata. This will allow a rebuild of the index in the space that the index previously occupied. Be aware that the disabling option only applies to non-clustered indexes.

Index Reorganization

An alternative to an index rebuild is to reorganize an index. This type of defragmentation happens just as it sounds. Data pages in the index are reordered across the pages already allocated to the index. After the reorganization is complete, the physical order of pages in an index match the logical order of pages. Indexes should be reorganized when they are not heavily fragmented. In general, indexes fragmented less than 30 percent are reorganization candidates.

To reorganize an index, the ALTER INDEX syntax is used (see Listing 6-21) with the REORGANIZE option. Along with that option, the reorganization allows for a single partition to be reorganized. The REBUILD option does not allow this.

Listing 6-21. Index Reorganization with ALTER INDEX

```
ALTER INDEX { index_name | ALL }
    ON <object>
    | REORGANIZE
      [ PARTITION = partition_number ]
      [ WITH ( LOB_COMPACTION = { ON | OFF } ) ]
```

There are a couple of benefits to using the REORGANIZE option. First, indexes are online or available for use by the Optimizer in a new execution plan or cached execution plans for the duration of the reorganization. Second, the process is designed around minimal resource usage which significantly lowers the chance that locking and blocking issues will occur during the transaction.

The downside to index reorganizations is that the reorganization only uses the data pages already allocated to the index. With fragmentation, the extents allocated to one index can often be intertwined with the extents allocated to other indexes. Reordering the data pages won't make the data pages any more contiguous that they currently are, but it will make certain that the pages allocated are sorted in the same order as the data itself.

Drop and Create

The third way to defragment an index is to simply drop the index and re-create it. I include this option for completeness but note that it is not widely practiced or advised. There are a few reasons that illustrate why dropping and creating can be a bad idea.

First, if the index is a clustered index, then all of the other indexes will need to be rebuilt when the clustered index is dropped. Clustered indexes and heaps use different structures for identifying rows and storing data. The non-clustered indexes on the table will need information on where the record is and will need to be recreated to obtain this information.

Next, if the index is a primary key or unique, there are likely other dependents on the index. For instance, the index may be referenced in a foreign key. Also, the index could be tied to a business rule, such as uniqueness, that cannot be removed from the table, even in a maintenance window.

The third reason to avoid this method is that it requires knowledge of all properties on an index. With the other strategies, the index retains all of the existing index properties. By having to recreate the index, there is a risk that a property or two may not be retained in the DDL for the index and important aspects of an index could be lost.

Lastly, after an index is dropped from that table, it cannot be used. This should be an obvious issue, but it's often overlooked when considering this option. The purpose of an index is usually the performance improvements that it brings; removing it from the table takes those improvements with it.

Defragmentation Strategies

So far we've discussed how fragmentation occurs, why it is an issue, and how it can be removed from indexes. It is important to apply this knowledge to the indexes in your databases. In this section, you will learn two ways in which the defragmentation of indexes can be automated.

Maintenance Plans

The first automation option available is defragmentation through maintenance plans, which offer the opportunity to quickly create and schedule maintenance for your indexes that will either reorganize or rebuild your indexes. For each of the types of index defragmentation, there is a task available in the maintenance plans.

There are a couple of ways in which maintenance plans can be created. For the purposes of brevity, we will assume that you are familiar with maintenance plans in SQL Server and thus will focus on the specific tasks related to defragmenting indexes.

Reorganize Index Task

The first task available is the Reorganize Index Task. This task provides a wrapper for the ALTER INDEX REORGANIZE syntax from the previous section. Once configured, this task will reorganize all of the indexes that match the criteria for the task.

There are a few properties that need to be configured when using the Reorganize Index Task (see Figure 6-15). These properties are

- **Connection:** The SQL Server instance the task will connect to when it executes.

- **Database(s):** The databases the task will connect to for reorganizing. The options for this property are

    - All databases

    - All system databases

    - All user database

    - These specific databases (A list of available databases is included and one must be selected.)

- **Object:** Determines whether the reorganization will be against tables, views, or tables and views.

- **Selection:** Specifies the tables or indexes affected by this task. Not available when tables and views is selected in the Object box.

- **Compact large objects:** Determines whether the reorganize uses the option `ALTER INDEX LOB_COMPACTION = ON`.

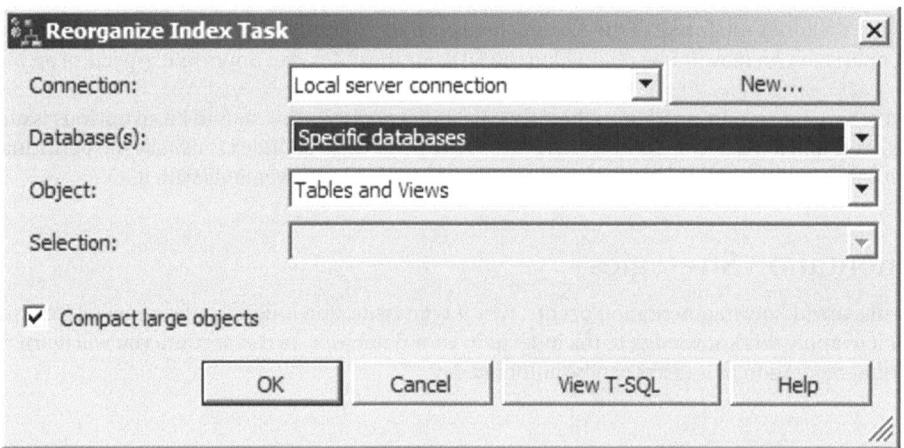

Figure 6-15. *Properties window for Reorganize Index Task*

The main issue with the Reorganize Index Task is that there isn't any filtering on the level of fragmentation or the size of the index. While indexes do remain online during reorganizations, there could be a fair amount of unnecessary work done.

Rebuild Index Task

The other task available is the Rebuild Index Task. This task provides a wrapper for the `ALTER INDEX REBUILD` syntax. Once configured, this task rebuilds all of the indexes that match the criteria for the task.

Similar to the Reorganize Index Task, the Rebuild Index Task has a number of properties that need to be configured before using it (see Figure 6-16). The properties available are

- **Connection:** The SQL Server instance the task will connect to when it executes.

- **Database(s):** The databases the task will connect to for rebuilding. The options for this property are

    - All databases

    - All system databases

    - All user database

    - These specific databases (A list of available databases is included and one must be selected.)

- **Object:** Determines whether the rebuild will be against tables, views, or tables and views.

- **Selection:** Specify the tables or indexes affected by this task. Not available when tables and views is selected in the Object box.

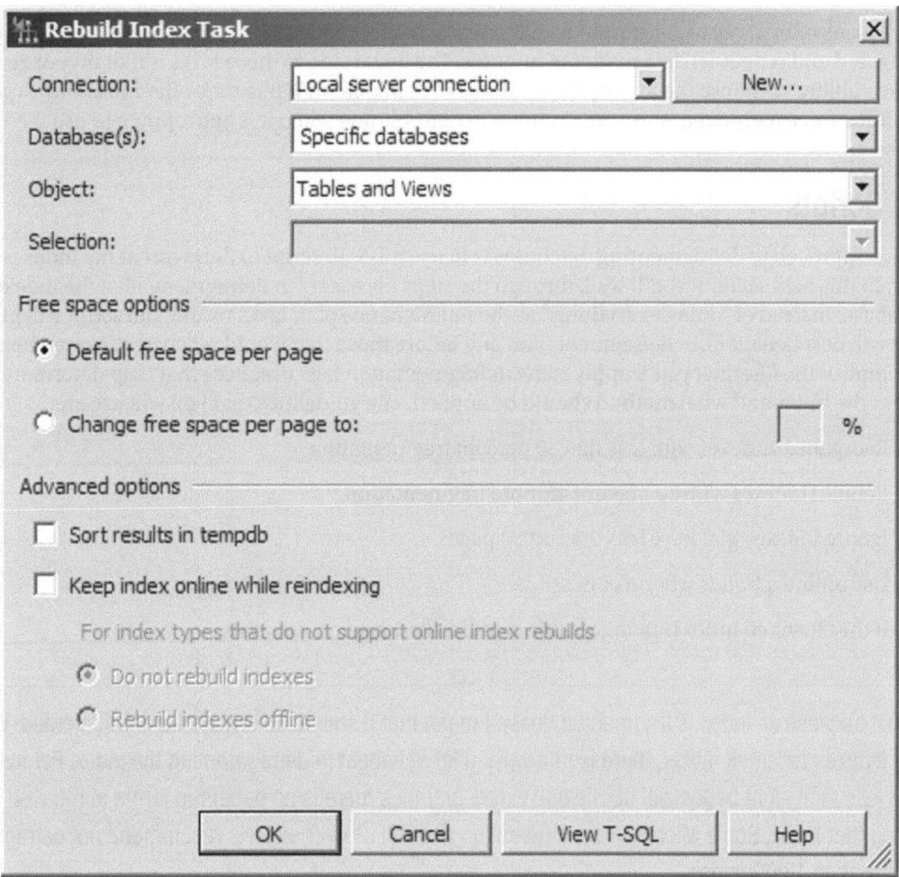

Figure 6-16. *Properties window for Rebuild Index Task*

- **Default free space per page:** Specifies whether the rebuild should use the current fill factor on the index.

- **Change free space per page to:** Allows the rebuild to specify a new fill factor when the index is rebuilt.

- **Sort results in tempdb:** Determines whether the rebuild uses the option `ALTER INDEX SORT_IN_TEMPDB = ON`.

- **Keep index online while reindexing:** Determines whether the rebuild uses the option `ALTER INDEX ONLINE = ON`. For indexes that cannot be rebuilt online, there is an additional option to determine whether to skip or rebuild the index offline.

The downside to the Rebuild Index Task is similar to that of the other index task: there are no options for filtering indexes based on fragmentation or size. This issue can be a bit more significant with the rebuild task. An index rebuild creates a new copy of the index in order to do the rebuild. If this task is configured to rebuild every index in a database, the task must then rewrite every index in the database every time the task executes. Depending on the frequency of transaction log backups, this could result in some significant log file growths overnight.

Maintenance Plan Summary

Maintenance plans offer a way to get started with removing fragmentation from your indexes right away. The tasks can be configured and scheduled in a matter of minutes. The down side to these tasks is that they are extremely limited in their ability to choose the appropriate indexes to defragment. While they offer the ability to get started today, their brute force nature requires some caution in determining when it is appropriate to use them.

T-SQL Scripts

An alternative approach to defragmenting databases is to use a T-SQL script to defragment the indexes intelligently. In this next section, you'll walk through the steps necessary to defragment all of the indexes in a single database. Instead of "doing everything," as the maintenance plan tasks would, the script will pick the indexes that will best benefit from defragmentation and ignore those that would receive little or no benefit.

To accomplish the filtering, you'll apply some defragmentation best practices that help determine whether to defragment the index and what method should be applied. The guidelines that you will use are

- Reorganize indexes with less that 30 percent fragmentation.

- Rebuild indexes with 30 percent or more fragmentation.

- Ignore indexes that have less than 1,000 pages.

- Use online rebuilds wherever possible.

- If the clustered index is being rebuilt, rebuild all indexes in the table.

■ **Note**   Just because an index is fragmented doesn't mean that it should be always be defragmented. When dealing with indexes for small tables, there isn't always a lot of benefit in defragmenting the index. For instance, an index having less than eight pages will fit into one extent and thus there is no benefit in terms of reduced I/O from defragmenting that index. Some Microsoft documentation and SQL Server experts recommend not defragmenting tables with less than 1,000 pages.

There are a few steps that a defragmentation script will perform to intelligently defragment the indexes. These steps are

1. Collect fragmentation data.

2. Determine what indexes to defragment.

3. Build defragmentation statement.

Before starting on the fragmentation steps, you need a template for the index maintenance script. The template, shown in Listing 6-22, declares a number of variables and utilize a CURSOR to loop through each of the indexes and perform the necessary index maintenance. The variables are set at the DECLARE statement with the thresholds defined at the start of this section. Also in the template is a table variable that is used to store intermediate results on the state of fragmentation in the database.

Listing 6-22. Index Defragmantion Script Template

```
DECLARE @MaxFragmentation TINYINT=30
,@MinimumPages SMALLINT=1000
,@SQL nvarchar(max)
,@ObjectName NVARCHAR(300)
,@IndexName NVARCHAR(300)
,@CurrentFragmentation DECIMAL(9, 6)

DECLARE @FragmentationState TABLE
(
SchemaName SYSNAME
,TableName SYSNAME
,object_id INT
,IndexName SYSNAME
,index_id INT
,page_count BIGINT
,avg_fragmentation_in_percent FLOAT
,avg_page_space_used_in_percent FLOAT
,type_desc VARCHAR(255)
)

INSERT INTO @FragmentationState
<Script to Collect Fragmenation Data (Listing 6-23)>

DECLARE INDEX_CURSE CURSOR LOCAL FAST_FORWARD FOR
<Script to Identify Fragmented Indexes (Listing 6-24)>

OPEN INDEX_CURSE

WHILE 1=1
BEGIN
  FETCH NEXT FROM INDEX_CURSE INTO @ObjectName, @IndexName
    ,@CurrentFragmentation
```

```
IF @@FETCH_STATUS <> 0
    BREAK

<Script to Build Index Defragmentation Statements (Listing 6-25)>

EXEC sp_ExecuteSQL @SQL
END

CLOSE INDEX_CURSE
DEALLOCATE INDEX_CURSE
```

To get started, you need to collect fragmentation data on the indexes and populate them into the `table` variable. In the script in Listing 6-23, the DMF sys.dm_db_index_physical_stats is used with the SAMPLED option. This option is used to minimize the impact that executing the DMF will have on the database. Included in the results are the schema, table, and index names to identify the index that is being reporting on, along with the object_id and index_id. Statistical columns on the index fragmentation from the DMF are included with in the columns `page_count`, `avg_fragmentation_in_percent`, and `avg_page_space_used_in_percent`. The last column in the results is `has_LOB_column`. This column is the result of a correlated sub-query that determines if any of the columns in the index are LOB types, which disallow online index rebuilds.

Listing 6-23. Script to Collect Fragmenation Data

```
SELECT
    s.name as SchemaName
    ,t.name as TableName
    ,t.object_id
    ,i.name as IndexName
    ,i.index_id
    ,x.page_count
    ,x.avg_fragmentation_in_percent
    ,x.avg_page_space_used_in_percent
    ,i.type_desc
FROM sys.dm_db_index_physical_stats(db_id(), NULL, NULL, NULL, 'SAMPLED') x
    INNER JOIN sys.tables t ON x.object_id = t.object_id
    INNER JOIN sys.schemas s ON t.schema_id = s.schema_id
    INNER JOIN sys.indexes i ON x.object_id = i.object_id AND x.index_id = i.index_id
WHERE x.index_id > 0
AND alloc_unit_type_desc = 'IN_ROW_DATA'
```

The results of the query in Listing 6-23 will vary for every reader. In general, the results should be similar to those in Figure 6-17, which include clustered, non-clustered, and XML indexes from the AdventureWorks database.

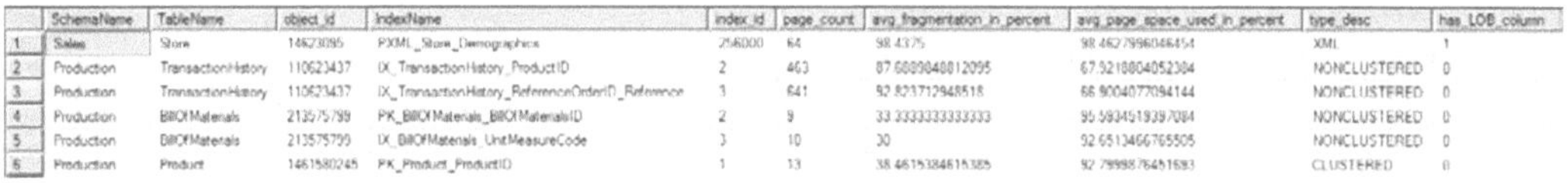

	SchemaName	TableName	object_id	IndexName	index_id	page_count	avg_fragmentation_in_percent	avg_page_space_used_in_percent	type_desc	has_LOB_column
1	Sales	Store	14623095	PXML_Store_Demographics	256000	64	98.4375	98.4627996044454	XML	1
2	Production	TransactionHistory	110623437	IX_TransactionHistory_ProductID	2	463	87.6889048812095	67.5218804052304	NONCLUSTERED	0
3	Production	TransactionHistory	110623437	IX_TransactionHistory_ReferenceOrderID_Reference	3	641	92.8237129485518	66.9004077094144	NONCLUSTERED	0
4	Production	BillOfMaterials	213575799	PK_BillOfMaterials_BillOfMaterialsID	2	9	33.3333333333333	95.5934519397084	NONCLUSTERED	0
5	Production	BillOfMaterials	213575799	IX_BillOfMaterials_UnitMeasureCode	3	10	30	92.6513466765505	NONCLUSTERED	0
6	Production	Product	1461580245	PK_Product_ProductID	1	13	38.4615384615385	92.7999876451683	CLUSTERED	0

Figure 6-17. *Properties window for Rebuild Index Task*

The next step in the defragmentation script is to build the list of indexes that need to be defragmented. The list of indexes, created through Listing 6-24, is used to populate the cursor. The cursor then loops through each of the indexes to perform the defragmentation. One point of interest in the script is that for clustered indexes, all of the underlying indexes will be rebuilt. This isn't a requirement when defragmenting indexes, but it is something that can be considered. When there are just a few indexes on a table, this may be a worthwhile way to manage them. As the count of indexes increases, this may become less appealing. The results from this query should look similar to those in Figure 6-18.

Listing 6-24. Script to Identify Fragmented Indexes

```
SELECT QUOTENAME(x.SchemaName)+'.'+QUOTENAME(x.TableName)
  ,CASE WHEN x.type_desc = 'CLUSTERED' THEN 'ALL'
    ELSE QUOTENAME(x.IndexName) END
  ,x.avg_fragmentation_in_percent
FROM  @FragmentationState
LEFT OUTER JOIN @FragmentationState y ON x.object_id = y.object_id AND y.index_id = 1
WHERE  (
      x.type_desc = 'CLUSTERED'
      AND y.type_desc = 'CLUSTERED'
      )
      OR y.index_id IS NULL
ORDER BY x.object_id
    ,x.index_id
```

	ObjectName	IndexName	avg_fragmentation_in_percent	has_LOB_column
1	[Sales].[Store]	[PXML_Store_Demographics]	98.4375	1
2	[Production].[TransactionHistory]	[IX_TransactionHistory_ProductID]	87.6889848812095	0
3	[Production].[TransactionHistory]	[IX_TransactionHistory_ReferenceOrderID_Reference...	92.823712948518	0
4	[Production].[BillOfMaterials]	[PK_BillOfMaterials_BillOfMaterialsID]	33.3333333333333	0
5	[Production].[BillOfMaterials]	[IX_BillOfMaterials_UnitMeasureCode]	30	0
6	[Production].[Product]	ALL	38.4615384615385	0

Figure 6-18. *Properties window for Rebuild Index Task*

The last part of the template is where the magic happens. In other words, the script in Listing 6-25 is used to construct the ALTER INDEX statement that is used to defragment the index. At this point, the level of fragmentation is checked to determine whether to issue a REBUILD or REORGANIZATION. For indexes that can support ONLINE index rebuilds, a CASE statement adds the appropriate syntax.

Listing 6-25. Script to Build Index Defragmentation Statements

```
SELECT @SQL='ALTER INDEX '
+@IndexName+' ON '+@ObjectName
+CASE WHEN @CurrentFragmentation <= 30
THEN ' REORGANIZE;'
ELSE ' REBUILD'
+CASE WHEN CONVERT(VARCHAR(100), SERVERPROPERTY('Edition')) LIKE 'Data Center%'
OR CONVERT(VARCHAR(100), SERVERPROPERTY('Edition')) LIKE 'Enterprise%'
OR CONVERT(VARCHAR(100), SERVERPROPERTY('Edition')) LIKE 'Developer%'
THEN ' WITH (ONLINE=ON, SORT_IN_TEMPDB=ON) '
END+';'
END
```

> ■ **Note**   One of the improvements to SQL Server 2012 Enterprise Edition is the ability to perform online index rebuilds when the index contains columns with large objects (LOB) data types.

Combining all of these pieces into the template from the beginning of this section to create an index defragmentation script that provides similar functionality to that of the maintenance plan tasks. With the ability to set the size and fragmentation levels in which the defragmentation occurs, this script removes the fragmentation from indexes that really need the work done on them vs. just defragmenting every index in the database. Using SQL Profiler on AdventureWorks to trace the output of the script reveals that the ALTER INDEX syntax for the results of the previous queries is similar to that in Listing 6-26.

Listing 6-26. Index Defragmentation Statements

```
ALTER INDEX [PXML_Store_Demographics] ON [Sales].[Store] REBUILD WITH (ONLINE=OFF, SORT_IN_
TEMPDB=ON) ;
ALTER INDEX [IX_TransactionHistory_ProductID] ON [Production].[TransactionHistory] REBUILD
WITH (ONLINE=ON, SORT_IN_TEMPDB=ON) ;
ALTER INDEX [IX_TransactionHistory_ReferenceOrderID_ReferenceOrderLineID] ON [Production].
[TransactionHistory] REBUILD WITH (ONLINE=ON, SORT_IN_TEMPDB=ON) ;
ALTER INDEX [PK_BillOfMaterials_BillOfMaterialsID] ON [Production].[BillOfMaterials] REBUILD
WITH (ONLINE=ON, SORT_IN_TEMPDB=ON) ;
ALTER INDEX [IX_BillOfMaterials_UnitMeasureCode] ON [Production].[BillOfMaterials] REORGANIZE;
ALTER INDEX ALL ON [Production].[Product] REBUILD WITH (ONLINE=ON, SORT_IN_TEMPDB=ON) ;
```

As the code in this section demonstrated, using a T-SQL script can be much more complicated that just using the maintenance plan tasks. The upside to the complexity is that once the script is complete, it can be wrapped in a stored procedure and used on all of your SQL Server instances. This script is meant as a first step in automating defragmentation with T-SQL scripts. It doesn't account for partitioned tables and doesn't check to see if the index is being used before rebuilding or reorganizing the index. On the upside, rather than driving a truck through your databases and re-indexing everything, a scripted solution can intelligently decide how and when to defragment your indexes.

> ■ **Note**   For a complete index defragmentation solution, check out Ola Hallengren's index maintenance scripts at http://ola.hallengren.com/Versions.html.

Preventing Fragmentation

Fragmentation within an index is not always foregone conclusion. There are some methods that can be utilized to mitigate the rate in which fragmentation occurs. When you have indexes that are often affected by fragmentation, it is advisable to investigate why the fragmentation is occurring. There a few strategies that can help mitigate fragmentation; these are fill factor, data typing, and default values.

Fill Factor

Fill factor is an option that can be used when building or rebuilding indexes. This property is used to determine how much space per page should be left available in the index when it is first created or the next time it is rebuilt. For instance, with a fill factor of 75, about 25 percent of every data page is left empty.

If an index encounters a significant or frequent amount of fragmentation, it is worthwhile to adjust the fill factor to mitigate the fragmentation. By doing this, the activities that are causing fragmentation should be less impactful, which should reduce the frequency that the index needs to be defragmented.

By default, SQL Server creates all indexes with a default of 0. This is a recommended value for both the server and database levels. Not all indexes are created equal, and fill factor should be applied as it is needed, not as a blanket insurance policy. Also, a fill factor of 0 is the same as fill factor 100.

The one downside of fill factor is that leaving space available in data pages means that the index will require more data pages for all of the records in the index. More pages means more I/O and possibly less utilization of the index if there are alternate indexes to select from.

Data Typing

A second way to avoid fragmentation is through appropriate data typing. This strategy applies to data types that can change length depending on the data that they contain. These are data types such as VARCHAR and NVARCHAR, which have lengths that can change over time.

In many cases, variable length data types are a great fit for columns in a table. Issues arise when the volatility of the data is high and the length of the data is volatile as well. As the data changes length, there can be page splits, which lead to fragmentation. If the length volatility occurs across significant portions of the index, then there may also be significant amounts of page splits, and thus fragmentation.

A good example of bad data typing comes from a previous experience with a data warehouse. The original design for one of the tables included a column with the data type of VARCHAR(10). The column was populated with dates in the format of yyyymmdd, with values similar to "20120401". As part of the import process, the date values were updated into a format of yyyy-mm-dd. When the import was moved to production and millions of rows were being processed at a time, the increase in the length of the column from 8 to 10 characters led to an astounding level of fragmentation due to page splits. Resolving the problem was a simple as changing the data type of the column from VARCHAR(10) to CHAR(10).

Such simple solutions can apply to many databases. It just requires a bit of investigation into why the fragmentation is occurring.

Default Values

The proper application of default values may not seem to be something that can assist in preventing fragmentation, but there are some scenarios in which it can have a significant effect on fragmentation. The poster child for this type of mitigation is when databases utilize the uniqueidentifier data type.

In most cases, uniqueidentifier values are generate using the NEWID() function. This function creates a GUID that should be unique across our entire planet. This is useful for generating unique identifiers for rows, but is likely scoped larger than that of your database. In many cases, the unique value probably needs to be unique for the server or just the table.

The main problem with the NEWID() function is that generating the GUID is not a sequential process. As was demonstrated at the beginning of the chapter, using this function to generate values for the clustered index key can lead to severe levels of fragmentation.

An alternative to the NEWID() function is the NEWSEQUENTIALID() function. This function returns a GUID just like the other function, but with a couple variations on how the values are generated. First, each GUID generated by the function on a server is sequential to the last value. The second variation is that GUID value generated is only unique to the server that is generating it. If another SQL Server instance generates GUID with this function for the same table, it is possible that duplicate values will be generated and the values will not be sequential since these are scoped to the server level.

With these restrictions in mind, if a table must use the uniqueidentifier data type, the NEWSEQUENTIALID() function is an excellent alternative to the NEWID() function. The values will be sequential and the amount of fragmentation encountered will be much lower and less frequent.

Index Statistics Maintenance

In Chapter 3, we discussed the statistics collected on indexes. These statistics provide crucial information that the query optimizer uses to compile execution plans for queries. When this information is out of date or inaccurate, the database will provide sub-optimal or inaccurate query plans.

For the most part, index statistics do not require much maintenance. In this section, you'll look at the processes within SQL Server that can be used to create and update statistics. You'll also look at how you can maintain statistics in situations where the automated processes cannot keep up with the rate of data change within an index.

Automatically Maintaining Statistics

The easiest way to build and maintain statistics in SQL Server is to just let SQL Server do it. There are three database properties that control whether SQL Server will automatically build and maintain statistics. These properties are

- AUTO_CREATE_STATISTICS

- AUTO_UPDATE_STATISTICS

- AUTO_UPDATE_STATISTICS_ASYNC

By default, the first two properties are enabled in databases. The last option is disabled by default. In most cases, all three of these properties should be enabled.

Automatic Creation

The first database property is AUTO_CREATE_STATISTICS. This database property directs SQL Server to automatically create single-column statistics that do not have statistics. From the perspective of indexes, this property does not have an impact. When indexes are created, a statistics object is created for the index.

Automatic Updating

The next two properties are AUTO_UPDATE_STATISTICS and AUTO_UPDATE_STATISTICS_ASYNC. At a high level, these two properties are quite similar. When an internal threshold is surpassed, SQL Server will initiate an update of the statistics object. The update occurs to keep the values within the statistics object current with the cardinality of values within the table.

The threshold for triggering a statistics update can change from table to table. The threshold is based on a couple of calculations relating to the count of rows that have changed. For an empty table, when more than 500 rows are added to the table, a statistics update will be triggered. If the table has more than 500 rows, then statistics will be updated when 500 rows plus 20 percent of the cardinality of rows have been modified. At this point, SQL Server will schedule an update to the statistics.

When the statistics update occurs, there are two modes in which it can be accomplished: synchronously and asynchronously. By default, statistics update synchronously. This means that when statistics are deemed out of date and required an update, the query optimizer will wait until after the statistics have been updated before it will compile an execution plan for the query. This is extremely useful for tables that have data that is very volatile. For instance, the statistics for a table before and after a TRUNCATE TABLE would be quite different. Optionally, statistics can be built asynchronously through enabling the AUTO_UPDATE_STATISTICS_ASYNC property. This changes how the query optimizer reacts when an update statistics event is triggered. Instead of waiting for the statistics update to complete, the query optimizer will compile an execution plan based on the existing statistics and use the update statistics for future queries after the update completes. For databases with high volumes of queries and data being pushed through, this is often the preferred manner of updating statistics. Instead of occasional pauses in transactional throughput, the queries will flow through unencumbered and plans will update as improved information is available.

If you are in an environment that disabled AUTO_UPDATE_STATISTICS in previous SQL Server versions, you should consider enabling it now with the AUTO_UPDATE_STATISTICS_ASYNC. The most common reason to disable AUTO_UPDATE_STATISTICS in the past was due to the delay caused by the update of statistics. With the option to enable AUTO_UPDATE_STATISTICS_ASYNC, those performance concerns can likely be mitigated.

Preventing Auto Update

Depending on the index on a table, there will be times in which automatically updating the indexes will do more harm than good. For instance, an automatic statistics update on a very large table may lead to performance issues while the statistics object is updated. In that situation, the existing statistics object may be good enough until the next maintenance window. There are a number of ways in which AUTO_UPDATE_STATISTICS can be disabled on an individual statistics object rather than across the entire database. These options are

- Executing sp_autostats system store procedure on the statistics object
- Using the NORECOMPUTE option on the UPDATE STATISTICS or CREATE STATISTICS statements.
- Using STATISTICS_NORECOMPUTE on the CREATE INDEX statement

Each of these options can be used to disable or enable the AUTO_UPDATE_STATISTICS option on indexes. Before disabling this feature, always be sure to validate that the statistics update is truly necessary.

Manually Maintaining Statistics

There will be times when the automated processes for maintaining statistics will not be good enough. This is often tied to situations where the data is changing but not enough has changed to trigger a statistics update. A good example of when this can happen is when update statements change the cardinality of the table without affecting a large number of rows. For instance, if 10 percent of a table was changed from a large number of values to a single value, then the plan for querying the data could end up being suboptimal. In situations like this, you need to be able to get in and manually update statistics. As with index fragmentation, there are two methods for manually maintaining statistics. These are

- Maintenance Plans
- T-SQL Scripts

In the next sections, you'll look at each of these methods and walk through how they can be implemented.

Maintenance Plans

Within maintenance plans, there is a task that allows statistics maintenance. This task is the Update Statistics Task, aptly named for exactly what it accomplishes. When using this task, there are a number of properties that can be configured to control its behavior (see Figure 6-19). The properties available are

- **Connection:** The SQL Server instance the task will connect to when it executes.
- **Database(s):** The databases the task will connect to for rebuilding. The options for this property are

- All databases

- All system databases

- All user database

- These specific databases (A list of available databases is included and one must be selected.)

- **Object:** Determines whether the rebuild will be against tables, views, or tables and Views.

- **Selection:** Specify the tables or indexes affected by this task. Not available when tables and views is selected in the Object box.

- **Update:** For each table, this property determines whether All existing statistics, Column statistics only (using WITH COLUMN clause), or Index statistics only (using WITH INDEX clause) are updated.

- **Scan Type:** A choice between a full scan of all leaf-level pages of the indexes or "Sample by," which will scan a percentage or number of rows to build the statistics object.

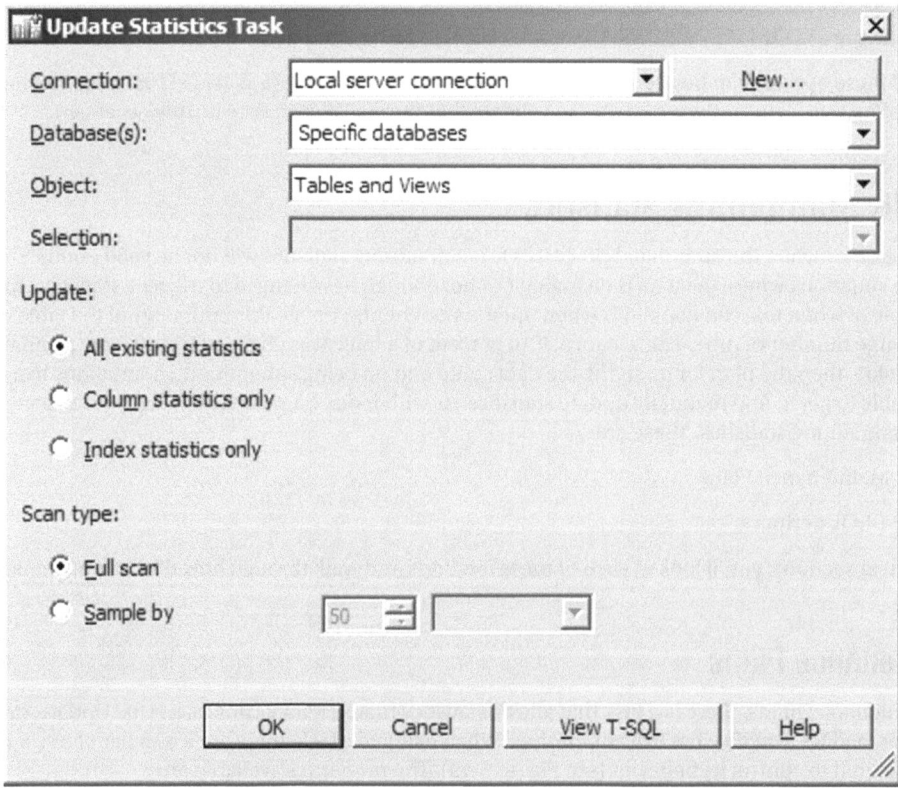

Figure 6-19. *Properties window for Update Statistics Task*

As with the maintenance plan tasks discussed earlier in this chapter, the tasks don't have deeper controls to help determine whether the statistics should be updated. A useful option would be to limit the statistics updates to a specified date range, which would reduce the number of statistics updated during each execution. For the most part, the lack of that option is not a deal-breaker. Statistics updates aren't like indexes where each update requires enough space to rebuild the entire index.

T-SQL Scripts

Through T-SQL there are a couple alternative approaches for updating statistics: through stored procedure or though DDL statements. Each of these approaches has pros and cons. In the next couple sections, you'll look at each one and why it may be a worthwhile approach.

Stored Procedure

Within the master database there is a system stored procedure named sp_updatestats that allows for updating all statistics within a database. Since it is a system stored procedure, it can be called from any database to update the statistics in the database in which it is called from.

When sp_updatestats is executed, it runs the UPDATE STATISTICS statement, described in the next section, using the ALL option. The stored procedure accepts a single parameter named resample, shown in Listing 6-27. The resample parameter accepts only the value resample. If this value is supplied, then the stored procedure uses the RESAMPLE option of UPDATE STATISTICS. Otherwise, the stored procedure uses the default sampling algorithm in SQL Server.

Listing 6-27. sp_updatestats Syntax

```
sp_updatestats [ [ @resample = ] 'resample']
```

One benefit to using sp_updatestats is that it will only update the statistics for items in which there has been modifications to the data. The internal counter that is used to trigger automatic statistics updates is checked to make certain that only statistics that have been changed will be updated.

In situations where a statistics update is needed, the sp_updatestats is a great tool for updating statistics on just those that have the potential for being out of date since the last update. Where the Update Statistics Task is an oversized blanket that smothers the entire database, sp_updatestats is a comforter that covers in just the right places.

DDL Command

The other option for updating statistics is through the DDL command UPDATE STATISTICS, shown in Listing 6-28. The UPDATE STATISTICS statement allows for finely tuned statistics updates on a per-statistics basis with a number of options for how to collect and build statistics information.

Listing 6-28. UPDATE STATISTICS Syntax

```
UPDATE STATISTICS table_or_indexed_view_name
    [
      {
        { index_or_statistics_name }
      | ( { index_or_statistics_name } [ ,...n ] )
            }
    ]
  [ WITH
```

```
        [
          [ FULLSCAN ]
          | SAMPLE number { PERCENT | ROWS } ]
          | RESAMPLE
        ]
        [ [ , ] [ ALL | COLUMNS | INDEX ]
        [ [ , ] NORECOMPUTE ]
      ] ;
```

The first parameter to set when using UPDATE STATISTICS is table_or_indexed_view_name. This parameter references the table in which the statistics will be updated. With the UPDATE STATISTICS command, only one table or view can have its statistics updated at a time.

The next parameter is index_or_statistics_name. This parameter is used to determine whether a single statistic, list of statistics, or all statistics on a table will be update. To update just a single statistic, include the name of the statistic after the name of the table or view. For a list of statistics, the names of the statistics are included in a comma-separated list within parenthesis. If no statistics are named, then all statistics will be considered for updating.

After the parameters are set, it is time to add applicable options to the UPDATE STATISTICS command. This is where the power and flexibility of the syntax really shines through. These parameters allow the statistics to be finely tuned to the data available in them to get the right statistics for the right table and the right index. The available options are

- **FULLSCAN:** When the statistics object is built, all rows and pages in the table or view are scanned. For large tables, this may have an effect on performance while creating the statistics. Basically, this is the same as performing a SAMPLE 100 PERCENT.

- **SAMPLE:** The statistics object is created using either a count or a percentage sample of the rows in the table or view. When the sample rate is not selected, SQL Server will determine an appropriate sample rate based on the number of rows in the table.

- **RESAMPLE:** Update the statistics using the sample rate from the last time that the statistics were updated. For instance, if that last update used a FULLSCAN, then a RESAMPLE will results in a FULLSCAN as well.

- **ALL | COLUMNS | INDEX:** Determines whether column statistics, index statistics, or both should be updated.

- **NORECOMPUTE:** Disables the option for the Query Optimizer to request an automatic update to the statistics. This is useful for locking in statistics that shouldn't change or are optimal with the current sample. Take caution when using this on tables that have frequent data modifications and make certain there are other mechanisms in place to update the statistics as needed.

The first three options in this list are mutually exclusive. You are only able to select one of the options. Selecting more than one of those options will generate an error.

Since UPDATE STATISTICS is a DDL command, it can easily be automated in a fashion similar to that used to defragment indexes. For brevity, a sample script is not included, but the template for the index fragmentation maintenance could be used as a starting point. As mentioned in the last section, sp_updatestats uses UPDATE STATISTICS under the covers. This DDL command is a powerful way to update statistics as needed in your databases without doing more than is really necessary. To continue the analogy from the last section, using UPDATE STATISTICS replaces the blanket and comforter with a handmade sweater.

Summary

In this chapter, you learned about a number of maintenance considerations that are part of indexing a table. These break down to managing the fragmentation of indexes and managing their statistics. With index fragmentation, you saw ways in which indexes can become fragmented, why it is an issue, and strategies to remove the fragmentation. These maintenance tasks are critical for making certain that SQL Server can use indexes to the best of its ability. Along with the maintenance activity, the statistics on the indexes must also be maintained. Out-of-date or inaccurate statistics can lead to execution plans that do not match the data in the table. Without proper execution plans, performance will suffer regardless of the indexes in place.

CHAPTER 7

■ ■ ■

Indexing Tools

When it comes to indexing, Microsoft has two tools built into SQL Server that can be used to help identify indexes that can improve database performance. These are the missing index Dynamic Management Objects (DMOs) and the Database Engine Tuning Advisor (DTA). Both tools are useful to assist with indexing databases and can provide valuable input when working on tuning a database.

This chapter will explain both indexing tools. We'll begin by explaining what they are and the capabilities they provide. Then we'll walk through how the tools can be used to provide assistance with indexing. Throughout the chapter, we will also look at the pros and cons in using each of the tools.

Missing Index DMOs

The missing index DMOs are a set of management objects that provide feedback from the query optimizer. When the query optimizer compiles an execution plan, it will determine what index would work for the current plan. If the index does not exist, it will store the information in the missing index DMOs.

There are a couple of benefits that the missing index DMOs provide. First, the missing index information is collected from the query optimizer without any action required on your part. Unlike extended events and other performance monitoring tools, you don't need to configure and enable it in order for information to be collected. The other thing to consider is that the missing index information is based on actual activity occurring on the SQL Server instance. The index suggestions aren't based on a test load you believe might happen in production but rather on the production load itself. As the usage patterns of the data in the databases change, so too will the missing index recommendations.

Along with the benefits provided by the missing index DMOs, there are a few considerations that must be taken into account when using them. The limitations on the missing index DMOs can be summarized into the following categories:

- Size of queue
- Depth of analysis
- Accuracy
- Type of indexes

The size of the queue for missing indexes is one of the limitations that is easy to miss. Regardless of the number of databases on the SQL Server instance, there can be no more than 500 missing index groups. Once 500 missing index groups have been identified, the query optimizer will stop reporting new missing index suggestions. It will not make any determinations to decide if a new possible missing index is of better quality than items already reported; the information is just not collected.

When considering the information in missing indexes, the depth of the analysis is a limitation that needs to be considered whenever you are reviewing the suggestions. The query optimizer only considers the current plan and whether the missing index would benefit the execution plan. Sometimes, adding the missing index to the database will result in a new plan with a new missing index suggestion. These suggestions are only a first pass at improving performance on an execution plan. The other half of this limitation is that the missing index details don't include tests to determine whether the order of the columns in the missing index suggestion is optimal. When looking at missing index suggestions, it will be necessary to test in order to determine the proper column order.

The third limitation of the missing index suggestion is the accuracy of the information returned with the statistics. There are two things that need to be considered with this limitation. First, when the queries use inequality predicates, the cost information is less accurate than those returned with equality predicates. Second, it is possible to return the same missing index suggestion with multiple cost estimates. How and where the missing index would be leveraged may change the cost estimate that is calculated. For each cost estimate, a missing index suggestion will be logged.

Lastly, the missing index tool is limited in the types of indexes it can suggest. The main limitation is index types and the inability of missing indexes to suggest clustered, XML, spatial, or column store indexes. The suggestions also will not include information on when to make an index filtered or not. Along these same lines, suggestions may, at times, contain only INCLUDE columns. When this happens, one of the INCLUDE columns will need to be designated as the key column.

■ **Note**   Missing index information for a table will be dropped whenever there are metadata operations made on the table. For instance, when a column is added to a table, the missing index information will be dropped. A less obvious example is when an index on a table changes. In this case as well, the missing index information will also be dropped.

Explaining the DMOs

There are four DMOs that can be used to return information on missing indexes. Each DMO provides a portion of the information needed to build indexes that the query optimizer can use to improve the performance of a query. The DMOs for missing indexes are:

- sys.dm_db_missing_index_details
- sys.dm_db_missing_index_columns
- sys.dm_db_missing_index_group_stats
- sys.dm_db_missing_index_group

In the next four sections, we'll review each of the dynamic management objects and look at how each provides information on how to identify missing indexes.

sys.dm_db_missing_index_details

The DMO sys.dm_db_missing_index_details is a dynamic management view that returns a list of missing index suggestions. Each row in the Dynamic Management View (DMV) provides a single suggested missing index. The columns in Table 7-1 provide information on the database and table to create the index on. It also includes the columns that should comprise the key and included columns for the index.

Table 7-1. Columns in sys.dm_db_missing_index_details

Column Name	Data Type	Description
index_handle	int	Unique identifier for each missing index suggestions. This is the key value for this DMV
database_id	smallint	Identifies the database where the table with the missing index resides
object_id	int	Identifies the table where the index is missing
equality_columns	nvarchar(4000)	Comma-separated list of columns that contribute to equality predicates
inequality_columns	nvarchar(4000)	Comma-separated list of columns that contribute to inequality predicates
included_columns	nvarchar(4000)	Comma-separated list of columns needed as covering columns for the query
statement	nvarchar(4000)	Name of the table where the index is missing

There are two columns in sys.dm_db_missing_index_details that are used to identify key columns on missing index suggestions. These are equality_columns and inequality_columns. The equality_columns are generated when there is a comparison in the query plan that makes a direct comparison. For instance, when the filter for a query is ColumnA = @Parameter, this is an equality predicate. The inequality_columns details are created when any nonequal filter is used in a query plan. Examples of this are when there are greater than, less than, or NOT IN comparisons being used.

When it comes to the included_columns information, this is generated when there are columns that are not part of the filter but that would be used to allow the index to cover the query request using a single index. Included columns are covered in more depth in Chapter 8. Suffice it to say, the use of included columns will help prevent the query plan from having to use a key lookup in the execution plan if the missing index is created.

sys.dm_db_missing_index_columns

The next DMO is sys.dm_db_missing_index_columns, which is a dynamic management function (DMF). This function returns a list of columns for each missing index listed in sys.dm_db_missing_index_details. To use the DMF, an index_handle is passed into the function as a parameter. Each row in the result set represents a column in the missing index suggestion from sys.dm_db_missing_index_details and repeats the information in equality_columns, inequality_columns, and included_columns. The output for sys.dm_db_missing_index_columns is listed in Table 7-2.

Table 7-2. *Columns in sys.dm_db_missing_index_columns*

Column Name	Data Type	Description
column_id	int	ID of the column
column_name	sysname	Name of the table column
column_usage	varchar(20)	Description of how the column will be used in the index

The primary information in this DMF is the column_usage column. For every row, this column will return one of the following values: EQUALITY, INEQUALITY, or INCLUDE. These values map to equality_columns, inequality_columns, and included_columns in sys.dm_db_missing_index_details. Depending on the type of usage in the former DMV, the use will be the same for this DMF.

sys.dm_db_missing_index_groups

The DMV sys.dm_db_missing_index_groups is the next missing index DMO. The DMV returns a list of missing index groups paired with missing index suggestions. The columns for sys.dm_db_missing_index_groups are listed in Table 7-3. Although this DMV supports the ability for many-to-many relationships within missing index suggestions, they are always made in a one-to-one relationship.

Table 7-3. *Columns in sys.dm_db_missing_index_groups*

Column Name	Data Type	Description
index_group_handle	int	Identifies a missing index group. This value joins to group_handle in sys.dm_db_missing_index_group_stats.
index_handle	int	Identifies a missing index handle. This value joins to index_handlein sys.dm_db_missing_index_details.

sys.dm_db_missing_index_group_stats

The last missing index DMO is the DMV sys.dm_db_missing_index_group_stats. The information in this DMV contains statistics on how the query optimizer would expect to use the missing index if it were built. From this, using the columns in Table 7-4, you can determine which missing indexes would provide the greatest benefit and the scope to which the index will be used.

Table 7-4. *Columns in sys.dm_db_missing_index_group_stats*

Column Name	Data Type	Description
group_handle	int	Unique identifier for each missing index group. This is the key value for this DMV. All queries that would benefit from using the missing index group are included in this group.
unique_compiles	bigint	Count of the execution plan compilations and recompilations that would benefit from this missing index group.
user_seeks	bigint	Count of seeks in user queries that would have occurred if the missing index had been built.
user_scans	bigint	Count of scans in user queries that would have occurred if the missing index had been built.
last_user_seek	datetime	Date and time of last user seek from user queries that would have occurred if the missing index had been built.
last_user_scan	datetime	Date and time of last user scans from user queries that would have occurred if the missing index had been built.
avg_total_user_cost	float	Average cost of the user queries that could be reduced by the index in the group.
avg_user_impact	float	Average percentage benefit that user queries could experience if this missing index group had been implemented.
system_seeks	bigint	Count of seeks in system queries that would have occurred if the missing index had been built.
system_scans	bigint	Count of scans in system queries that would have occurred if the missing index had been built.
last_system_seek	datetime	Date and time of last system seek from system queries that would have occurred if the missing index had been built.
last_system_scan	datetime	Date and time of last system scans from system queries that would have occurred if the missing index had been built.
avg_total_system_cost	float	Average cost of the system queries that could be reduced by the index in the group.
avg_system_impact	float	Average percentage benefit that system queries could experience if this missing index group had been implemented.

Using the DMOs

Now that the missing index DMOs have been explained, it is time to look at how they can be used together to provide missing index suggestions. You may have noticed that the results of the missing index DMOs have been referred to as suggestions instead of recommendations. This variation in wording is intentional. Typically, when someone receives a recommendation, it is fully thought through and ready to be implemented. This is not so with the missing index DMOs, thus we refer to them as suggestions.

With the suggestions from the missing index DMOs, we have a starting point to begin looking at and building new indexes. There are two things that are important to consider when looking at missing index suggestions. First, variations of each missing index suggestion may appear multiple times in the results. It is not recommended that each of these variations be implemented. Common patterns within the suggestions should be found. An index that covers a few of the suggestions is usually ideal. Second, when more than one column is suggested, the order of the columns needs to be tested to determine which is optimal.

To help explain how the missing index DMOs work and are related to one another, we'll walk through an example that includes a few SQL statements. These statements, shown in Listing 7-1, execute a few queries against the SalesOrderHeader table in the AdventureWorks database. For each of the queries, the filtering is on either the DueDate or OrderDate column or both.

Listing 7-1. SQL Statements to Generate Missing Index Suggestions

```
SELECT DueDate FROM Sales.SalesOrderHeader
WHERE DueDate = '2001-07-13 00:00:00.000'
AND OrderDate = '2001-07-13 00:00:00.000'
GO

SELECT DueDate FROM Sales.SalesOrderHeader
WHERE OrderDate Between '20010701' AND '20010731'
AND DueDate Between '20010701' AND '20010731'
GO

SELECT DueDate, OrderDate FROM Sales.SalesOrderHeader
WHERE DueDate Between '20010701' AND '20010731'
GO

SELECT CustomerID, OrderDate FROM Sales.SalesOrderHeader
WHERE DueDate Between '20010701' AND '20010731'
AND OrderDate Between '20010701' AND '20010731'
GO
```

If you examine the execution plan for any of the example queries, you'll see that they each use a clustered index scan to satisfy the query. The execution plan for the first query can be seen in Figure 7-1. In this execution plan, there is an indication that there is a missing index that could help improve the performance of the query.

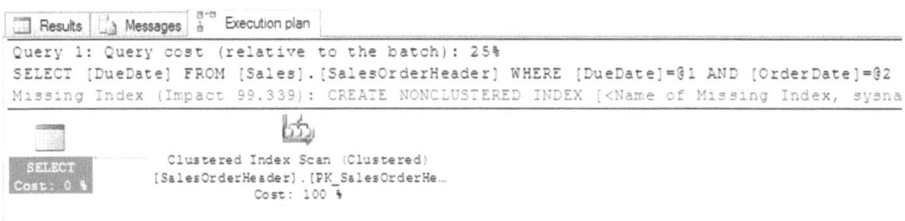

Figure 7-1. Execution plan for missing index SELECT query

To see more details on this missing index suggestion, you need to look at the missing index DMOs. A query against the missing index DMOs will look similar to Listing 7-2. The query includes the equality, inequality, and included column information that was described earlier. The query includes two calculations not previously described: the calculations for Impact and Score.

The Impact calculation helps identify missing index suggestions that will have the highest overall impact across multiple query executions. This is calculated by adding the potential seeks and scans on the missing index based on the average impact; the resulting value represents the total improvement across all queries that might have used the index. The higher the value, the more improvement the index could provide.

The Score calculation also helps to identify missing index suggestions that will improve query performance. The difference between the Impact and Score is the inclusion of the average total user cost. For the Score calculation, the average total user cost is multiplied by the Impact score and divided by 100. The inclusion of the cost value helps differentiate between expensive and inexpensive queries when deciding whether to consider the missing index. For instance, a missing index suggestion that provides an 80 percent improvement on queries with an average cost value of 1,000 would likely provide a better return that a 90 percent improvement for a query with an average cost value of 1.

Listing 7-2. Query for Missing Index DMOs

```
SELECT
  DB_NAME(database_id) AS database_name
  ,OBJECT_NAME(object_id, database_id) AS table_name
  ,mid.equality_columns
  ,mid.inequality_columns
  ,mid.included_columns
  ,(migs.user_seeks + migs.user_scans) * migs.avg_user_impact AS Impact
  ,migs.avg_total_user_cost * (migs.avg_user_impact / 100.0) * (migs.user_seeks + migs.user_
scans) AS Score
  ,migs.user_seeks
  ,migs.user_scans
FROM sys.dm_db_missing_index_details mid
    INNER JOIN sys.dm_db_missing_index_groups mig ON mid.index_handle = mig.index_handle
    INNER JOIN sys.dm_db_missing_index_group_stats migs ON mig.index_group_handle = migs.
group_handle
ORDER BY migs.avg_total_user_cost * (migs.avg_user_impact / 100.0) * (migs.user_seeks + migs.
user_scans) DESC
```

With the results from the missing index query, shown in Figure 7-2, there are a few items to consider from these suggestions. First, there are quite a few similarities between the suggestions. The predicate columns between each of the suggestions include the OrderDate and DueDate, except for one missing index. Since the column order has not been tested, the optimal column order could go either way. To satisfy the missing index suggestion, one possible index could have the key columns DueDate followed by OrderDate. This configuration would create an index that would satisfy all four of the missing index items.

	database_name	table_name	equality_columns	inequality_columns	included_columns	Impact	Score	user_seeks	user_scans
1	AdventureWorks	SalesOrderHeader	[OrderDate], [DueDate]	NULL	NULL	99.34	0.580982002328148	1	0
2	AdventureWorks	SalesOrderHeader	NULL	[OrderDate], [DueDate]	NULL	95.07	0.573957515967778	1	0
3	AdventureWorks	SalesOrderHeader	NULL	[OrderDate], [DueDate]	[CustomerID]	94.33	0.569489980869259	1	0
4	AdventureWorks	SalesOrderHeader	NULL	[DueDate]	[OrderDate]	94.91	0.555073503532963	1	0

Figure 7-2. *Results from missing index query*

The next item to look at is the included_columns. For two of the suggestions, there are included_columns listed. On the fourth missing index suggestion, it suggests including the column OrderDate. Since it will be one of the key columns of the index, it doesn't need to be included. The other column, from the third missing index suggestion, is the CustomerID column. While only one index needs this column, as an included column, the addition of this column would likely be negligible since it is a narrow column. We would also want to add this column to the index.

After looking at these results, we've walked you through four missing index suggestions and ended up with a suggestion for one index that can cover all four of the missing index items. If we build the index, using a DDL statement similar to that in Listing 7-3, we will end up with an index that solves these missing indexes. If you execute the queries in Listing 7-1 again, you can see this for yourself.

Listing 7-3. Index from Missing Index DMOs

```
CREATE NONCLUSTERED INDEX missing_index_SalesOrderHeader
ON Sales.SalesOrderHeader([DueDate], [OrderDate])
INCLUDE ([CustomerID])
```

Database Engine Tuning Advisor

The other indexing tool available in SQL Server is the DTA. This tool allows SQL Server to analyze workload that is stored in a file, a table, or the plan cache. The output of the DTA can assist in providing recommendations for indexing and configuring partitions for the workload. The chief benefit of using the tool is that it doesn't require a deep understanding of the underlying databases in order to make the recommendations.

Some of the core capabilities that the DTA can provide are:

- Recommend the best mix of indexes for databases by using the query optimizer to analyze queries in a workload.

- Recommend aligned or nonaligned partitions for databases referenced in a workload.

- Recommend indexed views for databases referenced in a workload.

- Analyze the effects of the proposed changes, including index usage, query distribution among tables, and query performance in the workload.

- Recommend ways to tune the database for a small set of problem queries.

- Allow you to customize the recommendation by specifying advanced options - such as disk space constraints.

- Provide reports that summarize the effects of implementing the recommendations for a given workload.

- Consider alternatives in which you supply possible design choices in the form of hypothetical configurations for DTA to evaluate.

Although the DTA has quite a few capabilities, there are also a number of limitations on the tools. Some of these limitations are:

- Not able to recommend indexes on system tables.

- Cannot add or drop unique indexes or indexes that enforce primary key or unique constraints.

- May provide variations in recommendations on some workloads. DTA samples data while it executes, which will influence the recommendations.

- Unable to tune database from SQL Server 7.0 or earlier.

- Unable to tune trace tables on remote servers.

- Constraints placed on tuning workloads can have a negative impact on suggestions if the tuning session exceeds the constraints.

■ **Note** The DTA often suffers a bad rap as an indexing tool. This is mostly due to abuse and misuse by others who have used it. When using the tool, be sure to validate any change that is recommended and test any changes thoroughly before applying them in a production environment.

Explaining DTA

There are two ways in which users can interact with the DTA. These are the graphical user interface (GUI) and the command-line utility. Both of these methods offer most of the same capabilities. Depending on your comfort level, either can be chosen.

The GUI tool, which we will use through most of this chapter, provides a wrapper for the DTA. It allows the user to select from the available options, and it enables you to view the tuning sessions that were previously executed. If you want to view tuning results, the GUI is very well suited. Tuning sessions can be configured and executed through the GUI.

The command-line utility provides the same capabilities as the GUI when it comes to configuring and executing sessions. The command-line utility can be configured either through switches or an XML configuration file. Both of these options allow database administrators (DBAs) and developers to build out processes to automate tuning activities for reviewing and analyzing workloads and to build out an index-tuning process that allows the DBA to work with results instead of going through the motions of setting up and configuring the tuning sessions. More about integrating the DTA utility into a performance tuning methodology will be discussed in Chapter 10.

With both tools, two general areas of configuration need to occur. The first determines how the tuning session will interact and makes suggestions with the physical design structures (PDS). The second determines which type of partitioning strategy DTA should employ when trying to tune the database.

There are two parts to the options on how physical design structure suggestions will be generated. The first option you will want to configure is which type of physical design structure can be utilized in the tuning. The options for this are:

- Indexes and indexed views
- Indexes (default option)
- Evaluate utilization of existing PDS only
- Indexed views
- Nonclustered indexes

Along with the following options, the tuning session can also consider whether the filtered indexes can be included in the suggestions. The other PDS option determines which objects to keep within the database. This option can help ensure that the tuning recommendations do not adversely affect tuning that was previously tested and deployed. The options for PDS items to retain in the database are:

- Do not keep any existing PDS
- Keep all existing PDS (default option)
- Keep aligned partitioning
- Keep indexes only
- Keep clustered indexes only

The other general option with when configuring DTA is how the tuning session will consider table partitioning. The options for table partition include:

- No partitioning (default option)
- Aligned partitioning
- Full partitioning

Outside these options, there are some advanced options that can be configured. These options configure how long the tuning session will run and how much memory the session can utilize. Also, for the index DDL, there is an option to determine whether the script for indexes will include online index rebuild options.

■ **Note** Before following along in the next section, run the code in Listing 7-1. If the index in Listing 7-3 has been created, drop the index using the DROP INDEX statement provided in Listing 7-4.

Listing 7-4. DDL Statement to Drop Index missing_index_SalesOrderHeader

```
DROP INDEX Sales.SalesOrderHeader.missing_index_SalesOrderHeader;
```

Using the DTA GUI

As mentioned earlier in the chapter, one of the ways to interact with DTA is through the GUI. In this section, we'll look at a scenario demonstrating how to use the DTA for index tuning. There are a few methods for launching the tool. The first option is within SQL Server Management Studio (SSMS). Within SSMS, you can choose Tools ➤ Database Engine Tuning Advisor from the toolbar. The other option is to select Microsoft SQL Server 2012 ➤ Performance Tools ➤ Database Engine Tuning Advisor from the Start menu.

After launching the DTA, you will be prompted to connect to a SQL Server. Once connected, the tool will open a new tuning session for configuration. A DTA session is shown in Figure 7-3.

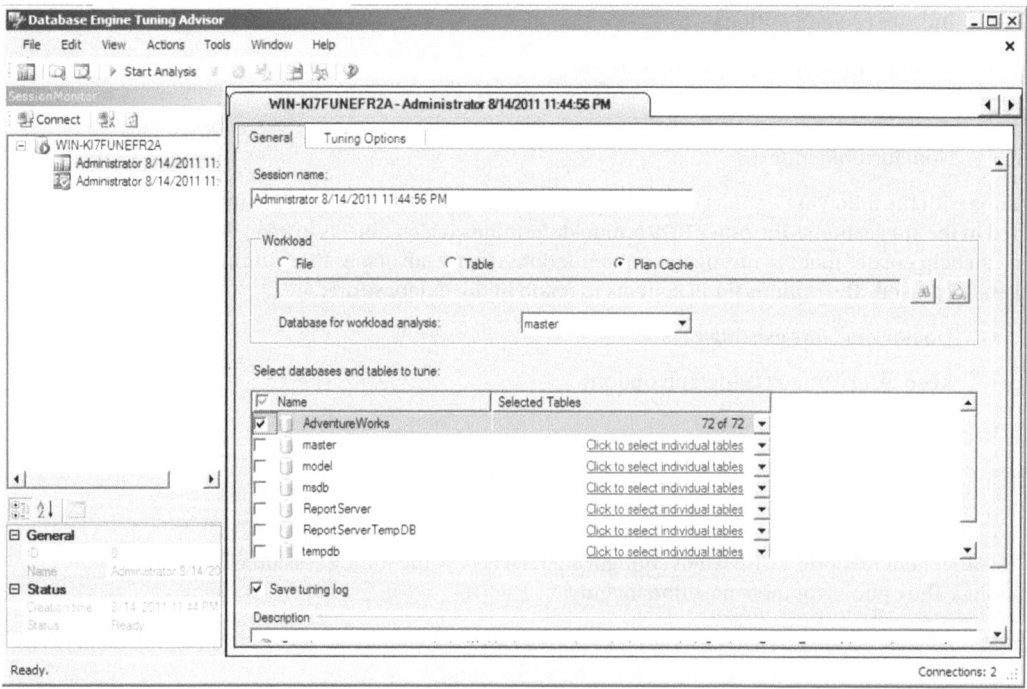

Figure 7-3. General configuration screen from the Database Engine Tuning Advisor

In the session launch screen on the General options tab, there are a few things to configure initially. To start there is the Session name. The Session name can be any value you desire. The default value includes your username with the date and time. Next select the type of workload that will be used. There are three options for the workload:

- *File*: A file containing SQL Trace output, an XML configuration, or SQL scripts.

- *Table*: SQL Server database table containing SQL Trace output. Before using the table, be sure the trace populating it has been completed.

- *Plan Cache*: The plan cache of the SQL Server that the tuning session is connected to. This capability is new to SQL Server 2012 and provides a powerful mechanism to tune execution plans that are being used in your SQL Server environment.

Each of the workloads can be used to provide recommendations. Through each of these workload sources, there is an opportunity to tune pretty much any type of workload that is needed. For the purposes of this exercise, select the Plan Cache option.

The next step is to select the database and tables to tune. With large databases, it will be critical to select only the tables that are a part of the workload and for which index recommendations are needed. When the DTA executes, it will generate statistics based on information in the table, and the less tables that need to be considered, the faster the tuning session can complete. Check the box in the "Select databases and tables to tune" section next to the AdventureWorks database before continuing.

■ **Caution**   Do not use the DTA in your production SQL Server environment. The tool uses some brute force tactics to identify index recommendations and create hypothetical indexes to support this work. Running the tool in production can adversely affect performance of other workloads on the server. Consider running the DTA from a command line and on a remote SQL Server for analyzing production databases. This option will be discussed in Chapter 10.

With the General options configured, the next step is to configure the Tuning Options. In the screen shown in Figure 7-4, deselect the Limit tuning time option. For the other options, leave them as the default selections. These should be:

- Physical Design Structures (PDS) to use in database ➤ Indexes

- Partitioning strategy to employ ➤ No partitioning

- Physical Design Structures (PDS) to keep in database ➤ Keep all existing PDS

The next step is to start the Database Engine Tuning Advisor. This can be accomplished through the toolbar or the menu, by selecting Actions ➤ Start Analysis. After starting the DTA, the Progress tab will open, as seen in Figure 7-5.

After a few minutes the tuning session will complete, though this will depend entirely on your computer's workload. With the indexes from Listing 7-1, the results should be similar to those in Figure 7-6. In these results, there are three items recommended. While the names will vary in your environment, the recommendations should generally be:

- Statistics on DueDate then OrderDate

- Index on DueDate including OrderDate

- Index on OrderDate then DueDate including CustomerID

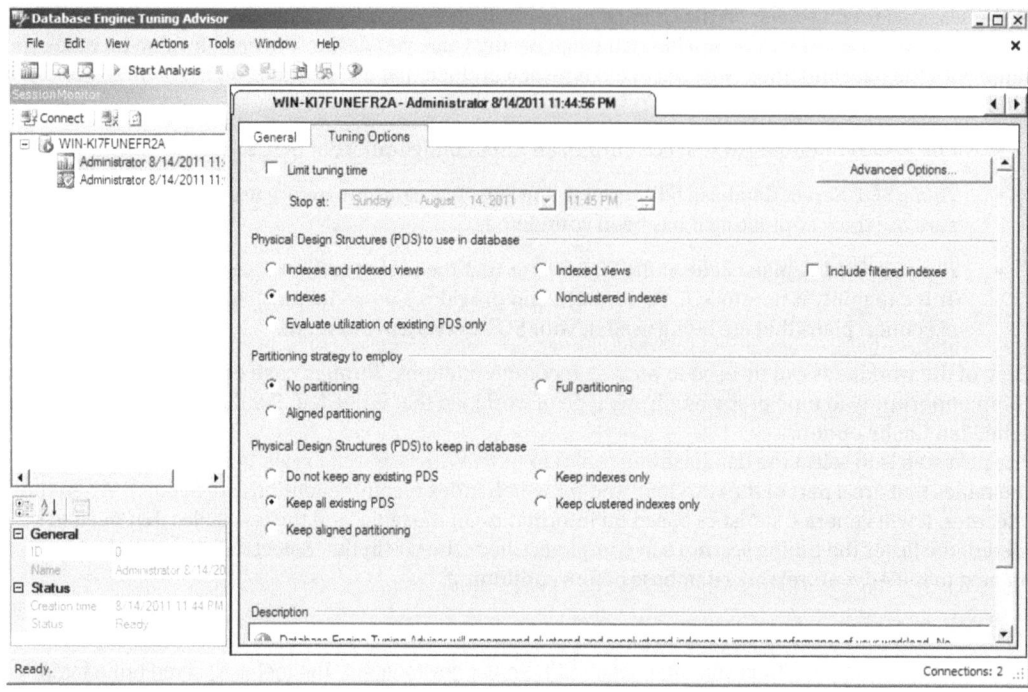

Figure 7-4. Tuning options configuration screen from Database Engine Tuning Advisor

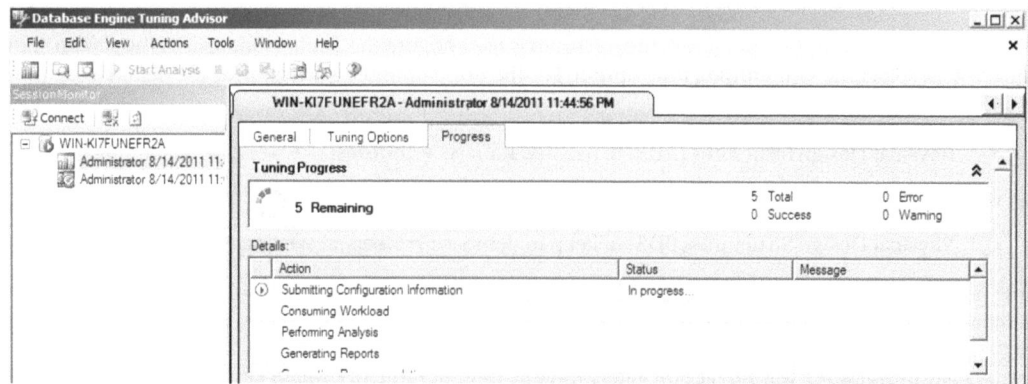

Figure 7-5. Progress screen from Database Engine Tuning Advisor

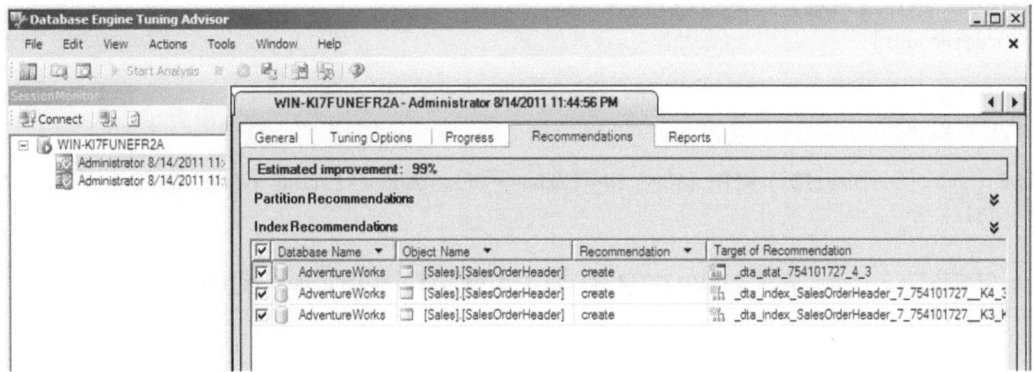

Figure 7-6. *Recommendations from Database Engine Tuning Advisor*

These indexes are similar to the suggestions previously found with the missing index DMOs. For each of the suggestions, you will need to go through the same considerations that were part of reviewing the suggestions from the missing index DMOs, such as "Can the recommendations be consolidated?" In this case, the two suggested indexes likely could be consolidated; of course, this will require testing to validate. To remove any item from the list of recommendations, simply deselect the checkbox and it will not be included in any of the recommendation outputs.

At this point, there are a few options that can be used to apply the indexes. These are:

- *Apply the indexes.* To apply the indexes: Select Actions in the menu bar and select Apply Recommendations. In the Apply Recommendations window that comes up, leave the default, Apply Now selected and click OK.

- *Apply the indexes in the future.* To apply the indexes in the future: Select Actions in the menu bar and select Apply Recommendations. In the Apply Recommendations window that comes up, select Schedule for later. Alter the scheduled date as desired and click OK. This will create the SQL Agent Job. Ensure the SQL Agent is running and the agent service account has the required permissions to apply the indexes.

- *Save recommendations.* To save recommendations: Select the Save Recommendations icon in the Menu bar, press the key combination Ctrl+S or select Actions in the Menu bar and then, Save Recommendations.

If the recommendations are saved, they will create a script like the one in Listing 7-5. Before applying indexes from the DTA, it is recommended that the names of the indexes be changed to match your organization's index naming standards. Also, when it comes to statistics, these are generally not created. SQL Server will create statistics as needed behind the scenes, removing the need for you to build your own statistics.

Listing 7-5. Database Engine Tuning Advisor Index Recommendations

```
use [AdventureWorks2012];
GO

CREATE NONCLUSTERED INDEX [_dta_index_SalesOrderHeader_7_754101727__K4_3] ON [Sales].
[SalesOrderHeader]
(
    [DueDate] ASC
)
INCLUDE ( [OrderDate]) WITH (SORT_IN_TEMPDB = OFF, DROP_EXISTING = OFF, ONLINE = OFF) ON [PRIMARY];
GO
```

```
CREATE NONCLUSTERED INDEX [_dta_index_SalesOrderHeader_7_754101727__K3_K4_11] ON [Sales].
[SalesOrderHeader]
(
    [OrderDate] ASC,
    [DueDate] ASC
)
INCLUDE (     [CustomerID]) WITH (SORT_IN_TEMPDB = OFF, DROP_EXISTING = OFF, ONLINE = OFF) ON
[PRIMARY];
GO

CREATE STATISTICS [_dta_stat_754101727_4_3] ON [Sales].[SalesOrderHeader]([DueDate],
[OrderDate]);
GO
```

By using the DTA through its GUI, you are able to make quick work of a workload. The recommendations returned provide a level of index tuning above using the missing index DMOs. In essence they provide a brute force indexing exercise to improve performance without improving code. Instead of spending many hours on tuning that can be resolved with a few new indexes, you can focus your time on performance tuning issues that are beyond just adding an index.

■ **Note**   When the DTA is terminated while processing, it will sometimes leave behind hypothetical indexes that were used while it was investigating possible indexes that could improve an environment. A hypothetical index is an index that only contains statistics and no data. These indexes can be identified through the is_hypothetical column in sys.indexes. If they exist in your environment, they should always be dropped.

Using the DTA Utility

The GUI isn't the only way to use the DTA within your SQL Server environment. The other method is through the command line with the DTA utility. What DTA utility lacks in an interactive interface, it makes up for with the flexibility to leverage the DTA utility in scripts and automation.

The syntax for using the DTA utility, shown in Listing 7-6, includes a number of arguments. These arguments, defined in Table 7-5, allow the DTA utility to contain the same features and flexibility of the GUI. Instead of clicking through a number of screens, the configuration information is passed in through the arguments.

Listing 7-6. DTA Utility Syntax

```
dta
[ -? ] |
[
    [ -S server_name[ \instance ] ]
    { { -U login_id [-P password ] } | -E }
    { -D database_name [ ,…n ] }
    [ -d database_name ]
    [ -Tl table_list | -Tf table_list_file ]
    { -if workload_file | -it workload_trace_table_name | -ip | -ipf }
    { -ssession_name | -IDsession_ID }
    [ -F ]
    [ -of output_script_file_name ]
    [ -or output_xml_report_file_name ]
    [ -ox output_XML_file_name ]
```

```
[ -rl analysis_report_list [ ,…n ] ]
[ -ix input_XML_file_name ]
[ -A time_for_tuning_in_minutes ]
[ -n number_of_events ]
[ -m minimum_improvement ]
[ -fa physical_design_structures_to_add ]
[ -fi ]
[ -fp partitioning_strategy ]
[ -fk keep_existing_option ]
[ -fx drop_only_mode ]
[ -B storage_size ]
[ -c max_key_columns_in_index ]
[ -C max_columns_in_index ]
[ -e | -e tuning_log_name ]
[ -N online_option]
[ -q ]
[ -u ]
[ -x ]
[ -a ]
]
```

Table 7-5. *DTA Utility Arguments*

Argument	Description
-?	Returns help information, including a list of all arguments.
-A	Provides a time limit, in minutes, in which the DTA utility will spend tuning the workload. The default time limit is 8 hours, or 640 minutes. Setting the limit to 0 will result in an unlimited tuning session.
-a	After the workload is tuned, the recommendations are applied without further prompting.
-B	Specifies the maximum size, in megabytes, that recommended indexes can consume. By default, this value is set to either three times the current raw data size or the free space on attached disk drives plus raw data size, whichever is smaller.
-c	Maximum number of key columns that DTA will recommend in an index. This value defaults to 16. The restriction does not include INCLUDED columns.
-C	Maximum number of columns that DTA will recommend in an index. The value defaults to 16, but can be raised as high as 1024, the maximum columns allowed in an index.
-d	Identifies the database that the DTA session connects to when the session begins. Only a single database can be specified for this argument.
-D	Identifies the databases that the DTA session will tune the workload against. One or more databases can be specified for this argument. To add multiple databases to a session, either include all the database names in a comma separated list in one argument or add one argument per database.
-e	Identifies the name of the logging table or file where the DTA session will output events that could not be tuned. When specifying a table name, use the three-part naming convention of [database_name].[schema_name].[table_name]. With an output file, the extension for the file should be .xml.

(continued)

Table 7-5. *(continued)*

Argument	Description
-E	Sets the database connection using a trusted connection. Required argument if -U is not used.
-F	Grants DTA permission to overwrite an output file if it already exists.
-fa	Identifies the types of physical design structures that the DTA session can include in the recommendations. The default value for this argument is IDX. The available values are: • IDX_IV: Indexes and indexed views. • IDX: Indexes only. • IX: Indexed views only. • NCL_IDX: Nonclustered indexes only.
-fi	Allows the DTA session to include recommendations for filtered indexes.
-fk	Sets the limitations on the existing physical design structures that the DTA session can modify in the recommendations. The available values are: • NONE: No existing structures. • ALL: All existing structures. • ALIGNED: All partition-aligned structures. • CL_IDX: All clustered indexes on tables. • IDX: All clustered and nonclustered indexes on tables.
-fp	Determines whether partitioning recommendations can be included in the DTA session recommendations. The default value for this argument is NONE. The available values are: • NONE: No partitioning. • FULL: Full partitioning. • ALIGNED: Aligned partitioning.
-fx	Limits the DTA session to only including recommendations to drop existing physical design structures. Lightly used indexes in the session are evaluated and recommendations for dropping them are provided. This argument cannot be used with the arguments -fa, -fp, or -fk ALL.
-ID	Sets a numerical identifier for the DTA session. Either this argument or -s must be specified.
-ip	Set the source of the workload for the DTA session to the plan cache. The top –n plan cache events for the databases specified with argument –D are analyzed.
-ipf	Sets the source of the workload for the DTA session to the plan cache. The top –n plan cache events for all databases are analyzed.
-if	Sets the source of the workload for the DTA session to a file source. The path and filename are passed in through this argument. The file must be SQL Server Profiler trace file (trc), SQL file (sql), or SQL Server trace file (log).

(continued)

Table 7-5. (*continued*)

Argument	Description
-it	Sets the source of the workload for the DTA session to a table. When specifying a table name, use the three-part naming convention of [database_name].dbo.[table_name]. The schema for the table must be dbo.
-ix	Identifies an XML file containing the configuration information for the DTA session. The XML file must conform to the DTASchema.xsd (which is located at http://schemas.microsoft.com/sqlserver/2004/07/dta/dtaschema.xsd).
-m	Sets the minimum percentage of improvement that a recommendation must provide.
-n	Sets the number of events in the workload that the DTA session should tune. When specified for a trace file, the order of the events selected is based on the decreasing order of duration.
-N	Determines whether the physical design structures are created online or offline. The available values are: • OFF: No objects are created online. • ON: All objects are created online. • MIXED: Objects are created where possible.
-of	Configures the DTA session to output the recommendations in a T-SQL format in the path and file specified.
-or	Configures the DTA session to output the recommendations to a report in an XML format. When a filename is not provided, a filename based on the session (-s) name will be used.
-ox	Configures the DTA session to output the recommendations in an XML format in the path and file specified.
-P	Sets the password to be used for the SQL login in the database connection. The DTA session will prompt the username (-U) argument used and the password is not provided.
-q	Sets the DTA session to execute in quiet mode.
-rl	Configures the reports that will be generated by the DTA session. One or more reports can be selected in a comma-separated list. The available values are: • ALL: All analysis reports • STMT_COST: Statement cost report. • EVT_FREQ: Event frequency report. • STMT_DET: Statement detail report. • CUR_STMT_IDX: Statement-index relations report (current configuration). • REC_STMT_IDX: Statement-index relations report (recommended configuration). • STMT_COSTRANGE: Statement cost range report. • CUR_IDX_USAGE: Index usage report (current configuration). • REC_IDX_USAGE: Index usage report (recommended configuration).

(continued)

Table 7-5. (continued)

Argument	Description
	• `CUR_IDX_DET`: Index detail report (current configuration).
	• `REC_IDX_DET`: Index detail report (recommended configuration).
	• `VIW_TAB`: View-table relations report.
	• `WKLD_ANL`: Workload analysis report.
	• `DB_ACCESS`: Database access report.
	• `TAB_ACCESS`: Table access report.
	• `COL_ACCESS`: Column access report.
`-S`	Sets the instance of SQL Server to be used for the DTA session.
`-s`	Sets the name of the DTA session.
`-Tf`	Identifies the name of a path and file containing a list of tables to be used for tuning. The file should contain one table per line using the three-part naming convention. After each table name, the number of rows can be specified to tune the workload for a scaled version of the table. If `-Tf` and `-Tl` are omitted, the DTA session will default to using all tables.
`-Tl`	Sets a list of tables to be used for tuning. Each table should be listed using the three-part naming convention, with each table name separated by a comma. If `-Tf` and `-Tl` are omitted, the DTA session will default to using all tables.
`-U`	Sets the username to be used for the SQL login in the database connection. Required argument `if` `-E` is not used.
`-u`	Launches the GUI interface for the DTA with all of the configuration values specified the to the DTA utility.
`-x`	Starts the DTA session and exists upon completion.

Using the DTA utility is fairly easy. To demonstrate, we'll look at two scenarios of using the tool that provide different outcomes. In the first scenario, we'll use the DTA utility to recommend indexing changes with only allowing nonclustered indexing changes. For the second scenario, the DTA utility will be configured to recommend any change to the indexing that would improve the performance of the workload. In both scenarios, we'll use the plan cache for SQL Server as the workload source. To populate the plan cache, execute the query in Listing 7-7.

Listing 7-7. Scenario Setup

```
USE AdventureWorks2012
GO

IF OBJECT_ID('dbo.SalesOrderDetail') IS NOT NULL
    DROP TABLE dbo.SalesOrderDetail;
SELECT SalesOrderID, SalesOrderDetailID, CarrierTrackingNumber, OrderQty, ProductID,
SpecialOfferID, UnitPrice, UnitPriceDiscount, LineTotal, rowguid, ModifiedDate
```

```
INTO dbo.SalesOrderDetail
FROM Sales.SalesOrderDetail;

CREATE CLUSTERED INDEX CL_SalesOrderDetail ON dbo.SalesOrderDetail(SalesOrderDetailID);

CREATE NONCLUSTERED INDEX IX_SalesOrderDetail ON dbo.SalesOrderDetail(SalesOrderID);
GO

SELECT SalesOrderID, CarrierTrackingNumber
INTO #temp
FROM dbo.SalesOrderDetail
WHERE SalesOrderID = 43660;
DROP TABLE #temp;
GO 1000

SELECT SalesOrderID, OrderQty
INTO #temp
FROM dbo.SalesOrderDetail
WHERE SalesOrderID = 43661;
DROP TABLE #temp;
GO 1000
```

For the first scenario, we'll build a command-line script similar to the one shown in Listing 7-8. For your environment, the server name (-S) will be different. The rest, however, will be the same. The database (-D and –d arguments) will be AdventureWorks2012. The source of the workload will be the plan cache (-ip argument). The name of the session (-s argument) is "First Scenario".

Listing 7-8. First Scenario DTA Utility Syntax

```
dta
-S STR8-SQL-12\SQL2012 -E
-D AdventureWorks2012
-d AdventureWorks2012
-ip
-s 'First Scenario'
-Tl AdventureWorks2012.dbo.SalesOrderDetail
-of 'C:\Temp\First Scenario.sql'
-fa NCL_IDX
-fp NONE
-fk ALL
```

With the DTA utility syntax prepared, the next step is to execute the script through the Command Prompt window. Depending on your SQL Server instance and the amount of information in the plan cache, the execution may take a few minutes. When it completes, the output in the Command Prompt window will look similar to the output shown in Figure 7-7. This output indicates that the file C:\Temp\First Scenario.sql contains the recommendations for tuning the query in Listing 7-7.

Based on the arguments passed into the DTA utility and the current workload, the recommendation from the First Scenario tuning session includes the creation of two nonclustered indexes and statistics on two columns, shown in Listing 7-9. These indexes function as covering indexes for the queries in Listing 7-7; as a result the Key Lookup is no longer required as part of the execution plan. The statistics provide information that SQL Server can use to build good plans for queries on the columns used in the query.

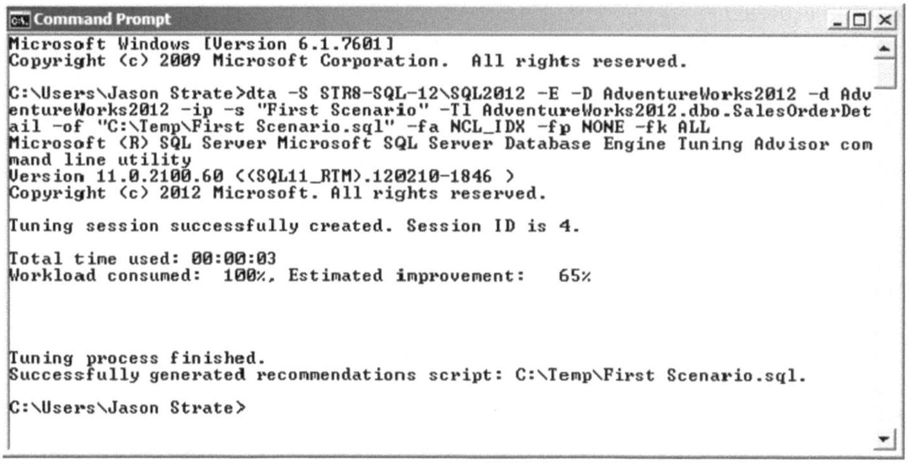

Figure 7-7. *Command Prompt for First Scenario*

Listing 7-9. First Scenario DTA Utility Output

```
use [AdventureWorks2012]
go

SET ANSI_PADDING ON

go

CREATE NONCLUSTERED INDEX [_dta_index_SalesOrderDetail_18_1591676718__K1_K2_3] ON [dbo].
[SalesOrderDetail]
(
    [SalesOrderID] ASC,
    [SalesOrderDetailID] ASC
)
INCLUDE (    [CarrierTrackingNumber]) WITH (SORT_IN_TEMPDB = OFF, DROP_EXISTING = OFF, ONLINE
= OFF) ON [PRIMARY]
go

CREATE NONCLUSTERED INDEX [_dta_index_SalesOrderDetail_18_1591676718__K1_K2_4] ON [dbo].
[SalesOrderDetail]
(
    [SalesOrderID] ASC,
    [SalesOrderDetailID] ASC
)
INCLUDE (    [OrderQty]) WITH (SORT_IN_TEMPDB = OFF, DROP_EXISTING = OFF, ONLINE = OFF) ON
[PRIMARY]
go

CREATE STATISTICS [_dta_stat_1591676718_2_1] ON [dbo].[SalesOrderDetail]([SalesOrderDetailID],
[SalesOrderID])
Go
```

The downside to the arguments that were selected in the First Scenario is that there isn't any information included that helps determine the value in adding this index and the statistics. For the next scenario, we'll demonstrate how to obtain that information along with moving deeper into providing recommendations on the physical structure of your databases.

To begin the next scenario, we'll use the same database and query. The arguments, though, will be modified slightly to accommodate the new goals, as shown in Listing 7-10 First, we'll change the name of the session (-s) to "Second Scenario". Next, change the allowed physical structure changes (argument -fa) from nonclustered indexes only (NCL_IDX) to indexes and indexed views (IDX_IV). The final change, for the reporting output, is to add the report list (argument -rl) to the script with the all-analysis reports (ALL) option.

Listing 7-10. Second Scenario DTA Utility Syntax

```
dta
-S STR8-SQL-12\SQL2012 -E
-D AdventureWorks2012
-d AdventureWorks2012
-ip
-s 'Second Scenario'
-Tl AdventureWorks2012.dbo.SalesOrderDetail
-of 'C:\Temp\Second Scenario.sql'
-fa IDX_IV
-fp NONE
-fk ALL
-rl ALL
```

Executing the DTA utility using the second scenario produces entirely different results from the first scenario. Instead of recommending nonclustered indexes, the second scenario recommends a change in the clustered key columns. With this solution, the DTA session identified the SalesOrderID column as the column frequently used to access data and recommended that as the clustered index. These recommendations are shown in Listing 7-11.

Listing 7-11. Second Scenario DTA Utility Output

```
use [AdventureWorks2012]
go

DROP INDEX [CL_SalesOrderDetail] ON [dbo].[SalesOrderDetail]
go

DROP INDEX [IX_SalesOrderDetail] ON [dbo].[SalesOrderDetail]
go

CREATE CLUSTERED INDEX [_dta_index_SalesOrderDetail_c_7_1348199853__K1] ON [dbo].
[SalesOrderDetail]
(
    [SalesOrderID] ASC
)WITH (SORT_IN_TEMPDB = OFF, DROP_EXISTING = OFF, ONLINE = OFF) ON [PRIMARY]
go

CREATE STATISTICS [_dta_stat_1348199853_1_2] ON [dbo].[SalesOrderDetail]([SalesOrderID],
[SalesOrderDetailID])
go
```

The one other difference with the second scenario is the creation of an XML report file. The session used the ALL option for the -rl argument, which includes all the reports listed for the argument in Table 7-5. These reports provide information regarding the statements that were tuned, the costs associated with the statements, the amount of improvement the recommendations provide, and much more (Figure 7-8). Through these reports, you are provided the information needed to make decisions about which recommendations to apply to your databases.

```xml
<?xml version="1.0" encoding="UTF-16"?>
- <DTAXML>
  - <DTAOutput>
    - <AnalysisReport>
      + <StatementCostReport>
      + <EventWeightReport>
      + <StatementDetailReport>
      + <StatementIndexReport Current="true">
      + <StatementIndexReport Current="false">
      - <StatementCostRangeReport>
        - <CostRange Percent="0% - 10%">
            <NumStatementsCurrent>0</NumStatementsCurrent>
            <NumStatementsRecommended>2</NumStatementsRecommended>
          </CostRange>
        - <CostRange Percent="11% - 20%">
            <NumStatementsCurrent>0</NumStatementsCurrent>
            <NumStatementsRecommended>0</NumStatementsRecommended>
          </CostRange>
        - <CostRange Percent="21% - 30%">
            <NumStatementsCurrent>0</NumStatementsCurrent>
            <NumStatementsRecommended>0</NumStatementsRecommended>
          </CostRange>
```

Figure 7-8. *Sample report output from DTA utility*

One thing to remember with the last two scenarios is that the table being tuned was tuned in a vacuum. There were no constraints or foreign key relationships on the table that need to be considered. In the real world, this won't be the way your database is designed, and foreign key relationships will affect how recommendations are provided. Also, the load for these scenarios only contained two queries. When building your workloads, be sure to use a sample that is representative of your environment.

Through the DTA scenarios provided in this section, we've laid a foundation for using tools in your index-tuning activities. Not only can the DTA identify missing indexes, but, given a workload, it can also help identify where clustered indexes and partitioning can assist with performance. The physical changes that DTA can provide could be extremely useful when you quickly need to address performance issues with a database.

Summary

This chapter has walked you through the use of the built-in indexing tools available in SQL Server. Each of these tools can be a great addition to your SQL Server tool belt. They allow you to dig in and start making informed indexing decisions without expending a lot of effort.

When it comes to the missing index DMOs, you are working with index suggestions based on existing activity on the SQL Server instance. These are real-world applications and they represent areas where you can almost immediately begin to build solutions to improve performance.

The DTA, while not as readily available as the missing index DMOs, allows you to tune indexes from a single query to a full workload with minimal effort. The new option to tune the contents of the plan cache allows you to leverage the work currently being done in an environment to build recommendations without the need to create a workload.

CHAPTER 8

Index Strategies

Indexing databases is often thought of as an art where the database is the canvas and the indexes are the paints that come together to form a beautiful tapestry of storage and performance. A little color here, a little color there, and paintings will take shape. In much the same way, a clustered index on a table and then a few non-clustered indexes can result in screaming performance as beautiful as any masterpiece. Going a little too abstract or minimalist with your indexing might make you feel good, but the performance will let you know it isn't too useful.

As colorful as this analogy is, there is more science behind designing and applying indexes than there is artistry. A few columns pulled together because they might work well together is often less beneficial than an index built upon well-established patterns. The indexes that are based on tried and true practices are often the best solutions. In this chapter, you'll walk through a number of patterns to help identify potential indexes.

Heaps

There are few valid cases for using heaps in your databases. The general rule of thumb for most DBAs is that all tables in database should be built with clustered indexes instead of heaps. While this practice rings true for most situations, there are situations when using a heap is acceptable. This section looks at one of these scenarios and discusses the other situations in generalities. The reason for being generic is that it is difficult to make blanket statements about when to use a heap instead of a clustered index (which will be explained more later in the section).

Temporary Objects

One of the situations in which heaps are useful is with temporary objects, such as temporary tables and table variables. When we use these objects, we often create them without thinking or considering building a clustered index on them. The result is that we use more heaps on tables than we think we do.

Consider for a moment the last time you created a table variable or a temporary table. Did the syntax for the object specifically create a CLUSTERED index or a PRIMARY KEY with the default configuration? If not, then the temporary object was created as a heap. This isn't necessarily a travesty. It is common in most workloads—not necessarily a call to arms to change your coding practices. As we'll demonstrate in the examples in this section, the performance between a temporary object with a heap or a clustered index can be immaterial.

For this example, let's start with a simple use case for a temporary table. The example uses the table Sales. SalesOrderHeader from which you'll retrieve a few rows based on a SalesPersonID and then insert them into a temporary table. The temporary table will be used to return all rows from Sales.SalesOrderDetail that match the results in the temporary table. Two versions of the example will be used to demonstrate how using a heap or a clustered index on the temporary table doesn't change the query execution.

In the first version of the example, shown in Listing 8-1, the temporary table is built using a heap. This is the method that people often use to create temporary objects. As the execution plan in Figure 8-1 shows, when the temporary table is accessed, identified by the arrow, a table scan is used to access the rows in the object. This behavior is expected with a heap. Since the rows aren't ordered, there is no way to access specific rows without checking all the rows first. To find all of the rows in Sales.SalesOrderDetail that match those in the temporary table, the execution plan uses a nested loop with an index seek.

Listing 8-1. Temporary Object with Heap

```
USE AdventureWorks2012
GO
CREATE TABLE #TempWithHeap
  (
  SalesOrderID INT
  );

INSERT INTO #TempWithHeap
SELECT SalesOrderID
FROM Sales.SalesOrderHeader
WHERE SalesPersonID = 283;

SELECT sod.* FROM Sales.SalesOrderDetail sod
  INNER JOIN #TempWithHeap t ON t.SalesOrderID = sod.SalesOrderID;
GO
```

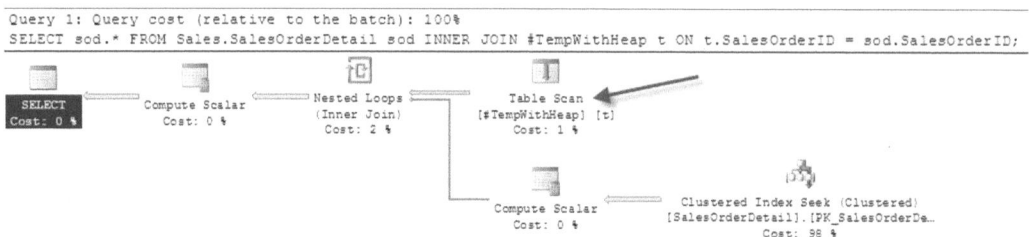

Figure 8-1. *Execution plan for Heap Temporary Object*

In the second version of the script, shown in Listing 8-2, the temporary table is created instead with a clustered index on the SalesOrderID column. The index is the only difference between the two scripts. This difference results in a slight change in the execution plans. The clustered index version of the execution plan is shown in Figure 8-2. The difference between the two plans is that instead of a table scan, there is a clustered index scan against the temporary table. While these are different operations, the work done by both is essentially the same. During query execution, all rows in the temporary object are accessed while joining them to rows in Sales.SalesOrderDetail.

Listing 8-2. Temporary Object with Clustered Index

```
USE AdventureWorks2012
GO
CREATE TABLE #TempWithClusteredIX
  (
  SalesOrderID INT PRIMARY KEY CLUSTERED
  )
INSERT INTO #TempWithClusteredIX
SELECT SalesOrderID
```

```
FROM Sales.SalesOrderHeader
WHERE SalesPersonID = 283

SELECT sod.* FROM Sales.SalesOrderDetail sod
INNER JOIN #TempWithClusteredIX t ON t.SalesOrderID = sod.SalesOrderID
GO
```

■ **Note**   Contrary to popular opinion, table variables can have clustered indexes on them. The requirement is that the clustered index is created when the variable is declared. DDL operations are not allowed on table variables after they are defined.

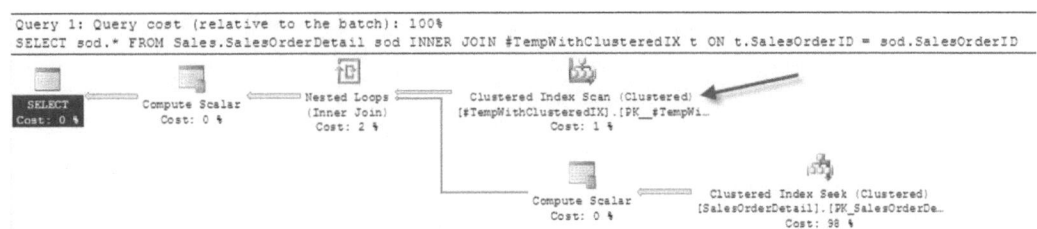

Figure 8-2. *Execution plan for clustered temporary object*

In queries similar to the example in this section, the execution plans for temporary tables with heaps and clustered indexes are nearly the same. As with all rules, there may be exceptions where performance will differ. A good example of when using a heap can affect performance is the T-SQL syntax that leverages a sort in its execution. Listing 8-3 shows a specific example using EXISTS in the WHERE clause. Figure 8-3 shows the execution plan for the query. Before the nested loop joins to resolve the EXISTS predicate, the data must first be sorted. In this case, the use of a heap has hindered the performance of the query because the heap table forces a sort operation. With small datasets, the performance difference may not be noticeable. As the size of dataset increases, little changes such as the inclusion of a sort operation can compound the performance of your queries.

Listing 8-3. EXISTS Example

```
SELECT sod.* FROM Sales.SalesOrderDetail sod
WHERE EXISTS (SELECT * FROM #TempWithHeap t WHERE t.SalesOrderID = sod.SalesOrderID);
GO
SELECT sod.* FROM Sales.SalesOrderDetail sod
WHERE EXISTS (SELECT * FROM #TempWithClusteredIX t WHERE t.SalesOrderID = sod.SalesOrderID);
```

Other Heap Scenarios

Generally, the other scenarios where using heaps makes sense are few and far between. In high insert environments, it might seem to make sense to use heaps to avoid the overhead of maintaining the B-Tree. The trouble with this scenario is that the gains on inserts are offset by the need to access the data, which requires other non-clustered indexes, which then have sort orders to maintain. When confronted with a situation for using heaps on your tables, first look at whether clustered indexes can be proven to be a burden on the storage of the data before using them.

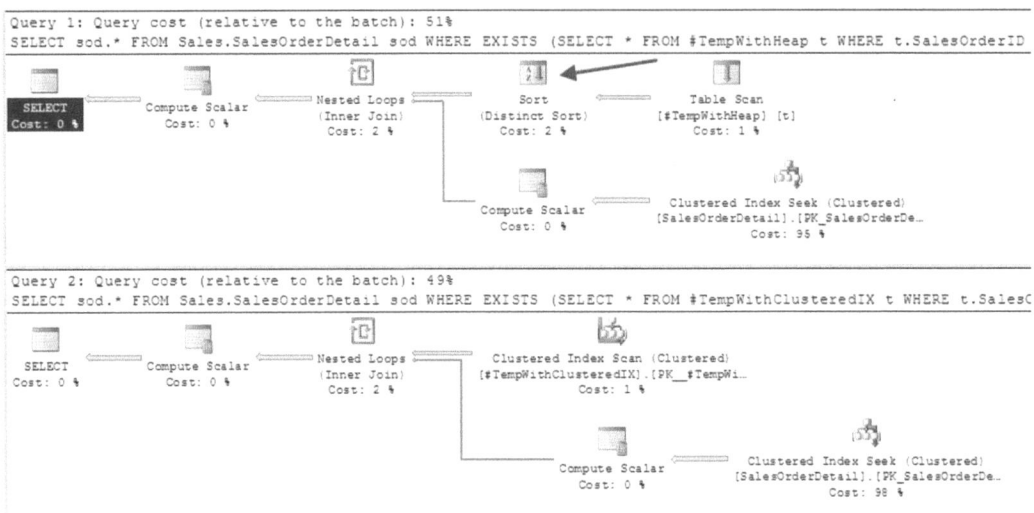

Figure 8-3. *EXISTS example execution plan*

The main point of this section is that heaps are used quite often in the real world. While most practices rail against their use, there are some cases and situations where they are a good fit. As the discussion moves into clustered indexes, you will see why it is usually a good idea to default to clustered indexes and use heaps in the situations where it either won't matter, like temporary objects, or where they outperform clustered indexes.

Clustered Indexes

Throughout this book, the value of and preference for using a clustered index as the structure for organizing the data page of a table has been discussed. Clustered indexes organize the data in their tables based on the key columns for the clustered index. All of the data pages for the index are stored logically according to the key columns. The benefit of this is optimal access to the data through the key columns.

New tables should nearly always be built with clustered indexes. The question, though, when building the tables is what should be selected for the key column(s) in the clustered index. There are a few characteristics that most often are attributed to well-defined clustered indexes. These are characteristics are

- Static
- Narrow
- Unique
- Ever-increasing

There are a number of reasons that each of these attributes help create a well-defined clustered index.

First, a clustered index should be static. The key column(s) defined for the clustered index should be expected to be static for the lifetime of the row. By using a static value, the position of the row in the index will not change when the row is updated. When non-static key column(s) are used, the position of the row in the clustered index can change, which would require the row to be inserted on a different page. Also, non-clustered indexes would need to be modified to change the key column(s) values stored in those indexes. All of this together leads to the potential for fragmentation of the clustered and non-clustered indexes on a table.

The next attribute that a clustered index should have is that it is narrow. Ideally, there should be only a single column for the clustered index key. These columns should be defined with the smallest data type reasonable for that data being stored in the table. Narrow clustered indexes are important because the clustered index key for every row is included into all non-clustered indexes associated with the table. The wider the clustered index key, the wider all non-clustered indexes will be and the more pages they will require. As discussed in other sections, the more pages in an index, the more resources are required to use the index. This can affect the performance of queries.

Clustered indexes should also be unique. Clustered indexes store a single row in a single location in the index; for duplicate rows within the key column(s) of a clustered index, the uniquifier provides the uniqueness required for the row. When the uniquifier is added to a row, it is extended by 4 bytes, which changes how narrow the clustered index is and results in the same concerns that are associated with a non-narrow clustered index. More information on the uniquifier can be found in Chapter 2.

Lastly, a well-defined clustered index will be based on an ever-increasing value. Using an ever-increasing clustered key causes new rows to be added to the end of the clustered index. Placing new rows at the end of the B-Tree reduces the fragmentation that would likely occur if the row was inserted in the middle of the clustered index.

One additional consideration when selecting the clustered index is that the data in the row will most frequently be accessed. Are there specific columns or values that will most often be used to retrieve rows from the table? If so, these column(s) are good candidates for the clustering index key. In the end, queries against the table will perform best when they can access data through the path of least resistance.

While considering the guidelines above for selecting clustered index strategies, there are a number of patterns that can be used to identify and model clustered indexes. The clustered index strategies are

- Identity Column
- Surrogate Key
- Foreign Key
- Multi-Column
- Globally Unique Identifier

In the rest of this section, we'll walk through each of the patterns, describing each and how to identify when to utilize the pattern.

Identity Column

The most frequent pattern of building a clustered index is to pair it with a column on a table that has been configured to be ever-increasing using either the IDENTITY property or the new SEQUENCE object. In this pattern, the IDENTITY column is often also the PRIMARY KEY on the table. The data type is often an integer, which includes tinyint, smallint, int, and bigint. The primary benefit of this pattern is that it achieves all of attributes of a well-defined clustered index. It is static, narrow, unique, and ever-increasing. When you consider how the data in the table will be accessed, in most cases the key value will most often be used to access rows in the table.

One distinction of the Identity Column pattern is that the column used for the clustered index key has no relationship between the data in the row and the clustered index key. To implement the pattern, a new column is added to the table that contains the IDENTITY property or SEQUENCE default. This column is then set as the clustered index key and often the PRIMARY KEY as well.

Examples of this pattern can be found in nearly all databases. Creating a table with this pattern would look similar to the CREATE TABLE statement in Listing 8-4. This table is built to contain fruit: two apple rows, a banana row, and grape row are inserted. The Color column would not have been a good clustering key since it does not identify the rows in the table. The FruitName column could have identified the rows in the table, except it isn't unique across the table, which would have required the uniquifier and led to a larger clustering key. Indexing the table to the Identity Column pattern, a FruitID column was created.

Listing 8-4. Creating and Populating Table for Identity Column Pattern

```
USE AdventureWorks2012
GO
CREATE TABLE dbo.IndexStrategiesFruit
(
FruitID int IDENTITY(1,1)
,FruitName varchar(25)
,Color varchar(10)
,CONSTRAINT PK_Fruit_FruitID PRIMARY KEY CLUSTERED (FruitID)
);

INSERT INTO dbo.IndexStrategiesFruit(FruitName, Color)
VALUES('Apple','Red'),('Banana','Yellow'),('Apple','Green'),('Grape','Green');

SELECT FruitID, FruitName, Color
FROM dbo.IndexStrategiesFruit;
```

One of the effects of using the Identity Column pattern is that the value for the clustering key has no relationship to the information that it represents. In the results from Listing 8-1, which are shown in Figure 8-4, the value of 1 is assigned to the first row inserted. Then, 2 is assigned for the next row, and so on. As more rows are added, the FruitID column increments and doesn't required any single piece of information in the record in order to designate the instance of information.

	FruitID	FruitName	Color
1	1	Apple	Red
2	2	Banana	Yellow
3	3	Apple	Green
4	4	Grape	Green

Figure 8-4. Results for Identity Column pattern

■ **Note**   A SEQUENCE is a new object in SQL Server 2012. Through sequences, ranges of numeric values can be generated, which are either ascending or descending. A SEQUENCE is not associated with any specific table.

Surrogate Key

In some cases, using a surrogate key in the data for the clustering key is as valid as adding an identity column to the table to use for the Identity Column pattern. A surrogate key is a column in the data that can uniquely identify one row from all of the other rows. The cases where using a surrogate key is valid can be identified when there is a surrogate key in the data that meets the attributes of a well-defined clustering key. When using surrogate keys for clustering keys, they are not likely to be ever-increasing but they should still be unique, narrow, and static.

A common example of when a surrogate key may be used instead of identity column is when looking at tables that contain one or two character abbreviations for the information they represent. These abbreviations may be for the status of an order, the size of a product, or a list of states or provinces. Compared to using an int, which is 4 bytes, in the Identity Column pattern, using a char(1) or char(2) data type with the Surrogate Key pattern will result in a clustering key that is more narrow than the former.

The Surrogate Key pattern also provides the additional benefit of providing an easier-to-decipher key value. When using the Identity Column pattern, there is no inherent meaning when the clustering key has the value of 1 or 7. These values are meaningless—intentionally so. With the Surrogate Key pattern, the abbreviations of "O" and "C" represent real information (Opened and Closed, respectively).

As a simple example of the Surrogate Key pattern, let's consider a table that contains states and their abbreviations. You'll also include the name of the country for the states. Listing 8-5 shows the SQL to create and populate the table. The table has a StateAbbreviation column, which is a char(2). Since this is a narrow, unique, and static value for each state, the clustered index is created on the column. Next, a few rows are added to the table for the four states that the fictitious database requires.

Listing 8-5. Creating and Populating Table for Surrogate Key Pattern

```
USE AdventureWorks2012
GO
CREATE TABLE dbo.IndexStrategiesSurrogate
(
StateAbbreviation char(2)
,StateName varchar(25)
,Country varchar(25)
,CONSTRAINT PK_State_StateAbbreviation PRIMARY KEY CLUSTERED (StateAbbreviation)
);

INSERT INTO dbo.IndexStrategiesSurrogate(StateAbbreviation, StateName, Country)
VALUES('MN','Minnesota','United States')
,('FL','Florida','United States')
,('WI','Wisconsin','United States')
,('NH','New Hampshire','United States');

SELECT StateAbbreviation, StateName, Country
FROM dbo.IndexStrategiesSurrogate;
```

In situations where the surrogate key matches the Surrogate Key pattern, the technique in Listing 8-5 can be a useful way of selecting the clustering key column. Reviewing the contents of dbo.IndexStrategiesSurrogate, shown in Figure 8-5, the four rows are in the table, and using StateAbbreviation in another table as a foreign key value can be useful since the value MN has some inherent meaning.

	StateAbbreviation	StateName	Country
1	FL	Florida	United States
2	MN	Minnesota	United States
3	NH	New Hampshire	United States
4	WI	Wisconsin	United States

Figure 8-5. Results for Surrogate Key pattern

This pattern may seem ideal and more worthwhile than the Identity Column pattern—especially since the value of the clustering key helps describe the data. However, there are a few downsides to using this pattern, which relate to the attributes that can make it a well-defined clustering key.

First, let's consider the uniqueness of the clustering key. Provided that the use cases for the database and table never change, there can be trust that the values will remain unique. What happens, though, when the database needs to be used in an international context? If states for other countries such as the Netherlands need to be included, there is a great potential for data issues. In the Netherlands, FL is the abbreviation for Flevopolder and NH is the abbreviation for Noord-Holland. Sending an order to Florida that should go to Flevopolder can have serious business consequences. In order to retain the uniqueness, something outside of the two-character abbreviation would need to be added to the surrogate key and clustering key.

Changing the surrogate would then affect the narrowness of the clustering key. There are probably two approaches that could be taken to address this problem. The first option is to add another column to the surrogate key to identify whether a state abbreviation belongs to one country or another. The other option is to increase the size of the state abbreviation to include a country abbreviation in the same column. With either of the solutions, the size of the clustering key will exceed the 4 bytes used to maintain a narrow clustering key through the use of an int data type and the Identity Column pattern.

Lastly, always consider whether surrogate keys are truly static. State abbreviations can change. While this doesn't happen too often—the last change in the United States happened in 1987 when state abbreviations were all standardized—it will happen occasionally with nearly all types of surrogate keys. One example is the country of Yugoslavia with its six republics, which became their own countries. Another is the Soviet Union, which evolved into the Russian Federation, which led to the formation of numerous other countries. As static as values such as state and country abbreviations may seem, on a grander scale there is variance. Also, looking to your applications, status codes that represent the states of a workflow may be accurate today but could have new and different meanings in the future.

The Surrogate Key pattern for selecting what an index does is a valid pattern for designing clustered indexes. As the example showed, it can be unique, narrow, and static. Look at the current and future applications of the table before using a surrogate key for the clustered index.

Foreign Key

One of the most often overlooked patterns for creating clustered indexes is to use a foreign key column in the clustering keys for the table. The Foreign Key pattern is not appropriate for all foreign keys but does have its use in designs where there is a one-to-many relationship between information in a header table and the related detail information. The Foreign Key pattern contains all of the attributes that are part of a well-defined clustering key. There are, though, a few caveats with a few of the attributes.

Implementing this pattern is very similar to the way you implement the Identity Column pattern. The pattern contains two tables that have columns with the IDENTITY property set on them. An example is in Listing 8-6. In the example, there are three tables created. The first is the header table, named dbo.IndexStrategiesHeader, with a clustered index built on the HeaderID column. The next table is first version of the detail table, named dbo.IndexStrategiesDetail_ICP. The table is designed as a child to the header table, the clustered index built using the Identity Column pattern, and an index on the HeaderID column is used to improve performance. The third table is also a detail table, named dbo.IndexStrategiesDetail_FKP; this table is designed using the Foreign Key pattern. Instead of clustering the table on the column with the IDENTITY property, the clustered index includes two columns. The first column is the column from the parent table, HeaderID, and the second is the primary key for this table, DetailID. To provide sample data, sys.indexes and sys.index_columns are used to populate all of the tables.

Listing 8-6. Creating and Populating Tables for Foreign Key Pattern

```
USE AdventureWorks2012
GO

CREATE TABLE dbo.IndexStrategiesHeader
(
HeaderID int IDENTITY(1,1)
,FillerData char(250)
,CONSTRAINT PK_Header_HeaderID PRIMARY KEY CLUSTERED (HeaderID)
);

CREATE TABLE dbo.IndexStrategiesDetail_ICP
(
```

```
DetailID int IDENTITY(1,1)
,HeaderID int
,FillerData char(500)
,CONSTRAINT PK_Detail_ICP_DetailID PRIMARY KEY CLUSTERED (DetailID)
,CONSTRAINT FK_Detail_ICP_HeaderID FOREIGN KEY (HeaderID) REFERENCES
IndexStrategiesHeader(HeaderID)
);
CREATE INDEX IX_Detail_ICP_HeaderID ON dbo.IndexStrategiesDetail_ICP (HeaderID)

CREATE TABLE dbo.IndexStrategiesDetail_FKP
(
DetailID int IDENTITY(1,1)
,HeaderID int
,FillerData char(500)
,CONSTRAINT PK_Detail_FKP_DetailID PRIMARY KEY NONCLUSTERED (DetailID)
,CONSTRAINT CLUS_Detail_FKP_HeaderIDDetailID UNIQUE CLUSTERED (HeaderID, DetailID)
,CONSTRAINT FK_Detail_FKP_HeaderID FOREIGN KEY (HeaderID) REFERENCES
IndexStrategiesHeader(HeaderID)
);
GO

INSERT INTO dbo.IndexStrategiesHeader(FillerData)
SELECT CONVERT(varchar,object_id)+name
FROM sys.indexes

INSERT INTO dbo.IndexStrategiesDetail_ICP
SELECT ish.HeaderID, CONVERT(varchar,ic.index_column_id)+'-'+FillerData
FROM dbo.IndexStrategiesHeader ish
    INNER JOIN sys.indexes i ON ish.FillerData = CONVERT(varchar,i.object_id)+i.name
    INNER JOIN sys.index_columns ic ON i.object_id = ic.object_id AND i.index_id = ic.index_id

INSERT INTO dbo.IndexStrategiesDetail_FKP
SELECT ish.HeaderID, CONVERT(varchar,ic.index_column_id)+'-'+FillerData
FROM dbo.IndexStrategiesHeader ish
    INNER JOIN sys.indexes i ON ish.FillerData = CONVERT(varchar,i.object_id)+i.name
    INNER JOIN sys.index_columns ic ON i.object_id = ic.object_id AND i.index_id = ic.index_id
```

At this point, you have three tables designed using the two clustered index patterns, Identity and Foreign Key. The key to this pattern is to design the table as such that in their common usage patterns the data will be returned as efficiently as possible. There are two use cases that are common in this type of a scenario. The first is returning the header and all of the detail rows for one row in the header table. The second is to return multiple rows from the header table and all of the related rows from the detail table.

First, let's examine the differences in performance for returning one row from the header table and all of the related detail rows. The code in Listing 8-7 executes this use case against both clustered indexing patterns. As expected, the dataset returned by both queries is the same. The difference lies in the statistics and query plan for the two queries. First, let's look at the statistics output when STATISTICS IO is used during the first use case (shown in Figure 8-6). The reads for the Identity Column pattern show that there were four reads as opposed to two reads by the Foreign Key pattern. While these numbers are low, this is a two-fold difference that could impact your database significantly if these are highly utilized queries. The big difference in execution, though, can be seen when reviewing the execution plans for the two queries (Figure 8-7). For the first query, to retrieve the results an index seek, key lookup, and nested loop are required against the detail table. Compare this to the second query, which obtains the same information using a clustered index seek. This example clearly indicates that the Foreign Key pattern performs better than the Identity Column pattern.

Listing 8-7. Single Header Row on Foreign Key Pattern

```
SELECT ish.HeaderID, ish.FillerData, isd.DetailID, isd.FillerData
FROM dbo.IndexStrategiesHeader ish
     INNER JOIN dbo.IndexStrategiesDetail_ICP isd ON ish.HeaderID = isd.HeaderID
WHERE ish.HeaderID = 10

SELECT ish.HeaderID, ish.FillerData, isd.DetailID, isd.FillerData
FROM dbo.IndexStrategiesHeader ish
    INNER JOIN dbo.IndexStrategiesDetail_FKP isd ON ish.HeaderID = isd.HeaderID
WHERE ish.HeaderID = 10
```

```
(1 row(s) affected)                                          Identity Column Pattern
Table 'IndexStrategiesDetail_ICP'. Scan count 1, logical reads 4, physical reads 0, read-ahead reads 0,
Table 'IndexStrategiesHeader'. Scan count 0, logical reads 2, physical reads 0, read-ahead reads 0, lob

(1 row(s) affected)

(1 row(s) affected)                                          Foreign Key Pattern
Table 'IndexStrategiesDetail_FKP'. Scan count 1, logical reads 2, physical reads 0, read-ahead reads 0,
Table 'IndexStrategiesHeader'. Scan count 0, logical reads 2, physical reads 0, read-ahead reads 0, lob

(1 row(s) affected)
```

Figure 8-6. *Results for single header row on foreign key pattern*

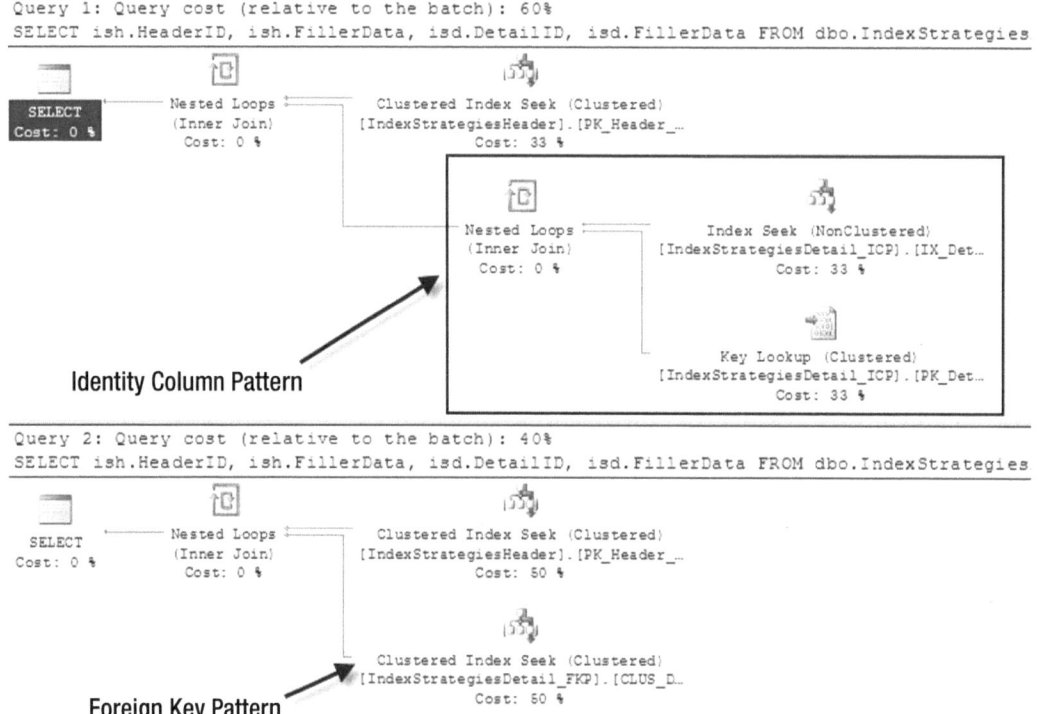

Figure 8-7. *Execution plans for single header row on foreign key pattern*

With the success of the first use case, let's examine the second use case. In this example, shown in Listing 8-8, the queries will retrieve multiple rows from the header table, and the data from the detail table that matches the HeaderID from the header rows. Again, the data returned by the queries using both of the clustered index patterns is the same and there are performance differences between the two executions. The first difference is in the STATISTICS IO output, shown in Figure 8-8. In the first execution, there are 158 reads on the header table and 44 reads on the detail table. Comparing those to the 4 reads on the header and 8 reads on the detail for the Foreign Key pattern, it's clear that the Foreign Key pattern performs better. In fact, the reads are a magnitude lower for the Foreign Key over the Identity Column pattern. The reason for the performance difference can be explained through the execution plan, shown in Figure 8-9. In the execution plan, the first query requires a Clustered Index Scan on the detail table to return the rows from the detail table. The second query, using the Foreign Key pattern, does not require this and uses a clustered index seek.

Listing 8-8. Multiple Header Row on Foreign Key Pattern

```
SELECT ish.HeaderID, ish.FillerData, isd.DetailID, isd.FillerData
FROM dbo.IndexStrategiesHeader ish
     INNER JOIN dbo.IndexStrategiesDetail_ICP isd ON ish.HeaderID = isd.HeaderID
WHERE ish.HeaderID BETWEEN 10 AND 50

SELECT ish.HeaderID, ish.FillerData, isd.DetailID, isd.FillerData
FROM dbo.IndexStrategiesHeader ish
     INNER JOIN dbo.IndexStrategiesDetail_FKP isd ON ish.HeaderID = isd.HeaderID
WHERE ish.HeaderID BETWEEN 10 AND 50
```

```
                                                            Identity Column Pattern
(79 row(s) affected)
Table 'IndexStrategiesHeader'. Scan count 0, logical reads 158, physical reads 0, read-ahead reads 0, lo
Table 'IndexStrategiesDetail_ICP'. Scan count 1, logical reads 44, physical reads 0, read-ahead reads 0,

(1 row(s) affected)
                                                            Foreign Key Pattern
(79 row(s) affected)
Table 'IndexStrategiesDetail_FKP'. Scan count 1, logical reads 8, physical reads 0, read-ahead reads 0,
Table 'IndexStrategiesHeader'. Scan count 1, logical reads 4, physical reads 0, read-ahead reads 0, lob

(1 row(s) affected)
```

Figure 8-8. *Results for multiple header row on foreign key pattern*

Through the two use cases in this section, you can see how the Foreign Key pattern can outperform the Identity Column pattern. However, there are things that need to be considered in databases before implementing this pattern. The chief question that needs to be answered is whether rows will be most often be retrieved going through the primary key of the detail table or its foreign key relationship to the header table. Not all foreign keys are suited for this clustered index pattern; it is only valid when there is a header-to-detail relationship between tables.

As mentioned, there are a few caveats regarding the attributes of a well-defined clustered index when using the Foreign Key pattern. In regards to being narrow, the pattern is not as narrow as the Identity Column pattern. Instead of a single integer-based column, two of them make up the clustering keys. When using the int data type, this will increase the size of the clustering key from 4 bytes to 8 bytes. While not an overly large value, it will impact the size of the non-clustered indexes on the table. In most cases, the clustering keys under the Foreign Key pattern will be static. There is a chance that the header row for some detail rows will need to change from time to time, maybe when two orders are logged and need to be merged for shipping. For this reason, the Foreign

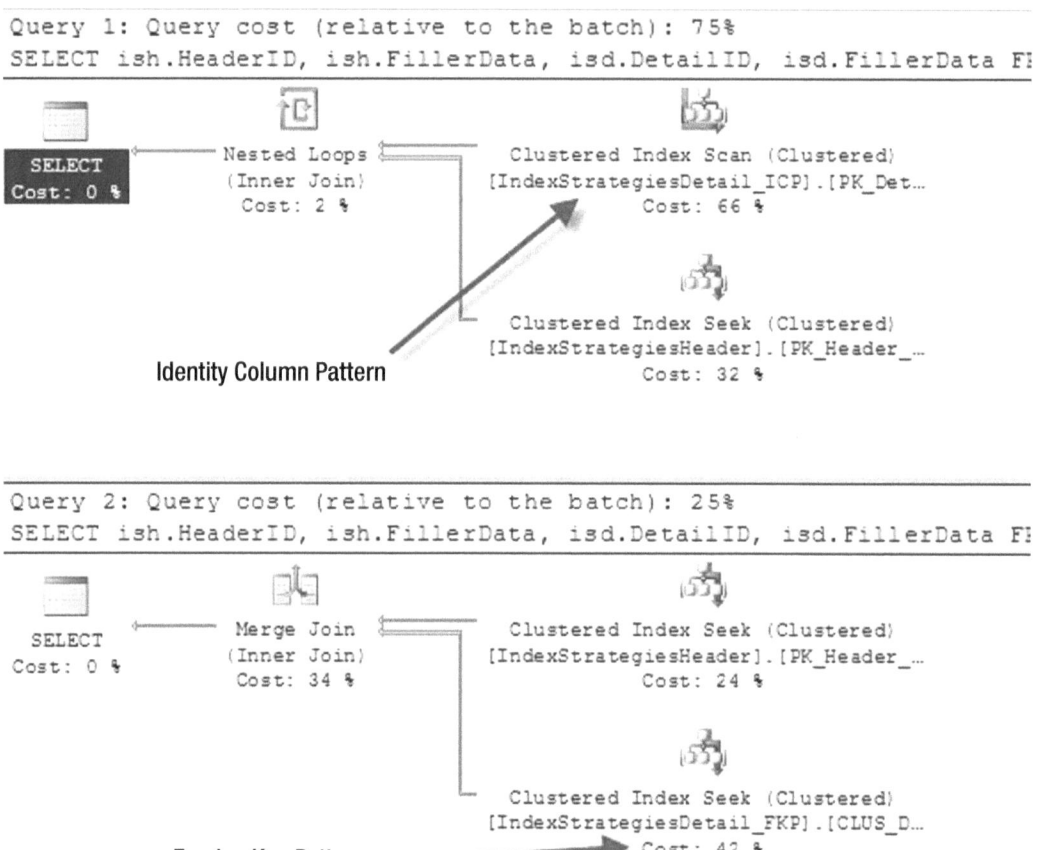

Figure 8-9. *Execution plans for multiple header row on foreign key pattern*

Key pattern isn't entirely static. The key can change but it shouldn't change very frequently. If there are frequent changes, you should reconsider using this clustered index pattern. The last attribute that has a caveat is whether the clustering keys are ever-increasing. In general, this should be the case. The typical insert pattern is to create a header and the detail records. In this situation, the header rows are created and inserted sequentially, followed by their detail records. If there is a delay in writing the detail records, or more detail records are added to a header row at a later date, the key won't be ever-increasing. As a result, there could be additional fragmentation and maintenance associated with this clustered index pattern

The Foreign Key pattern is not a clustered index pattern that will be applicable in all databases. When it is, though, it is quite beneficial and can alleviate performance issues that may not be as obvious as other issues. It is important to consider using this pattern when designing clustered indexes and to review the caveats associated with it to determine if it is the right fit.

Multiple Column

The next pattern that can be used to design clustered indexes is the Multiple Column pattern. In this pattern, two or more tables have a relationship to a third table that allows for many-to-many relationships to exist between the information. For instance, there might be a table that stores employee information and another that contains job roles. To represent the relationship, a third table is used. Through the Multiple Column pattern, instead of using a new column with the IDENTITY property on it, the columns used for the relationship serve as the clustering keys.

The Multiple Column pattern is similar to the Foreign Key pattern and provides many of the same performance enhancements that the previous pattern. As you will soon see, there is often one column or another in the many-to-many relationship table that is the best candidate for clustering key. Similar to the other patterns, this pattern also adheres to most of the attributes for a well-defined clustered index. The pattern is unique and mostly narrow and static; these properties will be apparent as you walk through an example of the Multiple Column pattern.

To demonstrate the Multiple Column pattern, let's begin by defining a few tables and their relationships. To start, there are tables that will store information about employees and job roles, named dbo.Employee and dbo.JobRole, respectively. Two tables named dbo.EmployeeJobRole_ICP and dbo.EmployeeJobRole_MCP are used to represent the Identity Column and Multiple Column patterns in the example relationships (see Listing 8-9). The example script includes insert statements to provide some sample data to use. Also, non-clustered are created on the tables to provide a real-world type scenario.

Listing 8-9. Multiple Column Pattern Script

```
USE AdventureWorks2012
GO

CREATE TABLE dbo.Employee (
EmployeeID int IDENTITY(1,1)
,EmployeeName varchar(100)
,FillerData varchar(1000)
,CONSTRAINT PK_Employee PRIMARY KEY CLUSTERED (EmployeeID));

CREATE INDEX IX_Employee_EmployeeName ON dbo.Employee(EmployeeName);

CREATE TABLE dbo.JobRole (
JobRoleID int IDENTITY(1,1)
,RoleName varchar(25)
,FillerData varchar(200)
,CONSTRAINT PK_JobRole PRIMARY KEY CLUSTERED (JobRoleID));

CREATE INDEX IX_JobRole_RoleName ON dbo.JobRole(RoleName);

CREATE TABLE dbo.EmployeeJobRole_ICP (
EmployeeJobRoleID int IDENTITY(1,1)
,EmployeeID int
,JobRoleID int
,CONSTRAINT PK_EmployeeJobRole_ICP PRIMARY KEY CLUSTERED (EmployeeJobRoleID)
,CONSTRAINT UIX_EmployeeJobRole_ICP UNIQUE (EmployeeID, JobRoleID))

CREATE INDEX IX_EmployeeJobRole_ICP_EmployeeID ON dbo.EmployeeJobRole_ICP(EmployeeID);
CREATE INDEX IX_EmployeeJobRole_ICP_JobRoleID ON dbo.EmployeeJobRole_ICP(JobRoleID);

CREATE TABLE dbo.EmployeeJobRole_MCP (
EmployeeJobRoleID int IDENTITY(1,1)
,EmployeeID int
,JobRoleID int
,CONSTRAINT PK_EmployeeJobRoleID PRIMARY KEY NONCLUSTERED (EmployeeJobRoleID)
,CONSTRAINT CUIX_EmployeeJobRole_ICP UNIQUE CLUSTERED (EmployeeID, JobRoleID));

CREATE INDEX IX_EmployeeJobRole_MCP_JobRoleID ON dbo.EmployeeJobRole_MCP(JobRoleID);

INSERT INTO dbo.Employee (EmployeeName)
SELECT OBJECT_SCHEMA_NAME(object_id)+'|'+name
FROM sys.tables;
```

```
INSERT INTO dbo.JobRole (RoleName)
VALUES ('Cook'),('Butcher'),('Candlestick Maker');

INSERT INTO dbo.EmployeeJobRole_ICP (EmployeeID, JobRoleID)
SELECT EmployeeID, 1 FROM dbo.Employee
UNION ALL SELECT EmployeeID, 2 FROM dbo.Employee WHERE EmployeeID / 4 = 1
UNION ALL SELECT EmployeeID, 3 FROM dbo.Employee WHERE EmployeeID / 8 = 1;

INSERT INTO dbo.EmployeeJobRole_MCP (EmployeeID, JobRoleID)
SELECT EmployeeID, 1 FROM dbo.Employee
UNION ALL SELECT EmployeeID, 2 FROM dbo.Employee WHERE EmployeeID / 4 = 1
UNION ALL SELECT EmployeeID, 3 FROM dbo.Employee WHERE EmployeeID / 8 = 1;
```

The first test against the example tables will look at querying against all three tables to retrieve information on employee names and job roles. These queries, shown in Listing 8-10, retrieve information based on the RoleName from dbo.JobRole. In the code, the two versions of the EmployeeJobRole table are created with different clustering keys. This results in a drastic difference in the execution plans, shown in Figure 8-10, from the test queries. The first execution plan using the table with the Identity Column pattern applied to it is more complex than the execution plan for the second query and has 61 percent of the cost compared to the other plan. The second plan, which has its clustering keys based on the Multiple Column pattern, has fewer operations and accounts for 39 percent of the execution. The main difference between the two plans is that using the Multiple Column pattern allows the clustered index to cover table access based on a column that is likely to be used to frequently access rows in the table, in this case the JobRoleID column. Using the other pattern does not provide this benefit and represents a data access path that will not likely be used, except maybe when needing to delete the row.

Listing 8-10. Script for Multiple Column Pattern

```
SELECT e.EmployeeName, jr.RoleName
FROM dbo.Employee e
INNER JOIN dbo.EmployeeJobRole_ICP ejr ON e.EmployeeID = ejr.EmployeeID
INNER JOIN dbo.JobRole jr ON ejr.JobRoleID = jr.JobRoleID
WHERE RoleName = 'Candlestick Maker'

SELECT e.EmployeeName, jr.RoleName
FROM dbo.Employee e
INNER JOIN dbo.EmployeeJobRole_MCP ejr ON e.EmployeeID = ejr.EmployeeID
INNER JOIN dbo.JobRole jr ON ejr.JobRoleID = jr.JobRoleID
WHERE RoleName = 'Candlestick Maker'
```

While the benefits are significant with the first test results, they are less impressive when looking at some other methods that can be used. For instance, if instead of using RoleName as the predicate, the EmployeeName was the predicate. The script in Listing 8-11 demonstrates this scenario. Contrary to the last test script, the results this time are no different than the other for either clustered index design (see Figure 8-11). The cause of the identical plans in the figure is based on the decision to optimize the clustering index keys in the Multiple Column pattern to favor the JobRoleID. When the EmployeeID column is used to access the data, the non-clustered index provides most of the heavy lifting, and a good, similar, plan for each query is created. The results of this second test do not discount the use of the Multiple Column pattern, but they do highlight that the column selected to lead the clustering key should be selected after performing tests with the expected workload.

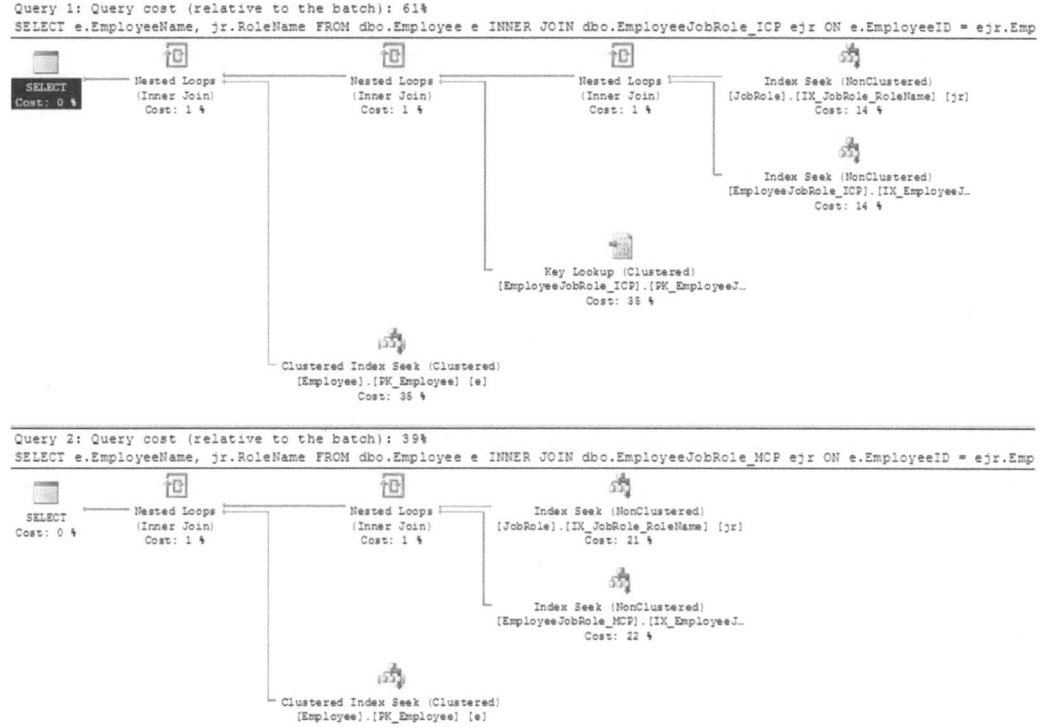

Figure 8-10. *Results for multiple column pattern*

Listing 8-11. Script for Multiple Column Pattern

```
SELECT e.EmployeeName, jr.RoleName
FROM dbo.Employee e
INNER JOIN dbo.EmployeeJobRole_ICP ejr ON e.EmployeeID = ejr.EmployeeID
INNER JOIN dbo.JobRole jr ON ejr.JobRoleID = jr.JobRoleID
WHERE EmployeeName = 'Purchasing|ShipMethod'

SELECT e.EmployeeName, jr.RoleName
FROM dbo.Employee e
INNER JOIN dbo.EmployeeJobRole_MCP ejr ON e.EmployeeID = ejr.EmployeeID
INNER JOIN dbo.JobRole jr ON ejr.JobRoleID = jr.JobRoleID
WHERE EmployeeName = 'Purchasing|ShipMethod'
```

There are various ways in which the Multiple Column pattern can be implemented. The key columns in the clustered index can be reversed, which would change the execution plans generated for the test scripts. While this pattern can be beneficial, be cautious when using it and fully understand the work load expected before using it.

To wrap up the Multiple Column pattern, let's review the attributes of a well-defined clustered index. First, the values are static. If there were to be a change, it would likely be deleting a record and inserting a new record. This is still effectively an update to mitigate this risk attempt to lead the clustered index with the value least likely to change or have variations in population. The second is whether the clustering key is narrow. In this example, the key was mostly narrow. It was comprised of two 4-byte columns. If using larger columns or more than two columns, carefully consider if this is the right approach. The next attribute is whether the values are unique. They are in this scenario and should be in any scenario in the real world. If not, then this pattern is naturally disqualified. As with the other non-Identity Column patterns, this pattern does not provide an ever-increasing clustering key.

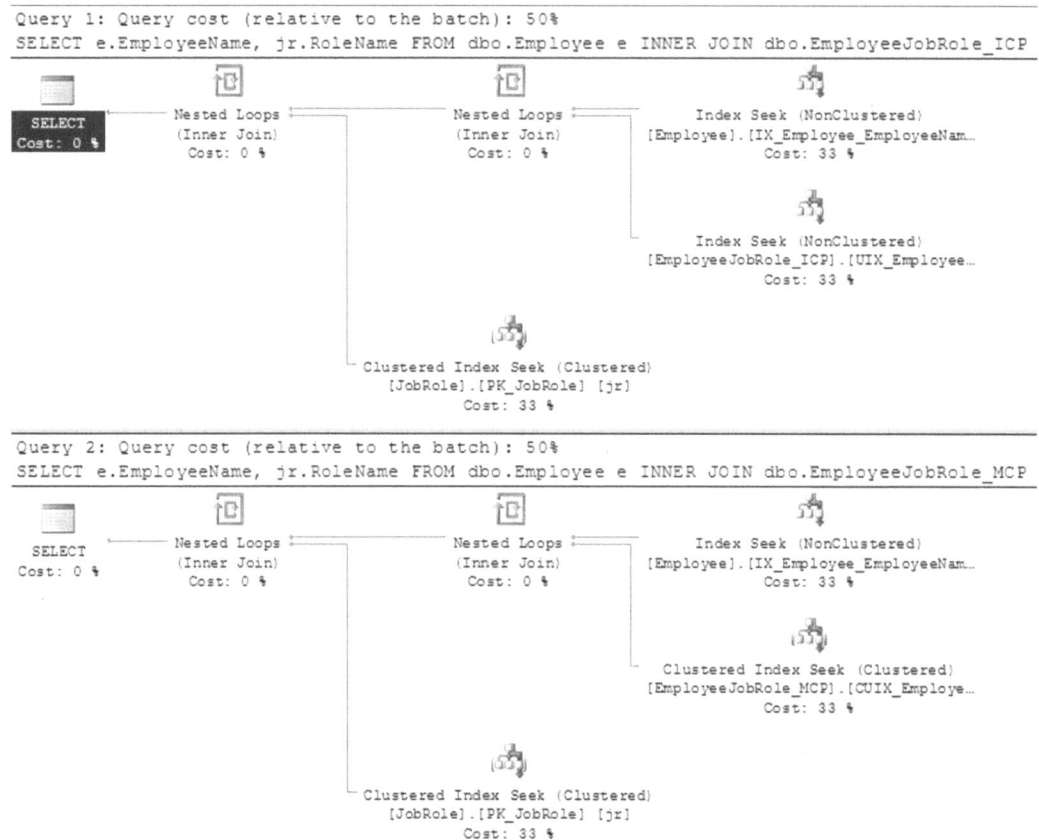

Figure 8-11. *Results for multiple column pattern*

As a final note, fact tables in data warehouses often succumb to the temptation to use the Multiple Column pattern. In these cases, all of the dimension keys in the fact table are placed in the clustered index. The aim in doing this is to enforce uniqueness on the fact rows. The effect is the creation of an extremely wide clustering key, which is then added to all of the non-clustered indexes on the table. Most likely, each of the dimension columns in the clustered key will have a separate index on the fact table. As a result, these indexes waste a lot of space and, because of their size, perform much worse than if the uniqueness on the fact table was constrained by a non-clustered unique index.

Globally Unique Identifier

The last, and definitely least beneficial, pattern for selecting a clustered index column is to use a Globally Unique Identifier, also known as a GUID. The GUID pattern involves using a uniquely generated value to provide a unique value for each row in a table. This value is not integer-based and is often chosen because it can be generated at any location (within the topology of an application) and has a guarantee that it will be unique. The problem this pattern solves is the need to be able to generate new unique values while disconnecting from the source that typically controls the list of unique values. Unfortunately, the GUID pattern causes nearly as many issues as it solves.

There are two main methods for generating GUID values. The first is through the NEWID() function. This function generates a 16-byte hexadecimal value that is partially based on the MAC address of the computer creating it at the time. Each value generated is unique and can start with any value from 0-9 or a-f. The next value created can be either ahead of or after the previous value in a sort. There is no guarantee that the next value is ever-increasing. The other option for generating a GUID is through NEWSEQUENTIALID(). This function also creates a 16-byte hexadecimal value. Unlike the other function, NEWSEQUENTIALID() creates new values that are greater than the previous value generated since the computer was last started. The last point is important: when the server restarts, it is likely that new values with NEWSEQUENTIALID() will be less than the value created before the restart.

As discussed, using the GUID pattern does not provide for an ever-increasing value. As mentioned, with either NEWID() or NEWSEQUENTIALID() there is no guarantee that the next value will always be greater than the last value. Along with that, it does not provide a narrow index. When storing a GUID as a uniqueidentifier, it requires 16 bytes of storage. This is the size of four ints or two bigints. Comparatively, the GUID is quite large, and that value will be placed in all non-clustered indexes on the table. The space used for the GUID pattern can sometimes be worse than this, though. In some cases, when the GUID pattern is poorly implemented, the GUID value is stored as characters that require 36 bytes to store or 72-bytes if using a Unicode data type.

Even with the failings of the GUID pattern, it does achieve some of the other attributes of a well-defined clustering key. First, the value is unique. With both the NEWID() and NEWSEQUENTIALID() functions, the values generated for the GUID value are unique. The value is also static, since the GUID value generated has no business, meaning there is no reason for it to change the value.

To demonstrate implementing the GUID pattern, let's examine its use on a table with a comparison to a couple other implementations. In this scenario, shown in Listing 8-12, there are three tables. Table dbo.IndexStrategiesGUID_ICP is designed using the Identity Column pattern. Table dbo.IndexStrategiesGUID_UniqueID is built with the GUID pattern using a uniqueidentifier, as best practices dictate. Lastly, the script contains table dbo.IndexStrategiesGUID_String, which uses a varchar(36) to store the GUID value. The last method is not the proper way to implement the GUID pattern and the analysis will help highlight that. With all three tables built, insert statements will populate 250,000 rows to each table. The final statement in the scenario retrieves the number of pages used by each of the tables.

Listing 8-12. Script for GUID Pattern Scenario

```
USE AdventureWorks2012
GO

CREATE TABLE dbo.IndexStrategiesGUID_ICP (
RowID int IDENTITY(1,1)
,FillerData varchar(1000)
,CONSTRAINT PK_IndexStrategiesGUID_ICP PRIMARY KEY CLUSTERED (RowID)
);

CREATE TABLE dbo.IndexStrategiesGUID_UniqueID (
RowID uniqueidentifier DEFAULT(NEWSEQUENTIALID())
,FillerData varchar(1000)
,CONSTRAINT PK_IndexStrategiesGUID_UniqueID PRIMARY KEY CLUSTERED (RowID)
);

CREATE TABLE dbo.IndexStrategiesGUID_String (
RowID varchar(36) DEFAULT(NEWID())
,FillerData varchar(1000)
,CONSTRAINT PK_IndexStrategiesGUID_String PRIMARY KEY CLUSTERED (RowID)
);

INSERT INTO dbo.IndexStrategiesGUID_ICP (FillerData)
SELECT TOP (250000) a1.name+a2.name
FROM sys.all_objects a1 CROSS JOIN sys.all_objects a2

INSERT INTO dbo.IndexStrategiesGUID_UniqueID (FillerData)
SELECT TOP (250000) a1.name+a2.name
```

```
FROM sys.all_objects a1 CROSS JOIN sys.all_objects a2

INSERT INTO dbo.IndexStrategiesGUID_String (FillerData)
SELECT TOP (250000) a1.name+a2.name
FROM sys.all_objects a1 CROSS JOIN sys.all_objects a2

SELECT OBJECT_NAME(object_ID) as table_name, in_row_used_page_count, in_row_reserved_page_count
FROM sys.dm_db_partition_stats
WHERE object_id IN (OBJECT_ID('dbo.IndexStrategiesGUID_ICP')
    ,OBJECT_ID('dbo.IndexStrategiesGUID_UniqueID')
    ,OBJECT_ID('dbo.IndexStrategiesGUID_String'))
```

	table_name	in_row_used_page_count	in_row_reserved_page_count
1	IndexStrategiesGUID_ICP	1875	1881
2	IndexStrategiesGUID_UniqueID	2257	2265
3	IndexStrategiesGUID_String	2965	2969

Figure 8-12. *Page counts for GUID pattern*

Unlike the other scenarios, the use of the GUID pattern is very much like the Identity Column pattern. There are two primary differences. First, the GUID pattern does not provide a narrow clustering key. For the clustering key with the uniqueidentifier data type, the change in size of the clustering key requires about 400 more pages to store the same information (see Figure 8-12). Even worse, when improperly storing the GUID in the varchar data type, the table requires about 1,100 more pages. Without a doubt, using the GUID pattern amounts to a lot of wasted space in the clustered index, which would also be included in any non-clustered indexes on the table. The other issue with the GUID pattern is tied in with the ever-increasing attribute of clustered indexes. As already discussed, GUIDs are not presented in an ordered fashion. The next value can be greater or less than the previous value and this leads to a random placement of rows within a table, which results in fragmentation. For more information on index fragmentation as a result of GUIDs, read Chapter 6.

In regards to the last two attributes of a well-defined clustering key, the GUID pattern does well with those. The value is static and should not be expected to change over time. The value is also unique. It should, in fact, be unique throughout the entire database. Even though the GUID pattern does achieve the two attributes of a well-defined clustered index, they do not mitigate the aforementioned issues with this pattern. The GUID pattern should be a pattern of last resort when determining how to build the clustered index for a table.

■ **Note**   Using the new sp_sequence_get_range stored procedure in conjunction with SEQUENCEs can be a valid replacement in applications using the Uniqueidentifier pattern that would like to migrate to using a Identity Column pattern for clustered index design.

Non-Clustered Indexes

In the last two sections, the discussion focused on heaps and clustered indexes, which are used to determine how to store the data. With heaps, the data is stored unsorted. With clustered indexes, data is sorted based on one set of columns. In nearly all databases, there will need to be other ways of accessing the data in the table that doesn't align with the sort order in which the data is stored. This is where non-clustered indexes come in. Non-clustered indexes provide another method for accessing data in addition to the heap or clustered index to locate data in a table.

In this section, you'll review a number of patterns that are associated with non-clustered indexes. These patterns will help identify when and where to consider building non-clustered indexes. For each pattern, you'll go through the chief components of the pattern and situations where it may be leveraged. Similar to the clustered index patterns, each non-clustered index pattern will included a scenario or two to demonstrate the benefit of the pattern. The non-clustered index patterns that will be discussed are

- Search Columns
- Index Intersection
- Multiple Column
- Covering Indexes
- Included Columns
- Filtered Indexes
- Foreign Keys

Before you review the patterns, there are a number of guidelines that will apply to all of the non-clustered indexes. These guidelines differ from the attributes of well-defined clustered indexes. With the attributes, one of the key goals was to adhere to them as much as possible. With the non-clustered indexing guidelines, they form a number of considerations that will help strengthen the case for an index but may not disqualify the use of the index. Some of the most common considerations to think of when designing indexes are

- **What is the frequency of change for the non-clustered index key columns?** The more frequent the data changes, the more often the row in the non-clustered may need to change its position in the index.

- **What frequent queries will the index improve?** The greater the overall lift an index provides, the better the database platform will operate as a whole.

- **What business needs does the index support?** Infrequently used indexes that support critical business operations can be sometimes be more important than frequently used indexes.

- **What is the cost in time to maintain the index versus the cost in time to query the data?** There can be a point where the performance gain from an indexes is outweighed by the time spent creating and defragmenting an index and the space that it requires.

As mentioned in the introduction, indexing can often feel like art. Fortunately, science or statistics can be used to demonstrate the value of indexes. As each of these patterns are reviewed, you'll look at scenarios where they can be applied and use some science, or metrics in this case, to determine whether the index provides value. The two things you will use to judge indexes will be reads during the execution and complexity of the execution plan.

Search Columns

The most basic and common pattern for designing non-clustered indexes is to build them based on defined or expected search patterns. The Search Columns pattern should be the most widely known pattern, but also happens to be easily, and often, overlooked.

If queries will be searching tables with contacts in them by first name, then index the first name column. If the address table will have searches against it by city or state, then index those columns. The primary goal of the Search Columns pattern is to reduce scans against the clustered index and move those operations to a non-clustered index that can provide more direct route to the data through a non-clustered index.

To demonstrate the Search Column pattern, let's use the first scenario mentioned in this section, a contact table. For simplicity, the examples will use a table named dbo.Contacts that contains data from the

AdventureWorks2012 table Person.Person (see Listing 8-13). There should be about 19,972 rows inserted into dbo.Contacts, though this will vary depending on the freshness of your AdventureWork2012 database.

Listing 8-13. Setup for Search Column Pattern

```
USE AdventureWorks2012
GO

CREATE TABLE dbo.Contacts (
ContactID int IDENTITY(1,1)
,FirstName nvarchar(50)
,LastName nvarchar(50)
,IsActive bit
,EmailAddress nvarchar(50)
,CertificationDate datetime
,FillerData char(1000)
,CONSTRAINT PK_Contacts PRIMARY KEY CLUSTERED (ContactID));

INSERT INTO dbo.Contacts (FirstName, LastName, IsActive, EmailAddress, CertificationDate)
SELECT pp.FirstName, pp.LastName, IIF(pp.BusinessEntityID/10=1,1,0), pea.EmailAddress,IIF(pp.
BusinessEntityID/10=1,pp.ModifiedDate,NULL)
FROM Person.Person pp
INNER JOIN Person.EmailAddress pea ON pp.BusinessEntityID = pea.BusinessEntityID;
```

With the table dbo.Contacts in place, the first test against the table is to query the table with no non-clustered indexes built on it. In the example, shown in Listing 8-14, the query is searching for rows with the first name of Catherine. Executing the query shows that there are 22 rows in dbo.Contacts that match the criteria (see Figure 8-13). To retrieve the 22 rows, SQL Server ended up reading 2,866 pages, which is all of the pages in the table. And as Figure 8-14 indicates, the page reads were the result of an index scan against PK_Contacts on dbo.Contacts. The aim of the query is to retrieve 22 out of the more than 19,000 rows, so checking every page in the table for rows with Catherine for the FirstName is not an optimal approach, and one that can be avoided.

Listing 8-14. Search Column Pattern

```
SET STATISTICS IO ON ;
SELECT ContactID, FirstName FROM dbo.Contacts
WHERE FirstName = 'Catherine';
SET STATISTICS IO OFF
```

```
(22 row(s) affected)
Table 'Contacts'. Scan count 1, logical reads 2866, physical reads 0, read-ahead reads 0, lob logical reads 0,

(1 row(s) affected)
```

Figure 8-13. Statistics IO results for Search Columns pattern

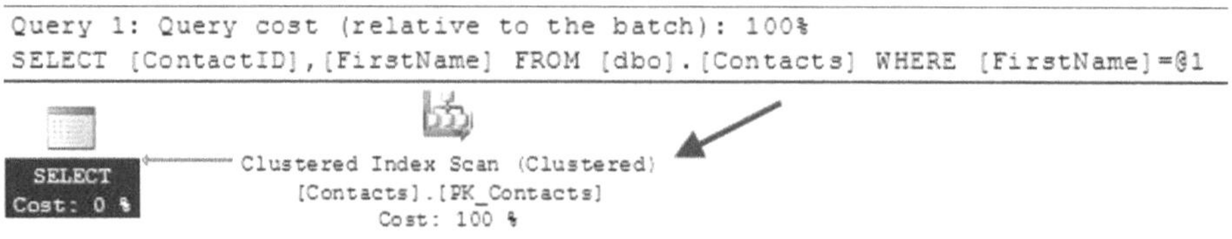

Figure 8-14. Execution plan for Search Columns pattern

Achieving the aim of retrieving all of the rows for Catherine optimally is relatively simple by adding a non-clustered index to dbo.Contacts. In the next script (Listing 8-15), a non-clustered index is created on the FirstName column. Besides the filter on FirstName, the query needs to also return ContactID. Since non-clustered indexes include the clustering index key, the value in ContactID is included in the index by default.

Executing the script in Listing 8-15 leads to substantially different results than before the non-clustered index was added to the table. Instead of reading every page in the table, the non-clustered index reduces the number of pages used for the query to two pages (Figure 8-15). The reduction here is significant, and highlights the power and value in using non-clustered indexes to provide more direct access to information in your tables on columns other than those in the clustered index keys. There is one other change in the execution: instead of a scan against PK_Index, the execution plan now uses an index seek against IC_Contacts_FirstName, shown in Figure 8-16. The change in the operator is further proof that the non-clustered index helped to improve the performance of the query.

Listing 8-15. Search Column Pattern

```
CREATE INDEX IX_Contacts_FirstName ON dbo.Contacts(FirstName);

SET STATISTICS IO ON
SELECT ContactID, FirstName FROM dbo.Contacts
WHERE FirstName = 'Catherine';
SET STATISTICS IO OFF;
```

```
(22 row(s) affected)
Table 'Contacts'. Scan count 1, logical reads 2, physical reads 0, read-ahead reads 0, lob logical reads 0,

(1 row(s) affected)
```

Figure 8-15. Statistics IO Results for Search Columns pattern

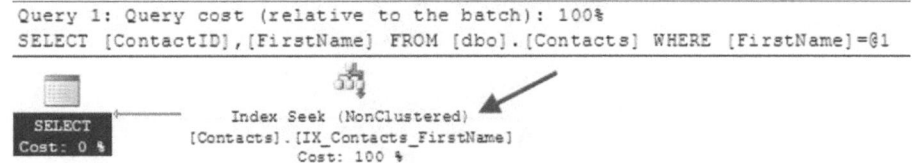

Figure 8-16. Execution plan for Search Columns pattern

Using the Search Columns pattern is probably the most important first step in applying non-clustered indexing patterns on your databases. It provides the alternative paths for accessing data that can be the difference between getting your data from a couple pages vs. thousands of pages. The Search Column example in this section shows building an index on a single column. The next few patterns will expand on this foundation.

Index Intersection

The aim of the Search Column is to create an index that will minimize the page reads for a query and improve the performance of it. Sometimes, though, the queries go beyond the single column example that was demonstrated. Additional columns may be a part of the predicate or returned in the SELECT statement. One of the ways to address this is to create non-clustered indexes that include the additional columns. When there are indexes that can satisfy each of the predicates in the WHERE clause, SQL Server can utilize multiple non-clustered indexes to find the rows between both that match on the clustering key. This operation is called Index Intersection.

To demonstrate the Index Intersection pattern, let's first review what happens when the filtering is expanded to cover multiple columns. The code in Listing 8-16 includes the expanded SELECT statement and WHERE clause expanding the predicate to include rows where LastName is Cox.

The change in the query results in a significant change in performance over the previous section's results. With the additional column in the query, there are 68 pages read to satisfy the query vs. the 2 pages when LastName was not included (Figure 8-17). The increase in pages read is due to the change in the execution plan (Figure 8-18). In the execution plan, an additional two operations are added to the execution of the query: a key lookup and nested loop. These operators are added because the index IX_Contacts_FirstName can't provide all of the information needed to satisfy the query. SQL Server determines that it is still cheaper to use the IX_Contacts_FirstName and look up the missing information from the clustered index than to scan the clustered index. The problem that you can run into is that for every row that matches on the non-clustered index, a lookup has to be done on the clustered index. While key lookups aren't always a problem, they can drive up the CPU and I/O costs for a query unnecessarily.

Listing 8-16. Index Intersection Pattern

```
SET STATISTICS IO ON
SELECT ContactID, FirstName, LastName FROM dbo.Contacts
WHERE FirstName = 'Catherine'
AND LastName = 'Cox'
SET STATISTICS IO OFF
```

```
(1 row(s) affected)
Table 'Contacts'. Scan count 1, logical reads 68, physical reads 0, read-ahead reads 0, lob logical reads 0,

(1 row(s) affected)
```

Figure 8-17. Statistics IO results for Index Intersections pattern

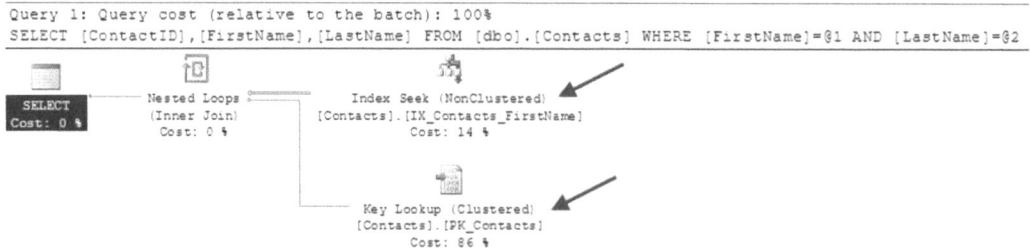

Figure 8-18. Execution plan for Index Intersections pattern

Leveraging the Index Intersection pattern is one of a few ways that the performance of the query in Listing 8-16 can be improved. Index intersection occurs when SQL Server can utilize multiple non-clustered indexes on the same table to satisfy the requirements for a query. In the case of the query in Listing 8-16, the most direct path for finding FirstNames was through the index IX_Contacts_FirstName. At that point, though, to filter and return the LastName column, SQL Server used the clustered index and performed a lookup on each row, similar to the image of the left side of Figure 8-19. Alternatively, if there had been an index for the LastName column, SQL Server could have used that index with IX_Contacts_FirstName. In essence, through index intersection, SQL Server is able to performn operations similar to joins between indexes on the same table to find rows that overlap between the two, as is show in the right side image in Figure 8-19.

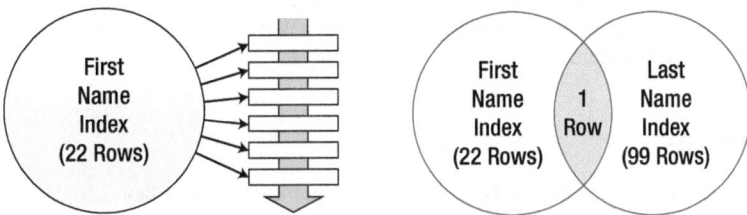

Figure 8-19. *Index seek with key lookup vs. two index seeks using index intersection*

To demonstrate the Index Intersection pattern and have SQL Server use index intersection, the next example creates an index on the LastName column (Listing 8-17). With the index IX_Contacts_LastName created, the results change significantly from when the index had not been created. The first significant change is in the number of reads. Instead of the 68 reads that occurred in the previous execution, there are only 5 reads (Figure 8-20). The cause of the reduction in reads is from SQL Server leveraging index intersection in the query plan (Figure 8-21). The indexes IX_Contacts_FirstName and IX_Contacts_LastName were used to satisfy the query without returning to the clustered index to retrieve data for the query. This happened because the two indexes can satisfy the query completely.

Listing 8-17. Index Intersection Pattern

```
CREATE INDEX IX_Contacts_LastName ON dbo.Contacts(LastName);

SET STATISTICS IO ON
SELECT ContactID, FirstName, LastName FROM dbo.Contacts
WHERE FirstName = 'Catherine'
AND LastName = 'Cox'
SET STATISTICS IO OFF
```

```
(1 row(s) affected)
Table 'Contacts'. Scan count 2, logical reads 5, physical reads 0, read-ahead reads 0, lob logical reads 0,

(1 row(s) affected)
```

Figure 8-20. *Statistics IO results for Index Intersections pattern*

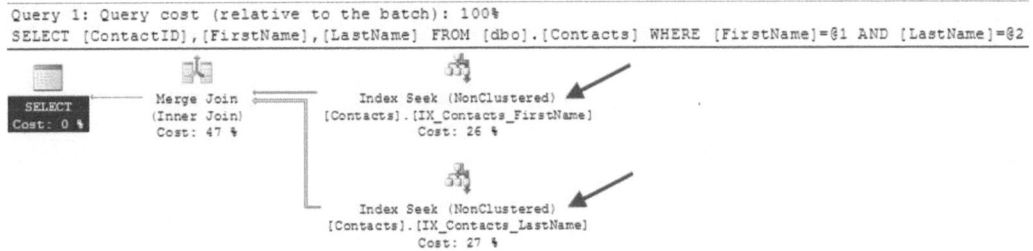

Figure 8-21. *Execution plan for Index Intersections pattern*

Index intersection is a feature of SQL Server that it uses to better satisfy queries when more than on non-clustered index from the same table can provide the results for the queries. When indexing for Index Intersection, the aim is to have multiple indexes based on the Search Column pattern that can be used together in numerous combinations to allow for a variety of filters. One key thing to remember with index intersection is that you can't tell SQL Server when to use index intersection; it will opt to use it when it is appropriate for the request, underlying indexes, and data.

Multiple Columns

The examples in the last two sections focused on indexes that included a single key column in the index. Non-clustered indexes, though, can have up to 16 columns. While being narrow was an attribute of a well-defined clustered index, the same attribute does not apply to non-clustered indexes. Instead, non-clustered indexes should contain as many columns as necessary to be used by the most queries as possible. If many queries will use the same columns as predicates, it is often a good idea to include them all in a single index.

A simple method for demonstrating an index using the Multiple Column pattern is to use the same query from the last section and apply this pattern to it. In that query, two indexes were built, one each on the FirstName and LastName columns. For the Multiple Column pattern, the new index will include both of the columns together (Listing 8-18).

As the statistics indicate (Figure 8-22), by using the Multiple Column pattern there is a reduction in the number of reads necessary to return the request results. Instead of five reads from the Index Intersection pattern, there are only two reads with the Multiple Column pattern. Additionally, the execution plan (shown in Figure 8-23) has been simplified. There is only an index seek on the index IX_Contacts_FirstNameLastName.

Listing 8-18. Multiple Column Pattern

```
CREATE INDEX IX_Contacts_FirstNameLastName ON dbo.Contacts(FirstName, LastName);

SET STATISTICS IO ON
SELECT ContactID, FirstName, LastName FROM dbo.Contacts
WHERE FirstName = 'Catherine'
AND LastName = 'Cox'
SET STATISTICS IO OFF
```

```
(1 row(s) affected)
Table 'Contacts'. Scan count 1, logical reads 2, physical reads 0, read-ahead reads 0, lob logical reads 0,

(1 row(s) affected)
```

Figure 8-22. *Statistics IO results for Multiple Columns pattern*

```
Query 1: Query cost (relative to the batch): 100%
SELECT [ContactID],[FirstName],[LastName] FROM [dbo].[Contacts] WHERE [FirstName]=@1 AND [LastName]=@2

    SELECT              Index Seek (NonClustered)
    Cost: 0 %        [Contacts].[IX_Contacts_FirstNameLa...
                              Cost: 100 %
```

Figure 8-23. *Execution plan for Multiple Columns pattern*

The Multiple Column pattern is as important to implement as the Search Column pattern when indexing your databases. This pattern can help reduce the number of indexes needed by putting the columns together that are most often used in predicated. While this pattern does contradict the Index Intersection pattern, the key between them is balance. In some cases, relying on index intersection on single column indexes will provide the best performance for a table with many variations on the query predicates. In other times, wider indexes with specific orders to the columns will be beneficial. Try both patterns and apply them in the manner that provides the best overall performance.

Covering Index

The next indexing pattern to be aware of is the Covering Index pattern. With the Covering Index pattern, columns outside of the predicates are added to an index's key columns to allow those values to be returned as part of the SELECT clauses of queries. This pattern has been a standard indexing practice for a while with SQL Server. Enhancements in how indexes can be created, though, make this pattern less useful than it was in the past. We are discussing it here because it is a common pattern that most already know.

To begin looking at the Covering Index pattern, you'll first need an example to define the problem that the index solves. To show the issue, the next test query will include the IsActive column in the SELECT list (Listing 8-19). With this column added, the I/O statistics increase again from two reads to five reads, shown in Figure 8-24. The change in performance is directly related to the change in the execution plan (see Figure 8-25) that includes a key lookup and nested loop. As with the previous examples, as items not included in the non-clustered index are added to the query, they need to be retrieved from the clustered index, which contains all of the data for the table.

Listing 8-19. Covering Index Pattern

```
SET STATISTICS IO ON
SELECT ContactID, FirstName, LastName, IsActive
FROM dbo.Contacts
WHERE FirstName = 'Catherine'
AND LastName = 'Cox'
SET STATISTICS IO OFF
```

```
(1 row(s) affected)
Table 'Contacts'. Scan count 1, logical reads 5, physical reads 0, read-ahead reads 0, lob logical reads 0,

(1 row(s) affected)
```

Figure 8-24. *Statistics IO results for Covering Index pattern*

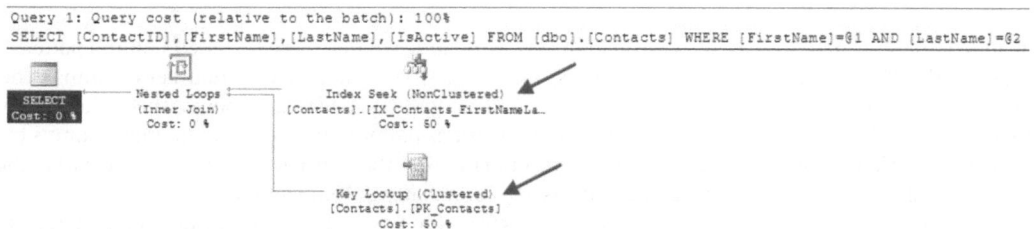

Figure 8-25. *Execution plan for Covering Index pattern*

Ideally, you want an index in place that can accommodate the filters on the index and can also rerun the columns requested in the SELECT list. The Covering Index pattern can fulfill these requirements. Even though IsActive is not one of the predicates for the query, it can be added to the index and SQL Server can use that key column to return the column values with the query. To demonstrate the Covering Index pattern, let's create an index that has FirstName, LastName, and IsActive as the key columns (see Listing 8-20). With the index IX_Contacts_FirstNameLastName in place, the reads return to two per execution (see Figure 8-26). The execution plan is also now using only an index seek (see Figure 8-27).

Listing 8-20. Covering Index Pattern

```
CREATE INDEX IX_Contacts_FirstNameLastNameIsActive ON dbo.Contacts(FirstName, LastName,
IsActive)

SET STATISTICS IO ON
SELECT ContactID, FirstName, LastName, IsActive FROM dbo.Contacts
WHERE FirstName = 'Catherine'
AND LastName = 'Cox'
SET STATISTICS IO OFF
```

```
(1 row(s) affected)
Table 'Contacts'. Scan count 1, logical reads 2, physical reads 0, read-ahead reads 0, lob logical reads 0,

(1 row(s) affected)
```

Figure 8-26. Statistics IO results for Covering Index pattern

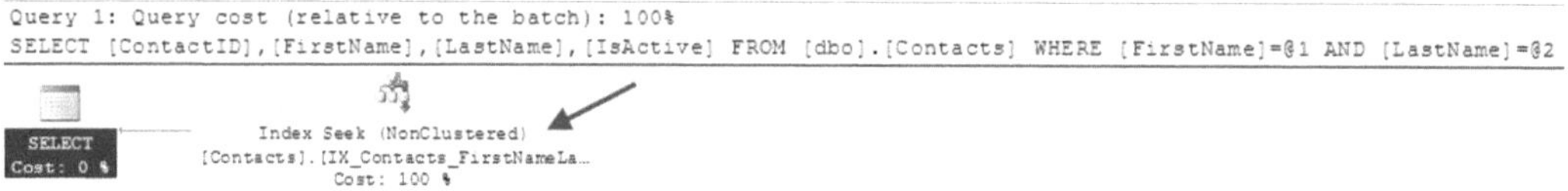

Figure 8-27. Execution plan for Covering Index pattern

The Covering Index pattern can be quite useful and has the potential to improve performance in a many areas. In the last few years, the use of this pattern has diminished. This change in use is primarily being driven by the availability of the option to include columns in indexes, which was introduced with SQL Server 2005.

Included Columns

The Included Columns pattern is a close cousin to the Covering Index pattern. The Included Column pattern leverages the INCLUDE clause of the CREATE and ALTER INDEX syntax. The clause allows non-key columns to be added to non-clustered indexes, similar to how non-key data is stored on clustered indexes. This is the primary difference between the Included Columns and the Covering Index patterns, where the additional columns in the Covering Index are key columns on the index. Like clustered indexes, the non-key columns that are part of the INCLUDE clause are not sorted, although they can be used as predicates in some queries.

The use case for the Included Columns pattern comes from the flexibility that it provides. It is generally the same as the Covering Index pattern and sometimes the names are used interchangeably. The key difference, which is demonstrated in this section, is that the Covering Index pattern is limited by the sort order of all of the columns in the index. The Included Columns pattern can avoid this potential issue by including non-key data, thereby increasing its flexibility of use.

Before demonstrating the flexibility of the Included Column pattern, let's first examine another index against the dbo.Contacts table. In Listing 8-21, the query is filtering just on FirstName of Catherine and returning the ContactID, FirstName, LastName, and EmailAddress columns. This query request differs from the other examples because it now includes the EmailAddress column. Since this column is not included in any of the other non-clustered indexes, none of them can fully satisfy the query. As a result, the execution plan utilizes IX_Contacts_FirstName to identify the Catherine rows and then looks up the rest of the data from the clustered index, shown in Figure 8-28. With the key lookup, the reads for the query also increase to 68 reads (see Figure 8-29), as they have in previous examples.

Listing 8-21. Included Columns Pattern

```
SET STATISTICS IO ON
SELECT ContactID, FirstName, LastName, EmailAddress FROM dbo.Contacts
WHERE FirstName = 'Catherine'
SET STATISTICS IO OFF
```

```
(22 row(s) affected)
Table 'Contacts'. Scan count 1, logical reads 68, physical reads 0, read-ahead reads 0, lob logical reads 0,

(1 row(s) affected)
```

Figure 8-28. *Statistics IO results for Included Columns pattern*

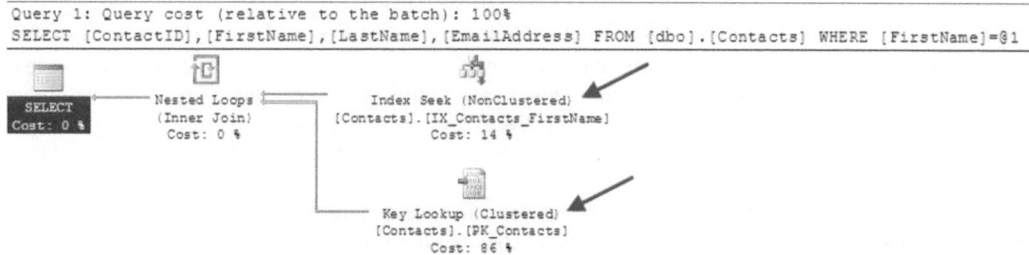

Figure 8-29. *Execution plan for Included Columns pattern*

To improve the performance of this query, another index based on either the Multiple Column or Covering Index patterns could be created. The trouble with these options, though, is that the resulting index would have the same limitations as the queries that they could improve. Instead, a new index based on the Included Column pattern will be created. This new index, shown in Listing 8-22, has FirstName as the key column and includes LastName, IsActive, and EmailAddress as the non-key columns. Even though the IsActive column is not used in the index, it is being included to allow additional flexibility for the index, which a later example in this section will utilize. With the index in place, the performance of the query in Listing 8-22 improves significantly. In this example, the reads drop from the previous 68 per execution to 3 reads (see Figure 8-30). In the execution plan, the key lookup and nested loop are no longer needed; instead there is just the index seek, which is now using the index IX_Contacts_FirstNameINC (see Figure 8-31).

Listing 8-22. Included Columns Pattern

```
CREATE INDEX IX_Contacts_FirstNameINC ON dbo.Contacts(FirstName)
        INCLUDE (LastName, IsActive, EmailAddress);
GO

SET STATISTICS IO ON;
SELECT ContactID, FirstName, LastName, EmailAddress FROM dbo.Contacts
WHERE FirstName = 'Catherine';
SET STATISTICS IO OFF;
GO
```

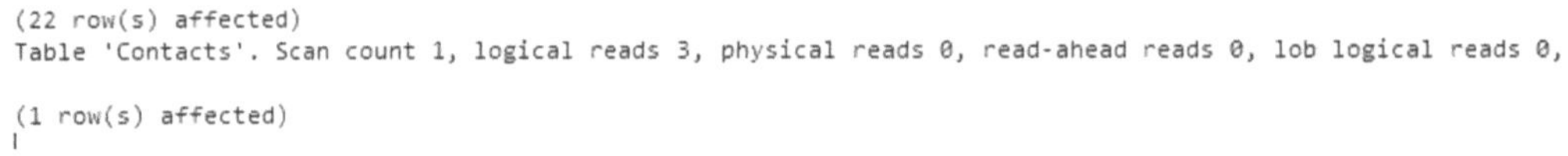

```
(22 row(s) affected)
Table 'Contacts'. Scan count 1, logical reads 3, physical reads 0, read-ahead reads 0, lob logical reads 0,

(1 row(s) affected)
```

Figure 8-30. *Statistics IO results for Included Column pattern*

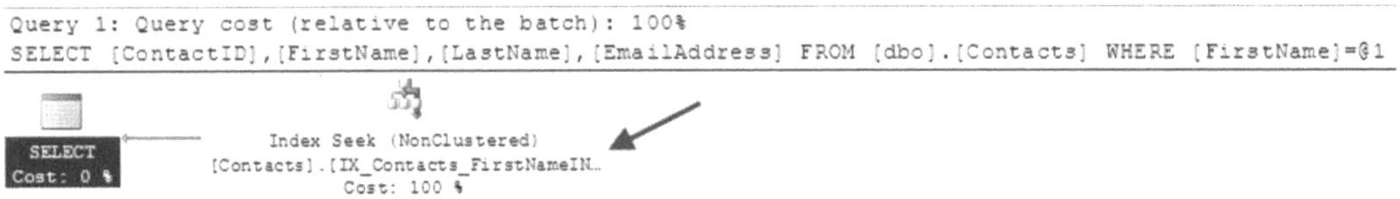

Figure 8-31. *Execution plan for Included Column pattern*

While the number of reads is slightly higher with an index created with the Included Columns pattern, there is flexibility with the index that offsets that difference. With each of the examples in this chapter, a new index has been added to the table dbo.Contacts. At this point, there are six indexes on the table, each serving a different purpose, and four leading with the same column, FirstName. Each of these indexes takes up space and requires maintenance when the data in dbo.Contacts is modified. In active tables, this amount of indexing could have a negative impact on all activity on the table.

The Included Columns pattern can assist with this issue. In cases where there are multiple indexes with the same leading key column, it is possible to consolidate those indexes into a single index using the Included Columns pattern with some of the key columns added to the index instead as non-key columns. To demonstrate, first remove all of the indexes that start with FirstName, except for the one created using the Included Column pattern (script provided in Listing 8-23).

Listing 8-23. Dropping Indexes in Included Columns Pattern

```
IF EXISTS(SELECT * FROM sys.indexes WHERE object_id = OBJECT_ID('dbo.Contacts')
AND name = 'IX_Contacts_FirstNameLastName')
        DROP INDEX IX_Contacts_FirstNameLastName ON dbo.Contacts
GO

IF EXISTS(SELECT * FROM sys.indexes WHERE object_id = OBJECT_ID('dbo.Contacts')
AND name = 'IX_Contacts_FirstNameLastNameIsActive')
        DROP INDEX IX_Contacts_FirstNameLastNameIsActive ON dbo.Contacts
GO
```

```
IF EXISTS(SELECT * FROM sys.indexes WHERE object_id = OBJECT_ID('dbo.Contacts')
AND name = 'IX_Contacts_FirstName')
        DROP INDEX IX_Contacts_FirstName ON dbo.Contacts
GO
```

The dbo.Contact table now has only three indexes on it. There is the clustered index on the ContactID column, a non-clustered index on LastName, and an index on FirstName with the columns LastName, IsActive, and EmailAddress included as data on the index. With these indexes in place, the queries from the previous patterns, shown in Listing 8-24, need to be tested against the table.

There are two points to pay attention to regarding how the queries perform with the Included Column pattern vs. with the other patterns. First, all of the execution plans for the queries, shown in Figure 8-32, are utilizing index seek operations. The seek operation is expected for the query that is just filtering on FirstName, but it can also be used when there is an additional filter on LastName. SQL Server can do this because underneath the index seek it is performing a range scan of the rows that match the first predicate, then removing the LastName results that don't have the value of Cox. The second item to notice is the number of reads for each of the queries, shown in Figure 8-33. The reads increased from two to three. While this constitutes a 50 percent increase in reads, the performance change is not significant enough to justify creating four indexes when one index can adequately provide the needed performance.

Listing 8-24. Other Queries Against Included Columns Pattern

```
SET STATISTICS IO ON
SELECT ContactID, FirstName FROM dbo.Contacts
WHERE FirstName = 'Catherine';

SELECT ContactID, FirstName, LastName FROM dbo.Contacts
WHERE FirstName = 'Catherine'
AND LastName = 'Cox'

SELECT ContactID, FirstName, LastName, IsActive FROM dbo.Contacts
WHERE FirstName = 'Catherine'
AND LastName = 'Cox'
SET STATISTICS IO OFF
```

```
(22 row(s) affected)
Table 'Contacts'. Scan count 1, logical reads 3, physical reads 0, read-ahead reads 0, lob logical reads 0,

(1 row(s) affected)

(1 row(s) affected)
Table 'Contacts'. Scan count 1, logical reads 3, physical reads 0, read-ahead reads 0, lob logical reads 0,

(1 row(s) affected)

(1 row(s) affected)
Table 'Contacts'. Scan count 1, logical reads 3, physical reads 0, read-ahead reads 0, lob logical reads 0,

(1 row(s) affected)
```

Figure 8-32. *Statistics IO results for Included Column pattern*

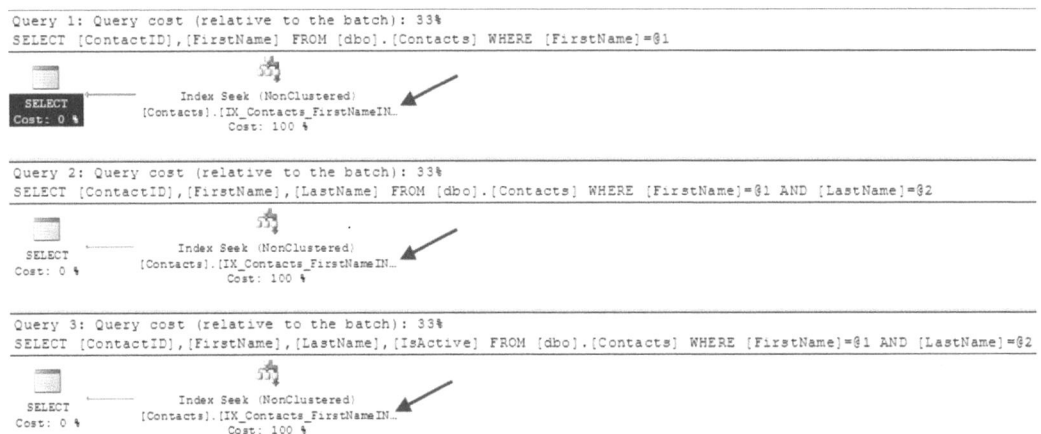

Figure 8-33. *Execution plan for Included Column pattern*

The Included Columns pattern for building non-clustered indexes is an important pattern to utilize when creating indexes. When used with specific queries that result in lookup operations, it provides improved read and execution performance. It also provides opportunities to consolidate similar queries to reduce the number of indexes on the table while still providing performance improvements over situations where the indexes do not exist.

Filtered Indexes

In some tables in your databases, there are rows with certain values that will rarely, or never, be returned in resultset as a part of the applications using the databases. In these cases, it might be beneficial to remove the rows as an option to be returned by the resultset. In some other situations, it may be useful to identify a subset of data in a table and create indexes. Instead of querying across millions or billions of records in the table, you can utilize indexes that cover the hundreds or thousands of rows that the query needs to return results. Both of these situations identify scenarios where using the Filtered Indexes pattern can help improve performance.

The Filtered Indexes pattern utilizes, as the name suggests, the filtered index feature that was introduced with SQL Server 2005. When using filtered indexes, a WHERE clause is added to a non-clustered index to reduce the rows that are contained within the index. By only including rows that match the filter of the WHERE clause, the query engine only has to consider those rows in building an execution plan; moreover, the cost of scanning a range of rows is less expensive than if all of the rows were included in the index.

To illustrate the value in using filtered indexes, consider a scenario where only a small subset of the table has values in the column that is being filtered. Listing 8-25 considers variations of a query. In the first version, the rows where CertificationDate has a value are returned. The second version returns only rows that have a CertificationDate between January 1, 2005 and February 1, 2005. With both of these queries, there is no index on the table that will provide an optimal plan for execution since all 2,866 pages of the index are accessed during execution (see Figure 8-34). Examining both execution plans (Figure 8-35) shows that a clustered index scan of dbo.Contacts is utilized to find the rows that match the CertificationDate predicate. An index on the CertificationDate column could, as the Missing Index hint suggests, improve the performance of the query.

Listing 8-25. Filtered Index Pattern

```
SET STATISTICS IO ON
SELECT ContactID, FirstName, LastName, CertificationDate
```

```
FROM dbo.Contacts
WHERE CertificationDate IS NOT NULL
ORDER BY CertificationDate

SELECT ContactID, FirstName, LastName, CertificationDate
FROM dbo.Contacts
WHERE CertificationDate BETWEEN '20050101' AND '20050201'
ORDER BY CertificationDate
SET STATISTICS IO OFF
```

```
(1 row(s) affected)

(10 row(s) affected)
Table 'Contacts'. Scan count 1, logical reads 2866, physical reads 0, read-ahead reads 0, lob logical reads 0,

(1 row(s) affected)

(2 row(s) affected)
Table 'Contacts'. Scan count 1, logical reads 2866, physical reads 0, read-ahead reads 0, lob logical reads 0,

(1 row(s) affected)
```

***Figure 8-34.** Statistics IO results for Filtered Index pattern*

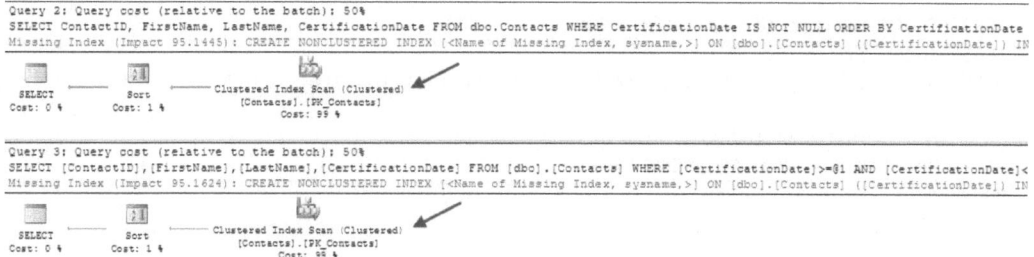

***Figure 8-35.** Execution plan for Filtered Index pattern*

Before applying the Missing Index suggestion, you should consider how the index will be use in this and future queries. In this scenario, assume that there will never be a query that uses CertificationDate when the value is NULL. Does it make sense then to store the empty values for all of the NULL rows in the index? Given the stated assumption, it doesn't make sense, thus doing so would waste space in the database and potentially lead to execution plans that were not optimal if the index on CertificationDate was skipped because the reads for a scan were high enough that other indexes were selected.

In this scenario, it makes sense to filter the rows in the index. To do so, the index is created like any other index, except that a WHERE clause is added to the index (see Listing 8-26). When creating filtered indexes, there are a few things to keep in mind about the WHERE clause. To start with, the WHERE clause must be deterministic. It can't change over time depending on the results of functions within the clause. For instance, the GETDATE()function can't be used since the value returned changes every millisecond. The second restriction is that only simple comparison logic is allowed. This means that the BETWEEN and LIKE comparisons can't be used. For more information on the restrictions and limitations with filtered indexes, refer to Chapter 2.

Executing the CertificationDate queries from Listing 8-26 shows that the filtered index provides a significant impact on the performance for the query. In regards to the reads incurred, there are now only 2 reads as opposed to the 2,866 reads before the index was applied (see Figure 8-36). Also, the execution plans now use index seeks for both queries instead of the clustered index scans, as shown in Figure 8-37. While these results are to be expected, the other consideration with the index is that the new index is only comprised of two pages. As you can see in Figure 8-38, the number of pages required for the entire index is substantially less that the clustered index and the other non-clustered indexes.

Listing 8-26. Filtered Index Pattern

```
USE AdventureWorks2012
GO

CREATE INDEX IX_Contacts_CertificationDate ON dbo.Contacts(CertificationDate)
      INCLUDE (FirstName, LastName)
      WHERE CertificationDate IS NOT NULL;

SET STATISTICS IO ON
SELECT ContactID, FirstName, LastName, CertificationDate
FROM dbo.Contacts
WHERE CertificationDate IS NOT NULL
ORDER BY CertificationDate

SELECT ContactID, FirstName, LastName, CertificationDate
FROM dbo.Contacts
WHERE CertificationDate BETWEEN '20050101' AND '20050201'
ORDER BY CertificationDate
SET STATISTICS IO OFF

SELECT OBJECT_NAME(object_id) as table_name
      ,CASE index_id
      WHEN INDEXPROPERTY(object_id , 'IX_Contacts_CertificationDate', 'IndexID') THEN 'Filtered
Index'
    WHEN 1 THEN 'Clustered Index'
    ELSE 'Other Indexes' END As index_type
    ,index_id
    ,in_row_data_page_count
    ,in_row_reserved_page_count
    ,in_row_used_page_count
FROM sys.dm_db_partition_stats
WHERE object_id = OBJECT_ID('dbo.Contacts')
```

```
        (10 row(s) affected)
        Table 'Contacts'. Scan count 1, logical reads 2, physical reads 0, read-ahead reads 0, lob logical reads 0,

        (1 row(s) affected)

        (2 row(s) affected)
        Table 'Contacts'. Scan count 1, logical reads 2, physical reads 0, read-ahead reads 0, lob logical reads 0,

        (1 row(s) affected)
```

Figure 8-36. *Statistics IO results for Filtered Index pattern*

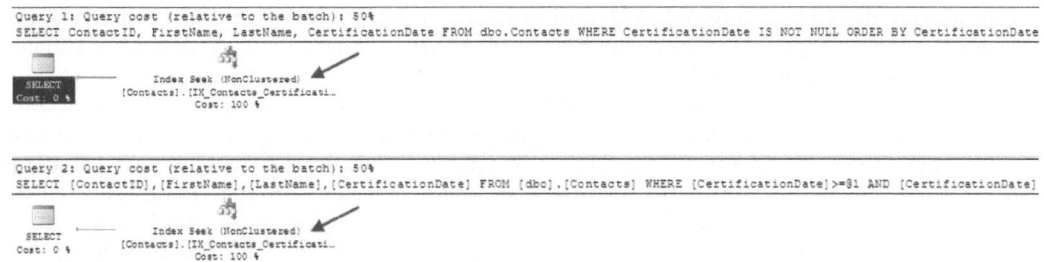

```
Query 1: Query cost (relative to the batch): 50%
SELECT ContactID, FirstName, LastName, CertificationDate FROM dbo.Contacts WHERE CertificationDate IS NOT NULL ORDER BY CertificationDate
```

```
      SELECT            Index Seek (NonClustered)
      Cost: 0 %         [Contacts].[IX_Contacts_Certificati...
                                   Cost: 100 %
```

```
Query 2: Query cost (relative to the batch): 50%
SELECT [ContactID],[FirstName],[LastName],[CertificationDate] FROM [dbo].[Contacts] WHERE [CertificationDate]>=@1 AND [CertificationDate]
```

```
      SELECT            Index Seek (NonClustered)
      Cost: 0 %         [Contacts].[IX_Contacts_Certificati...
                                   Cost: 100 %
```

Figure 8-37. *Execution plan for Filtered Index pattern*

	table_name	index_type	index_id	in_row_data_page_count	in_row_reserved_page_count	in_row_used_page_count
1	Contacts	Clustered Index	1	2854	2873	2866
2	Contacts	Other Indexes	5	63	73	65
3	Contacts	Filtered Index	6	1	2	2
4	Contacts	Other Indexes	8	242	257	244

Figure 8-38. *Page count comparison for filtered index*

Only including a subset of the rows in a table within an index has a number of advantages. One advantage is that the since the index is smaller, there are less pages in the index, which translate directly to lower storage requirements for the database. Along the same lines, if there are fewer pages in the index, there are fewer opportunities for index fragmentation and less effort required to maintain the indexes. The final advantage of filtered indexes relates to performance and plan quality. Since the values in the filtered index are limited, the statistics for the index are limited as well. Since there are fewer pages to traverse in the filtered index, a scan against a filtered index is almost always less of an issue than a scan on the clustered index or heap.

There are a few situations where using the Filtered Index pattern can and should be used when creating indexes. The first situation is when you need to place an index on a column that is configured as sparse. In this case, the expected number of rows that will have the value will be small compared to the total number of rows. One of the benefits of using sparse columns is avoiding the storage costs associated with storing NULL values in these columns. Make certain that the indexes on these columns don't store the NULL values by not using filtered indexes. The second situation is when you need to enforce uniqueness on a column that can have multiple NULL values in it. Creating the filtered index as unique where the key columns are not NULL will bypass the restrictions on uniqueness that allow only a single NULL value in the columns. In this case, you can ensure that social security numbers in a table are unique when they are provided.

The last situation that is a good fit for filtered indexes is when queries need to be run that don't fit the normal index profile for a table. In this case, there might be a query for a one-off report that needs to retrieve a few thousand rows from the database. Instead of running the report and dealing with the potential scan of the clustered index or heap, create filtered indexes that mimic the predicates of the query. This will allow the query to be quickly executed, without having to spend the time building indexes that contain values the query would never have considered.

As this section has detailed, the Filtered Index pattern is one that can be useful in a variety of situations. Be sure to consider it your indexing. Often, when the first use for a filtered index is found, there are others that start appearing and you'll identify situations with selecting and modifying data, as above, that can benefit from its use.

Foreign Keys

The last non-clustered index pattern is the Foreign Key pattern. This is the only pattern that relates directly back to objects in the database design. Foreign keys provide a mechanism to constrain values in one table to the values in rows in another table. This relationship provides referential integrity that is critical in most database deployments. However, foreign keys can sometimes be the cause of performance issues in databases without anyone realizing that they are interfering with performance.

Since foreign keys provide a constraint on the values that are possible for a column, there is a check that is done when the values need to be validated. There are two types of validations that can occur with a foreign key. The first happens on the parent table, dbo.ParentTable, and the second on the child table, dbo.ChildTable (see Figure 8-39). Validations occur on dbo.ParentTable whenever rows are modified in dbo.ChildTable. In these cases, the ParentID value from dbo.ChildTable is validated with a lookup of the value in dbo.ParentTable. Usually, this does not result in a performance issue, since ParentID in dbo.ParentTable will likely be the primary key in the table and also the column upon which the table is clustered. The other validations occur on dbo.ChildTable when there are modifications to dbo.ParentTable. For instance, if one of the rows in dbo.ParentTable were to be deleted, then dbo.ChildTable would need to be checked to see if the ParentID value is being used in that table. This validation is where the Foreign Key pattern needs to be applied.

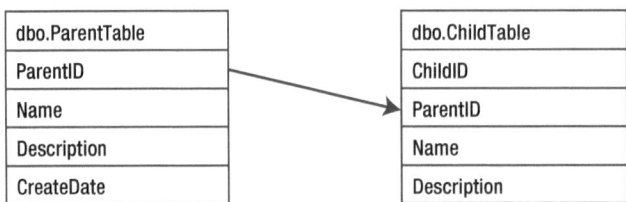

Figure 8-39. Foreign key relationship

To demonstrate the Foreign Key pattern, you will first need a couple tables for the examples. The code in Listing 8-27 builds two tables, dbo.Customer and dbo.SalesOrderHeader. For these tables, a foreign key relationship exists between them on the CustomerID columns. For every dbo.SalesOrderHeader row, there is a customer associated with the row. Conversely, every row in dbo.Customer can relate to one or more rows in dbo.SalesOrderHeader.

Listing 8-27. Setup for Foreign Key Pattern

```
USE AdventureWorks2012
GO

CREATE TABLE dbo.Customer(
      CustomerID int
      ,FillterData char(1000)
      ,CONSTRAINT PK_Customer_CustomerID PRIMARY KEY CLUSTERED (CustomerID)
      );

CREATE TABLE dbo.SalesOrderHeader(
      SalesOrderID int
      ,OrderDate datetime
      ,DueDate datetime
      ,CustomerID int
      ,FillterData char(1000)
      ,CONSTRAINT PK_SalesOrderHeader_SalesOrderID PRIMARY KEY CLUSTERED (SalesOrderID)
      ,CONSTRAINT GK_SalesOrderHeader_CustomerID_FROM_Customer FOREIGN KEY (CustomerID)
REFERENCES dbo.Customer(CustomerID)
      );
```

```
INSERT INTO dbo.Customer (CustomerID)
SELECT CustomerID
FROM Sales.Customer;

INSERT INTO dbo.SalesOrderHeader (SalesOrderID, OrderDate, DueDate, CustomerID)
SELECT SalesOrderID, OrderDate, DueDate, CustomerID
FROM Sales.SalesOrderHeader;
```

In the example, you want to observe what happens in dbo.SalesOrderHeader when a row in dbo.Customer is modified. To demonstrate activity on dbo.Customer, the script in Listing 8-28 executes a DELETE on the table on the row where CustomerID equals 701. This row should have no rows in dbo.SalesOrderHeader. Even though this is the case, the foreign key does require that a check be made to determine whether there are rows in dbo.SalesOrderHeader for that CustomerID. If so, then SQL Server would error on the delete. Since there are no rows in dbo.SalesOrderHeader, the row in dbo.Customer can be deleted.

The execution identifies a couple potential performance problems with the delete. First, with only one row being deleted, there are a total of 4,516 reads (see Figure 8-40). Of the reads, 3 occur on dbo.Customer, while 4,513 occur on dbo.SalesOrderHeader. The reason for this is the Clustered Index Scan that had to occur on dbo.SalesOrderHeader (shown in Figure 8-41). The scan occurred because the only way to check which rows were using Customer equal to 701 is to scan all the rows in the table. There is no index that can provide a faster path to verifying if the value was being used.

Listing 8-28. Foreign Key Pattern

```
SELECT MAX(c.CustomerID)
      FROM dbo.Customer c
      LEFT OUTER JOIN dbo.SalesOrderHeader soh ON c.CustomerID = soh.CustomerID
      WHERE soh.CustomerID IS NULL;

SET STATISTICS IO ON
DELETE FROM dbo.Customer
WHERE CustomerID = 701
SET STATISTICS IO OFF
```

```
Table 'SalesOrderHeader'. Scan count 1, logical reads 4513, physical reads 0, read-ahead reads 0, lob logical reads 0, lob physical
Table 'Customer'. Scan count 0, logical reads 3, physical reads 0, read-ahead reads 0, lob logical reads 0, lob physical reads 0, lo
```

Figure 8-40. Statistics IO results for Foreign Key pattern

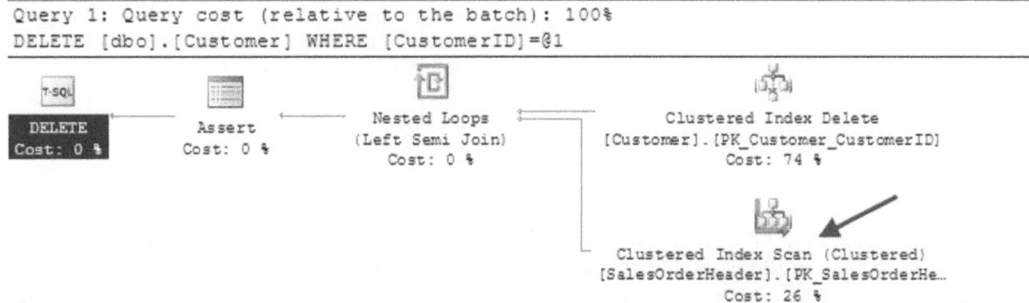

Figure 8-41. Execution plan for Foreign Key pattern

Improving the performance of the DELETE on dbo.Customer can be done simply through the Foreign Key pattern. An index built on dbo.SalesOrderHeader on the CustomerID column will provide a reference point for validation with the next delete operation (see Listing 8-29). Reviewing the execution with the index in place yields quite different results. Instead of 4,513 reads on dbo.SalesOrderHeader, there are now only 2 reads against that table (see Figure 8-42). This change is, of course, due to the index that was created on the CustomerID column (see Figure 8-43). Instead of a clustered index scan, the delete operation can utilize an index seek on dbo.SalesOrderHeader.

Listing 8-29. Foreign Key Pattern

```
CREATE INDEX IS_SalesOrderHeader_CustomerID ON dbo.SalesOrderHeader(CustomerID)
GO

SELECT MAX(c.CustomerID)
    FROM dbo.Customer c
    LEFT OUTER JOIN dbo.SalesOrderHeader soh ON c.CustomerID = soh.CustomerID
    WHERE soh.CustomerID IS NULL;

SET STATISTICS IO ON
DELETE FROM dbo.Customer
WHERE CustomerID = 700
SET STATISTICS IO OFF
```

```
Table 'SalesOrderHeader'. Scan count 1, logical reads 2, physical reads 0, read-ahead reads 0, lob logical reads 0,
Table 'Customer'. Scan count 0, logical reads 3, physical reads 0, read-ahead reads 0, lob logical reads 0, lob phys

(1 row(s) affected)
```

Figure 8-42. *Statistics IO results for Foreign Key pattern*

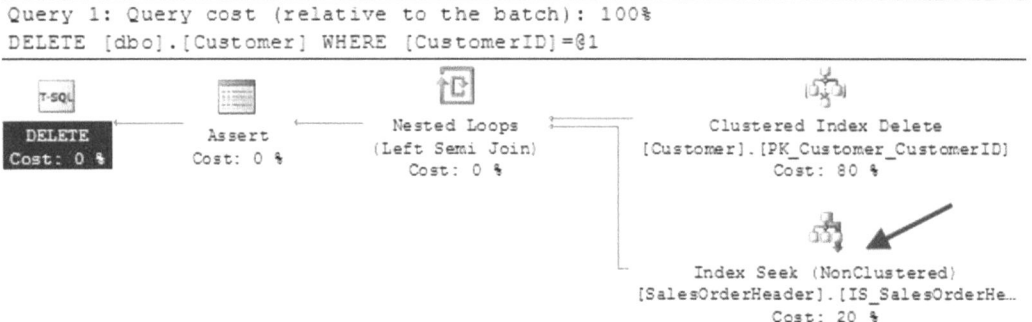

Figure 8-43. *Execution plan for Foreign Key pattern*

The Foreign Key pattern is important to keep in mind with building foreign key relationships between tables. The purpose of those relationships is to validate data, and you need to be certain that the indexes to support that activity are in place. Don't use this pattern as an excuse to remove validation from your databases; instead use it as an opportunity to properly index your databases. If the column needs to be queried to validate and constrain the data, it will likely be accessed by applications when the data needs to be used for other purposes.

ColumnStore Index

As the size of databases has grown, there have been more and more situations where clustered and non-clustered indexes don't adequately provide the performance needed for calculating results. This is primarily a pain with large data warehouses, and for this problem the ColumnStore index was introduced in SQL Server 2012. Previous chapters discussed how the ColumnStore utilizes column-based storage vs. row-based storage. This section looks at some guidelines for recognizing when to build a ColumnStore index. After the guidelines, an example implementing a ColumnStore index will be provided.

■ **Note**   The ColumnStore examples in this section utilize the Microsoft Contoso BI Demo Dataset for Retail Industry. This database has a fact table with more than 8 million records. It is available for download at http://www. microsoft.com/download/en/details.aspx?displaylang=en&id=18279.

The key to using ColumnStore indexes is to be able to properly identify the situations where they should be applied. While it could be useful with some OLTP databases to use the ColumnStore index, this is not the target audience. While the performance of the ColumnStore index could be useful in an OLTP database, the restrictions associated with this index type prevents using it in a meaningful way in OLTP databases. The ColumnStore index is primarily designed for use with data warehouses. With the column-wise storage and built-in compression, this index type provides a way to get to the data requested as fast as possible without having to load columns that are not part of the query. Within you data warehouse, ColumnStore indexes are geared towards fact tables vs. dimension tables. ColumnStore indexes really prove their worth when they are used on large tables. The larger the table, the more a ColumnStore index will be able to improve performance over traditional indexes.

When a scenario for using a ColumnStore index is discovered, there are a number of guidelines to remember when building the index. First, the order of the columns in the ColumnStore index does not matter. Each column is stored separate from the other columns, and there are no relationships between them until they are materialized together again during execution. The next thing to remember is that all columns in the table should be included in the ColumnStore index. Since there can be only one ColumnStore index on a table, everything needs to be included in order for all of the columns to leverage the index.

As mentioned in previous chapters, there are a number of limitations regarding the use of ColumnStore indexes. The main limitation of this index type is the restriction on data modifications on the index. All ColumnStore indexes are read-only, and any table or partition that has a ColumnStore index built upon it will be placed in a read-only state. Another limitation of the ColumnStore index is length of time that it takes to create the index. In many cases, it takes 4-5 times longer to create a ColumnStore index than it does to build a regular non-clustered index. For more information on ColumnStore indexes, see Chapter 2.

Before demonstrating the ColumnStore index, let's look at a demonstration of a query against a data warehouse with traditional indexing. In Listing 8-30, the query is summarizing `SalesQuantity` values by `CalendarQuarter` and `ProductCategoryName`. Executing the query does not take a substantial amount of time; Figure 8-44 shows an elapsed time of 3.5 seconds, with a little less than 20,000 reads. The results are reasonable for the current volume of records, but consider if the table had 10 or 100 times as many rows. At what point would the 3.5 seconds of execution grow outside acceptable execution time?

■ **Note**   Due to the size of the execution plans, they are not being included in the ColumnStore index examples.

Listing 8-30. ColumnStore Index

```
USE ContosoRetailDW
GO
```

```
SET STATISTICS IO ON
SET STATISTICS TIME ON
SELECT dd.CalendarQuarter
      ,dpc.ProductCategoryName
      ,COUNT(*) As TotalRows
      ,SUM(SalesQuantity) AS TotalSales
FROM dbo.FactSales fs
      INNER JOIN dbo.DimDate dd ON fs.DateKey = dd.Datekey
      INNER JOIN dbo.DimProduct dp ON fs.ProductKey = dp.ProductKey
      INNER JOIN dbo.DimProductSubcategory dps ON dp.ProductSubcategoryKey = dps.
ProductSubcategoryKey
      INNER JOIN dbo.DimProductCategory dpc ON dps.ProductCategoryKey = dpc.ProductCategoryKey
GROUP BY dd.CalendarQuarter
      ,dpc.ProductCategoryName
SET STATISTICS IO OFF
SET STATISTICS TIME OFF
```

```
(96 row(s) affected)
Table 'DimDate'. Scan count 5, logical reads 334, physical reads 0, read-ahead reads 0, lob logical reads 0, lob physical
Table 'DimProductCategory'. Scan count 0, logical reads 88, physical reads 0, read-ahead reads 0, lob logical reads 0, lob
Table 'DimProductSubcategory'. Scan count 1, logical reads 3, physical reads 0, read-ahead reads 0, lob logical reads 0, 1
Table 'Worktable'. Scan count 0, logical reads 0, physical reads 0, read-ahead reads 0, lob logical reads 0, lob physical
Table 'DimProduct'. Scan count 5, logical reads 370, physical reads 0, read-ahead reads 0, lob logical reads 0, lob physic
Table 'FactSales'. Scan count 5, logical reads 19056, physical reads 0, read-ahead reads 0, lob logical reads 0, lob physi
Table 'Worktable'. Scan count 0, logical reads 0, physical reads 0, read-ahead reads 0, lob logical reads 0, lob physical

SQL Server Execution Times:
   CPU time = 10627 ms,  elapsed time = 3571 ms.

SQL Server Execution Times:
   CPU time = 0 ms,  elapsed time = 0 ms.
```

Figure 8-44. *Statistics IO results for ColumnStore*

To test the performance with a ColumnStore index on dbo.FactSales, let's add a new index to the table. As stated in the guidelines in this section, all of the columns in dbo.FactSales are added to the ColumnStore index, showing in Listing 8-31. With the index in place, the performance of the query changes dramatically. From a timing perspective, the query completes in 424ms, shown in Figure 8-45, which is an improvement of over eight times the performance without the ColumnStore index.

One item of peculiarity is the number of reads reported from the execution. STATISTICS IO reports that there are no reads performed on dbo.FactSales. This is incorrect; there are reads on dbo.FactSales. Currently, STATISTICS IO does not provide any results for the ColumnStore index and this is by design for SQL Server 2012. To obtain the reads for the query, you can use SQL Profiler. In this example, the Profiler reports that the number of reads for the query is 3,643, which is five times less than with traditional indexing.

Listing 8-31. ColumnStore Index

```
USE ContosoRetailDW
GO

CREATE COLUMNSTORE INDEX IX_FactSales_CStore ON dbo.FactSales (
    SalesKey, DateKey, channelKey, StoreKey, ProductKey, PromotionKey, CurrencyKey, UnitCost,
UnitPrice,
    SalesQuantity, ReturnQuantity, ReturnAmount, DiscountQuantity, DiscountAmount, TotalCost,
SalesAmount,
```

```
        ETLLoadID, LoadDate, UpdateDate)
GO

SET STATISTICS IO ON
SET STATISTICS TIME ON
SELECT dd.CalendarQuarter
        ,dpc.ProductCategoryName
        , COUNT(*) As TotalRows
        ,SUM(SalesQuantity) AS TotalSales
FROM dbo.FactSales fs
        INNER JOIN dbo.DimDate dd ON fs.DateKey = dd.Datekey
        INNER JOIN dbo.DimProduct dp ON fs.ProductKey = dp.ProductKey
        INNER JOIN dbo.DimProductSubcategory dps ON dp.ProductSubcategoryKey = dps.
ProductSubcategoryKey
        INNER JOIN dbo.DimProductCategory dpc ON dps.ProductCategoryKey = dpc.ProductCategoryKey
GROUP BY dd.CalendarQuarter
        ,dpc.ProductCategoryName
SET STATISTICS IO OFF
SET STATISTICS TIME OFF
```

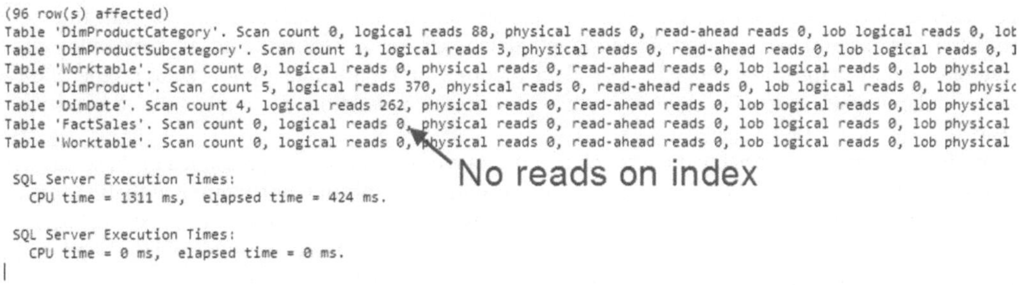

```
(96 row(s) affected)
Table 'DimProductCategory'. Scan count 0, logical reads 88, physical reads 0, read-ahead reads 0, lob logical reads 0, lot
Table 'DimProductSubcategory'. Scan count 1, logical reads 3, physical reads 0, read-ahead reads 0, lob logical reads 0, ]
Table 'Worktable'. Scan count 0, logical reads 0, physical reads 0, read-ahead reads 0, lob logical reads 0, lob physical
Table 'DimProduct'. Scan count 5, logical reads 370, physical reads 0, read-ahead reads 0, lob logical reads 0, lob physic
Table 'DimDate'. Scan count 4, logical reads 262, physical reads 0, read-ahead reads 0, lob logical reads 0, lob physical
Table 'FactSales'. Scan count 0, logical reads 0, physical reads 0, read-ahead reads 0, lob logical reads 0, lob physical
Table 'Worktable'. Scan count 0, logical reads 0, physical reads 0, read-ahead reads 0, lob logical reads 0, lob physical

    SQL Server Execution Times:
        CPU time = 1311 ms,  elapsed time = 424 ms.

    SQL Server Execution Times:
        CPU time = 0 ms,  elapsed time = 0 ms.
```

No reads on index

Figure 8-45. Statistics IO results for ColumnStore index

While new to SQL Server, ColumnStore indexes are a significant improvement in the way in which data warehouses are indexed. These performance improvements also open opportunities to scale the databases even further. Scenarios where only millions of rows are able to be summarized in results will now be able to scale to billions of rows.

Index Storage Strategies

The strategies in the chapter up to this point have primarily focused on improving the performance queries using indexes through the key and non-key column design of the index. There are other options that can be used in conjunction to column selection that can be considered in the design of indexes. These alternative strategies all relate to the way in which indexes are stored in the database.

There are two options available for addressing how an index stores its data. The basic premise for both of these options is that the smaller the index, the fewer pages that it will contain and the fewer reads and writes that will be required when querying the data. The first option available is row compression and the second is page compression. Both of these options provide the potential for substantial storage savings and performance improvements.

■ **Note**   The use of row and page compression is limited to SQL Server 2012 Enterprise Edition.

Row Compression

The first way to reduce the size of an index is by reducing the size of the row in the index. Row compression achieves this by altering the way in which data is stored in a row. Row compression can be used on heaps or clustered and non-clustered indexes. There are a few things that occur on a row when row compression is enabled. These are

- Modification of the metadata for the row.

- Fixed-length character data is stored in a variable length format.

- Numeric-based data types are stored in variable length format.

With the metadata changes, the information stored for each column is generally reduced compared to a non-row compression record. Excessive bits in the row overhead are removed and the information is streamlined to reduce waste. There is an exception to this change, though: some of the changes to fixed-length data types may result in a larger row overhead to accommodate for the additional information required for data length and offset values.

For fixed-length character data, white space is removed from the end of values in the column. This information is not lost and the behavior of fixed-length data types, such as char and nchar, are unaffected. The difference is only in the manner in which the data is stored. For binary data, trailing zeros on the value are removed, similar to white space. Information on the characters removed from a column is stored in the row overhead.

Numeric data types are probably the most changed data types with row compression. For these data types, the data type is stored in the smallest form possible for the data type. This means a column with the bigint data type, which typically requires 8 bytes, would only require 1 byte if the value stored is between 0 and 255. At the value 256, the column would then store the value in 2 bytes. This progression continues until the need to store the value in 8 bytes is reached. This applies to all of the numeric-based data types, which include smallint, int, bigint, decimal, numeric, smallmoney, money, float, real, datetime, datetime2, datetimeoffset, and timestamp.

To demonstrate, you first need a table on which to implement compression and this is provided in Listing 8-32. This script creates two tables, dbo.NoCompression and dbo.RowCompression. Let's use these tables to demonstrate the effect of row compression on the size of the table, through the clustered index, and on query performance.

Listing 8-32. Setup for Row Compression

```
USE AdventureWorks2012
GO

IF OBJECT_ID('dbo.NoCompression') IS NOT NULL
  DROP TABLE dbo.NoCompression

IF OBJECT_ID('dbo.RowCompression') IS NOT NULL
  DROP TABLE dbo.RowCompression

SELECT SalesOrderID
    ,SalesOrderDetailID
    ,CarrierTrackingNumber
    ,OrderQty
    ,ProductID
```

```
    ,SpecialOfferID
    ,UnitPrice
    ,UnitPriceDiscount
    ,LineTotal
    ,rowguid
    ,ModifiedDate
INTO dbo.NoCompression
FROM Sales.SalesOrderDetail

SELECT SalesOrderID
    ,SalesOrderDetailID
    ,CarrierTrackingNumber
    ,OrderQty
    ,ProductID
    ,SpecialOfferID
    ,UnitPrice
    ,UnitPriceDiscount
    ,LineTotal
    ,rowguid
    ,ModifiedDate
INTO dbo.RowCompression
FROM Sales.SalesOrderDetail
```

Implementation of row compression relies on the use of DATA_COMPRESSION index options on the CREATE or ALTER INDEX statements. Compression can be used on either clustered or non-clustered indexes. For row compression, the ROW option is shown in Listing 8-33. In this example, a clustered index is added to both of the example tables. The impact of using row compression on this table is impressive; there is a reduction of over 33 percent in the number pages required for the clustered index (see Figure 8-46).

Listing 8-33. Implementing Row Compression

```
USE AdventureWorks2012
GO

CREATE CLUSTERED INDEX CLIX_NoCompression ON dbo.NoCompression
    (SalesOrderID, SalesOrderDetailID);

CREATE CLUSTERED INDEX CLIX_RowCompression ON dbo.RowCompression
    (SalesOrderID, SalesOrderDetailID)
  WITH (DATA_COMPRESSION = ROW);

SELECT OBJECT_NAME(object_id) AS table_name
    ,in_row_reserved_page_count
FROM sys.dm_db_partition_stats
WHERE object_id IN (OBJECT_ID('dbo.NoCompression'),OBJECT_ID('dbo.RowCompression'))
```

	table_name	in_row_reserved_page_count
1	NoCompression	1558
2	RowCompression	1014

Figure 8-46. *Row compression output*

Storage isn't the only place where there is an improvement; there is also an improvement in query performance. To demonstrate this benefit, execute the code in Listing 8-34. In this script, two queries are executed against the tables from the previous example. While the business rules for the queries are identical, the same 33 percent reduction in page reads for the table with row compression is realized. By just adding compression to the index, the resources required for the query are reduced and performance is improved without a change to the query design (Figure 8-47).

Listing 8-34. Row Compression Query

```
USE AdventureWorks2012
GO

SET STATISTICS IO ON

SELECT SalesOrderID, SalesOrderDetailID, CarrierTrackingNumber
FROM dbo.NoCompression
WHERE SalesOrderID BETWEEN 51500 AND 52000

SELECT SalesOrderID, SalesOrderDetailID, CarrierTrackingNumber
FROM dbo.RowCompression
WHERE SalesOrderID BETWEEN 51500 AND 52000
```

```
(4569 row(s) affected)
Table 'NoCompression'. Scan count 1, logical reads 66, physical reads 0, read-ahead reads 0, lob logical reads 0,

(4569 row(s) affected)
Table 'RowCompression'. Scan count 1, logical reads 43, physical reads 0, read-ahead reads 0, lob logical reads 0,
```

Figure 8-47. *Row compression query statistics*

There are a number of things that need to be considered when implementing row compression on an index. First, the amount of compression achieved by any use of compression will vary depending on the data types implemented and the data that is being stored. The improvement will, and should be expected to, vary per table and over time. Compression can't be enabled if the maximum possible size of the row exceeds 8060 bytes (including the size of the data and the row overhead). Non-clustered indexes will not inherit the compression settings of the clustered index or heap; this must be specified when the index is created. However, clustered indexes will inherit the compression settings of the heap they are being created on if none is specified.

Row compression is a useful mechanism for altering how indexes are stored. They reduce the size of rows, which has the dual benefit of improving query performance and reducing storage requirements for indexes. The main thing to be concerned with when implementing row compression is the additional overhead associated with its use; this overhead materializes as an increase in CPU utilization.

Page Compression

The other method to reduce the size of an index is by using variable length data types and removing repeating values on a page. SQL Server accomplishes this through the page compression option on indexes. Like row compression, this compression type can be applied to heaps or clustered and non-clustered indexes. There are three components to page compression. These are

- Row compression
- Prefix compression
- Dictionary compression

The row compression component of page compression is identical to the row compression option. Before compressing a page, the row on the page is first compressed.

The next step in page compression is accomplished through prefix compression. Prefix compression scans columns and removes similar values and groups them in the page header. For instance, if a number of columns start with "abc", this value is placed in the page header and the value is replaced in the column with a location identify what values has been replaced. If another column contains the value "abcd", a reference to the "abc" value in the page header is included changing the column value to "0d". This is continued for all columns to remove the most prevalent patterns and reduce the information stored per row of the column

The last step in page compression is the dictionary compression. Through dictionary compression, the values in all columns are checked for repeating values. Continuing the previous example, if there are values in two columns across multiple rows that match the "0d" value, then that value is placed in the page header and a reference to the value is stored in those columns. This is done across the entire page, reducing the repeated prefix compressed values.

For a demonstration of the benefits of page compression, let's expand on the example from the row compression section. To start the example, execute the script in Listing 8-35. This creates the dbo. PageCompression table similar to the tables from the previous example.

Listing 8-35. Setup for Page Compression

```
USE AdventureWorks2012
GO

IF OBJECT_ID('dbo.PageCompression') IS NOT NULL
    DROP TABLE dbo.PageCompression

SELECT SalesOrderID
    ,SalesOrderDetailID
    ,CarrierTrackingNumber
    ,OrderQty
    ,ProductID
    ,SpecialOfferID
    ,UnitPrice
    ,UnitPriceDiscount
    ,LineTotal
    ,rowguid
    ,ModifiedDate
INTO dbo.PageCompression
FROM Sales.SalesOrderDetail
```

Implementing page compression is nearly the same as row compression. Both utilize the DATA_ COMPRESSION option with the use of the PAGE option for page compression. To see the effect of page compression on the tables, execute the code in Listing 8-36. In this example, the effect of page compression has significantly more impact on the table than was observed with row compression. This time the number of pages used by the table decreases by 50 percent, as shown in Figure 8-48.

Listing 8-36. Implementing Page Compression

```
USE AdventureWorks2012
GO

CREATE CLUSTERED INDEX CLIX_PageCompression ON dbo.PageCompression
    (SalesOrderID, SalesOrderDetailID)
    WITH (DATA_COMPRESSION = PAGE);

SELECT OBJECT_NAME(object_id) AS table_name
    ,in_row_reserved_page_count
```

```
FROM sys.dm_db_partition_stats
WHERE object_id IN (OBJECT_ID('dbo.NoCompression'),OBJECT_ID('dbo.PageCompression'))
```

	table_name	in_row_reserved_page_count
1	NoCompression	1558
2	PageCompression	702

Figure 8-48. *Page compression output*

The improvements from page compression are not limited to just storage of the index. These improvement continue on to query the table. Comparing the previous results against dbo.NoCompression to those against dbo. PageCompression (script in Listing 8-37) shows that the savings in reads continues with page compression. In this case, the reads decreased to 29 (see Figure 8-49), which is a more than 50 percent decrease in I/O cost.

Listing 8-37. Page Compression Query

```
USE AdventureWorks2012
GO

SET STATISTICS IO ON

SELECT SalesOrderID, SalesOrderDetailID, CarrierTrackingNumber
FROM dbo.PageCompression
WHERE SalesOrderID BETWEEN 51500 AND 52000
```

```
(4569 row(s) affected)
Table 'PageCompression'. Scan count 1, logical reads 29, physical reads 0, read-ahead reads 0, lob logical reads 0,
```

Figure 8-49. *Page compression query statistics*

The considerations for page compression are similar in nature to those for row compression with the addition of a few additional items. First, due to the nature in which page compression is implemented, there are times when the SQL Server will decide that the rate of compression for a page is not sufficient to justify the cost of compressing the page. In these cases, SQL Server will attempt to compress the page, but will record a failure of the page compression and store the page without the benefit of page compression over row compression. It is important to monitor the rate in which page compression attempts do not succeed, since they can indicate when there is low value in using page compression on an index. This is discussed further in Chapter 3.

Next, the CPU cost for page compression is much higher than with row compression or without compression. If there are not sufficient CPU resources available, this can lead to other performance issues. Lastly, page compression is not ideal for tables and indexes that expect frequent data modifications. Compressing and uncompressing a page to modify a single row can have a significant impact on CPU.

Both row and page compression can provide substantial cost savings to indexing solutions. Consider both when looking at index designs. Doing so will provide performance improvements in situations where other solutions may not have yielded the desired results.

■ **Note**   Additional considerations related to compression can be found in the Books Online topic "Data Compression" at http://msdn.microsoft.com/en-us/library/cc280449.aspx.

Indexed Views

In many cases, the way in which data is stored in the database does not fully represent the information that the users need to retrieve from the database. To solve this, you can build queries to pull the data that users need together into resultsets that they can more easily consume. In the process of performing these activities, you can aggregate data to provide the results at the level of detail in which users require.

As an example, users may want to see the total amount sold for a product across all of the orders in a database, but without including information on the detail items. In most situations, retrieving this information is not an issue. However, in some cases, performing that aggregation on the fly can create bottlenecks in the database. While indexes can assist in streamlining the aggregations, they sometimes do not provide the needed cost improvement to achieve the required performance.

One possible solution for this issue is to created indexes on a view in the database. The view can be created to provide the summary and aggregations that are required, and an index can be used to materialize the information in the view into an aggregated form. When indexing a view, the results of the query are stored in the database in much the same way as any table is stored. By storing this information ahead of time, queries that use the aggregations in the view can obtain improved response time.

Before looking at how to implement a view, let's first walk through the problem outlined above with retrieving summary information for products. In this case, suppose that there is a need for summary information for all products at the product sub-category level. The query for this, provided in Listing 8-38, would need to provide a sum aggregation of all of the LineTotal OrderQty values and then an average of the UnitPrice. While the number of reads for the query aren't substantially high (see Figure 8-50), suppose that in this database it was considered too high for a query to be released into production. Examining the execution plan, provided in Figure 8-51, you see that while not overly complicated, the plan includes a number of steps and would not be considered a trivial plan.

Listing 8-38. Query Example

```
USE AdventureWorks2012
GO

IF OBJECT_ID('dbo.ProductSubcategorySummary') IS NOT NULL
    DROP VIEW dbo.ProductSubcategorySummary

SET STATISTICS IO ON

SELECT psc.Name
    ,SUM(sod.LineTotal) AS SumLineTotal
    ,SUM(sod.OrderQty) AS SumOrderQty
    ,AVG(sod.UnitPrice) AS AvgUnitPrice
FROM dbo.SalesOrderDetail sod
    INNER JOIN Production.Product p ON sod.ProductID = p.ProductID
    INNER JOIN Production.ProductSubcategory psc ON p.ProductSubcategoryID = psc.
ProductSubcategoryID
GROUP BY psc.Name
ORDER BY psc.Name;
```

```
(35 row(s) affected)
Table 'ProductSubcategory'. Scan count 1, logical reads 2, physical reads 0, read-ahead reads 0, lob logical reads 0, lob physical 
Table 'Worktable'. Scan count 0, logical reads 0, physical reads 0, read-ahead reads 0, lob logical reads 0, lob physical reads 0, 
Table 'SalesOrderDetail'. Scan count 1, logical reads 1513, physical reads 0, read-ahead reads 0, lob logical reads 0, lob physical 
Table 'Product'. Scan count 1, logical reads 15, physical reads 0, read-ahead reads 0, lob logical reads 0, lob physical reads 0, l

(1 row(s) affected)
```

Figure 8-50. *Statistics IO results for Indexed View*

Figure 8-51. *Execution plan for Indexed View*

As mentioned, a solution for this performance problem can be found through creating a view for the query in Listing 8-39 and adding an index to the view. There are a number of things to consider when add indexes to views. Some of the more important considerations are

- All columns in the view must be deterministic.

- The view must be created using the SCHEMA_BINDING view option.

- The clustered index must be created as unique.

- Tables referenced in the view must use two-part naming.

- If aggregating values, the COUNT_BIG() function must be included.

- Some aggregations, such as AVG(), are disallowed in indexed views.

Additional consideration when creating indexed views are included in the Books Online topic Create Indexed Views (http://msdn.microsoft.com/en-us/library/ms191432.aspx).

The first step in creating an indexed view is to create the underlying view. Given the considerations listed, the query in Listing 8-38 cannot be directly turned into a view. The query must be changed to remove the AVG function and include the COUNT_BIG function. While this change removes one of the required data elements from the output, you will be able to calculate that value after indexing the view. Along with that, the view definition must include the WITH SCHEMABINDING option. The end result is the view definition in Listing 8-39. The last step is to create a unique clustered index on the table using the Name column from the Production.ProductSubcategory table.

Listing 8-39. Indexed View

```
USE AdventureWorks2012
GO

CREATE VIEW dbo.ProductSubcategorySummary
WITH SCHEMABINDING
AS
SELECT psc.Name
```

```
    ,SUM(sod.LineTotal) AS SumLineTotal
    ,SUM(sod.OrderQty) AS SumOrderQty
    ,SUM(sod.UnitPrice) AS TotalUnitPrice
    ,COUNT_BIG(*) AS Occurances
FROM dbo.SalesOrderDetail sod
  INNER JOIN Production.Product p ON sod.ProductID = p.ProductID
  INNER JOIN Production.ProductSubcategory psc ON p.ProductSubcategoryID = psc.
ProductSubcategoryID
GROUP BY psc.Name;
GO

CREATE UNIQUE CLUSTERED INDEX CLIX_ProductSubcategorySummary
    ON dbo.ProductSubcategorySummary(Name)
```

With the indexed view in place, the next step is to test how the view performs compared to the original query. Before executing the code in Listing 8-40, first look at the second query that is using the TotalUnitPrice and Occurrances columns to generate AvgUnitPrice. While you can't include the AVG function in the definitions for indexed views, you can arrive at the same results with minimal effort.

After executing the queries in Listing 8-40, you will notice that the queries performed substantially better than in the example in Listing 8-38. Instead of over 1,500 reads, there are only 2 reads required (see Figure 8-52) and the execution plan (Figure 8-53) is quite a bit simpler. Instead of numerous operators, the plan was simplified to three operators.

Listing 8-40. Query the Indexed View

```
USE AdventureWorks2012
GO
SET STATISTICS IO ON

SELECT psc.Name
    ,SUM(sod.LineTotal) AS SumLineTotal
    ,SUM(sod.OrderQty) AS SumOrderQty
    ,AVG(sod.UnitPrice) AS AvgUnitPrice
FROM dbo.SalesOrderDetail sod
  INNER JOIN Production.Product p ON sod.ProductID = p.ProductID
  INNER JOIN Production.ProductSubcategory psc ON p.ProductSubcategoryID = psc.
ProductSubcategoryID
GROUP BY psc.Name
ORDER BY psc.Name;

SELECT Name
    ,SumLineTotal
    ,SumOrderQty
    ,TotalUnitPrice / Occurances AS AvgUnitPrice
FROM dbo.ProductSubcategorySummary
ORDER BY Name;
```

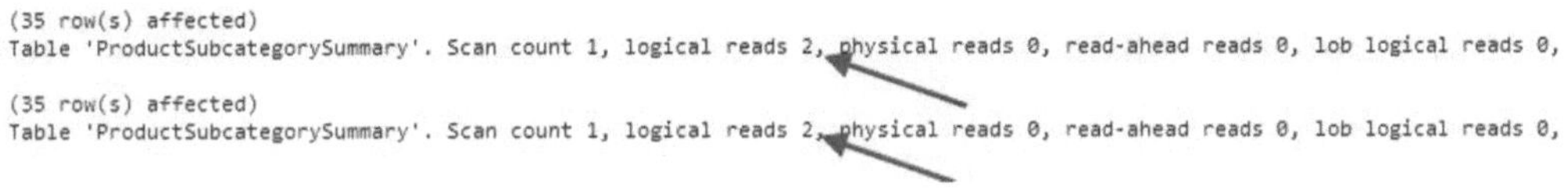

```
        (35 row(s) affected)
        Table 'ProductSubcategorySummary'. Scan count 1, logical reads 2, physical reads 0, read-ahead reads 0, lob logical reads 0,

        (35 row(s) affected)
        Table 'ProductSubcategorySummary'. Scan count 1, logical reads 2, physical reads 0, read-ahead reads 0, lob logical reads 0,
```

Figure 8-52. *Statistics IO results for Indexed View*

```
Query 1: Query cost (relative to the batch): 50%
SELECT psc.Name ,SUM(sod.LineTotal) AS SumLineTotal ,SUM(sod.OrderQty) AS SumOrderQty ,AVG(sod.Unit
```

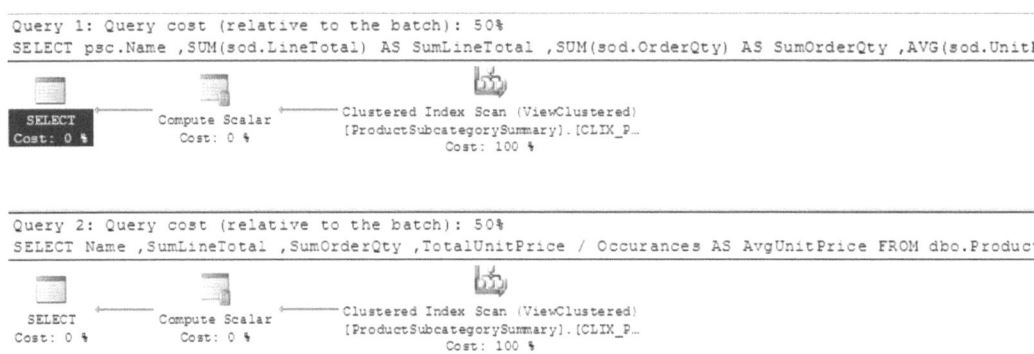

```
Query 2: Query cost (relative to the batch): 50%
SELECT Name ,SumLineTotal ,SumOrderQty ,TotalUnitPrice / Occurances AS AvgUnitPrice FROM dbo.Produc
```

Figure 8-53. *Execution plan for Indexed View pattern*

Another peculiar thing occurred in the execution that you may notice. Both the query against the base tables and the query against the view performed identically after implementing the indexed view. This is one of the added benefits of indexed views. When SQL Server is determining the execution plan for the first query, it is able to deduce that there is an indexed view that can cover the same logic as the query, even though the calculation for the average column is not the same.

Indexed views are an extremely useful tool when multiple tables need to be joined together in a single unit to reduce the IO required to join the data at runtime. While there are a number of restrictions associated with indexed views, there are numerous benefits, including the ability use indexed views in situations like the one in Listing 8-40. When you have view and queries with the same shape that are used frequently, consider whether an include of the view can provide the benefit that indexes on the base tables does not provide.

Summary

This chapter focused on how and when to apply indexes to tables in a number of situations. Each example demonstrated how to apply a particular index pattern to the situation to improve the performance with indexing. The chapter covered the limited, yet valid, instances for using heaps. It then went on to identify the various options and manners for building clustered indexes. With non-clustered indexes, the example demonstrated the options for adding to your clustered indexes to add performance on columns outside of the clustering key. The chapter also included an example of implementing ColumnStore indexes and a discussion on when to apply this type of index. Overall, these patterns provide the groundwork for identifying the types of indexes that are required on tables in databases and they provide the basis for being able to compare and contrast one index to another.

CHAPTER 9

Query Strategies

In the last chapter, you looked at strategies to identify potential indexes for your databases. That, though, is often only half of the story. Once the indexes have been created, you would expect performance within the database to improve, leading you then to the next bottleneck. Unfortunately, coding practices and selectivity can sometimes negatively influence the application of indexes to queries. And sometimes how the database and tables are being accessed will prevent the use of some of the most beneficial indexes in your databases.

This chapter covers a number of querying strategies where indexes may not be used as you may have expected. These scenarios are

- LIKE Comparison

- Concatenation

- Computed Columns

- Scalar Functions

- Data Conversions

In each scenario, you'll look at the circumstances around them and why they don't work as expected. Then you'll see some ways to mitigate the issues and some tips on how to use the right index in the right place. By the end of the chapter, you'll be more prepared to recognize situations that will hamper your ability to index the database for performance, and you'll have the tools to begin mitigating these risks.

LIKE Comparison

When looking at the impact of queries on the use of indexes, the first place to start is with the LIKE comparison. The LIKE comparison allows searches in columns on any single character or pattern. If you need to find all the values in a table that start with the letters "AAA" or "BBB," the LIKE comparison provides this functionality. In these searches, the query can read through the index and find the values that match to the characters or pattern, since the index is sorted. Problems can arise when using this comparison in queries to find values that contain or end with a character or pattern.

In this situation, the sort of the index becomes immaterial because statistics are only collected on the left edge of character values. The likelihood that the letter "B" appears in the first value in the index is equal to it appearing in the last value in the index. In order to determine which records in the table have a "B" in the column, all rows must be checked. There are no statistics available to identify the expected likelihood of occurrences. Without reliable statistics to use, SQL Server will not know what index to use to satisfy a query and may end up using a poor execution plan.

To understand the problems that can occur with the LIKE comparison, you'll walk through a few demonstrations that show the both scenarios and their related statistics. Let's start with querying the Person. Address table for records where AddressLine1 starts with 710(see Listing 9-1). A review of the STATISTICS IO output in Figure 9-1 shows the query required three logical reads. Examining the execution plan in Figure 9-2 shows an index seek on the non-clustered index, which results in three logical reads.

Listing 9-1. Query for Addresses Beginning with 710

```
USE AdventureWorks2012
GO

SET STATISTICS IO ON;

SELECT AddressID, AddressLine1, AddressLine2, City, StateProvinceID, PostalCode
FROM Person.Address
WHERE AddressLine1 LIKE '710%';
```

```
(15 row(s) affected)
Table 'Address'. Scan count 1, logical reads 3, physical reads 0, read-ahead reads 0, lob logical reads 0,

(1 row(s) affected)
```

Figure 9-1. *STATISTICS IO for addresses beginning with 710*

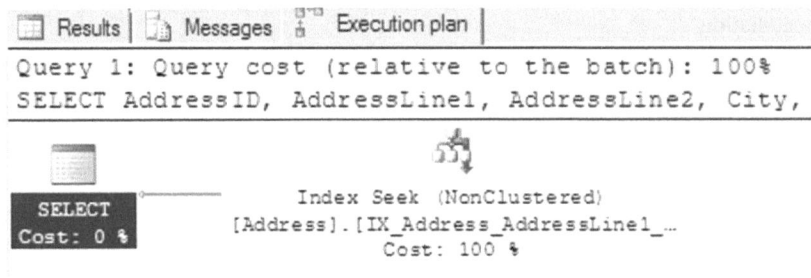

Figure 9-2. *Execution plan for addresses beginning with 710*

In this situation, the LIKE comparison worked well and the execution plan, statistics, and I/O were all appropriate for the request. Unfortunately, as mentioned, this isn't the only manner in which LIKE comparisons can be used. The comparison can be used to find values within a column. Consider a scenario where you need to find all of the addresses that match a specific name of a road, such as "Cynthia" (see Listing 9-2). With this query, the execution plan uses a scan, shown in Figure 9-4, on the non-clustered index and requires 216 logical reads, from Figure 9-3.

Listing 9-2. Query for Addresses Containing "Cynthia"

```
USE AdventureWorks2012
GO

SET STATISTICS IO ON;

SELECT AddressID, AddressLine1, AddressLine2, City, StateProvinceID, PostalCode
FROM Person.Address
WHERE AddressLine1 LIKE '%Cynthia%';
```

```
(6 row(s) affected)
Table 'Address'. Scan count 1, logical reads 216, physical reads 0, read-ahead reads 1, lob logical reads 0,
|
```

Figure 9-3. *STATISTICS IO for addresses containing "Cynthia"*

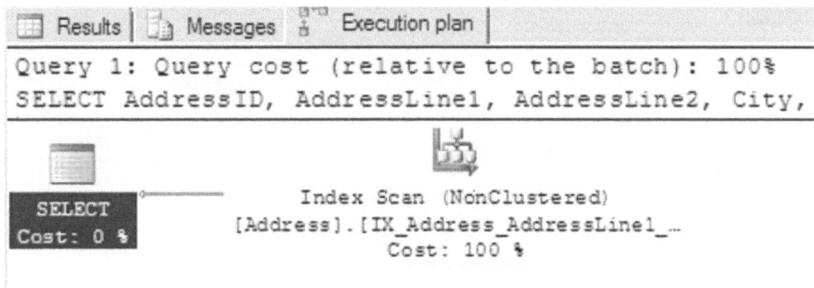

Figure 9-4. *Execution plan for addresses containing "Cynthia"*

In this scenario, the table and index were both small. The difference between an index seek and an index scan was not too extreme. Consider if this scenario was happening in your production system with one of the larger tables in your databases. Instead of being able to quickly filter out records that match the search values, SQL Server is required to look through all rows, which could potentially lead to blocking and deadlocking issues.

A popular method of avoiding this situation is to declare that wildcards are never allowed on the left edge of searches. Unfortunately, this is a fairly unrealistic expectation. There are few business managers in the world that would agree to require their users to enter all possible street number combinations in an attempt to find every address that matched the street name search. Just reading it here sounds silly.

A less popular but much more appropriate and useful solution to this scenario is to create a fulltext index on the table. A contributing factor to fulltext indexes being less popular than non-clustered indexes is due to the difference in building and creating them, which has made them less familiar to most people. With a fulltext index, words within one or more columns are catalogued, along with their position in the table. This enables the query to search quickly for the discrete values within a column value without having to check all the records in an index.

To use a fulltext index on the Person.Address table, a fulltext catalog must first be built, as shown in Listing 9-3. After that, the fulltext index is created and includes the column that will be searched in the queries. Lastly, the query needs to be modified to use one of the fulltext predicate functions. In this example, you will be using the CONTAINS function.

Listing 9-3. Query for Addresses Using CONTAINS

```
USE AdventureWorks2012
GO

SET STATISTICS IO ON;

CREATE FULLTEXT CATALOG ftQueryStrategies AS DEFAULT;

CREATE FULLTEXT INDEX ON Person.Address(AddressLine1)
KEY INDEX PK_Address_AddressID;
GO

SELECT AddressID, AddressLine1, AddressLine2, City, StateProvinceID, PostalCode
FROM Person.Address
WHERE CONTAINS (AddressLine1,'Cynthia');
```

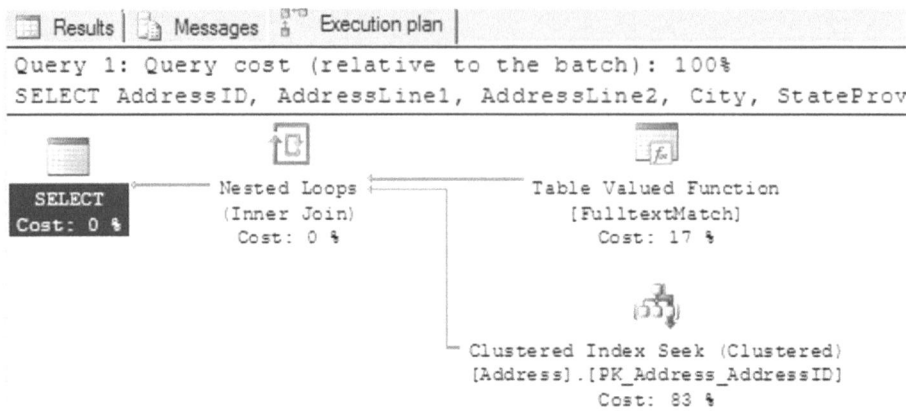

Figure 9-5. *Execution plan for addresses using CONTAINS*

With the fulltext index in place, the performance of the search for streets named Cynthia is similar to the first search where the query was looking for addresses starting with 710. In the execution plan in Figure 9-5, instead of a scan of the non-clustered index, the query is using a seek operation on the clustered index with a table valued function lookup against the fulltext index. As a result, instead of the 216 logical reads when using the LIKE comparison, using the fulltext index only requires 12 logical reads. The difference in reads provides a substantial improvement in performance over the first search attempt.

For more information on fulltext indexes, read Chapter 4.

Concatenation

Another scenario that can wreak havoc on indexing strategies is the use of concatenation. *Concatenation* is when two or more values are appended to one another. When this happens in a WHERE clause, it can often lead to poor performance that wasn't expected.

To demonstrate this scenario, consider a query for someone with the name Gustavo Achong. Searching for this value requires using the FirstName and LastName columns, which are concatenated together with a space between the columns. The query is in Listing 9-4. A script to build and index on these columns is also included in the code listing. The execution plan generated for this query, shown in Figure 9-7, shows that the new index is used but that the index is being scanned instead of a seek operation being used. Even though the leading left edge of the index matches the left side values of the concatenated values, the index is not able to determine where in the index to find the values. This results in the index using 99 logical reads to return the query results, shown in Figure 9-6.

Listing 9-4. Query with Concatenation

```
USE AdventureWorks2012
GO

SET STATISTICS IO ON;

CREATE INDEX IX_PersonContact_FirstNameLastName ON Person.Person (FirstName, LastName)
GO

SELECT BusinessEntityID, FirstName, LastName
FROM Person.Person
WHERE FirstName + ' ' + LastName = 'Gustavo Achong'
```

```
(1 row(s) affected)
Table 'Person'. Scan count 1, logical reads 99, physical reads 0, read-ahead reads 7, lob logical reads 0,
```

Figure 9-6. *STATISTICS IO for concatentation*

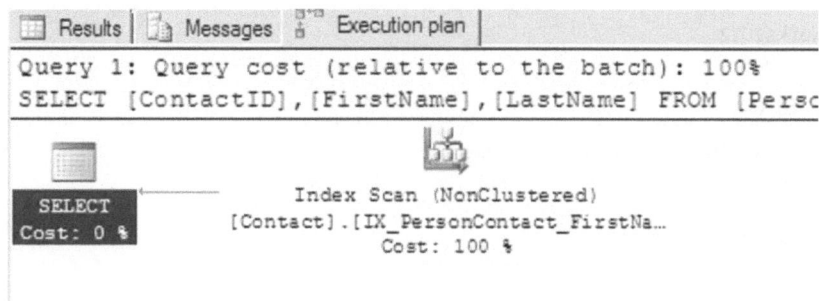

Figure 9-7. *Execution plan for concatentation*

As mentioned, using a scan on the index is not necessarily a bad thing. However, using a scan when there are a lot of concurrent users or data modifications occurring could lead to a performance issue. When it comes to larger tables with millions or more records, this can possibly lead to a lack of scalability for the database.

You might think that removing the space between the first and last name is a good idea (see Listing 9-5). The major issue with this solution is that it doesn't work. As the execution plan in Figure 9-8 shows, it's nearly identical to the one with the space in the concatenated value.

Listing 9-5. Concatenation Without Spaces

```
USE AdventureWorks2012
GO

SET STATISTICS IO ON;

SELECT BusinessEntityID, FirstName, LastName
FROM Person.Person
WHERE FirstName + LastName = 'GustavoAchong';
```

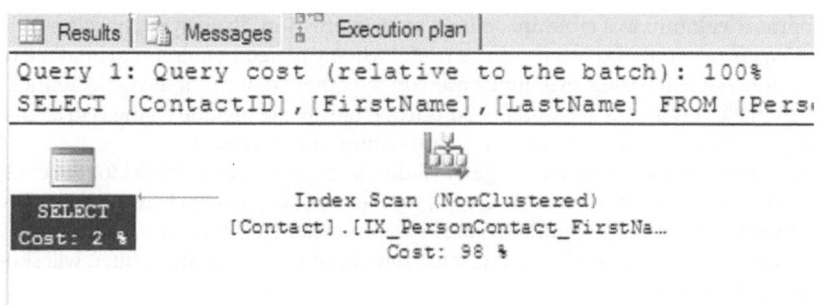

Figure 9-8. *Execution plan for concatenation without spaces*

Probably the best way to fix issues with concatenated values is to remove the need to concatenate. Instead of searching for the value Gustavo Achong, instead search for the first name Gustavo and the last name Achong (see Listing 9-6). When this change is made, the query is then able to use a seek operation on the non-clustered index and return the results with only two logical reads. These results are a definite improvement over when the values were concatenated together. See Figure 9-9 for the execution plan.

Listing 9-6. Query with Concatenation Removed

```
USE AdventureWorks2012
GO

SET STATISTICS IO ON;

SELECT BusinessEntityID, FirstName, LastName
FROM Person.Person
WHERE FirstName = 'Gustavo'
AND LastName = 'Achong';
```

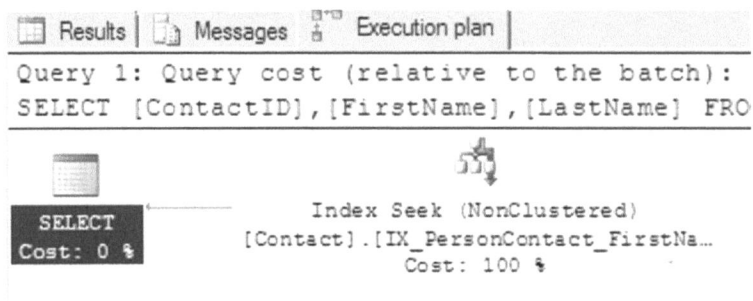

Figure 9-9. *Execution plan with concatenation removed*

At times, you won't have the option to remove concatenation from a query. In these cases, there is another way to resolve index performance issues: the concatenated values can be added to the table as a computed column. This solution, along with some of its issues, is discussed in the next section.

Computed Columns

Sometimes one or more columns in a table are defined as an expression. These types of columns are referred to as *computed columns*. Computed columns can be useful when you need a column to hold the result of a function or calculation that will change over time based on the other columns in the table. Rather than spending the people cycles to make certain that all modifications to a table always include changes to all of the related columns, the components can be changed and the results computed afterwards.

Note that computed columns cannot leverage the indexes on the source columns for the computed column. To demonstrate, add two computed columns to the Person.Person table using Listing 9-7. The first column will concatenate FirstName and LastName together, as they were concatenated in the last section. The second column will multiply ContactID by EmailPromotion; this calculation doesn't mean anything but it will show how this can be used with other calculation types.

Listing 9-7. Add Computed Columns to Person.Person

```
USE AdventureWorks2012
GO

ALTER TABLE Person.Person
ADD FirstLaseName AS (FirstName + ' ' + LastName)
,CalculateValue AS (BusinessEntityID * EmailPromotion);
```

With the columns in place, the next step is to execute a couple of queries against the table. Execute two queries against the table using Listing 9-8. The first query is similar to the first and last name query from the last section (when searching for Gustavo Achong). The second query will return all records with the CalculatedValue of 198.

Listing 9-8. Computed Column Queries

```
USE AdventureWorks2012
GO

SELECT BusinessEntityID, FirstName, LastName, FirstLaseName
FROM Person.Person
WHERE FirstLaseName = 'Gustavo Achong';

SELECT BusinessEntityID, CalculateValue
FROM Person.Person
WHERE CalculateValue = 198;
```

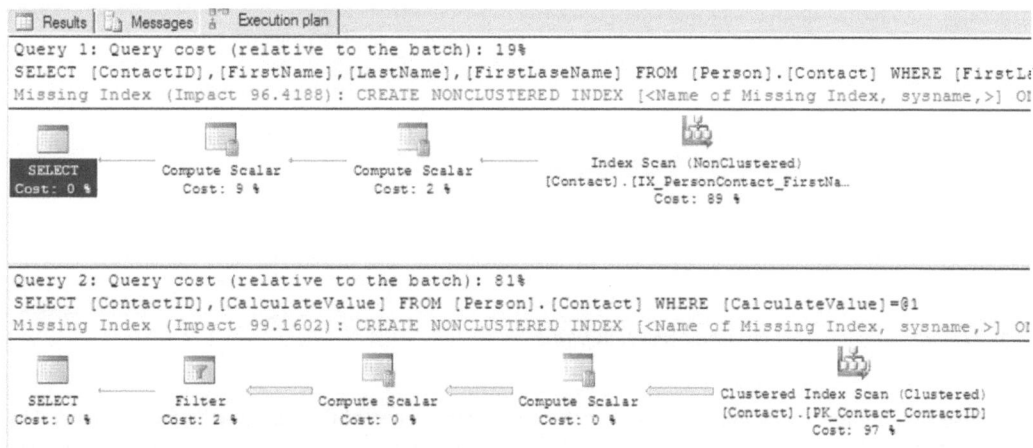

Figure 9-10. Computed column execution plans

After executing both queries, the execution plans in Figure 9-10 show that both used scan operations to return the query results. These results are less than ideal for the same reasons mentioned earlier in this chapter: in some situations they can lead to blocking and utilize more I/O than should be necessary for the query request.

An indexing option available for computed columns is to index the computed columns themselves. As the query for FirstLastName shows, the query can use any of the indexes on the table. The restriction is that they can't use them any better than if the expression for the computed column was in the query itself. Indexing the computed columns, as shown in Listing 9-9, provides the necessary distribution and record information to allow queries, such as those in Listing 9-8, to use seeks instead of scans. The index materializes the values in the computed column, allowing quick access to the data. The execution plan is shown in Figure 9-11.

■ **Note**   When indexing a computed column, the expression for the column must be deterministic. This means that every time the expression executes with the same variables, it will always return the same results. As an example, using GETDATE() in a computed column expression would not be deterministic.

Listing 9-9. Computed Column Indexes

```
USE AdventureWorks2012
GO

CREATE INDEX IX_PersonPerson_FirstLaseName ON Person.Person(FirstLaseName);
CREATE INDEX IX_PersonPerson_CalculateValue ON Person.Person(CalculateValue);
```

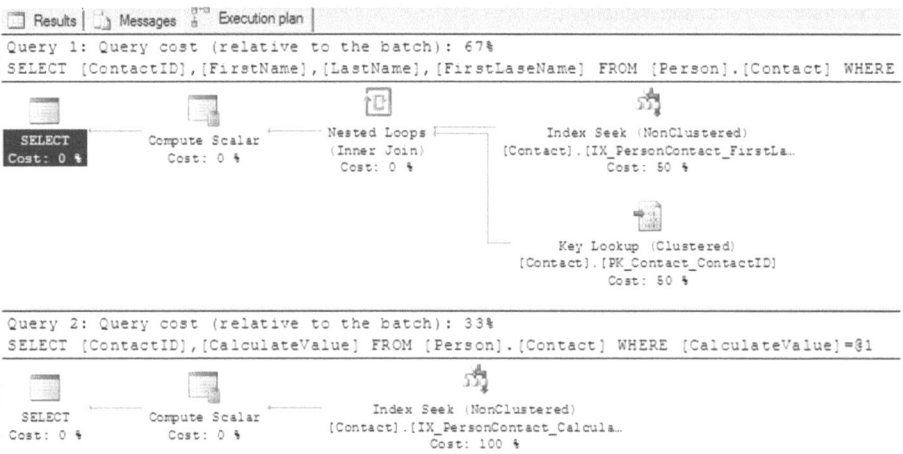

Figure 9-11. Indexed computed column execution plans

As this section demonstrates, computed columns can be extremely useful when expressions are needed to define values as part of a table. For instance, if an application can only send in searches where the first and last name were combined, computed columns can provide the data in the format that the application is sending. The columns can use underlying indexes to return results but can't use the statistics for those indexes due to the expression in the column definition. To index these types of columns, the computed column itself must be indexed.

Scalar Functions

The last few sections discussed filtering query results by searching within column values or by combining values across columns. This section looks at the effect of scalar functions used in the WHERE clauses of queries. Scalar functions provide the ability to transform values to other values that can be more useful than the original value when querying the database.

There are numerous scalar functions within SQL Server that allow modifications of dates (DATEADD or DATEDIFF) to string functions to extract portions of character date (SUBSTRING or LTRIM) to mathematical functions (CEILING and FLOOR). These are just a few of the scalar functions that are available within SQL Server. User-defined scalar functions can also be created and used in WHERE clause. The trouble with both system and user-defined scalar functions is that they change the values in the index to something other than what was indexed by SQL Server. Because the values of the calculations are not known until runtime, the Query Optimizer does not have statistics to determine the frequency of values in the index or information on where the calculated values are located in the index or table.

To demonstrate the effect of scalar functions on queries, consider the two queries in Listing 9-10 that return information from Person.Person. Both queries will return all rows that have the value Gustavo in the FirstName column. The difference between the two queries is that the second query will use the RTRIM function in the WHERE clause on the FirstName column.

Listing 9-10. Queries on FirstName Gustavo

```
USE AdventureWorks2012
GO

SELECT BusinessEntityID, FirstName, LastName
FROM Person.Person
WHERE FirstName = 'Gustavo';

SELECT BusinessEntityID, FirstName, LastName
FROM Person.Person
WHERE RTRIM(FirstName) = 'Gustavo';
```

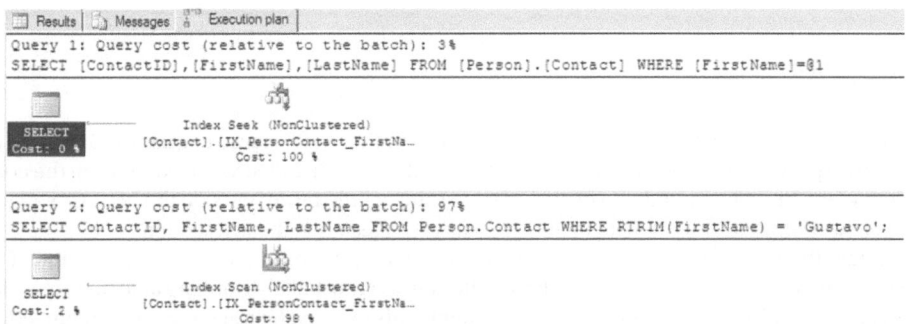

Figure 9-12. *Execution plans for Gustavo queries*

As the execution plan in Figure 9-12 shows, when the scalar function is added to the WHERE clause, the execution plan utilizes an index scan instead of an index seek. In this example, just excluding the scalar function, as in the first query, can provide the same results as with the function in place. That won't be the case for all queries, but the way to allow indexes to be best used is to move the scalar function from the key columns to the parameters of a query.

A good example of how scalar functions can be moved off of key columns and into the parameters is when the functions MONTH and YEAR are used. Suppose a query needs to return all of the sales orders for the year 2001 and for December. This could be accomplished with the first SELECT query in Listing 9-11. Unfortunately, using the MONTH and YEAR functions change the value of OrderDate and the index that was built cannot be used (see the first execution plan in Figure 9-13). This issue can be avoided by changing the query in such a way that, instead of using the functions, you filter against a range of values, such as in the second SELECT statement in Listing 9-11. As the second execution shows, the query is able to return the results with a seek instead of a scan, providing a significant reduction in reads.

Listing 9-11. Queries on FirstName Gustavo

```
USE AdventureWorks2012
GO

CREATE INDEX IX_SalesSalesOrderHeader_OrderDate ON Sales.SalesOrderHeader(OrderDate);

SELECT SalesOrderID, OrderDate
FROM Sales.SalesOrderHeader
WHERE MONTH(OrderDate) = 12
AND YEAR(OrderDate) = 2006;

SELECT SalesOrderID, OrderDate
FROM Sales.SalesOrderHeader
WHERE OrderDate BETWEEN '20061201' AND '20061231';
```

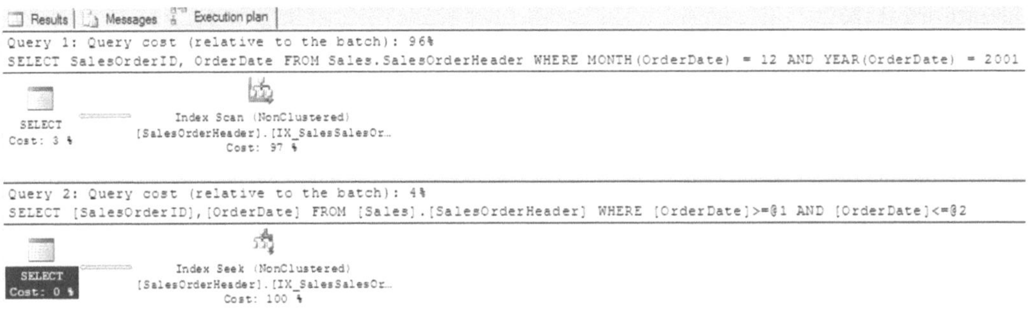

Figure 9-13. *Execution plans for date queries*

It won't always be possible to remove scalar functions from the WHERE clause of queries. One good example of this is if leading spaces were added to a column that should not be included when comparing the column values to parameters. In such a situation, you will need to think a little more "outside the box." One possible solution is to use a computed column with an index on it, as suggested in the last section.

The important thing to remember when dealing with scalar functions in the WHERE clause is that if the function changes the value of a column, any index on the column most likely won't be able to be used for the query. If the table is small and the queries will be infrequent, this may not be a significant problem. For larger systems, this may be the reason behind unexpected high numbers of scans on indexes.

Data Conversion

One last area where queries can negatively affect how indexes are used is when the data types of columns change within a JOIN operation or WHERE clause. When data types don't match in either of those conditions, SQL Server needs to convert the values in the columns to the same data types. If the data conversion is not included in the syntax of the query, SQL Server will attempt the data conversion behind the scenes.

The reason that data conversions can have a negative effect on query performance is along the same lines as the issues related to scalar functions. If a column in an index needs to be changed from varchar to int, the statistics and other information for this index won't be useful in determining the frequency and location of values. For instance, the number 10 and the string "10" would likely be sorted into entirely different positions in the same index.

Listing 9-12. Data Conversion Setup

```
USE AdventureWorks2012
GO

SELECT BusinessEntityID
  ,CAST(FirstName as varchar(50)) as FirstName
  ,CAST(MiddleName as varchar(50)) as MiddleName
  ,CAST(LastName as varchar(50)) as LastName
INTO PersonPerson
FROM Person.Person;

CREATE CLUSTERED INDEX IX_PersonPerson_ContactID ON PersonPerson (BusinessEntityID);

CREATE INDEX IX_PersonContact_FirstName ON PersonPerson(FirstName);
```

To illustrate the effect that data conversions can have on a query, start by executing the code in Listing 9-12. This script will create a table with varchar data in it. It will then add two indexes to the table that will be used in the demonstration queries. The two sample queries, shown in Listing 9-13, will be used to show how data conversions can affect the performance and utilization of an index. For both queries, the RECOMPILE option is being utilized to prevent bad parameter sniffing, which occurs when the option is not being used.

The first SELECT query uses the @FirstName variable with the nvarchar data type. This data type does not match the data type for the column in the table PersonContact, so the column in the table must be converted from varchar to nvarchar. The execution plan for the query (Figure 9-14) shows that the query is using an index seek on the non-clustered index to satisfy the query, and the predicate is converting the data in the column to nvarchar, with a key lookup on the clustered index for the columns not in the non-clustered index. Also note that the cost for the first query is 40 percent of the total batch, which is just the two queries.

Listing 9-13. Implicit Conversion Queries

```
USE AdventureWorks2012
GO
SET STATISTICS IO ON

DECLARE @FirstName nvarchar(100)
SET @FirstName = 'Katherine';

SELECT * FROM PersonPerson
WHERE FirstName = @FirstName
OPTION (RECOMPILE);
GO

DECLARE @FirstName varchar(100)
SET @FirstName = 'Katherine';

SELECT * FROM PersonPerson
WHERE FirstName = @FirstName
```

■ **Note** The additional information shown for the operators in the execution plans is available in the Properties window in SQL Server Management Studio. The Properties windows is full of useful information about the operations from the columns that are used for estimated and actual row counts.

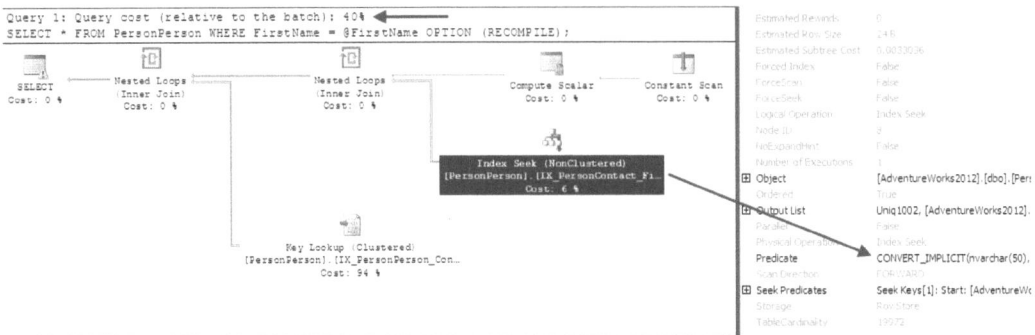

Figure 9-14. *Execution plans with implicit data conversion*

One other item to note in the execution plan in Figure 9-15 is the warning included on the SELECT operation for the first query. With the release of SQL Server 2012 there are now new warning messages included in execution plans that contain implicit conversions. The warning message appears as a yellow triangle with an exclamation point in it. Hovering over the operator will display properties of the operator and the warning message. These messages include information detailing what column is being converted and the issue associated with the problem. In this case, the issue is "CardinalityEstimate." In other words, SQL Server doesn't have statistics necessary to build an execution plan that knows the frequency of the values in the predicate.

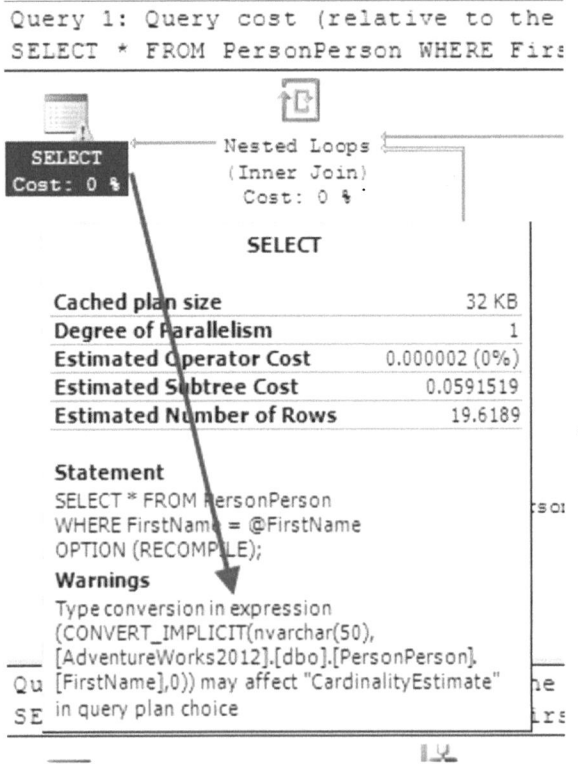

Figure 9-15. *Warning included with implicit conversion*

The second SELECT query in Listing 9-13 uses a variable with a varchar data type. Since this data type already matches the data type of the column in the table, the non-clustered index that can be used. As the execution plan in Figure 9-16 shows, with matching data types the query optimizer can build a plan that knows where the rows in the index are and can perform a seek to obtain them.

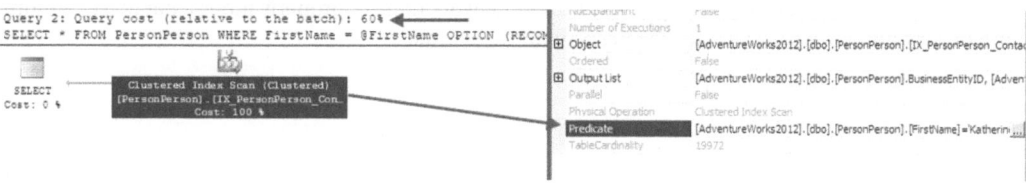

Figure 9-16. Execution plans without data conversion

Interestingly enough, the cost of the second plan is 60 percent of the batch, which should mean that the second plan performed more poorly than the first. This isn't the case, though, as you can see if you review the logical reads from STATISTICS IO, shown in Figure 9-17. For the first query, the number of reads was 201 logical reads. The second query had only 99 reads. The difference in the reads is due to the CardinalityEstimation issue. The execution plan didn't know the frequency from statistics in which "Katherine" would appear in the index. It estimated that there would be far fewer rows that there were, so it built a plan with an index seek and key lookup to return the rows. The operations required to satisfy that plan resulted in more than twice the number of reads than if the entire table was scanned for the value.

```
(99 row(s) affected)
Table 'PersonPerson'. Scan count 1, logical reads 201, physical reads 0, read-ahead reads 0, lob logical reads 0,

(1 row(s) affected)

(99 row(s) affected)
Table 'PersonPerson'. Scan count 1, logical reads 89, physical reads 0, read-ahead reads 0, lob logical reads 0,

(1 row(s) affected)
```

Figure 9-17. STATISTICS IO for implicit conversion queries

In this section, the discussion mostly focused on implicit data conversions. While these can be more silent that explicit data conversions, the same concepts and mitigations apply to these data conversions. Since they are more intentional, they should be less frequent. Even so, when performing data conversions, pay close attention to the data types because how they are changed will impact query performance and index utilization.

Summary

In this chapter, you examined the effect that queries can have on whether indexes can provide the expected performance improvements. There are times when a specific type of index may not be appropriate for a situation, such as searching for values within character values in large tables. In other situations, applying the right type of index or function in the right place can have a significant impact on whether the query can utilize an index.

In many of the examples in this chapter, the offending usage of an index was when it utilized a scan on the index instead of a seek operation. For these scenarios, index seeks were the ideal index operation. This won't always be the case and there are situations where scans against an index are significantly more ideal than seek operations. It's important to remember what type of transactions the environment is geared for and the size of the tables that are being accessed.

The main take-away from this chapter is that you should take care when writing queries. The choices made when developing database code can completely unravel the work done to properly index a database. Be sure to compliment your indexes with code that leverages them to their max.

CHAPTER 10

■ ■ ■

Index Analysis

Throughout this book, we've discussed what indexes are, what they do, patterns for building them, and many other aspects for determining how a SQL Server database should be indexed. All of that information is necessary for the last piece in indexing your databases, which is the process of actually applying indexes. To do this, you need a process for applying that knowledge to determine the indexes that are best for your environment and provide the greatest gain to performance.

In this chapter, we'll discuss a general practice that can be used to build an indexing methodology. We'll look at the steps necessary to manage indexes and provide methods for identifying opportunities and issues with indexes. This methodology can be applied to a single database, server, or your entire SQL Server environment. Regardless of the type of operations or business that the database supports, the same methodology for building indexes can be used.

Indexing Method

Before you can begin creating and dropping indexes, you first need a process to determine what to create and drop. This process needs to provide a way to observe your databases and determine the indexes that are appropriate for your databases. As mentioned in previous chapters, indexing should be more of a science than an art. The information needed to properly index a database is available; through some research, the indexes needed can be identified. Similar to how scientists use the scientific method to prove theories, database administrators can use an Indexing Method to prove what indexes a database requires.

The Indexing Method used in this book is comprised of three phases: Monitor, Analyze, and Implement (see Figure 10-1). Within each component are a number of steps that, when completed, help to provide the appropriate indexing for the database. At the completion of the Implement phase, the Indexing Method restarts the first phase, making indexing a continuous and iterative process.

When starting with the Monitor phase, the primary activity is to observe the indexes. The observations entail reviewing both the performance and behavior of the indexes. SQL Server will use the indexes that it finds most beneficial from those available. By observing this behavior, you can identify the indexes that are most often used and how they are used.

After the observations, the Analyze phase of the Indexing Method begins. In the Analyze phase, the statistics collected in the previous phase are used to determine what indexes are best suited for the database. The goal is to identify what indexes need to be created, dropped, and modified. Along with this, the impacts of any indexing changes are also identified.

The last phase of the Indexing Method is the Implementation phase. In this phase, the indexes from the last phase are applied to the databases. For every database and environment, the implementation path will be different. For instance, the process for deploying indexes on third-party databases differs from applications owned by your company. Within this phase, though, there are core concepts that apply to all environments;

outside of physically building the indexes, you will need to communicate the change plan and possible effects of the change. Then, you need to track the changes over time. There is more to implementing indexes that just executing a CREATE INDEX statement.

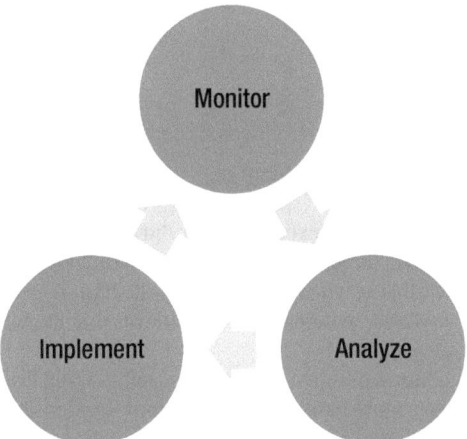

Figure 10-1. Indexing Method cycle

After the last phase completes, the Indexing Method resumes with the first phase. In this way, indexing is a continuous and iterative process. The indexes that provide the best performance today may not be the best indexes for tomorrow. Two events primarily contribute to the need for changing indexes over time. The first is data usage, where the functions and features of applications can change over time, so the purpose of the application can also change. Second, the data population and distribution can, and usually will, change over time. With these changes, indexes may shift out of usage and other data access paths may be required. Data changes aren't the only things that can cause index use to change; the optimization in a future SQL Server version or service pack may change how the optimizer uses indexes.

Now that you know the basics of the Indexing Method, let's begin by walking through each phase and the considerations and actions that should be taken for each. This chapter will provide a number of options for pulling together the proper indexes for your environment. As you learn more about indexing and your databases, you may find other ways to look at performance and usage statistics that provide more, or better informed, guidance.

Monitor

As discussed in the introduction, the first phase of the Indexing Method is to collect information. The goal of this phase is to collect information regarding the indexes in your databases. This information will come from a variety of sources. The sources for monitoring should be familiar, as they are often used with tasks similar to indexing, such as performance tuning. For some sources, the information will be collected over time to provide an idea of general trends. For other sources, a snapshot at a specific point in time is sufficient. It is important to collect information over time to provide a baseline against which to compare performance; this will help you know when changes in indexing are required.

As mentioned, there are a number of sources from which information will be collected during the Monitoring phase. The sources that will be discussed in this chapter are

- Performance Counters

- Dynamic Management Objects

- SQL Trace

For each of these sources, the subsequent sections will describe what is to be collected and provide guidance on how to collect this information. At the end of the section, you will have a framework that is capable of providing the information necessary to start the Analyze phase.

■ **Note**   All of the monitoring information from this chapter will be collected in a database named `IndexingMethod`. The scripts can be run in that database or your own performance monitoring database.

Performance Counters

The first source of monitoring information for indexes is SQL Server performance counters. Performance counters are metrics provided by Microsoft to measure the rate of events or state of resources within applications and hardware on the server. With some of the performance counters, there are some general guidelines that can be used to indicate when a problem with indexing may exist. For the others, changes in the rate or level of the performance counter may indicate a need to change the indexing on a server.

The primary issue with using performance counters is that they represent the server, or SQL Server instance, level state of the counters. They do not indicate at a database or table level where possible indexing issues may be occurring. This level of detail, though, is acceptable and useful when considering the other tools available for monitoring your indexing and identifying potential indexing needs. One advantage to collecting counter information at this level is that you are forced to consider the whole picture and the effect of all of the indexes on performance. In an isolated situation, a couple of poor performing indexes on a tables might be acceptable. However, in conjunction with a few tables with poor indexes, the aggregate performance may reach a tipping point where the indexes need to be addressed. With the server-level statistics provided by performance counters, you will be able to identify when this point has been reached.

There are a large number of performance counters available for both SQL Server and Windows Server. From the perspective of indexing, though, many of the performance counters can be eliminated. The performance counters that are most useful are those that map to operations related to how indexes operate or are accessed, such as forwarded records and index searches. For a definition of the performance counters that are most useful with indexing, see Table 10-1. The reasons for collecting each of the counters will be discussed in the Analyze phase.

There are a number of ways to collect performance counters. For the monitoring in this chapter, you'll use the DMV `sys.dm_os_performance_counters`. This DMV returns a row for all of the SQL Server counters for an instance. The values returned are the raw values for the counters, so depending on the type of counter the value can be a point-in-time state value or an ever accumulating aggregate.

To begin collecting performance counter information for monitoring, you'll first need to create a table for storing this information. The table definition in Listing 10-1 provides for this need. When collecting the performance counters, you will use a table that stores the counter name with the value and then datestamps each row to identify when the information was collected.

Table 10-1. *Index-related Performance Counters*

Option Name	Description
Access Methods\Forwarded Records/sec	Number of records per second fetched through forwarded record pointers.
Access Methods\FreeSpace Scans/sec	Number of scans per second that were initiated to search for free space in which to insert a new record fragment.
Access Methods\Full Scans/sec	Number of unrestricted full scans per second. These can be either base-table or full-index scans.
Access Methods\Index Searches/sec	Number of index searches per second. These are used to start range scans and single index record fetches and to reposition an index.
Access Methods\Page Splits/sec	Number of page splits per second that occur as the result of overflowing index pages.
Buffer Manager\Page Lookups/sec	Number of requests to find a page in the buffer pool.
Locks(*)\Lock Wait Time (ms)	Total wait time (in milliseconds) for locks in the last second.
Locks(*)\Lock Waits/sec	Number of lock requests per second that required the caller to wait.
Locks(*)\Number of Deadlocks/sec	Number of lock requests per second that resulted in a deadlock.
SQL Statistics\ Batch Requests/sec	Number of Transact-SQL command batches received per second.

Listing 10-1. Performance Counter Snapshot Table

```
USE IndexingMethod
GO

CREATE TABLE dbo.IndexingCounters
  (
  counter_id INT IDENTITY(1, 1)
  ,create_date DATETIME
  ,server_name VARCHAR(128) NOT NULL
  ,object_name VARCHAR(128) NOT NULL
  ,counter_name VARCHAR(128) NOT NULL
  ,instance_name VARCHAR(128) NULL
  ,Calculated_Counter_value FLOAT NULL
  ,CONSTRAINT PK_IndexingCounters PRIMARY KEY CLUSTERED (counter_id)
  )
GO

CREATE NONCLUSTERED INDEX IX_IndexingCounters_CounterName
  ON dbo.IndexingCounters (counter_name)
  INCLUDE (create_date,server_name,object_name,Calculated_Counter_value)
```

For the purposes of collecting information for monitoring indexing, you'll take the information from sys.dm_os_performance_counters and calculate the appropriate values from the DMV. These would be the same values that would be available when viewing performance counter information from other tools, such as Performance Monitor. There are a few steps required in order to populate dbo.IndexingCounters. As mentioned, the DMV contains raw counter values. To calculate these values properly, it is necessary to take a snapshot of the values in the DMV and then wait a number of seconds before calculating the counter value. In Listing 10-2, the counter value is calculated after ten seconds. Once the time has expired, the counters are calculated and inserted into the dbo.IndexingCounters tables. This script should be scheduled and executed frequently. Ideally, you should collect this information every one to five minutes.

■ **Note**   Performance counter information can be collected more frequently. For instance, Performance Monitor defaults to every 15 seconds. For the purposes of index monitoring, that frequency is not necessary.

Listing 10-2. Performance Counter Snapshot Script

```
USE IndexingMethod
GO

IF OBJECT_ID('tempdb..#Delta') IS NOT NULL
  DROP TABLE #Delta

SELECT object_name
  ,counter_name
  ,instance_name
  ,cntr_value
INTO #Delta
FROM sys.dm_os_performance_counters opc
WHERE counter_name LIKE '%/sec%'
OR counter_name LIKE '%KB/s%';

WAITFOR DELAY '00:00:10'

INSERT INTO dbo.IndexingCounters
(create_date, server_name, object_name, counter_name, instance_name, Calculated_Counter_value)
SELECT GETDATE()
  ,LEFT(opc.object_name,CHARINDEX(':',opc.object_name)-1)
  ,SUBSTRING(opc.object_name,1+CHARINDEX(':',opc.object_name), LEN(opc.object_name))
  ,opc.counter_name
  ,opc.instance_name
  ,CASE WHEN opc.cntr_type = 537003264
   THEN CONVERT(FLOAT, opc.cntr_value) / coalesce(x.cntr_RatioBaseValue,-1)
   WHEN b.cntr_value IS NOT NULL
   THEN (opc.cntr_value - b.cntr_value)/5.
   ELSE opc.cntr_value -- The values of the other counter types are already calculated.
   END  as Calculated_Counter_value
FROM sys.dm_os_performance_counters opc
  LEFT OUTER JOIN (
  SELECT CASE cntr_value WHEN 0 THEN 1
     ELSE cntr_value END as cntr_RatioBaseValue
    ,SUBSTRING(counter_name, 1, PATINDEX('% Base%', counter_name)) as counter_name_fixed
    ,counter_name
    ,[object_name]
    ,instance_name
    ,cntr_type
  FROM sys.dm_os_performance_counters
  WHERE cntr_type = 1073939712 ) as x
```

```
        ON opc.counter_name = x.counter_name_fixed
        AND opc.[object_name] = x.[object_name]
        AND opc.instance_name = x.instance_name
    LEFT OUTER JOIN #Delta b
     ON opc.counter_name = b.counter_name
    AND opc.object_name = b.object_name
    AND opc.instance_name = b.instance_name
WHERE opc.cntr_type <> 1073939712
AND ((opc.[object_name] LIKE '%Access Methods%'
    AND (opc.counter_name LIKE '%Forwarded Records/sec';
    OR opc.counter_name LIKE '%FreeSpace Scans/sec%'
    OR opc.counter_name LIKE '%Full Scans/sec%'
    OR opc.counter_name LIKE '%Index Searches/sec%'
    OR opc.counter_name LIKE '%Page Splits/sec%'))
OR (opc.[object_name] LIKE '%Buffer Manager%'
    AND (opc.counter_name LIKE '%Page life expectancy%'
    OR opc.counter_name LIKE '%Page lookups/sec%'))
OR (opc.[object_name] LIKE '%Locks%'
    AND (opc.counter_name LIKE '%Lock Wait Time (ms)%'
    OR opc.counter_name LIKE '%Lock Waits/sec%'
    OR opc.counter_name LIKE '%Number of Deadlocks/sec%'))
OR (opc.[object_name] LIKE '%SQL Statistics%'
    AND opc.counter_name LIKE '%Batch Requests/sec%'))
```

The first time you collect performance counters for your indexes, you won't be able to compare the counters to other reasonable values for your SQL Server. As time goes on, though, you can retain previous performance counter samples to make comparisons. As part of monitoring, you will be responsible for identifying periods in which values for the performance counters represent the typical activity for your environment. To store these values, insert them into a table similar to the one in Listing 10-3. This table has start and end dates to indicate the range that the baseline represents. Also, there are minimum, maximum, average, and standard deviation columns to store values from the collected counters. The minimum and maximum values allow you to understand the range in which the performance counters vary. The average value provides an idea of what the counter value will be when it is "good." The standard deviation allows you to understand the variability of the counter values. The lower the number, the more frequently the counter values cluster around the average value. Higher values is indicate that the counter values vary more frequently and are often nearer to the minimum and maximum values.

Listing 10-3. Performance Counter Baseline Table

```
USE IndexingMethod
GO

CREATE TABLE dbo.IndexingCountersBaseline
  (
  counter_baseline_id INT IDENTITY(1, 1)
  ,start_date DATETIME
  ,end_date DATETIME
  ,server_name VARCHAR(128) NOT NULL
  ,object_name VARCHAR(128) NOT NULL
  ,counter_name VARCHAR(128) NOT NULL
  ,instance_name VARCHAR(128) NULL
  ,minimum_counter_value FLOAT NULL
```

```
    ,maximum_counter_value FLOAT NULL
    ,average_counter_value FLOAT NULL
    ,standard_deviation_counter_value FLOAT NULL
    ,CONSTRAINT PK_IndexingCountersBaseline
      PRIMARY KEY CLUSTERED (counter_baseline_id)
    )
GO
```

When populating the values into dbo.IndexingCountersBaseline, there are two steps to the population process. First, you need to collect a sample from the performance counters that represents a typical week. If there are no typical weeks, pick this week and collect samples for it. Once you have the typical week, the next step is to aggregate the information into the baseline table. Aggregating the information is a matter of summarizing the information in the table dbo.IndexingCounters for a range of days. In Listing 10-4, the data is from March 1 to March 15, 2012. The next step is to validate the baseline. Just because the average for the past week states that Forwarded Records/sec are at 100 doesn't mean that value is good for your baseline. Use your experience with your servers and databases to influence the values in the baseline. Make adjustments to the baseline as needed if there is a recent trend below or above what is normal.

Listing 10-4. Populate Counter Baseline Table

```
USE IndexingMethod
GO

DECLARE @StartDate DATETIME = '20120301'
  ,@EndDate DATETIME = '20120325'

INSERT INTO dbo.IndexingCountersBaseline
    (
    start_date
    ,end_date
    ,server_name
    ,object_name
    ,counter_name
    ,instance_name
    ,minimum_counter_value
    ,maximum_counter_value
    ,average_counter_value
    ,standard_deviation_counter_value
    )
    SELECT MIN(create_date)
        ,MAX(create_date)
        ,server_name
        ,object_name
        ,counter_name
        ,instance_name
        ,MIN(calculated_Counter_value)
        ,MAX(calculated_Counter_value)
        ,AVG(calculated_Counter_value)
        ,STDEV(calculated_Counter_value)
    FROM  dbo.IndexingCounters
    WHERE create_date BETWEEN @StartDate AND @EndDate
```

```
GROUP BY server_name
    ,object_name
    ,counter_name
    ,instance_name
```

There are other ways to collect and view performance counters for your SQL Server instances. The Windows application Performance Monitor can be used to view performance counters in real time. It can also be used to log performance counters to a binary or text file. The command-line utility Logman can be used to interact with Performance Monitor to create data collectors, and start and stop them as needed. Also, PowerShell is a possibility for assisting in the collection of performance counters.

All of these alternatives are valid options for collecting performance counters on your databases and indexes. The key is that if you want to monitor your indexes, you must collect the information necessary to know when potential indexing issues may arise. Pick a tool that you are comfortable with and start collecting these counters today.

Dynamic Management Objects

Some of the best indexing performance information for monitoring indexing are included in Dynamic Management Objects (DMOs). The DMOs contain information on logical and physical uses for the indexes and overall physical structure. For monitoring, there are four DMOs that provide information on the usage of the indexes: `sys.dm_db_index_usage_stats`, `sys.dm_db_index_operational_stats`, `sys.dm_db_index_physical_stats`, and `sys.dm_os_wait_stats`. In this section, you'll walk through a process to monitor your indexes using each of these DMOs.

The first three following sections will discuss the sys.dm_db_index_* DMOs. These were previously discussed in Chapter 3 where the contents of the DMOs were defined and demonstrated. One thing to remember with these DMOs is that they can be flushed through various operations on the server, such as restarting the service or re-creating the index. The fourth DMO, `sys.dm_os_wait_stats`, relates to index monitoring and provides information that can help during index analysis.

■ **Warning** The indexing DMOs don't have information at the row level to precisely indicate when the information collected for the index has been reset. Due to this, there can be situations where the statistics reported can be slightly higher or lower than they actually are. While this shouldn't greatly affect the outcome during analysis, it is something to keep in mind.

Index Usage Stats

The DMO `sys.dm_db_index_usage_stats` provides information on how indexes are being used and when the index was last used. This information can be useful when you want to track if indexes are being used and which operations are being executed against the index.

The monitoring process for this DMO, which is similar to the other DMOs, consists of the following steps:

1. Create a table to hold snapshot information.

2. Insert the current state of the DMO into the snapshot table.

3. Compare the most recent snapshot to the previous snapshot and insert the delta between the rows in the output into a history table.

To build the process, you'll first need to create the snapshot and history tables. The schema for these tables will be identical and will contain all of the columns from the DMO and a create_date column (see Listing 10-5). For consistency with the source DMO, the columns for the table will match the schema of the DMO.

Listing 10-5. Index Usage Stats Snapshot Tables Stats

```
USE IndexingMethod
GO

CREATE TABLE dbo.index_usage_stats_snapshot
   (
   snapshot_id INT IDENTITY(1,1)
   ,create_date DATETIME
   ,database_id SMALLINT NOT NULL
   ,object_id INT NOT NULL
   ,index_id INT NOT NULL
   ,user_seeks BIGINT NOT NULL
   ,user_scans BIGINT NOT NULL
   ,user_lookups BIGINT NOT NULL
   ,user_updates BIGINT NOT NULL
   ,last_user_seek DATETIME
   ,last_user_scan DATETIME
   ,last_user_lookup DATETIME
   ,last_user_update DATETIME
   ,system_seeks BIGINT NOT NULL
   ,system_scans BIGINT NOT NULL
   ,system_lookups BIGINT NOT NULL
   ,system_updates BIGINT NOT NULL
   ,last_system_seek DATETIME
   ,last_system_scan DATETIME
   ,last_system_lookup DATETIME
   ,last_system_update DATETIME
   ,CONSTRAINT PK_IndexUsageStatsSnapshot
     PRIMARY KEY CLUSTERED (snapshot_id)
   ,CONSTRAINT UQ_IndexUsageStatsSnapshot
     UNIQUE (create_date, database_id, object_id, index_id)
   );

CREATE TABLE dbo.index_usage_stats_history
   (
   history_id INT IDENTITY(1,1)
   ,create_date DATETIME
   ,database_id SMALLINT NOT NULL
   ,object_id INT NOT NULL
   ,index_id INT NOT NULL
   ,user_seeks BIGINT NOT NULL
   ,user_scans BIGINT NOT NULL
   ,user_lookups BIGINT NOT NULL
   ,user_updates BIGINT NOT NULL
   ,last_user_seek DATETIME
   ,last_user_scan DATETIME
   ,last_user_lookup DATETIME
   ,last_user_update DATETIME
```

```
    ,system_seeks BIGINT NOT NULL
    ,system_scans BIGINT NOT NULL
    ,system_lookups BIGINT NOT NULL
    ,system_updates BIGINT NOT NULL
    ,last_system_seek DATETIME
    ,last_system_scan DATETIME
    ,last_system_lookup DATETIME
    ,last_system_update DATETIME
    ,CONSTRAINT PK_IndexUsageStatsHistory
      PRIMARY KEY CLUSTERED (history_id)
    ,CONSTRAINT UQ_IndexUsageStatsHistory
      UNIQUE (create_date, database_id, object_id, index_id)
    );
```

The next piece in capturing a history of index usage stats is collecting the current values in sys.dm_db_index_usage_stats. Similar to the performance monitor script, the collection query, shown in Listing 10-6, needs to be scheduled to run every about every 4 hours. The activity in your environment and rate in which indexes are modified should help determine the frequency in which the information is captured. Be certain to schedule a snapshot prior to any index defragmentation processes to capture information that might be lost when indexes are rebuilt.

Listing 10-6. Index Usage Stats Snapshot Population

```
USE IndexingMethod
GO

INSERT INTO dbo.index_usage_stats_snapshot
    SELECT GETDATE()
        ,database_id
        ,object_id
        ,index_id
        ,user_seeks
        ,user_scans
        ,user_lookups
        ,user_updates
        ,last_user_seek
        ,last_user_scan
        ,last_user_lookup
        ,last_user_update
        ,system_seeks
        ,system_scans
        ,system_lookups
        ,system_updates
        ,last_system_seek
        ,last_system_scan
        ,last_system_lookup
        ,last_system_update
    FROM  sys.dm_db_index_usage_stats
```

After populating the snapshot for the index usage stats, the delta between the most recent and the previous snapshot needs to be inserted into the index_usage_stats_history table. Since there isn't anything in the rows from sys.dm_db_index_usage_stats to identify when the stats for the index have been reset, the process for identifying when a delta between two entries for an index exists is to remove the row if any of the statistics on the index return a negative value. The resulting query, shown in Listing 10-7, implements this logic along with removing any rows where no new activity has happened.

Listing 10-7. Index Usage Stats Snapshot Population

```
USE IndexingMethod
GO

WITH  IndexUsageCTE
     AS ( SELECT
          DENSE_RANK() OVER ( ORDER BY create_date DESC ) AS HistoryID
          ,create_date
          ,database_id
          ,object_id
          ,index_id
          ,user_seeks
          ,user_scans
          ,user_lookups
          ,user_updates
          ,last_user_seek
          ,last_user_scan
          ,last_user_lookup
          ,last_user_update
          ,system_seeks
          ,system_scans
          ,system_lookups
          ,system_updates
          ,last_system_seek
          ,last_system_scan
          ,last_system_lookup
          ,last_system_update
          FROM
          dbo.index_usage_stats_snapshot
          )
INSERT INTO dbo.index_usage_stats_history
SELECT i1.create_date
  ,i1.database_id
  ,i1.object_id
  ,i1.index_id
  ,i1.user_seeks - COALESCE(i2.user_seeks, 0)
  ,i1.user_scans - COALESCE(i2.user_scans, 0)
  ,i1.user_lookups - COALESCE(i2.user_lookups, 0)
  ,i1.user_updates - COALESCE(i2.user_updates, 0)
  ,i1.last_user_seek
  ,i1.last_user_scan
  ,i1.last_user_lookup
  ,i1.last_user_update
  ,i1.system_seeks - COALESCE(i2.system_seeks, 0)
  ,i1.system_scans - COALESCE(i2.system_scans, 0)
  ,i1.system_lookups - COALESCE(i2.system_lookups, 0)
  ,i1.system_updates - COALESCE(i2.system_updates, 0)
  ,i1.last_system_seek
```

```
    ,i1.last_system_scan
    ,i1.last_system_lookup
    ,i1.last_system_update
FROM
  IndexUsageCTE i1
  LEFT OUTER JOIN IndexUsageCTE i2
        ON i1.database_id = i2.database_id
            AND i1.object_id = i2.object_id
            AND i1.index_id = i2.index_id
            AND i2.HistoryID = 2
            --Verify no rows are less than 0
            AND NOT ( i1.system_seeks - COALESCE(i2.system_seeks, 0) < 0
                AND i1.system_scans - COALESCE(i2.system_scans, 0) < 0
                AND i1.system_lookups - COALESCE(i2.system_lookups, 0) < 0
                AND i1.system_updates - COALESCE(i2.system_updates, 0) < 0
                AND i1.user_seeks - COALESCE(i2.user_seeks, 0) < 0
                AND i1.user_scans - COALESCE(i2.user_scans, 0) < 0
                AND i1.user_lookups - COALESCE(i2.user_lookups, 0) < 0
                AND i1.user_updates - COALESCE(i2.user_updates, 0) < 0
                )

WHERE
  i1.HistoryID = 1
--Only include rows are greater than 0
  AND ( i1.system_seeks - COALESCE(i2.system_seeks, 0) > 0
     OR i1.system_scans - COALESCE(i2.system_scans, 0) > 0
     OR i1.system_lookups - COALESCE(i2.system_lookups, 0) > 0
     OR i1.system_updates - COALESCE(i2.system_updates, 0) > 0
     OR i1.user_seeks - COALESCE(i2.user_seeks, 0) > 0
     OR i1.user_scans - COALESCE(i2.user_scans, 0) > 0
     OR i1.user_lookups - COALESCE(i2.user_lookups, 0) > 0
     OR i1.user_updates - COALESCE(i2.user_updates, 0) > 0
     )
```

Index Operational Stats

The DMO sys.dm_db_index_operational_stats provides information on the physical operations that happen on indexes during plan execution. This information can be useful for tracking the physical plan operations that occur when indexes are used and the rates for those operations. One of the other things this DMO monitors is the success rate in which compression operates.

As mentioned in the last section, the process for monitoring this DMO involves a few simple steps. First, you'll create tables to store snapshot and history information on the DMO output. Then, periodic snapshots of the DMO output are inserted into the snapshot table. After the snapshot is retrieved, the delta between the current and previous snapshot is inserted into the history table.

The process utilizes a snapshot and history table that is nearly identical to the schema of sys.dm_db_index_operational_stats. The chief variance in the schema is the addition of a create_date column, used to identify when the snapshot occurred. The code in Listing 10-8 provides the schema required for the snapshot and history tables.

Listing 10-8. Index Operational Stats Snapshot Tables Stats

```
USE IndexingMethod
GO

CREATE TABLE dbo.index_operational_stats_snapshot (
   snapshot_id INT IDENTITY(1,1)
   ,create_date DATETIME
   ,database_id SMALLINT NOT NULL
   ,object_id INT NOT NULL
   ,index_id INT NOT NULL
   ,partition_number INT NOT NULL
   ,leaf_insert_count BIGINT NOT NULL
   ,leaf_delete_count BIGINT NOT NULL
   ,leaf_update_count BIGINT NOT NULL
   ,leaf_ghost_count BIGINT NOT NULL
   ,nonleaf_insert_count BIGINT NOT NULL
   ,nonleaf_delete_count BIGINT NOT NULL
   ,nonleaf_update_count BIGINT NOT NULL
   ,leaf_allocation_count BIGINT NOT NULL
   ,nonleaf_allocation_count BIGINT NOT NULL
   ,leaf_page_merge_count BIGINT NOT NULL
   ,nonleaf_page_merge_count BIGINT NOT NULL
   ,range_scan_count BIGINT NOT NULL
   ,singleton_lookup_count BIGINT NOT NULL
   ,forwarded_fetch_count BIGINT NOT NULL
   ,lob_fetch_in_pages BIGINT NOT NULL
   ,lob_fetch_in_bytes BIGINT NOT NULL
   ,lob_orphan_create_count BIGINT NOT NULL
   ,lob_orphan_insert_count BIGINT NOT NULL
   ,row_overflow_fetch_in_pages BIGINT NOT NULL
   ,row_overflow_fetch_in_bytes BIGINT NOT NULL
   ,column_value_push_off_row_count BIGINT NOT NULL
   ,column_value_pull_in_row_count BIGINT NOT NULL
   ,row_lock_count BIGINT NOT NULL
   ,row_lock_wait_count BIGINT NOT NULL
   ,row_lock_wait_in_ms BIGINT NOT NULL
   ,page_lock_count BIGINT NOT NULL
   ,page_lock_wait_count BIGINT NOT NULL
   ,page_lock_wait_in_ms BIGINT NOT NULL
   ,index_lock_promotion_attempt_count BIGINT NOT NULL
   ,index_lock_promotion_count BIGINT NOT NULL
   ,page_latch_wait_count BIGINT NOT NULL
   ,page_latch_wait_in_ms BIGINT NOT NULL
   ,page_io_latch_wait_count BIGINT NOT NULL
   ,page_io_latch_wait_in_ms BIGINT NOT NULL
   ,tree_page_latch_wait_count BIGINT NOT NULL
   ,tree_page_latch_wait_in_ms BIGINT NOT NULL
   ,tree_page_io_latch_wait_count BIGINT NOT NULL
   ,tree_page_io_latch_wait_in_ms BIGINT NOT NULL
   ,page_compression_attempt_count BIGINT NOT NULL
   ,page_compression_success_count BIGINT NOT NULL
```

```
      ,CONSTRAINT PK_IndexOperationalStatsSnapshot
        PRIMARY KEY CLUSTERED (snapshot_id)
      ,CONSTRAINT UQ_IndexOperationalStatsSnapshot
        UNIQUE (create_date, database_id, object_id, index_id, partition_number)
    );

CREATE TABLE dbo.index_operational_stats_history (
    history_id INT IDENTITY(1,1)
    ,create_date DATETIME
    ,database_id SMALLINT NOT NULL
    ,object_id INT NOT NULL
    ,index_id INT NOT NULL
    ,partition_number INT NOT NULL
    ,leaf_insert_count BIGINT NOT NULL
    ,leaf_delete_count BIGINT NOT NULL
    ,leaf_update_count BIGINT NOT NULL
    ,leaf_ghost_count BIGINT NOT NULL
    ,nonleaf_insert_count BIGINT NOT NULL
    ,nonleaf_delete_count BIGINT NOT NULL
    ,nonleaf_update_count BIGINT NOT NULL
    ,leaf_allocation_count BIGINT NOT NULL
    ,nonleaf_allocation_count BIGINT NOT NULL
    ,leaf_page_merge_count BIGINT NOT NULL
    ,nonleaf_page_merge_count BIGINT NOT NULL
    ,range_scan_count BIGINT NOT NULL
    ,singleton_lookup_count BIGINT NOT NULL
    ,forwarded_fetch_count BIGINT NOT NULL
    ,lob_fetch_in_pages BIGINT NOT NULL
    ,lob_fetch_in_bytes BIGINT NOT NULL
    ,lob_orphan_create_count BIGINT NOT NULL
    ,lob_orphan_insert_count BIGINT NOT NULL
    ,row_overflow_fetch_in_pages BIGINT NOT NULL
    ,row_overflow_fetch_in_bytes BIGINT NOT NULL
    ,column_value_push_off_row_count BIGINT NOT NULL
    ,column_value_pull_in_row_count BIGINT NOT NULL
    ,row_lock_count BIGINT NOT NULL
    ,row_lock_wait_count BIGINT NOT NULL
    ,row_lock_wait_in_ms BIGINT NOT NULL
    ,page_lock_count BIGINT NOT NULL
    ,page_lock_wait_count BIGINT NOT NULL
    ,page_lock_wait_in_ms BIGINT NOT NULL
    ,index_lock_promotion_attempt_count BIGINT NOT NULL
    ,index_lock_promotion_count BIGINT NOT NULL
    ,page_latch_wait_count BIGINT NOT NULL
    ,page_latch_wait_in_ms BIGINT NOT NULL
    ,page_io_latch_wait_count BIGINT NOT NULL
    ,page_io_latch_wait_in_ms BIGINT NOT NULL
    ,tree_page_latch_wait_count BIGINT NOT NULL
    ,tree_page_latch_wait_in_ms BIGINT NOT NULL
    ,tree_page_io_latch_wait_count BIGINT NOT NULL
    ,tree_page_io_latch_wait_in_ms BIGINT NOT NULL
    ,page_compression_attempt_count BIGINT NOT NULL
```

```
,page_compression_success_count BIGINT NOT NULL
,CONSTRAINT PK_IndexOperationalStatsHistory
  PRIMARY KEY CLUSTERED (history_id)
,CONSTRAINT UQ_IndexOperationalStatsHistory
  UNIQUE (create_date, database_id, object_id, index_id, partition_number)
);
```

With the tables in place, the next step is to capture a current snapshot of the information in sys.dm_db_index_operational_stats. The information can be populated using the script in Listing 10-9. Since the Indexing Method is geared towards capturing information on indexing for all databases on the server, the values for the parameters for sys.dm_db_index_operational_stats are set to NULL. This will return results for all partitions of all indexes on all tables in all databases on the server. Like the index usage stats, this information should be captured about every four hours with one of the scheduled points being before the index maintenance on the server.

Listing 10-9. Index Operational Stats Snapshot Population

```
USE IndexingMethod
GO

INSERT INTO dbo.index_operational_stats_snapshot
SELECT
  GETDATE()
  ,database_id
  ,object_id
  ,index_id
  ,partition_number
  ,leaf_insert_count
  ,leaf_delete_count
  ,leaf_update_count
  ,leaf_ghost_count
  ,nonleaf_insert_count
  ,nonleaf_delete_count
  ,nonleaf_update_count
  ,leaf_allocation_count
  ,nonleaf_allocation_count
  ,leaf_page_merge_count
  ,nonleaf_page_merge_count
  ,range_scan_count
  ,singleton_lookup_count
  ,forwarded_fetch_count
  ,lob_fetch_in_pages
  ,lob_fetch_in_bytes
  ,lob_orphan_create_count
  ,lob_orphan_insert_count
  ,row_overflow_fetch_in_pages
  ,row_overflow_fetch_in_bytes
  ,column_value_push_off_row_count
  ,column_value_pull_in_row_count
  ,row_lock_count
  ,row_lock_wait_count
  ,row_lock_wait_in_ms
  ,page_lock_count
```

```
    ,page_lock_wait_count
    ,page_lock_wait_in_ms
    ,index_lock_promotion_attempt_count
    ,index_lock_promotion_count
    ,page_latch_wait_count
    ,page_latch_wait_in_ms
    ,page_io_latch_wait_count
    ,page_io_latch_wait_in_ms
    ,tree_page_latch_wait_count
    ,tree_page_latch_wait_in_ms
    ,tree_page_io_latch_wait_count
    ,tree_page_io_latch_wait_in_ms
    ,page_compression_attempt_count
    ,page_compression_success_count
FROM sys.dm_db_index_operational_stats(NULL,NULL,NULL,NULL)
```

The step after populating the snapshot is populating the history table. As before, the purpose of history table is to store statistics on the deltas between two snapshots. The deltas provide information on which operations occurred and they also help to timebox those operations so that, if needed, more focus can be placed on operations during core vs. non-core hours. The business rule identifying when the statistics have been reset is similar to index usage stats: if any of the statistics on the index return a negative value, the row from the previous snapshot will be ignored. Also, any rows that return all zero values will not be included. The code used to generate the history delta is included in Listing 10-10.

Listing 10-10. Index Operational Stats Snapshot Population

```
USE IndexingMethod
GO

WITH IndexOperationalCTE
AS ( SELECT
    DENSE_RANK() OVER ( ORDER BY create_date DESC ) AS HistoryID
    ,create_date
    ,database_id
    ,object_id
    ,index_id
    ,partition_number
    ,leaf_insert_count
    ,leaf_delete_count
    ,leaf_update_count
    ,leaf_ghost_count
    ,nonleaf_insert_count
    ,nonleaf_delete_count
    ,nonleaf_update_count
    ,leaf_allocation_count
    ,nonleaf_allocation_count
    ,leaf_page_merge_count
    ,nonleaf_page_merge_count
    ,range_scan_count
    ,singleton_lookup_count
    ,forwarded_fetch_count
    ,lob_fetch_in_pages
    ,lob_fetch_in_bytes
```

```
      ,lob_orphan_create_count
      ,lob_orphan_insert_count
      ,row_overflow_fetch_in_pages
      ,row_overflow_fetch_in_bytes
      ,column_value_push_off_row_count
      ,column_value_pull_in_row_count
      ,row_lock_count
      ,row_lock_wait_count
      ,row_lock_wait_in_ms
      ,page_lock_count
      ,page_lock_wait_count
      ,page_lock_wait_in_ms
      ,index_lock_promotion_attempt_count
      ,index_lock_promotion_count
      ,page_latch_wait_count
      ,page_latch_wait_in_ms
      ,page_io_latch_wait_count
      ,page_io_latch_wait_in_ms
      ,tree_page_latch_wait_count
      ,tree_page_latch_wait_in_ms
      ,tree_page_io_latch_wait_count
      ,tree_page_io_latch_wait_in_ms
      ,page_compression_attempt_count
      ,page_compression_success_count
      FROM
      dbo.index_operational_stats_snapshot
      )
INSERT INTO dbo.index_operational_stats_history
SELECT i1.create_date
      ,i1.database_id
      ,i1.object_id
      ,i1.index_id
      ,i1.partition_number
      ,i1.leaf_insert_count - COALESCE(i2.leaf_insert_count, 0)
      ,i1.leaf_delete_count - COALESCE(i2.leaf_delete_count, 0)
      ,i1.leaf_update_count - COALESCE(i2.leaf_update_count, 0)
      ,i1.leaf_ghost_count - COALESCE(i2.leaf_ghost_count, 0)
      ,i1.nonleaf_insert_count - COALESCE(i2.nonleaf_insert_count, 0)
      ,i1.nonleaf_delete_count - COALESCE(i2.nonleaf_delete_count, 0)
      ,i1.nonleaf_update_count - COALESCE(i2.nonleaf_update_count, 0)
      ,i1.leaf_allocation_count - COALESCE(i2.leaf_allocation_count, 0)
      ,i1.nonleaf_allocation_count - COALESCE(i2.nonleaf_allocation_count, 0)
      ,i1.leaf_page_merge_count - COALESCE(i2.leaf_page_merge_count, 0)
      ,i1.nonleaf_page_merge_count - COALESCE(i2.nonleaf_page_merge_count, 0)
      ,i1.range_scan_count - COALESCE(i2.range_scan_count, 0)
      ,i1.singleton_lookup_count - COALESCE(i2.singleton_lookup_count, 0)
      ,i1.forwarded_fetch_count - COALESCE(i2.forwarded_fetch_count, 0)
      ,i1.lob_fetch_in_pages - COALESCE(i2.lob_fetch_in_pages, 0)
      ,i1.lob_fetch_in_bytes - COALESCE(i2.lob_fetch_in_bytes, 0)
      ,i1.lob_orphan_create_count - COALESCE(i2.lob_orphan_create_count, 0)
      ,i1.lob_orphan_insert_count - COALESCE(i2.lob_orphan_insert_count, 0)
```

```
      ,i1.row_overflow_fetch_in_pages - COALESCE(i2.row_overflow_fetch_in_pages, 0)
      ,i1.row_overflow_fetch_in_bytes - COALESCE(i2.row_overflow_fetch_in_bytes, 0)
      ,i1.column_value_push_off_row_count - COALESCE(i2.column_value_push_off_row_count, 0)
      ,i1.column_value_pull_in_row_count - COALESCE(i2.column_value_pull_in_row_count, 0)
      ,i1.row_lock_count - COALESCE(i2.row_lock_count, 0)
      ,i1.row_lock_wait_count - COALESCE(i2.row_lock_wait_count, 0)
      ,i1.row_lock_wait_in_ms - COALESCE(i2.row_lock_wait_in_ms, 0)
      ,i1.page_lock_count - COALESCE(i2.page_lock_count, 0)
      ,i1.page_lock_wait_count - COALESCE(i2.page_lock_wait_count, 0)
      ,i1.page_lock_wait_in_ms - COALESCE(i2.page_lock_wait_in_ms, 0)
      ,i1.index_lock_promotion_attempt_count - COALESCE(i2.index_lock_promotion_attempt_count, 0)
      ,i1.index_lock_promotion_count - COALESCE(i2.index_lock_promotion_count, 0)
      ,i1.page_latch_wait_count - COALESCE(i2.page_latch_wait_count, 0)
      ,i1.page_latch_wait_in_ms - COALESCE(i2.page_latch_wait_in_ms, 0)
      ,i1.page_io_latch_wait_count - COALESCE(i2.page_io_latch_wait_count, 0)
      ,i1.page_io_latch_wait_in_ms - COALESCE(i2.page_io_latch_wait_in_ms, 0)
      ,i1.tree_page_latch_wait_count - COALESCE(i2.tree_page_latch_wait_count, 0)
      ,i1.tree_page_latch_wait_in_ms - COALESCE(i2.tree_page_latch_wait_in_ms, 0)
      ,i1.tree_page_io_latch_wait_count - COALESCE(i2.tree_page_io_latch_wait_count, 0)
      ,i1.tree_page_io_latch_wait_in_ms - COALESCE(i2.tree_page_io_latch_wait_in_ms, 0)
      ,i1.page_compression_attempt_count - COALESCE(i2.page_compression_attempt_count, 0)
      ,i1.page_compression_success_count - COALESCE(i2.page_compression_success_count, 0)
FROM IndexOperationalCTE i1
LEFT OUTER JOIN IndexOperationalCTE i2
    ON i1.database_id = i2.database_id
    AND i1.object_id = i2.object_id
    AND i1.index_id = i2.index_id
  AND i1.partition_number = i2.partition_number
    AND i2.HistoryID = 2
--Verify no rows are less than 0
AND NOT ( i1.leaf_insert_count - COALESCE(i2.leaf_insert_count, 0) < 0
  AND i1.leaf_delete_count - COALESCE(i2.leaf_delete_count, 0) < 0
  AND i1.leaf_update_count - COALESCE(i2.leaf_update_count, 0) < 0
  AND i1.leaf_ghost_count - COALESCE(i2.leaf_ghost_count, 0) < 0
  AND i1.nonleaf_insert_count - COALESCE(i2.nonleaf_insert_count, 0) < 0
  AND i1.nonleaf_delete_count - COALESCE(i2.nonleaf_delete_count, 0) < 0
  AND i1.nonleaf_update_count - COALESCE(i2.nonleaf_update_count, 0) < 0
  AND i1.leaf_allocation_count - COALESCE(i2.leaf_allocation_count, 0) < 0
  AND i1.nonleaf_allocation_count - COALESCE(i2.nonleaf_allocation_count, 0) < 0
  AND i1.leaf_page_merge_count - COALESCE(i2.leaf_page_merge_count, 0) < 0
  AND i1.nonleaf_page_merge_count - COALESCE(i2.nonleaf_page_merge_count, 0) < 0
  AND i1.range_scan_count - COALESCE(i2.range_scan_count, 0) < 0
  AND i1.singleton_lookup_count - COALESCE(i2.singleton_lookup_count, 0) < 0
  AND i1.forwarded_fetch_count - COALESCE(i2.forwarded_fetch_count, 0) < 0
  AND i1.lob_fetch_in_pages - COALESCE(i2.lob_fetch_in_pages, 0) < 0
  AND i1.lob_fetch_in_bytes - COALESCE(i2.lob_fetch_in_bytes, 0) < 0
  AND i1.lob_orphan_create_count - COALESCE(i2.lob_orphan_create_count, 0) < 0
  AND i1.lob_orphan_insert_count - COALESCE(i2.lob_orphan_insert_count, 0) < 0
  AND i1.row_overflow_fetch_in_pages - COALESCE(i2.row_overflow_fetch_in_pages, 0) < 0
  AND i1.row_overflow_fetch_in_bytes - COALESCE(i2.row_overflow_fetch_in_bytes, 0) < 0
  AND i1.column_value_push_off_row_count - COALESCE(i2.column_value_push_off_row_count, 0) < 0
```

```
    AND i1.column_value_pull_in_row_count - COALESCE(i2.column_value_pull_in_row_count, 0) < 0
    AND i1.row_lock_count - COALESCE(i2.row_lock_count, 0) < 0
    AND i1.row_lock_wait_count - COALESCE(i2.row_lock_wait_count, 0) < 0
    AND i1.row_lock_wait_in_ms - COALESCE(i2.row_lock_wait_in_ms, 0) < 0
    AND i1.page_lock_count - COALESCE(i2.page_lock_count, 0) < 0
    AND i1.page_lock_wait_count - COALESCE(i2.page_lock_wait_count, 0) < 0
    AND i1.page_lock_wait_in_ms - COALESCE(i2.page_lock_wait_in_ms, 0) < 0
    AND i1.index_lock_promotion_attempt_count - COALESCE(i2.index_lock_promotion_attempt_count, 0) < 0
    AND i1.index_lock_promotion_count - COALESCE(i2.index_lock_promotion_count, 0) < 0
    AND i1.page_latch_wait_count - COALESCE(i2.page_latch_wait_count, 0) < 0
    AND i1.page_latch_wait_in_ms - COALESCE(i2.page_latch_wait_in_ms, 0) < 0
    AND i1.page_io_latch_wait_count - COALESCE(i2.page_io_latch_wait_count, 0) < 0
    AND i1.page_io_latch_wait_in_ms - COALESCE(i2.page_io_latch_wait_in_ms, 0) < 0
    AND i1.tree_page_latch_wait_count - COALESCE(i2.tree_page_latch_wait_count, 0) < 0
    AND i1.tree_page_latch_wait_in_ms - COALESCE(i2.tree_page_latch_wait_in_ms, 0) < 0
    AND i1.tree_page_io_latch_wait_count - COALESCE(i2.tree_page_io_latch_wait_count, 0) < 0
    AND i1.tree_page_io_latch_wait_in_ms - COALESCE(i2.tree_page_io_latch_wait_in_ms, 0) < 0
    AND i1.page_compression_attempt_count - COALESCE(i2.page_compression_attempt_count, 0) < 0
    AND i1.page_compression_success_count - COALESCE(i2.page_compression_success_count, 0) < 0)
WHERE i1.HistoryID = 1
--Only include rows are greater than 0
AND ( i1.leaf_insert_count - COALESCE(i2.leaf_insert_count, 0) > 0
   OR i1.leaf_delete_count - COALESCE(i2.leaf_delete_count, 0) > 0
   OR i1.leaf_update_count - COALESCE(i2.leaf_update_count, 0) > 0
   OR i1.leaf_ghost_count - COALESCE(i2.leaf_ghost_count, 0) > 0
   OR i1.nonleaf_insert_count - COALESCE(i2.nonleaf_insert_count, 0) > 0
   OR i1.nonleaf_delete_count - COALESCE(i2.nonleaf_delete_count, 0) > 0
   OR i1.nonleaf_update_count - COALESCE(i2.nonleaf_update_count, 0) > 0
   OR i1.leaf_allocation_count - COALESCE(i2.leaf_allocation_count, 0) > 0
   OR i1.nonleaf_allocation_count - COALESCE(i2.nonleaf_allocation_count, 0) > 0
   OR i1.leaf_page_merge_count - COALESCE(i2.leaf_page_merge_count, 0) > 0
   OR i1.nonleaf_page_merge_count - COALESCE(i2.nonleaf_page_merge_count, 0) > 0
   OR i1.range_scan_count - COALESCE(i2.range_scan_count, 0) > 0
   OR i1.singleton_lookup_count - COALESCE(i2.singleton_lookup_count, 0) > 0
   OR i1.forwarded_fetch_count - COALESCE(i2.forwarded_fetch_count, 0) > 0
   OR i1.lob_fetch_in_pages - COALESCE(i2.lob_fetch_in_pages, 0) > 0
   OR i1.lob_fetch_in_bytes - COALESCE(i2.lob_fetch_in_bytes, 0) > 0
   OR i1.lob_orphan_create_count - COALESCE(i2.lob_orphan_create_count, 0) > 0
   OR i1.lob_orphan_insert_count - COALESCE(i2.lob_orphan_insert_count, 0) > 0
   OR i1.row_overflow_fetch_in_pages - COALESCE(i2.row_overflow_fetch_in_pages, 0) > 0
   OR i1.row_overflow_fetch_in_bytes - COALESCE(i2.row_overflow_fetch_in_bytes, 0) > 0
   OR i1.column_value_push_off_row_count - COALESCE(i2.column_value_push_off_row_count, 0) > 0
   OR i1.column_value_pull_in_row_count - COALESCE(i2.column_value_pull_in_row_count, 0) > 0
   OR i1.row_lock_count - COALESCE(i2.row_lock_count, 0) > 0
   OR i1.row_lock_wait_count - COALESCE(i2.row_lock_wait_count, 0) > 0
   OR i1.row_lock_wait_in_ms - COALESCE(i2.row_lock_wait_in_ms, 0) > 0
   OR i1.page_lock_count - COALESCE(i2.page_lock_count, 0) > 0
   OR i1.page_lock_wait_count - COALESCE(i2.page_lock_wait_count, 0) > 0
   OR i1.page_lock_wait_in_ms - COALESCE(i2.page_lock_wait_in_ms, 0) > 0
   OR i1.index_lock_promotion_attempt_count - COALESCE(i2.index_lock_promotion_attempt_count, 0) > 0
   OR i1.index_lock_promotion_count - COALESCE(i2.index_lock_promotion_count, 0) > 0
```

```
    OR i1.page_latch_wait_count - COALESCE(i2.page_latch_wait_count, 0) > 0
    OR i1.page_latch_wait_in_ms - COALESCE(i2.page_latch_wait_in_ms, 0) > 0
    OR i1.page_io_latch_wait_count - COALESCE(i2.page_io_latch_wait_count, 0) > 0
    OR i1.page_io_latch_wait_in_ms - COALESCE(i2.page_io_latch_wait_in_ms, 0) > 0
    OR i1.tree_page_latch_wait_count - COALESCE(i2.tree_page_latch_wait_count, 0) > 0
    OR i1.tree_page_latch_wait_in_ms - COALESCE(i2.tree_page_latch_wait_in_ms, 0) > 0
    OR i1.tree_page_io_latch_wait_count - COALESCE(i2.tree_page_io_latch_wait_count, 0) > 0
    OR i1.tree_page_io_latch_wait_in_ms - COALESCE(i2.tree_page_io_latch_wait_in_ms, 0) > 0
    OR i1.page_compression_attempt_count - COALESCE(i2.page_compression_attempt_count, 0) > 0
    OR i1.page_compression_success_count - COALESCE(i2.page_compression_success_count, 0) > 0)
```

Index Physical Stats

The indexing DMO for monitoring indexes is sys.dm_db_index_physical_stats. This DMO provides statistics on the current physical structure of the indexes in the databases. The value of this information is in determining the fragmentation of the index, which is discussed more in Chapter 6. From a Monitor phase perspective, you are collecting the physical statistics to aid the Analyze phase. The goal is to identify potential issues that may be affecting the efficiency in how the index is stored, or vice versa, thus impacting query performance because of how the index is stored.

With the physical stats DMO, the statistics are collected a bit differently than with the other DMOs. The main difference between this DMO and the other is the impact that can be placed on the database while collecting the information. While the other two reference in-memory tables, index_physical_stats reads the pages in the index to determine the actual fragmentation and physical layout of the indexes. More on the impact of using sys.dm_db_index_physical_stats is found in Chapter 3. To accommodate this difference, the statistics are only stored in a history table; the deltas between the points in which the history is retrieved is not determined. Also, due to the nature of the statistics contained in the DMO, there would be little value in calculating delta values.

The first piece needed to begin collecting statistics on index physical stats is the previously mentioned history table. This table, shown in Listing 10-11, uses the same schema as the DMO with the addition of the create_date column.

■ **Tip**   When generating the table schema needed for the DMOs, a table-valued function new to SQL Server 2012 was utilized. The function sys.dm_exec_describe_first_result_set can be used to identify the column names and data types for a query.

Listing 10-11. Index Physical Stats History Table

```
USE IndexingMethod
GO

CREATE TABLE dbo.index_physical_stats_history
  (
  history_id INT IDENTITY(1,1)
  ,create_date DATETIME
  ,database_id SMALLINT
  ,object_id INT
  ,index_id INT
  ,partition_number INT
  ,index_type_desc NVARCHAR(60)
  ,alloc_unit_type_desc NVARCHAR(60)
```

```
    ,index_depth TINYINT
    ,index_level TINYINT
    ,avg_fragmentation_in_percent FLOAT
    ,fragment_count BIGINT
    ,avg_fragment_size_in_pages FLOAT
    ,page_count BIGINT
    ,avg_page_space_used_in_percent FLOAT
    ,record_count BIGINT
    ,ghost_record_count BIGINT
    ,version_ghost_record_count BIGINT
    ,min_record_size_in_bytes INT
    ,max_record_size_in_bytes INT
    ,avg_record_size_in_bytes FLOAT
    ,forwarded_record_count BIGINT
    ,compressed_page_count BIGINT
    ,CONSTRAINT PK_IndexPhysicalStatsHistory PRIMARY KEY CLUSTERED (history_id)
    ,CONSTRAINT UQ_IndexPhysicalStatsHistory UNIQUE (create_date, database_id, object_id, index_
id, partition_number, alloc_unit_type_desc, index_depth, index_level)
    ) ;
```

The collection of the history for index_physical_stats differs from the previous two DMOs. Since it's just history, there is no need to capture the snapshot information to build the delta between the two snapshots for the history. Instead, the current statistics are inserted directly into the history table, as shown in Listing 10-12. Also, since index_physical_stats performs physical operations on the index while collecting the statistics, there are a few things to keep in mind when generating the history information. First, the script will collect information from each database independently from the other databases through a CURSOR-drive loop. This provides a batched separation between the collections of statistics for each database and limits the impact of the DMO. Second, you should be certain that the query is executed during non-core hours. The start of the daily maintenance window would be ideal. It is important that this information is collected prior to defragmentation or re-indexing since these operations will change the information provided by the DMO. Usually, this information is collected as a step in the defragmentation process, which is discussed in Chapter 6.

Listing 10-12. Index Physical Stats History Population

```
USE IndexingMethod
GO

DECLARE @DatabaseID INT
DECLARE DatabaseList CURSOR FAST_FORWARD FOR
  SELECT database_id
  FROM sys.databases
  WHERE state_desc = 'ONLINE';

OPEN DatabaseList
FETCH NEXT FROM DatabaseList INTO @DatabaseID;

WHILE @@FETCH_STATUS = 0
BEGIN

  INSERT INTO dbo.index_physical_stats_history
    (create_date, database_id, object_id, index_id, partition_number
    , index_type_desc, alloc_unit_type_desc, index_depth, index_level
    , avg_fragmentation_in_percent, fragment_count, avg_fragment_size_in_pages
    , page_count, avg_page_space_used_in_percent, record_count
```

```
  , ghost_record_count, version_ghost_record_count, min_record_size_in_bytes
  , max_record_size_in_bytes, avg_record_size_in_bytes, forwarded_record_count
  , compressed_page_count)
SELECT
  GETDATE()
  ,database_id
  ,object_id
  ,index_id
  ,partition_number
  ,index_type_desc
  ,alloc_unit_type_desc
  ,index_depth
  ,index_level
  ,avg_fragmentation_in_percent
  ,fragment_count
  ,avg_fragment_size_in_pages
  ,page_count
  ,avg_page_space_used_in_percent
  ,record_count
  ,ghost_record_count
  ,version_ghost_record_count
  ,min_record_size_in_bytes
  ,max_record_size_in_bytes
  ,avg_record_size_in_bytes
  ,forwarded_record_count
  ,compressed_page_count
  FROM sys.dm_db_index_physical_stats(@DatabaseID, NULL, NULL, NULL, 'SAMPLED')

  FETCH NEXT FROM DatabaseList INTO @DatabaseID;
END

CLOSE DatabaseList
DEALLOCATE DatabaseList
```

Wait Statistics

One other DMO that provides information related to indexing is sys.dm_os_wait_stats. This DMO collects information related to resources that SQL Server is waiting for in order to start or continue executing a query or other request. Most performance tuning methodologies include a process for collecting and analyzing wait statistics. From an indexing perspective, there are a number of wait resources that can indicate that there may be indexing issues on the SQL Server instance. By monitoring these statistics, you can be informed when these issues may exist. Table 10-2 provides a short list of wait types that most often indicate that indexing issues may exist.

Similar to performance counters, wait statistics are general indicators of health that reflect information about the SQL Server instance as a whole. They do not point directly to resources; instead, they collect information on when there was a wait for a specific resource on the SQL Server instance.

■ **Note** Many performance monitoring tools from third-party vendors collect wait statistics as a part of their monitoring. If there is a tool already installed in your environment, check to see if wait statistics information can be retrieved from that tool.

Table 10-2. *Index Related Wait Statistics*

Option Name	Description
CXPACKET	Used to synchronize threads involved in a parallel query. This wait type only means a parallel query is processing with either an unbalanced workload or a worker is blocked by a preceding request.
IO_COMPLETION	Used to indicate a wait for I/O for operation (typically synchronous) like sorts and various situations where the engine needs to do a synchronous I/O. This wait type represents non-data page I/Os.
LCK_M_*	Occurs when a task is waiting to acquire a lock on an index or table.
PAGEIOLATCH_*	Occurs when a task is waiting on a latch for a buffer that is in an I/O request. Long waits may indicate problems with the disk subsystem.

The process for collecting wait statistics follows the pattern of using snapshot and history tables. To do this, the data will be collected first in a snapshot table with the deltas between snapshots stored in a history table. The snapshot and history tables, shown in Listing 10-13, contain the columns needed to support the snapshot and history patterns.

Listing 10-13. Wait Statistics Snapshot and History Table

```
USE IndexingMethod
GO

CREATE TABLE dbo.wait_stats_snapshot
  (
   wait_stats_snapshot_id INT IDENTITY(1, 1)
  ,create_date DATETIME
  ,wait_type NVARCHAR(60) NOT NULL
  ,waiting_tasks_count BIGINT NOT NULL
  ,wait_time_ms BIGINT NOT NULL
  ,max_wait_time_ms BIGINT NOT NULL
  ,signal_wait_time_ms BIGINT NOT NULL
  ,CONSTRAINT PK_wait_stats_snapshot PRIMARY KEY CLUSTERED
    (wait_stats_snapshot_id)
  ) ;

CREATE TABLE dbo.wait_stats_history
  (
   wait_stats_history_id INT IDENTITY(1, 1)
  ,create_date DATETIME
  ,wait_type NVARCHAR(60) NOT NULL
  ,waiting_tasks_count BIGINT NOT NULL
  ,wait_time_ms BIGINT NOT NULL
  ,max_wait_time_ms BIGINT NOT NULL
  ,signal_wait_time_ms BIGINT NOT NULL
  ,CONSTRAINT PK_wait_stats_history PRIMARY KEY CLUSTERED
    (wait_stats_history_id)
  ) ;
```

To collect the wait statistics information, the output from sys.dm_os_wait_stats is queried. Unlike the other DMOs discussed in this chapter, there is some summarization of the information that needs to occur prior to inserting the data. In previous versions of SQL Server, the wait_stats DMO contains two rows for the wait type MISCELLANEOUS. To accommodate for this variance, the sample script in Listing 10-14 uses aggregations to get around the issue. Another difference between wait_stats_snapshot and the other snapshots is the frequency in which the information should be collected. Wait_stats reports information on when requested resources were not available. Being able to tie this information down to specific times of the day can be critical. As such, wait_stats information should be collected about once every hour.

Listing 10-14. Wait Statistics Snapshot Population

```
USE IndexingMethod
GO

INSERT INTO dbo.wait_stats_snapshot (
  create_date
  ,wait_type
  ,waiting_tasks_count
  ,wait_time_ms
  ,max_wait_time_ms
  ,signal_wait_time_ms)
SELECT GETDATE()
  ,wait_type
  ,waiting_tasks_count
  ,wait_time_ms
  ,max_wait_time_ms
  ,signal_wait_time_ms
FROM sys.dm_os_wait_stats
```

With each snapshot collected, the delta between it and the previous snapshot needs to be added in the wait_stats_history table. For determining when the information in sys.dm_os_wait_stats has been reset, the column waiting_tasks_count is utilized. If the value in the column is lower than the previous snapshot, the information in the DMO is reset. The code for populating the history table is provided in Listing 10-15.

While there are only a few wait types that point towards indexing issues, the history table will show results for all of the wait types that are encountered. The reason is that waits on resources need to be compared to the total number of other waits that occur. For instance, if CXPACKET is the lowest relative wait on the server, there isn't much value in researching the queries and determining the indexing that could reduce the occurrence this wait type, since other issues would likely impact performance more significantly.

Listing 10-15. Wait Statistics History Population

```
USE IndexingMethod
GO

WITH  WaitStatCTE
    AS ( SELECT
          create_date
          ,DENSE_RANK() OVER ( ORDER BY create_date DESC ) AS HistoryID
          ,wait_type
          ,waiting_tasks_count
          ,wait_time_ms
          ,max_wait_time_ms
          ,signal_wait_time_ms
          FROM
```

```
        dbo.wait_stats_snapshot
        )
INSERT INTO dbo.wait_stats_history
SELECT
  w1.create_date
  ,w1.wait_type
  ,w1.waiting_tasks_count - COALESCE(w2.waiting_tasks_count, 0)
  ,w1.wait_time_ms - COALESCE(w2.wait_time_ms, 0)
  ,w1.max_wait_time_ms - COALESCE(w2.max_wait_time_ms, 0)
  ,w1.signal_wait_time_ms - COALESCE(w2.signal_wait_time_ms, 0)
FROM
  WaitStatCTE w1
  LEFT OUTER JOIN WaitStatCTE w2 ON w1.wait_type = w2.wait_type
    AND w1.waiting_tasks_count >= COALESCE(w2.waiting_tasks_count,0)
    AND w2.HistoryID = 2
WHERE
  w1.HistoryID = 1
  AND w1.waiting_tasks_count - COALESCE(w2.waiting_tasks_count, 0) > 0
```

Data Cleanup

While all of the information in the Monitor phase is needed for the Analyze phase, this information is not needed indefinitely. The process for monitoring would not be complete without tasks in place to clean up the information collected after a reasonable amount of time. A generally acceptable schedule for cleaning up information is to purge snapshots after 3 days and history information after 90 days.

The snapshot information is used simply to prepare the history information and is really not needed after the delta is created. Since SQL Agent jobs can error, and collection points may be a day apart from the previous, a three day window generally provides the leeway needed to support the process and accommodate for any issues that may arise.

The data in the history tables is more crucial than the snapshot information and needs to be kept longer. This information feeds the activities in the Analyze phase. The window for retaining this information should match the amount of time that it generally takes to go through the Indexing Method three or more times. This way, the information retained can be used for reference in a few cycles of the process.

When scheduling the cleanup process, it should be at least daily and during non-core processing hours. This will minimize the amount of information deleted in each execution and reduce the possible contention of the delete with other activity on the server. The delete script, shown in Listing 10-16, covers each of the tables discussed throughout this section.

Listing 10-16. Index Monitoring Snapshot and History Cleanup

```
USE IndexingMethod
GO

DECLARE @SnapshotDays INT = 3
  ,@HistoryDays INT = 90

DELETE FROM dbo.index_usage_stats_snapshot
WHERE create_date < DATEADD(d, -@SnapshotDays, GETDATE())

DELETE FROM dbo.index_usage_stats_history
WHERE create_date < DATEADD(d, -@HistoryDays, GETDATE())
```

```
DELETE FROM dbo.index_operational_stats_snapshot
WHERE create_date < DATEADD(d, -@SnapshotDays, GETDATE())

DELETE FROM dbo.index_operational_stats_history
WHERE create_date < DATEADD(d, -@HistoryDays, GETDATE())

DELETE FROM dbo.index_physical_stats_history
WHERE create_date < DATEADD(d, -@HistoryDays, GETDATE())

DELETE FROM dbo.wait_stats_snapshot
WHERE create_date < DATEADD(d, -@SnapshotDays, GETDATE())

DELETE FROM dbo.wait_stats_history
WHERE create_date < DATEADD(d, -@HistoryDays, GETDATE())
```

SQL Trace

The last set of information that should be collected during the Monitor phase is a SQL Trace session. The purpose of using the trace information is to collect SQL statements that represent production activity that can be used during the Analyze phase to identify indexes that could be useful based on the query activity in your production environment and on the data that is being stored there. While the statistics collected so far provide information on the effect of activity on indexes and other resource use on the SQL Server instance, SQL Trace collects the activity that is causing those statistics.

There are a few areas to be careful of when collecting information with SQL Trace. First, SQL Trace will likely collect a lot of information, and this will need to be accommodated. In other words, the more active the server and the databases, the larger the trace (.trc) files will be. Along these same lines, don't collect the trace information on drives that are already heavily used or dedicated to data or transaction log files. Doing this can, and likely will, impact the performance of I/O on those files. The end goal for monitoring is to improve the performance of the system; care needs to be taken to minimize the impact of monitoring.

Finally, SQL Trace and SQL Profiler are deprecated in SQL Server 2012. This doesn't mean that these tools no longer function, but they are slated for removal in a future SQL Server release. While SQL Trace is deprecated, it is still the ideal tool for collecting trace information, which will later be used with the Database Engine Tuning Advisor.

■ **Note**   It is always advisable to keep apprised of deprecated features within SQL Server. For more information on Deprecated Features, see Books Online at `http://technet.microsoft.com/en-us/library/ms143729(v=sql.110).aspx`.

There are four basic steps to creating a SQL Trace session.

1. Build the trace session.

2. Assign the events and columns to the session.

3. Add filters to the session.

4. Start the SQL Trace session.

The next few pages will cover these steps and describe the components used in creating the SQL Trace session.

To begin monitoring with SQL Trace, a trace session must first be created. Sessions are created using the sp_trace_create stored procedure. This procedure accepts a number of parameters that configure how the session will collect information. In the example session, shown in Listing 10-17, the SQL Trace session will create files that automatically failover when they reach the 50MB file size limit. The file size is limited to allow better file management. It's easier to copy 50MB files compared to files that are 1GB or more. Also, the trace files are being created in c:\temp with the file name IndexingMethod. Note that this name can be changed to anything that suits the needs of the server and databases you are monitoring.

Listing 10-17. Create SQL Trace Session

```
USE master
GO

-- Create a Queue
DECLARE @rc INT
  ,@TraceID int
  ,@maxfilesize BIGINT = 50 --Maximum .trc file size in MB
  ,@FileName NVARCHAR(256) = 'c:\temp\IndexingMethod' --File name and path, minus the extension

EXEC @rc = sp_trace_create @TraceID output, 0, @FileName, @maxfilesize, NULL
if (@rc != 0) RAISERROR('Error creating trace file',16,1)

SELECT * FROM sys.traces WHERE id = @TraceID
```

After creating the SQL Trace session, the next step is to add events to the session. There are two events that will collect the information that is of most value to index monitoring: RPC:Completed and SQL:BatchCompleted. The RPC:Completed returns results whenever a remote procedure call completes; the best example of this is the completion of a stored procedure. The other event, SQL:BatchCompleted, occurs when ad-hoc and prepared batches are completed. Between these two events, all of the completed SQL statements on the server will be collected.

To add events to the SQL Trace session, the sp_trace_set event stored procedure is used. The stored procedure adds events and the column requested from the event to the trace with each execution of the stored procedure. For two events with 15 columns each, the stored procedure will need to be executed 30 times. For the example session, shown in Listing 10-18, the following columns are being collected for each of the sessions:

ApplicationName

ClientProcessID

CPU

DatabaseID

DatabaseName

Duration

EndTime

HostName

LoginName

NTUserName

Reads

SPID

StartTime

TextData

Writes

The codes for the events and columns can be found in system catalog views. Events are listed in the view sys.trace_events. The columns available are listed in sys.trace_columns. The columns view also includes an indicator to identify if the values from the column can be filtered, which is useful in the next step in creating SQL Trace sessions.

Listing 10-18. Add Events and Columns to SQL Trace Session

```
USE master
GO

DECLARE @on INT = 1
   ,@FileName NVARCHAR(256) = 'c:\temp\IndexingMethod'
   ,@TraceID INT

SET @TraceID = (SELECT id FROM sys.traces WHERE path LIKE @FileName+'%')

-- RPC:Completed
exec sp_trace_setevent @TraceID, 10, 1, @on
exec sp_trace_setevent @TraceID, 10, 10, @on
exec sp_trace_setevent @TraceID, 10, 11, @on
exec sp_trace_setevent @TraceID, 10, 12, @on
exec sp_trace_setevent @TraceID, 10, 13, @on
exec sp_trace_setevent @TraceID, 10, 14, @on
exec sp_trace_setevent @TraceID, 10, 15, @on
exec sp_trace_setevent @TraceID, 10, 16, @on
exec sp_trace_setevent @TraceID, 10, 17, @on
exec sp_trace_setevent @TraceID, 10, 18, @on
exec sp_trace_setevent @TraceID, 10, 3, @on
exec sp_trace_setevent @TraceID, 10, 35, @on
exec sp_trace_setevent @TraceID, 10, 6, @on
exec sp_trace_setevent @TraceID, 10, 8, @on
exec sp_trace_setevent @TraceID, 10, 9, @on

--SQL:BatchCompleted
exec sp_trace_setevent @TraceID, 12, 1, @on
exec sp_trace_setevent @TraceID, 12, 10, @on
exec sp_trace_setevent @TraceID, 12, 11, @on
exec sp_trace_setevent @TraceID, 12, 12, @on
exec sp_trace_setevent @TraceID, 12, 13, @on
exec sp_trace_setevent @TraceID, 12, 14, @on
exec sp_trace_setevent @TraceID, 12, 15, @on
exec sp_trace_setevent @TraceID, 12, 16, @on
exec sp_trace_setevent @TraceID, 12, 17, @on
exec sp_trace_setevent @TraceID, 12, 18, @on
exec sp_trace_setevent @TraceID, 12, 3, @on
exec sp_trace_setevent @TraceID, 12, 35, @on
exec sp_trace_setevent @TraceID, 12, 6, @on
exec sp_trace_setevent @TraceID, 12, 8, @on
exec sp_trace_setevent @TraceID, 12, 9, @on
```

The next step is to filter out unneeded events from the SQL Trace session. There is no need to collect all statements all the time for all databases and all applications with every SQL Trace session. In fact, in Listing 10-19, events from the system databases, those with database ID less than 5, are removed from the session. The stored procedure for filtering SQL Trace sessions is sp_trace_setfilter. The stored procedure accepts the ID for columns from sys.trace_columns. Columns not included in the events can be filtered, and filters apply to all events.

Listing 10-19. Add Filters to SQL Trace Session

```
USE master
GO

DECLARE @intfilter INT = 5
  ,@FileName NVARCHAR(256) = 'c:\temp\IndexingMethod'
  ,@TraceID INT

SET @TraceID = (SELECT id FROM sys.traces WHERE path LIKE @FileName+'%')

--Remove system databases from output
EXEC sp_trace_setfilter @TraceID, 3, 0, 4, @intfilter
```

The last step in setting up the monitoring for SQL Trace is to start the trace. This task is accomplished using the sp_trace_setstatus stored procedure, shown in Listing 10-20. Through this procedure, SQL Trace sessions can be started, paused, and stopped. Once the trace is started, it will start to create .trc files in the file location provided and the configuration for SQL Trace monitoring will be complete. When the collection period for the SQL Trace session completes, this script will be used with the status code 2 instead of 1 to terminate the session. This script is provided in Listing 10-21.

Listing 10-20. Start SQL Trace Session

```
USE master
GO

DECLARE @FileName NVARCHAR(256) = 'c:\temp\IndexingMethod'
  ,@TraceID INT

SET @TraceID = (SELECT id FROM sys.traces WHERE path LIKE @FileName+'%')

-- Set the trace status to start
exec sp_trace_setstatus @TraceID, 1
```

■ **Note** SQL Server experts often find it unfashionable to use the Database Engine Tuning Advisor, instead preferring to manually analyze the database and determine the indexes needed. This preference misses the opportunity to uncover low hanging fruit or situations where changing the location of the clustered index can improve performance.

Listing 10-21. Stop SQL Trace Session

```
USE master
GO

DECLARE @FileName NVARCHAR(256) = 'c:\temp\IndexingMethod'
  ,@TraceID INT

SET @TraceID = (SELECT id FROM sys.traces WHERE path LIKE @FileName+'%')

-- Set the trace status to stop
exec sp_trace_setstatus @TraceID, 0
```

The SQL Trace session example in this section is fairly basic. In your environment, you may need to have a more intelligent process that collects information in each trace file for a specified amount of time instead of using a file size to control the file rollover rate. These types of changes to collecting information from SQL Trace for monitoring indexes should have no impact on your ability to use the SQL Trace information for the purposes intended later in this chapter. There is one last item to consider with the SQL Trace information. Trace information does not need to constantly be gathered, like Performance Counter and DMO information. Instead, the SQL Trace information is often better suited to being collected for a four to eight hour period that represents a regular day of activity on your database platform. With SQL Trace, you can collect too much information, which can overwhelm the analyze phase and delay indexing recommendations.

If you've followed along in the chapter thus far, the components needed to monitor index performance and needs will be implemented and ready for future analysis. You'll want to gather statistics for a short time before progressing to the next phase of the Indexing Method. Once the information has been collected, the next phase is the Analyze phase.

Analyze

The next phase of the Indexing Method is to analyze the information. In this phase, you will take all of the information gathered during the Monitor phase and use it to analyze the state of performance and the value of the existing indexes. The end goal of the Analyze phase is to build a list of indexes to create, modify, and, potentially, drop from the databases. In many cases, the analysis of the indexes will border on art. There are many judgment calls in which you will use previous performance to anticipate future indexing needs. In the end, though, with every change proposed there will be supporting evidence before and after the indexing solutions to statistically support or disprove the value of the index.

The general layout of the Analyze phase is broken out into a number of components. Each component contains a process in which the analysis will start from high levels to identify the needed focus and hone the analysis into existing issues. The analysis components are

- Review of server state
- Schema discovery
- Database Engine Tuning Advisor
- Unused indexes
- Index plan usage

Before any exercise in analyzing the indexes of a database can take place, you first need to know the current deployment state. The tactics that can be used for a database in deployment vs. a database already deployed to the production environment will be roughly the same. There is a significant difference between the two, though, when it comes to where and how the statistics are gathered.

For the database that has not been developed, the focus will be on how users are expected to use the database and application after it is deployed. Tests and workloads against the database will focus on validating that the indexing in the database supports those activities. The activity that is chosen for the testing will likely be the result of estimations and projections of what users will do with the application. Determining the activity will be the responsibility of the business analysts that develop the requirements for the application.

Once the database has been deployed, the monitoring shifts from what the activity could be to what the activity is. The rate in which users adopt features and what the distribution of the data is with that activity will be known. At this point, the indexes developed during testing and planning may not be correct for the workload. The first round of using the Indexing Method on the database after deployment may lead to significant indexing changes. The key with indexing databases that have been deployed is that the analysis needs to be against the statistics of the workload in production. Doing so will provide you with the necessary guidance for implementing indexes that provide the best benefit to the database and pair them with the features that users are using and the frequency in which they use them.

Going through the Analyze phase with databases in either deployment states will provide a set of indexes that are optimal for what you currently know and understand about the database. When the indexes are applied, your mileage with them can, and will, vary. An index may provide the perfect access path for data for the activity in the database last month. But with the new release, new clients, or changes in user behavior, they may not continue to be optimal. As is often heard with stock purchases, past performance may not yield similar future results.

Fortunately, with a well practiced use of the Indexing Method, you will be able to provide the indexing your environment needs. In this chapter, the focus is on databases that are already deployed to production. As mentioned, these tactics will work with databases and servers in both states, development and production, but for simplicity, a production environment will be the default perspective and approach.

As you move through each of the areas in the index analysis, you will get a list of indexes to either create, modify, delete, or investigate further. For the indexes that require further investigation, you will use subsequent portions of the Analyze phase to determine how to progress and handle the index.

Review of Server State

The first step in the Analyze phase is to review the state of the server. Review both the host server environment and the SQL Server instance environment to identify if there are conditions indicating that there may be indexing issues. By starting at a high level and not looking directly at tables and individual indexes, you can avoid getting blinded by the trees in the forest. Often, when there are hundreds of indexes in dozens of databases, it is easy to get overly focused on an index or table that looks poorly indexed, only to later discover that the table has less than a hundred rows in a database with billions of rows in other tables.

When analyzing the server state, you will look at the following three areas:

- Performance counters

- Wait statistics

- Buffer allocation

Each of these areas provides an idea of where to start focusing the index analysis process. They let the database platform tell you where the performance issues related to indexing may reside.

Performance Counters

The first set of information collected in the Monitor phase was the performance counters. Naturally, you want to look at these first in the Analyze phase. Tracking performance counters over a monitoring period and over time will not provide prescriptive guidance on what to do about indexing issues, but they will provide a point for discovering performance issues and thus where to begin.

For each of the counters, we'll discuss some general guidelines. These guidelines are generalities that you should take with a grain of salt. Use them to initially guide whether the counter is outside what might be normal on other database platforms. If there is a reason that counters on your platform trend higher than typical, that is the purpose and point in maintaining the baseline tables. Work with the counter values that are valid for your environment as opposed to those that work best for others.

There are two ways in which performance counters should be analyzed. The first is to use Excel and/or PowerPivot to view graphs and trend lines based on the performance counters. The second is to review the performance counters with a query that takes a snapshot of the information in the performance counter table (defined in the "Performance Counters" subsection of the "Monitor" section). The second approach is the approach used in this chapter. The guidelines for the snapshot queries apply to both approaches.

■ **Note**   For simplicity, the snapshot analysis queries in this section will be scoped to the database level. In most cases, you will need to execute them against every database on the SQL Server instance. Options for accomplishing this are using sp_MSForEachDB or extending the cursors.

Access Methods\Forwarded Records/sec

As discussed in Chapter 2, forwarded records occur when heap records are updated and no longer fit on the page in which they were originally stored. In these situations, a pointer is placed in the original record to the new record location. The performance counter Forwarded Records/sec measures the rate in which forwarded rows are accessed on the server. Generally, the ratio of Forwarded Records/sec should not exceed 10% of Batch Requests/sec. This ratio can be a misnomer, since Forward Records represent the access of data at the row level and Batch Requests represent a higher scoped operation. The ratio, though, provides an indicator of when the balance of Forwarded Records may be exceeding an advisable level.

The snapshot query for Forwarded Records, shown in Listing 10-22, provides columns for the Forward Records/sec counter and the ratio calculation. In this query, the values are aggregated into minimum, average, and maximum values. The ratio is calculated on each set of collected counters and aggregated after that calculation. The final column, PctViolation, shows the percentage of time in which the Forward-Records-to-Batch-Requests ratio exceeds the 10 percent guideline.

Listing 10-22. Forwarded Records Counter Analysis

```
USE IndexingMethod
GO

WITH CounterSummary
AS (
  SELECT create_date
    ,server_name
    ,MAX(CASE WHEN counter_name = 'Forwarded Records/sec'
      THEN Calculated_Counter_value END) ForwardedRecords
    ,MAX(CASE WHEN counter_name = 'Forwarded Records/sec'
      THEN Calculated_Counter_value END)
      / (NULLIF(MAX(CASE WHEN counter_name = 'Batch Requests/sec'
      THEN Calculated_Counter_value END),0) * 10) AS ForwardedRecordRatio
  FROM dbo.IndexingCounters
  WHERE counter_name IN ('Forwarded Records/sec','Batch Requests/sec')
  GROUP BY create_date
    ,server_name
)
SELECT server_name
  ,MIN(ForwardedRecords) AS MinForwardedRecords
  ,AVG(ForwardedRecords) AS AvgForwardedRecords
  ,MAX(ForwardedRecords) AS MaxForwardedRecords
  ,MIN(ForwardedRecordRatio) AS MinForwardedRecordRatio
  ,AVG(ForwardedRecordRatio) AS AvgForwardedRecordRatio
  ,MAX(ForwardedRecordRatio) AS MaxForwardedRecordRatio
  ,100.*SUM(CASE WHEN ForwardedRecordRatio > 1 THEN 1 END)
    /COUNT(*) AS PctViolation
FROM CounterSummary
GROUP BY server_name
```

When reviewing the output from the snapshot query, there are a few things to ask about the information returned. First, review the minimum and maximum values for the counter and ratio. Is the minimum value close or at zero? How high is the maximum? How does it compared to previous values collected during monitoring? Is the average value for the counter and ratio closer to the minimum or maximum value? If the volume and peaks of forwarded records is increasing, then further analysis is warranted. Next, consider the PctViolation column. Is the percentage greater than 1%? If so, further analysis of forwarded records is warranted. If there is a need to dig deeper into Forward Records, the next step is to move the analysis from the server level to the databases.

To provide an example of some forwarded record activity, execute the script in Listing 10-23. This script will create a table with a heap. Then it will insert records into the table and update those records, causing records to be expanded, leading to record forwarding. Finally, a query will access the forwarded records causing forwarded record access operations.

Listing 10-23. Forwarded Records Example

```
USE [IndexingMethod]
GO
CREATE TABLE dbo.HeapExample
  (ID INT IDENTITY
  ,FillerData VARCHAR(2000)
  )

INSERT INTO dbo.HeapExample (FillerData)
SELECT REPLICATE('X',100)
FROM sys.all_objects

UPDATE dbo.HeapExample
SET FillerData = REPLICATE('X',2000)
WHERE ID % 5 = 1
GO

SELECT *
FROM dbo.HeapExample
WHERE ID % 3 = 1
GO 2
```

Once determining that Forwarded Record analysis needs to go into the database, the process will leverage information available in the DMO. There are two DMOs that will help to determine the scope and extent of forwarded records issues. These are sys.dm_db_index_physical_stats and sys.dm_db_index_operational_stats. For the analysis, the sys.dm_db_index_operational_stats information will come from the monitoring table dbo.index_operational_stats_history. The analysis process, shown in Listing 10-24, involves identifying all of the heaps in a database and then checking the physical structure of the heap. This information is then joined to the information collected in dbo.index_operational_stats_history. The physical stature of the index is retrieved from sys.dm_db_index_operational_stats because the DETAILED option for the DMO is required in order to get the forwarded record information.

Listing 10-24. Forwarded Records Snapshot Query

```
IF OBJECT_ID('tempdb..#HeapList') IS NOT NULL
  DROP TABLE #HeapList

CREATE TABLE #HeapList
  (
   database_id int
  ,object_id int
  ,page_count INT
```

```
  ,avg_page_space_used_in_percent DECIMAL(6,3)
  ,record_count INT
  ,forwarded_record_count INT
  )

DECLARE HEAP_CURS CURSOR FORWARD_ONLY FOR
  SELECT object_id
  FROM sys.indexes i
  WHERE index_id = 0

DECLARE @IndexID INT

OPEN HEAP_CURS
FETCH NEXT FROM HEAP_CURS INTO @IndexID

WHILE @@FETCH_STATUS = 0
BEGIN
  INSERT INTO #HeapList
  SELECT
    DB_ID()
    ,object_id
    ,page_count
    ,CAST(avg_page_space_used_in_percent AS DECIMAL(6,3))
    ,record_count
    ,forwarded_record_count
  FROM
    sys.dm_db_index_physical_stats(DB_ID(), @IndexID, 0, NULL,'DETAILED') ;

  FETCH NEXT FROM HEAP_CURS INTO @IndexID
END

CLOSE HEAP_CURS
DEALLOCATE HEAP_CURS

SELECT
  QUOTENAME(DB_NAME(database_id))
  ,QUOTENAME(OBJECT_SCHEMA_NAME(object_id)) + '.'
    + QUOTENAME(OBJECT_NAME(object_id)) AS ObjectName
  ,page_count
  ,avg_page_space_used_in_percent
  ,record_count
  ,forwarded_record_count
  ,x.forwarded_fetch_count
  ,CAST(100.*forwarded_record_count/record_count AS DECIMAL(6,3)) AS forwarded_record_pct
  ,CAST(1.*x.forwarded_fetch_count/forwarded_record_count AS DECIMAL(12,3)) AS forwarded_row_ratio
FROM #HeapList h
  CROSS APPLY(
    SELECT SUM(forwarded_fetch_count) AS forwarded_fetch_count
    FROM IndexingMethod.dbo.index_operational_stats_history i
    WHERE h.database_id = i.database_id
    AND h.object_id = i.OBJECT_ID
    AND i.index_id = 0) x
WHERE forwarded_record_count > 0
ORDER BY page_count DESC
```

The results of the snapshot query, shown in Figure 10-2, provide information on all of the heaps in a database that have any forwarded records. Through these results, the heaps that have issues with forwarding and forwarded records can be identified. The first columns to pay attention to are page_count and record_count. Heaps with many records with forwarded record issues will be more important than those with few rows. It is worthwhile to focus on those tables that will provide the greatest relief to forwarded records when investigating this counter. The columns forwarded_record_count and forwarded_fetch_count provide a count of the number of records in a table that have been forwarded and the number of times those forwarded records have been accessed, respectively. These columns provide a scope to the size of the problem. The last columns to look at are forwarded_record_pct and forwarded_row_ratio. These columns detail the percentage of columns that are forwarded and how many times each of the forwarded rows has been accessed.

In the example table, the statistics do indicate that there is an issue with forwarded records. The table has more than 16% of its rows forwarded. Each of these rows has been accessed three times. From the code sample, there have been only three queries executed on the table, meaning that 100% of data access has resulted in all forwarded rows being accessed. When analyzing the indexes in this database, mitigating the forwarded records for this table would be worthwhile. Do pay special attention to whether forwarded records are being accessed. Mitigating forwarded records on a table that has very high forwarded records but no forwarded record access would not be worth the effort and would have no impact on the Forwarded Records/sec counter.

(No column name)	ObjectName	page_count	avg_page_space_used_in_percent	record_count	forwarded_record_count	forwarded_fetch_count	forwarded_record_pct	forwarded_row_ratio
1	[IndexingMethod]	[dbo].[HeapExample] 171	76.056	2517	420	1260	16.687	3.000

Figure 10-2. Forwarded record snapshot query results

When heaps that have forwarded record issues have been identified, there are generally two ways in which the forwarded record can be mitigated. The first approach is to change the data types for the columns that are variable to fixed length data types. For instance, the varchar data type would be changed to char. This approach is not always ideal since it can result in more space being required by the table and some queries may not accommodate the extra space at the end of character fields and could return incorrect results. The second option is to add a clustered index to the table. which would remove the heap as the organizational method for storing the data in the table. The downside to this approach is in identifying the appropriate key column to cluster the table on. If there is a PRIMARY KEY on the table, it can usually suffice as the clustering index key. There is a third option. The heap can be rebuilt, which will rewrite the heap back to the database file and remove all of the forwarded records (using the script in Listing 10-25). This is generally considered a poor approach to resolving forwarded records in heaps since it doesn't provide a meaningful permanent fix to the issue. Remember, forwarded records aren't necessarily bad. They do, though, provide a potential performance problem when the ratio of operations for forwarded records starts to increase as compared to batch requests.

Listing 10-25. Rebuild Heap Script

```
USE [IndexingMethod]
GO

    ALTER TABLE dbo.HeapExample REBUILD
```

Access Methods\FreeSpace Scans/sec

The performance counter FreeSpace Scans/sec is another performance counter that is related to heaps. This counter represents the activity that happens when records are being inserted into a table with a heap. During inserts into heaps, there can be activity on the GAM, SGAM, and PFS pages. If the rate of inserts is high enough, contention can happen on these pages. Analyzing the values of the FreeSpace Scan/sec counter provides an opportunity to keep track of this activity, determine when the volume of activity is increasing, and determine when heaps may need to be analyzed further.

The query to analyze the FreeSpace Scans/sec counter is provided in Listing 10-26. It provides a snapshot of FreeSpace Scan activity on the SQL Server instance. The query provides aggregations of the counter with minimum, average, and maximum values. Similar to the last counter, this counter also follows recommended guidelines of one FreeSpace Scan/sec for every ten Batch Requests. The PctViolation column measures the percentage of time that the counter exceeds the guideline.

Listing 10-26. FreeSpace Scans Counter Analysis

```
USE IndexingMethod
GO

WITH CounterSummary
AS (
  SELECT create_date
    ,server_name
    ,MAX(CASE WHEN counter_name = 'FreeSpace Scans/sec'
      THEN Calculated_Counter_value END) FreeSpaceScans
    ,MAX(CASE WHEN counter_name = 'FreeSpace Scans/sec'
      THEN Calculated_Counter_value END)
      / (NULLIF(MAX(CASE WHEN counter_name = 'Batch Requests/sec'
      THEN Calculated_Counter_value END),0) * 10) AS ForwardedRecordRatio
  FROM dbo.IndexingCounters
  WHERE counter_name IN ('FreeSpace Scans/sec','Batch Requests/sec')
  GROUP BY create_date
    ,server_name
)
SELECT server_name
  ,MIN(FreeSpaceScans) AS MinFreeSpaceScans
  ,AVG(FreeSpaceScans) AS AvgFreeSpaceScans
  ,MAX(FreeSpaceScans) AS MaxFreeSpaceScans
  ,MIN(ForwardedRecordRatio) AS MinForwardedRecordRatio
  ,AVG(ForwardedRecordRatio) AS AvgForwardedRecordRatio
  ,MAX(ForwardedRecordRatio) AS MaxForwardedRecordRatio
  ,100.*SUM(CASE WHEN ForwardedRecordRatio > 1 THEN 1 END)/COUNT(*) AS PctViolation
FROM CounterSummary
GROUP BY server_name
```

When the FreeSpace Scans/sec number is high, the analysis will focus on determining which heaps in the databases have the highest rate of inserts. To identify the tables with the highest inserts on heaps, use the information in the monitoring tables from sys.dm_db_index_operational_stats. The column with the information on inserts is leaf_insert_count. The query in Listing 10-27 provides a list of the heaps in the monitoring table dbo.index_operational_stats_history with the most indexes.

Listing 10-27. FreeSpace Scans Snapshot Query

```
USE IndexingMethod
GO

SELECT
  QUOTENAME(DB_NAME(database_id)) AS database_name
  ,QUOTENAME(OBJECT_SCHEMA_NAME(object_id, database_id)) + '.'
    + QUOTENAME(OBJECT_NAME(object_id, database_id)) AS ObjectName
  , SUM(leaf_insert_count) AS leaf_insert_count
  , SUM(leaf_allocation_count) AS leaf_allocation_count
```

```
FROM dbo.index_operational_stats_history
WHERE index_id = 0
AND database_id > 4
GROUP BY object_id, database_id
ORDER BY leaf_insert_count DESC
```

Reviewing the table in the demonstration script in Listing 10-24 with the FreeSpace Scan snapshot query yields the results in Figure 10-3. As this example shows, there were 4,204 inserts into the heap. While only a single table is shown in the results, the tables that appear at the height of this list are going to be the ones most often contributing to FreeSpace Scans/sec.

	database_name	ObjectName	leaf_insert_count	leaf_allocation_count
1	[IndexingMethod]	[dbo].[HeapExample]	4204	171

Figure 10-3. FreeSpace Scan/sec snapshot query results

Once the contributing heaps are identified, the best method for mitigating the heaps is to create a clustered index on the tables with the most inserts. Since the counter is based on scans of free space on the GAM, SGAM, and PFS pages, building clustered indexes on the heap tables will move the allocation of pages to IAM pages, which are dedicated to each clustered index.

Access Methods\Full Scans/sec

Through the performance counter Full Scans/sec, the number of full scans on clustered and non-clustered indexes and heaps are measured. Within execution plans, this counter is triggered during index scans and table scans. The higher the rate in which full scans are performed, the more likely that there can be performance issues related to full scans. From a performance perspective, this can impact Page Life Expectancy as data is churned in memory, and there may be I/O contention as data needs to be brought into memory.

Using the query in Listing 10-28, the current state of Full Scans/sec can be analyzed for the current monitoring window. As with the previous counters, it is important to consider the relationship between this counter and the Batch Requests/sec counter. When the ratio of Full Scans/sec to Batch Requests/sec exceeds one for every thousand, there may be an issue with Full Scans/sec, which merits further review.

Listing 10-28. Full Scans Counter Analysis

```
USE IndexingMethod
GO

WITH CounterSummary
AS (
  SELECT create_date
    ,server_name
    ,MAX(CASE WHEN counter_name = 'Full Scans/sec'
      THEN Calculated_Counter_value END) FullScans
    ,MAX(CASE WHEN counter_name = 'Full Scans/sec'
      THEN Calculated_Counter_value END)
      / (NULLIF(MAX(CASE WHEN counter_name = 'Batch Requests/sec'
      THEN Calculated_Counter_value END),0) * 1000) AS FullRatio
  FROM dbo.IndexingCounters
  WHERE counter_name IN ('Full Scans/sec','Batch Requests/sec')
  GROUP BY create_date
    ,server_name
)
```

```
SELECT server_name
  ,MIN(FullScans) AS MinFullScans
  ,AVG(FullScans) AS AvgFullScans
  ,MAX(FullScans) AS MaxFullScans
  ,MIN(FullRatio) AS MinFullRatio
  ,AVG(FullRatio) AS AvgFullRatio
  ,MAX(FullRatio) AS MaxFullRatio
  ,100.*SUM(CASE WHEN FullRatio > 1 THEN 1 ELSE 0 END)/COUNT(*) AS PctViolation
FROM CounterSummary
GROUP BY server_name
```

Before demonstrating how to examine the underlying causes for high Full Scans/sec counter values, let's set up some example statistics. Listing 10-29 will provide a number of full scans that can be collected through the monitoring process detailed in the previous section. Be certain to execute the scripts that collect the monitoring information after executing the example script.

Listing 10-29. Full Scans Example Query

```
USE AdventureWorks2012
GO

SELECT * FROM Sales.SalesOrderHeader
GO 10
```

To dig deeper into Full Scan/sec issues, the primary goal is to identify which of the indexes this counter is being affected by. Once the indexes are identified, they need to be analyzed to determine if they are the proper index for that operation or if there are other performance tuning tactics required to reduce the use of the index in a full scan operation. The DMO to use for investigating full scans is sys.dm_db_index_usage_stats from the monitoring tables; this is the dbo.index_usage_stats_history table.

The indexes can be identified using the query shown in Listing 10-30. The snapshot results exclude any indexes with no rows in them. Those indexes are still being utilized for full scans, but mitigating the scans on those indexes would not greatly impact performance. To sort the results, the number of scans on the indexes is multiplied by the number of rows in the table. Sorting in this manner weighs the output to put focus on those indexes that might not have a high impact on reducing the Full Scans/sec but will provide the greatest lift to index performance.

Listing 10-30. Full Scans Snapshot Query

```
USE IndexingMethod
GO

SELECT QUOTENAME(DB_NAME(uh.database_id)) AS database_name
  ,QUOTENAME(OBJECT_SCHEMA_NAME(uh.object_id, uh.database_id)) + '.'
    + QUOTENAME(OBJECT_NAME(uh.object_id, uh.database_id)) AS ObjectName
  ,uh.index_id
  ,SUM(uh.user_scans) AS user_scans
  ,SUM(uh.user_seeks) AS user_seeks
  ,x.record_count
FROM dbo.index_usage_stats_history uh
  CROSS APPLY (
    SELECT DENSE_RANK() OVER (ORDER BY ph.create_date DESC) AS RankID
      ,ph.record_count
    FROM dbo.index_physical_stats_history ph
```

```
     WHERE ph.database_id = uh.database_id AND ph.object_id = uh.object_id AND ph.index_id =
uh.index_id) x
WHERE uh.database_id > 4
AND x.RankID = 1
GROUP BY uh.database_id, uh.object_id, uh.index_id, x.record_count
ORDER BY SUM(uh.user_scans) * x.record_count DESC
GO
```

The results of the full scans snapshot query will look similar to the output in Figure 10-4. With this output, the next step is to identify which indexes require further analysis. The purpose of the current analysis is to identify problem indexes for later analysis. Once identified, the next step is to determine where they are being utilized and how to mitigate the full scans in those places. The next step is in the section "Determining Index Plan Usage," which is later in this chapter.

	database_name	ObjectName	index_id	user_scans	user_seeks	record_count
1	[AdventureWorks2012]	[Sales].[SalesOrderHeader]	1	14	1	31465
2	[AdventureWorks]	[Sales].[SalesOrderHeader]	1	11	0	31465
3	[ReportServer$SQL2012]	[dbo].[Catalog]	1	651	0	332
4	[ReportServer$SQL2012]	[dbo].[Catalog]	1	651	0	46
5	[MVP]	[dbo].[SQLServerMVP]	0	52	0	310

Figure 10-4. FreeSpace scan snapshot query results

Access Methods\Index Searches/sec

The alternative to scanning indexes is to perform a seek against the index. The performance counter Index Searches/sec provides reporting on the rate of index seek on the SQL Server instance. This can include operations such as range scans and key lookups. In most environments, it is preferable to have high Index Searches/sec counter values. Along those lines, the higher this performance counter is in relationship to Full Scans/sec, the better.

The analysis of Index Searches/sec will begin with reviewing the performance counter information collected over time (shown in Listing 10-31). As mentioned, the ratio of Index Searches/sec to Full Scans/sec is one of the metrics that can be used to evaluate whether Index Searches/sec is indicating a potential indexing issue. The guideline for evaluating the ratio between the two counters is to look for 1,000 Index Searches/sec for every one Full Scans/sec. The analysis query provides this calculation, along with determine the amount of time in which the counter values exceeded this ratio, through the column PctViolation.

Listing 10-31. Index Searches Counter Analysis

```
USE IndexingMethod
GO

WITH CounterSummary
AS (
  SELECT create_date
    ,server_name
    ,MAX(CASE WHEN counter_name = 'Index Searches/sec'
      THEN Calculated_Counter_value END) IndexSearches
    ,MAX(CASE WHEN counter_name = 'Index Searches/sec'
      THEN Calculated_Counter_value END)
      / (NULLIF(MAX(CASE WHEN counter_name = 'Full Scans/sec'
      THEN Calculated_Counter_value END),0) * 1000) AS SearchToScanRatio
  FROM dbo.IndexingCounters
```

```
  WHERE counter_name IN ('Index Searches/sec','Full Scans/sec')
  GROUP BY create_date
    ,server_name
)
SELECT server_name
  ,MIN(IndexSearches) AS MinIndexSearches
  ,AVG(IndexSearches) AS AvgIndexSearches
  ,MAX(IndexSearches) AS MaxIndexSearches
  ,MIN(SearchToScanRatio) AS MinSearchToScanRatio
  ,AVG(SearchToScanRatio) AS AvgSearchToScanRatio
  ,MAX(SearchToScanRatio) AS MaxSearchToScanRatio
  ,100.*SUM(CASE WHEN SearchToScanRatio > 1 THEN 1 END)/COUNT(*) AS PctViolation
FROM CounterSummary
GROUP BY server_name
```

If the analysis indicates an issue with Index Searches, the first step is to verify that the analysis for Full Scans/sec in the last section was completed. That analysis will provide the most insight into which indexes have many full scans, which would contribute to high ratios for Index Searches/sec.

Once that analysis is complete, you can begin to identify where there are issues with the ratios of scans-to-seeks at the index level. Using the query in Listing 10-32, indexes with a high ratio of scans to seeks can be identified. Similar to the performance counter guideline of 1,000 seeks to every one scan, the query returns results for those indexes with less than 1,000 seeks for every scan. Since full scan issues should have been identified in the last section, the analysis also removes any indexes that do not have seeks against them.

Listing 10-32. Index Searches Snapshot Query

```
USE IndexingMethod
GO

SELECT QUOTENAME(DB_NAME(uh.database_id)) AS database_name
  ,QUOTENAME(OBJECT_SCHEMA_NAME(uh.object_id, uh.database_id)) + '.'
    + QUOTENAME(OBJECT_NAME(uh.object_id, uh.database_id)) AS ObjectName
  ,uh.index_id
  ,SUM(uh.user_scans) AS user_scans
  ,SUM(uh.user_seeks) AS user_seeks
  ,1.*SUM(uh.user_seeks)/NULLIF(SUM(uh.user_scans),0) AS SeekScanRatio
  ,x.record_count
FROM dbo.index_usage_stats_history uh
  CROSS APPLY (
    SELECT DENSE_RANK() OVER (ORDER BY ph.create_date DESC) AS RankID
      ,ph.record_count
    FROM dbo.index_physical_stats_history ph
    WHERE ph.database_id = uh.database_id AND ph.object_id = uh.object_id AND ph.index_id =
uh.index_id) x
WHERE uh.database_id > 4
AND x.RankID = 1
AND x.record_count > 0
GROUP BY uh.database_id, uh.object_id, uh.index_id, x.record_count
HAVING 1.*SUM(uh.user_seeks)/NULLIF(SUM(uh.user_scans),0) < 1000
AND SUM(uh.user_seeks) > 0
ORDER BY 1.*SUM(uh.user_seeks)/NULLIF(SUM(uh.user_scans),0) DESC, SUM(uh.user_scans) DESC
GO
```

Viewing the results of the snapshot query, shown in Figure 10-5, there are a few indexes identified where the seek-to-scan ratio is quite low. For instance, in the AdventureWorks2012 database, the table Sales. SalesOrderHeader has 1,016 scans for every one seek. Indexes such as this are easy to determine as needing further analysis. Similar to the last section, the next steps will be to do further analysis, similar to that provided in section "Determining Index Plan Usage."

	database_name	ObjectName	index_id	user_scans	user_seeks	Seek Scan Ratio	record_count
1	[Report Server$SQL2012]	[dbo].[Segment]	2	2	233	116.50000000000000000	57
2	[Report Server$SQL2012]	[dbo].[SegmentedChunk]	2	2	233	116.50000000000000000	45
3	[Report Server$SQL2012]	[dbo].[SegmentedChunk]	3	2	231	115.50000000000000000	45
4	[Report Server$SQL2012]	[dbo].[Chunk Segment Mapping]	2	2	231	115.50000000000000000	57
5	[Report Server$SQL2012]	[dbo].[Chunk Segment Mapping]	3	4	233	58.25000000000000000	57
6	[Report Server$SQL2012]	[dbo].[Keys]	1	15	10	0.66666666666666666	2
7	[Report Server$SQL2012]	[dbo].[Keys]	1	15	10	0.66666666666666666	4
8	[Report Server$SQL2012]	[dbo].[SnapshotData]	1	237	2	0.00843881856540084	39
9	[Adventure Works2012]	[Sales].[SalesOrderHeader]	1	1016	1	0.00098425196850393	31465

Figure 10-5. Index Search snapshot query sample results

During further analysis, there are a few things you'll want to pay attention to that might indicate an issue with the indexes identified. First is the current seek vs. scan behavior new to the index; in other words, has the variance been on a common trend that has slowly been getting worse? If the change is sudden, there could be a plan that is no longer using the index as it once did, maybe because of a coding change or bad parameter sniffing. Second is when the change has been gradual; look at increased data volumes and whether a query or feature within the database is being used more than it was previously. This can also hint at changes in how people are using the database and its applications, which is sometimes gradual until it reaches the point where indexing, and the performance they support, suffers.

Access Methods\Page Splits/sec

Similar to how clustered indexes are the other side of heaps, page splits are the other side of forwarded records. An in-depth discussion of page splits is included in Chapter 2. For the purposes of this chapter, though, page splits occur when a clustered or non-clustered index needs to make room in the ordering of the pages of the index to place data into its proper position. Page splits can be resource intensive as the single page is divided between two or more pages and involves locking and, potentially, blocking. The more frequent the page splits, the more likely that indexes will incur blocking and performance will suffer. Also, the fragmentation caused by page splits reduces the size of reads that can be performed in single operations.

To begin analyzing the performance counters for a page split, the counter Page Splits/sec is utilized. The query in Listing 10-33 provides a method for summarizing page split activity. The query includes the minimum, maximum and average level of the performance counter. Along with that, a ratio of Page Splits/sec to Batch Requests/sec is included. When identifying if there are issues with page splits on a SQL Server instance, the general rule of thumb is to look for times in which there is more than one page split/sec for every 20 batch requests/sec. Of course, as with the other counter, pay attention to the amount of time, through PctViolation, that the counter exceeded the threshold.

Listing 10-33. Page Splits Counter Analysis

```
USE IndexingMethod
GO

WITH CounterSummary
AS (
```

```
  SELECT create_date
    ,server_name
    ,MAX(CASE WHEN counter_name = 'Page Splits/sec'
      THEN Calculated_Counter_value END) PageSplits
    ,MAX(CASE WHEN counter_name = 'Page Splits/sec'
      THEN Calculated_Counter_value END)
      / (NULLIF(MAX(CASE WHEN counter_name = 'Batch Requests/sec'
      THEN Calculated_Counter_value END),0) * 20) AS FullRatio
  FROM dbo.IndexingCounters
  WHERE counter_name IN ('Page Splits/sec','Batch Requests/sec')
  GROUP BY create_date
    ,server_name
)
SELECT server_name
  ,MIN(PageSplits) AS MinPageSplits
  ,AVG(PageSplits) AS AvgPageSplits
  ,MAX(PageSplits) AS MaxPageSplits
  ,MIN(FullRatio) AS MinFullRatio
  ,AVG(FullRatio) AS AvgFullRatio
  ,MAX(FullRatio) AS MaxFullRatio
  ,100.*SUM(CASE WHEN FullRatio > 1 THEN 1 ELSE 0 END)/COUNT(*) AS PctViolation
FROM CounterSummary
GROUP BY server_name
```

To determine the indexes that are being affected by page splits, there are a few values that can be considered. A couple of the values come from sys.dm_db_index_operational_stats or dbo.index_operational_stats_history from the Monitor phase. These columns report each page allocation that occurs on an index, whether from inserts at the end of the B-tree or page splits in the middle of it. Since you only care about operations that are part of page splits, the next two columns provide information on whether fragmentation from page splits is occurring. To determine fragmentation, the column avg_fragmentation_in_percent from sys.dm_db_index_physical_stats is included in the monitoring table dbo.index_physical_stats_history. For the average fragmentation, there are two values returned. The first is the last fragmentation value reported for the index, the second is the average of all of the fragmentation values collected. See Listing 10-34.

Listing 10-34. Page Splits Snapshot Query

```
USE IndexingMethod
GO

SELECT
  QUOTENAME(DB_NAME(database_id)) AS database_name
  ,QUOTENAME(OBJECT_SCHEMA_NAME(object_id, database_id)) + '.'
    + QUOTENAME(OBJECT_NAME(object_id, database_id)) AS ObjectName
  , SUM(leaf_allocation_count) AS leaf_insert_count
  , SUM(nonleaf_allocation_count) AS nonleaf_allocation_count
  , MAX(CASE WHEN RankID=1 THEN x.avg_fragmentation_in_percent END) AS last_fragmenation
  , AVG(x.avg_fragmentation_in_percent) AS average_fragmenation
FROM dbo.index_operational_stats_history oh
  CROSS APPLY (
    SELECT DENSE_RANK() OVER (ORDER BY ph.create_date DESC) AS RankID
      ,CAST(ph.avg_fragmentation_in_percent AS DECIMAL(6,3)) AS avg_fragmentation_in_percent
    FROM dbo.index_physical_stats_history ph
```

```
          WHERE ph.database_id = oh.database_id AND ph.object_id = oh.object_id AND ph.index_id =
oh.index_id) x
WHERE database_id > 4
AND oh.index_id <> 0
AND (leaf_allocation_count > 0 OR nonleaf_allocation_count > 0)
GROUP BY object_id, database_id
ORDER BY leaf_insert_count DESC
```

Investigating page splits in this manner provides a way to see the number of allocations and pairs that information with fragmentation. A table with low fragmentation and a high leaf_insert_count, such as the table dbo.IndexingCounters shown in Figure 10-6 is not a concern from a page split perspective. On the other hand, dbo.index_operational_stats_history does show a high amount of fragmentation and leaf_insert_count. It would be worthwhile to investigate that index further.

	database_name	ObjectName	leaf_insert_count	nonleaf_allocation_count	last_fragmenation	average_fragmenation
1	[IndexingMethod]	[dbo].[IndexingCounters]	103020	580	12.465	5.537421
2	[IndexingMethod]	[dbo].[index_operational_stats_snapshot]	3920	35	72.065	61.680400
3	[IndexingMethod]	[dbo].[index_operational_stats_history]	815	5	96.591	96.952600
4	[IndexingMethod]	[dbo].[index_physical_stats_history]	695	10	7.500	9.746200
5	[IndexingMethod]	[dbo].[index_usage_stats_snapshot]	165	5	78.788	79.078600
6	[IndexingMethod]	[dbo].[index_usage_stats_history]	70	5	28.571	37.841000

Figure 10-6. *Page Split snapshot query sample results*

With the indexes requiring more analysis identified, the next step is mitigation. There are a number of ways to mitigate page splits on indexes. The first is to review the fragmentation history for the index. If the index needs to be rebuilt on a regular basis, one of the first things that can be done is to decrease the fill factor on the index. Reducing the fill factor will increase the space remaining on pages after rebuilding indexes, which will reduce the likelihood for page splits. The second strategy for reducing fragmentation is to consider the columns in the index. Are the columns highly volatile and do the values change dramatically? For instance, an index on create_date would likely not have page split issues. But one on update_date would be prone to fragmentation. If the usage rates for the index don't justify the index, it might be worthwhile to remove that index. Or, in multi-column indexes, move the volatile columns to the right side of the index or add them as included columns. A third approach to mitigating page splits can be to identify where the index is being used, through techniques such as those discussed in the section "Determining Index Plan Usage." One final approach to mitigating page splits on indexes is to review the data types being used by the index. In some cases a variable data type might be better suited to being a fixed length data type, similar to what was proposed previously in the "Forward Records/sec" section.

Buffer Manager\Page lookups/sec

The performance counter Page Lookups/sec measures the number of requests made in the SQL Server instance to retrieve individual pages from the buffer pool. When this counter is high, it often means that there is inefficiency in query plans, which can often be addressed through execution plan analysis. Often, high levels of Page Lookups/sec are attributed to plans with large numbers Page Lookups and Row Lookups per execution. Generally speaking, in terms of performance issues, the number of Page Lookups/sec should not exceed a ratio of 100 operations for each Batch Request/sec.

The initial analysis of Page Lookups/sec involves looking at both Page Lookups/sec and Batch Request/sec. To start, use the query shown in Listing 10-35; the analysis will include the minimum, maximum, and average Page Lookups/sec over the data from the monitoring period. Next, the minimum, maximum, and average of the ratio is included, with the PctViolation column, for the ratio of Page Lookups/sec-to-Batch Request/sec in each time period. The violation calculation verified whether the ratio of operations exceed 100 to 1.

Listing 10-35. Page Lookups Counter Analysis

```
USE IndexingMethod
GO

WITH CounterSummary
AS (
  SELECT create_date
    ,server_name
    ,MAX(CASE WHEN counter_name = 'Page Lookups/sec'
      THEN Calculated_Counter_value END) PageLookups
    ,MAX(CASE WHEN counter_name = 'Page Lookups/sec'
      THEN Calculated_Counter_value END)
      / (NULLIF(MAX(CASE WHEN counter_name = 'Batch Requests/sec'
      THEN Calculated_Counter_value END),0) * 100) AS PageLookupRatio
  FROM dbo.IndexingCounters
  WHERE counter_name IN ('Page Lookups/sec','Batch Requests/sec')
  GROUP BY create_date
    ,server_name
)
SELECT server_name
  ,MIN(PageLookups) AS MinPageLookups
  ,AVG(PageLookups) AS AvgPageLookups
  ,MAX(PageLookups) AS MaxPageLookups
  ,MIN(PageLookupRatio) AS MinPageLookupRatio
  ,AVG(PageLookupRatio) AS AvgPageLookupRatio
  ,MAX(PageLookupRatio) AS MaxPageLookupRatio
  ,100.*SUM(CASE WHEN PageLookupRatio > 1 THEN 1 ELSE 0 END)/COUNT(*) AS PctViolation
FROM CounterSummary
GROUP BY server_name
```

As with the other counters, when the analysis dictates that there are potential problems with the counter, the next step is to dig deeper. There are three approaches that can be taken to address high Page Lookups/sec. The first is to query `sys.dm_exec_query_stats` to identify queries that are executed often with high I/O; more information on this DMV can be found at `http://msdn.microsoft.com/en-us/library/ms189741.aspx`. Those queries need to reviewed and a determination needs to be made whether the queries are utilizing an excessive amount of I/O. Another approach is to review the database in the SQL Server instance for missing indexes; this approach is discussed further in the section "Missing Indexes." The third approach, which will be detailed in this section, is to review the occurrences of lookups on clustered indexes and heaps.

To investigate lookups on clustered indexes and heaps, the primary source for this information is the DMO `sys.dm_db_index_usage_stats`. Thanks to the Monitor phase, this information is available in the table `dbo.index_usage_stats_history`. To perform the analysis, use the query in Listing 10-36; you'll review lookups, seeks, and scans that have occurred from a user perspective. With these values, the query calculates the ratio of user lookups to user seeks and returns all that have a ratio higher than 100 to 1.

Listing 10-36. Page Lookups Snapshot Query

```
USE IndexingMethod
GO

SELECT QUOTENAME(DB_NAME(uh.database_id)) AS database_name
  ,QUOTENAME(OBJECT_SCHEMA_NAME(uh.object_id, uh.database_id)) + '.'
    + QUOTENAME(OBJECT_NAME(uh.object_id, uh.database_id)) AS ObjectName
  ,uh.index_id
```

```
    ,SUM(uh.user_lookups) AS user_lookups
    ,SUM(uh.user_seeks) AS user_seeks
    ,SUM(uh.user_scans) AS user_scans
    ,x.record_count
    ,CAST(1. * SUM(uh.user_lookups) / IIF(SUM(uh.user_seeks)=0,1,SUM(uh.user_seeks)) AS
DECIMAL(18,2)) AS LookupSeekRatio
FROM dbo.index_usage_stats_history uh
  CROSS APPLY (
    SELECT DENSE_RANK() OVER (ORDER BY ph.create_date DESC) AS RankID
      ,ph.record_count
    FROM dbo.index_physical_stats_history ph
    WHERE ph.database_id = uh.database_id AND ph.object_id = uh.object_id AND ph.index_id =
uh.index_id) x
WHERE uh.database_id > 4
AND x.RankID = 1
AND x.record_count > 0
GROUP BY uh.database_id, uh.object_id, uh.index_id, x.record_count
HAVING CAST(1. * SUM(uh.user_lookups) / IIF(SUM(uh.user_seeks)=0,1,SUM(uh.user_seeks)) AS
DECIMAL(18,2)) > 100
ORDER BY 1. * SUM(uh.user_lookups) / IIF(SUM(uh.user_seeks)=0,1,SUM(uh.user_seeks)) DESC
GO
```

Once indexes with issues are identified, the next step is to determine how and where the indexes are being used. For that, refer to the section "Determining Index Plan Usage."

Locks(*)\Lock Wait Time (ms)

Some performance counters can be used to determine if there is pressure on the indexes based on their usage. One such counter is Lock Wait Time (ms). This counter measures the amount of time, in milliseconds, that SQL Server spends waiting to implement a lock on a table, index, or page. There aren't any good values for this counter. Generally, the lower this value, the better, but what "low" means is entirely dependent on the database platform and the applications that are accessing it.

Since there are no guidelines for the level at which the values from Lock Wait Time(ms) are good or bad, the best method for evaluating the counter is to compared it to the baseline values. In this case, collecting a baseline becomes incredibly important in terms of being able to monitor when index performance related to lock wait time has occurred. Using the query in Listing 10-37, the Lock Wait Time (ms) is compared to the available baseline values. For both the baseline and the values from the monitoring period, an aggregate of the counter values is provided for the minimum, maximum, average, and standard deviation. These aggregations assist in providing a profile of the state of the counter and whether it has increased or decreased compared to the baseline.

Listing 10-37. Lock Wait Time Counter Analysis

```
USE IndexingMethod
GO

WITH CounterSummary
AS (
  SELECT create_date
    ,server_name
    ,instance_name
    ,MAX(CASE WHEN counter_name = 'Lock Wait Time (ms)'
      THEN Calculated_Counter_value END)/1000 LockWaitTime
```

```
  FROM dbo.IndexingCounters
  WHERE counter_name = 'Lock Wait Time (ms)'
  GROUP BY create_date
    ,server_name
    ,instance_name
)
SELECT
  CONVERT(VARCHAR(50), MAX(create_date), 101) AS CounterDate
  ,server_name
  ,instance_name
  ,MIN(LockWaitTime) AS MinLockWaitTime
  ,AVG(LockWaitTime) AS AvgLockWaitTime
  ,MAX(LockWaitTime) AS MaxLockWaitTime
  ,STDEV(LockWaitTime) AS StdDevLockWaitTime
FROM CounterSummary
GROUP BY server_name, instance_name
UNION ALL
SELECT 'Baseline: '+CONVERT(VARCHAR(50), start_date, 101)
  +' -->'+CONVERT(VARCHAR(50), end_date, 101)
  ,server_name
  ,instance_name
  ,minimum_counter_value/1000
  ,maximum_counter_value/1000
  ,average_counter_value/1000
  ,standard_deviation_counter_value/1000
FROM dbo.IndexingCountersBaseline
WHERE counter_name = 'Lock Wait Time (ms)'
ORDER BY instance_name, CounterDate DESC
```

As an example, in Figure 10-7, the average and maximum lock wait times have increased from the baseline values. In a production environment, an increase in the average lock wait over the baseline of about 8 seconds is cause for concern. Also, the increase in the range to the maximum value is something to investigate. Based on these results, the duration of time spent waiting to acquire locks is increasing, which is likely going to impact users.

	CounterDate	server_name	instance_name	MinLockWaitTime	AvgLockWaitTime	MaxLockWaitTime	StdDevLockWaitTime
1	Baseline: 03/20/2012 --> 03/20/2012	MSSQL$SQL2012	_Total	74.875	74.875	74.875	0
2	04/01/2012	MSSQL$SQL2012	_Total	74.875	82.5821157793422	92.782	7.1423035977518

Figure 10-7. *Lock Wait Time counter analysis sample results*

In this case, it would be advisable to investigate the lock wait time further. To do so, you will want to investigate which indexes in the SQL Server instance are generating the most lock wait time by using the query in Listing 10-38. This information is found in the DMO sys.dm_db_index_operational_stats or the monitoring table dbo.index_operational_stats_history. The columns reviewed for Lock Wait Time are row_lock_wait_count, row_lock_wait_count, row_lock_wait_count, and page_lock_wait_in_ms. These columns report the number of waits per index and the time for those waits. As the columns indicate, there are locks at both the row and page level, most often the variations between the lock types correlate with seek and scan operations on the index.

Listing 10-38. Lock Wait Time Snapshot Query

```
USE IndexingMethod
GO

SELECT
  QUOTENAME(DB_NAME(database_id)) AS database_name
  ,QUOTENAME(OBJECT_SCHEMA_NAME(object_id, database_id)) + '.'
    + QUOTENAME(OBJECT_NAME(object_id, database_id)) AS ObjectName
  ,index_id
  ,SUM(row_lock_wait_count) AS row_lock_wait_count
  ,SUM(row_lock_wait_in_ms) / 1000. AS row_lock_wait_in_sec
  ,ISNULL(SUM(row_lock_wait_in_ms)
    / NULLIF(SUM(row_lock_wait_count),0)
    / 1000.,0) AS avg_row_lock_wait_in_sec
  ,SUM(page_lock_wait_count) AS page_lock_wait_count
  ,SUM(page_lock_wait_in_ms) / 1000. AS page_lock_wait_in_sec
  ,ISNULL(SUM(page_lock_wait_in_ms)
    / NULLIF(SUM(page_lock_wait_count),0)
    / 1000.,0) AS avg_page_lock_wait_in_sec
FROM dbo.index_operational_stats_history oh
WHERE database_id > 4
AND (row_lock_wait_in_ms > 0 OR page_lock_wait_in_ms > 0)
GROUP BY database_id, object_id, index_id
```

Looking at the results of the snapshot query, shown in Figure 10-8, there are a couple things to point out. First, in this example, all of the locks are occurring across the pages of the table, not at the row level. This can result in larger scale blocking since more than the rows being accessed will be locked. Also, the average page lock is about 7 seconds. For most environments, this is an excessive amount of time for locking. Based on this information, you should definitely further investigate the clustered index (index_id=1) on the table Person.Person.

	database_name	ObjectName	index_id	row_lock_wait_count	row_lock_wait_in_sec	avg_row_lock_wait_in_sec	page_lock_wait_count	page_lock_wait_in_sec	avg_page_lock_wait_in_sec
1	[AdventureWorks2012]	[Person].[Person]	1	0	0.000000	0.000000	2	14.798000	7.399000

Figure 10-8. Lock Wait Time index analysis sample results

When you need to dig deeper into an index and its usage, the next step is to follow the previously state recommendation. Determine which execution plans are utilizing the index using the information in section "Determining Index Plan Usage" and optimize either the query of the structure or the index to reduce locking. In some cases, if the index is not critical to the table, it might be better to remove the index and allow other indexes to satisfy the query.

Locks(*)\Lock Waits/sec

The next counter, Lock Waits/sec, has a very similar approach for analysis to that of Lock Wait Time (ms). With Lock Waits/sec, the counter measures the number of lock requests that could not be satisfied immediately. For these requests, SQL Server waited until the row or page was available for the lock before granting the lock. As with the other counter, this counter also does not have any specific guidelines on what "good" values are. For these, you should turn to the baseline and compare and contrast against it to determine when the counter is outside normal operations.

The analysis of Lock Waits/sec includes the same minimum, maximum, average, and standard deviation aggregations as was used for Lock Wait Time(ms). These values are aggregated for both the per-counter table dbo.IndexingCounters and the baseline table dbo.IndexingCountersBaseline, shown in Listing 10-39. The results from the query are displayed in Figure 10-9.

Listing 10-39. Lock Waits Counter Analysis

```
USE IndexingMethod
GO

WITH CounterSummary
AS (
  SELECT create_date
    ,server_name
    ,instance_name
    ,MAX(CASE WHEN counter_name = 'Lock Waits/sec'
      THEN Calculated_Counter_value END) LockWaits
  FROM dbo.IndexingCounters
  WHERE counter_name = 'Lock Waits/sec'
  GROUP BY create_date
    ,server_name
    ,instance_name
)
SELECT
  CONVERT(VARCHAR(50), MAX(create_date), 101) AS CounterDate
  ,server_name
  ,instance_name
  ,MIN(LockWaits) AS MinLockWait
  ,AVG(LockWaits) AS AvgLockWait
  ,MAX(LockWaits) AS MaxLockWait
  ,STDEV(LockWaits) AS StdDevLockWait
FROM CounterSummary
GROUP BY server_name, instance_name
UNION ALL
SELECT 'Baseline: '+CONVERT(VARCHAR(50), start_date, 101)
  +' -->'+CONVERT(VARCHAR(50), end_date, 101)
  ,server_name
  ,instance_name
  ,minimum_counter_value/1000
  ,maximum_counter_value/1000
  ,average_counter_value/1000
  ,standard_deviation_counter_value/1000
FROM dbo.IndexingCountersBaseline
WHERE counter_name = 'Lock Waits/sec'
ORDER BY instance_name, CounterDate DESC
```

There will be times, such as those included in Figure 10-9, when Lock Wait/sec is not an issue, but there were issues with Lock Wait Time(ms). Those cases point to long duration blocking situations. On the other hand, Lock Wait/sec is important to monitor since it will indicate when there is widespread blocking. The blocking may not be long in duration, but it is widespread; a single long block can cause significant performance issues.

	CounterDate	server_name	instance_name	MinLockWait	AvgLockWait	MaxLockWait	StdDevLockWait
1	Baseline: 03/20/2012 --> 03/20/2012	MSSQL$SQL2012	_Total	0	0	0	0
2	04/02/2012	MSSQL$SQL2012	_Total	0	0.000127132111452484	0.8	0.00920584362462753
3	Baseline: 03/20/2012 --> 03/20/2012	MSSQL$SQL2012	AllocUnit	0	0	0	0
4	04/02/2012	MSSQL$SQL2012	AllocUnit	0	0	0	0
5	Baseline: 03/20/2012 --> 03/20/2012	MSSQL$SQL2012	Application	0	0	0	0
6	04/02/2012	MSSQL$SQL2012	Application	0	0	0	0
7	Baseline: 03/20/2012 --> 03/20/2012	MSSQL$SQL2012	Database	0	0	0	0
8	04/02/2012	MSSQL$SQL2012	Database	0	8.47547409683229E-05	0.8	0.00823430584655794

Figure 10-9. *Lock Waits counter analysis Sample results*

In a situation with wide-spread blocking, as indicated by high amounts of Lock Wait/sec, the analysis will require investigating the statistics of indexes using the DMO sys.dm_db_index_operational stats. With the Monitor phase, this information will be available in the table dbo.index_operational_stats_history. Using the query in Listing 10-40, the count and percentage of locks that wait can be determined. As with Lock Wait Time(ms), this counter analysis also looks at statistics at the row and page level.

Listing 10-40. Lock Waits Snapshot Query

```
USE IndexingMethod
GO

SELECT
  QUOTENAME(DB_NAME(database_id)) AS database_name
  ,QUOTENAME(OBJECT_SCHEMA_NAME(object_id, database_id)) + '.'
    + QUOTENAME(OBJECT_NAME(object_id, database_id)) AS ObjectName
  ,index_id
  ,SUM(row_lock_count) AS row_lock_count
  ,SUM(row_lock_wait_count) AS row_lock_wait_count
  ,ISNULL(SUM(row_lock_wait_count)
    / NULLIF(SUM(row_lock_count),0),0) AS pct_row_lock_wait
  ,SUM(page_lock_count) AS page_lock_count
  ,SUM(page_lock_wait_count) AS page_lock_wait_count
  ,ISNULL(SUM(page_lock_wait_count)
    / NULLIF(SUM(page_lock_count),0),0) AS pct_page_lock_wait
FROM dbo.index_operational_stats_history oh
WHERE database_id > 4
AND (row_lock_wait_in_ms > 0 OR page_lock_wait_in_ms > 0)
GROUP BY database_id, object_id, index_id
```

Indexes that have a high percentage of lock waits to locks are prime for index tuning. Often, when there are excessive lock waits on a database, the end users will see slowness to the applications and in some of the worse cases, timeouts in the application. The aim of analyzing this counter is to identify indexes that can be optimized and then to investigate where the indexes are being used. As with other sections, refer to the section "Determining Index Plan Usage" to identify where the indexes are being utilized. Once this is done, address the causes for the locks and tune the indexes and queries to reduce the locking on the index.

Locks(*)\Number of Deadlocks/sec

In extreme cases, poor indexing and excess lock blocking can lead to deadlocks. Deadlocks occur in situations where locks have been placed by two or more transactions in which the locking order of one of the transactions is prevented from acquiring and/or releasing its locks because of the locks of the other transactions. There are a number of ways to address deadlocking, one of which is to improve indexing.

To determine if deadlocks are occurring on the SQL Server instance, review the performance counters collected during the Monitor phase. The query in Listing 10-41 provides an overview of the deadlock rate during the monitoring window. The query returns aggregate values for the minimum, average, maximum, and standard deviation for the deadlocks on the server.

Listing 10-41. Number of Deadlocks Counter Analysis

```
USE IndexingMethod
GO

WITH CounterSummary
AS (
  SELECT create_date
    ,server_name
    ,Calculated_Counter_value AS NumberDeadlocks
  FROM dbo.IndexingCounters
  WHERE counter_name = 'Number of Deadlocks/sec'
)
SELECT server_name
  ,MIN(NumberDeadlocks) AS MinNumberDeadlocks
  ,AVG(NumberDeadlocks) AS AvgNumberDeadlocks
  ,MAX(NumberDeadlocks) AS MaxNumberDeadlocks
  ,STDEV(NumberDeadlocks) AS StdDevNumberDeadlocks
FROM CounterSummary
GROUP BY server_name
```

In general, a well-tuned database platform should not have any deadlocks occurring. When they occur, each should be investigate to determine the root cause for the deadlock. Before a deadlock can be examined, though, the deadlock first needs to be retrieved. There are a number of ways in which deadlock information can be collected from SQL Servers. These include trace flags, SQL Profiler, and event notifications. Another method is through extended events, using the built in system_health session. The query in Listing 10-42 returns a list of all of the deadlocks that are currently in the ring_buffer for that session.

Listing 10-42. System-Health Deadlock Query

```
USE IndexingMethod
GO

WITH deadlock
AS (
  SELECT CAST(target_data AS XML) AS target_data
  FROM sys.dm_xe_session_targets st
    INNER JOIN sys.dm_xe_sessions s ON s.address = st.event_session_address
  WHERE name = 'system_health'
  AND target_name = 'ring_buffer'
)
SELECT
  c.value('(@timestamp)[1]', 'datetime') AS event_timestamp
  ,c.query('data/value/deadlock')
FROM deadlock d
  CROSS APPLY target_data.nodes('//RingBufferTarget/event') AS t(c)
WHERE c.exist('.[@name = "xml_deadlock_report"]') = 1
```

When deadlocks have been identified, they are returned in an XML document. For most, reading the XML documents is not a natural way to examine a deadlock. Instead, it is often preferable to review the deadlock graph that is associated with the deadlock, such as the one shown in Figure 10-10. To obtain a deadlock graph for any of the deadlocks returned by Listing 10-42, open the deadlock XML document in SQL Server Management Studio and then save the file with an XDL extension. When the file is re-opened, it will open with the deadlock graph instead of as an XML document.

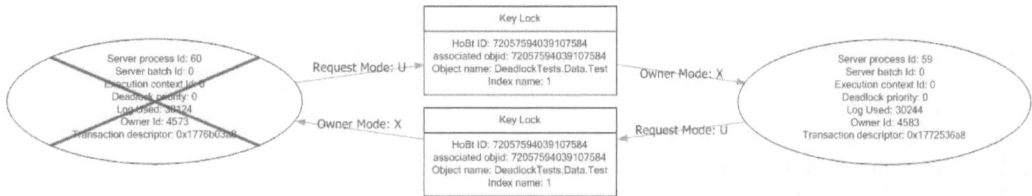

Figure 10-10. Deadlock graph in SQL Server Management Studio

Once deadlocks are identified, you must determine their cause to determine how to prevent them from reoccurring. A common issue that causes deadlocks is the order of operations between numerous transactions. This cause is often difficult to resolve since it may require rewriting parts applications. To address deadlocks, one of the easiest approaches is to decrease the amount of time in which the transaction occurs. Indexing the tables that are accessed is a typical approach that can resolve deadlocks in many cases by shrinking the window in which deadlocks can be created.

Wait Statistics

The analysis process for wait statistics is similar to that of performance counters. For both sets of data, the information points to areas where resources are potentially being taxed and identifying the resources and indicating next steps. A lot of the same processes for performance counters apply to wait statistics. The one main difference between the two sets of information is that wait statistics are looked at as a whole and their value is determined as a relationship of themselves to other wait statistics on the SQL Server instance.

Due to this difference, when reviewing wait statistics, there is only a single query required for analysis of the wait stats. Before using the wait statistics analysis query, provided in Listing 10-43, there are a few aspects to wait statistics analysis that should be explained. First, as the list of ignore wait stats shows, there are some wait states that accumulate regardless of the activity on the server. For these, there isn't any value in investigating behavior related to them, either because they are just the ticking of CPU time on the server or they are related to internal operations that can't be affected. Second, the value in wait statistics is in looking at them in relationship to the time that has transpired on the server. While one wait state being higher than another is important, without know the amount of time that has transpired, there is no scale by which to measure the pressure the wait state is having on the server. To accommodate for this, the waits from the first set of results in the monitoring table is ignored, and the date between then and the last collection point is used to calculate the time that has transpired. The length of time that a wait state occurred compared to the total time provides the values needed to determine the pressure of the wait state on the SQL Server instance.

Listing 10-43. Wait Statistics Analysis Query

```
USE IndexingMethod
GO

WITH WaitStats
AS (
  SELECT DENSE_RANK() OVER (ORDER BY w.create_date ASC) AS RankID
    ,create_date
    ,wait_type
    ,waiting_tasks_count
    ,wait_time_ms
    ,max_wait_time_ms
    ,signal_wait_time_ms
    ,MIN(create_date) OVER() AS min_create_date
    ,MAX(create_date) OVER() AS max_create_date
  FROM dbo.wait_stats_history w
  WHERE wait_type NOT IN ('CLR_SEMAPHORE','LAZYWRITER_SLEEP','RESOURCE_QUEUE'
    ,'SLEEP_TASK','SLEEP_SYSTEMTASK','SQLTRACE_BUFFER_FLUSH','WAITFOR'
    ,'LOGMGR_QUEUE','CHECKPOINT_QUEUE','REQUEST_FOR_DEADLOCK_SEARCH'
    ,'XE_TIMER_EVENT','BROKER_TO_FLUSH','BROKER_TASK_STOP','CLR_MANUAL_EVENT'
    ,'CLR_AUTO_EVENT','DISPATCHER_QUEUE_SEMAPHORE', 'FT_IFTS_SCHEDULER_IDLE_WAIT'
    ,'XE_DISPATCHER_WAIT', 'XE_DISPATCHER_JOIN', 'SQLTRACE_INCREMENTAL_FLUSH_SLEEP'
    ,'ONDEMAND_TASK_QUEUE', 'BROKER_EVENTHANDLER', 'SLEEP_BPOOL_FLUSH'
    ,'DIRTY_PAGE_POLL','HADR_FILESTREAM_IOMGR_IOCOMPLETION')
)
SELECT
  wait_type
  ,DATEDIFF(ms, min_create_date, max_create_date) AS total_time_ms
  ,SUM(waiting_tasks_count) AS waiting_tasks_count
  ,SUM(wait_time_ms) AS wait_time_ms
  ,CAST(1.*SUM(wait_time_ms)/SUM(waiting_tasks_count) AS DECIMAL(18,3)) AS avg_wait_time_ms
  ,CAST(100.*SUM(wait_time_ms)/DATEDIFF(ms, min_create_date, max_create_date) AS DECIMAL(18,3))
AS pct_time_in_wait
  ,SUM(signal_wait_time_ms) AS signal_wait_time_ms
  ,CAST(100.*SUM(signal_wait_time_ms)/NULLIF(SUM(wait_time_ms),0) AS DECIMAL(18,3)) AS pct_time_
runnable
FROM WaitStats
WHERE RankID <> 1
GROUP BY wait_type, min_create_date, max_create_date
ORDER BY SUM(wait_time_ms) DESC
```

The query includes a number of calculations to help identify when there are issues with specific wait types. To best understand the information provided, see the definitions provided in Table 10-3. These calculations and their definitions will help focus the performance issues related to wait statistics.

When reviewing the results of the wait statistics query, shown in Figure 10-11, there are two thresholds to watch. First, if any of the waits exceed 5% of the total wait time, there is likely a bottleneck related to that wait type and further investigation into the wait should happen. Similarly, if any of the waits exceed 1% of the time, they should be considered for further analysis, but not before reviewing the items with higher waits. One thing to pay close attention to when reviewing wait statistics is that if the time spent on the wait is mostly due to signal wait time, then the resource contention can be better resolved by first focusing on CPU pressure on the server.

Table 10-3. *Wait Statistics Query Column Definitions*

Option Name	Description
wait_type	The wait statistics that incurred the wait.
total_time_ms	Total amount of time measured by the query in milliseconds.
waiting_tasks_count	Count of the number of waits for this wait type.
wait_time_ms	Time in milliseconds accumulated for this wait type. This includes the time spent on signal_wait_time_ms.
avg_wait_time_ms	Average time per wait type in milliseconds.
pct_time_in_wait	Percent of total time spent for this wait type.
signal_wait_time_ms	Time in milliseconds accumulated after the wait type was available and no longer waiting before it was running. This is the time spent in the RUNNABLE state.
pct_time_runnable	Percent of time spent for this wait type in the RUNNABLE state.

	wait_type	total_time_ms	waiting_tasks_count	wait_time_ms	avg_wait_time_ms	pct_time_in_wait	signal_wait_time_ms	pct_time_runnable
1	LCK_M_S	14224286	15	888830	59255.333	6.249	958	0.108
2	WRITELOG	14224286	15165	398890	26.303	2.804	6618	1.659
3	PAGEIOLATCH_UP	14224286	3679	336800	91.547	2.368	581	0.173
4	CXPACKET	14224286	11835	332920	28.130	2.341	0	0.000
5	ASYNC_NETWORK_IO	14224286	3457	305240	88.295	2.146	12788	4.189
6	PREEMPTIVE_OS_WAITFORSINGLEOBJECT	14224286	225	208060	924.711	1.463	0	0.000
7	SOS_SCHEDULER_YIELD	14224286	115600	200060	1.731	1.406	19746	9.870
8	PREEMPTIVE_OS_AUTHENTICATIONOPS	14224286	71239	132590	1.861	0.932	0	0.000
9	ASYNC_IO_COMPLETION	14224286	16	89360	5585.000	0.628	1	0.001
10	LCK_M_IX	14224286	1	88010	88010.000	0.619	85	0.097

Figure 10-11. *Wait statistics analysis output*

Once wait states with issues have been identified, the next step is to review the wait and the recommended courses of actions for the wait. Since this chapter focuses on more index-centric wait types, we'll focus on those definitions. To learn more about the other wait types, review the Books Online topic for sys.dm_os_wait_stats (Transact-SQL).

CXPACKET

The CXPACKET wait type occurs when there are waits due to parallel query execution, otherwise known as *parallelism*. There are two main scenarios when parallel queries can experience CXPACKET waits. The first is when one of the threads from the parallel query is blocked by a thread already on the scheduler. The second is when one of the threads from the parallel query takes longer to execute that the rest of the threads and the rest of the threads have to wait for the slower thread to complete. The first cause is the more common cause for parallel waits, but it is outside the scope of this book. The second cause, though, can be addressed through indexing. And often, by addressing the second reason for CXPACKET waits, the first cause of parallel waits can be mitigated.

Two approaches that are common for addressing CXPACKET waits is to adjust the max degree of parallelism and cost threshold for parallelism server properties. As with the first cause of parallelism waits, addressing parallelism with these server properties is outside the context of the book. There are valid approaches for utilizing these two properties, but our focus is on indexing rather than constraining the degree and cost of parallelism. For a simple explanation, the max degree of parallelism limits the total number of cores that any single query can use during parallel processing. Alternatively, the cost threshold for parallelism increases the threshold in which SQL Server determines that a query can use parallelism, without limiting the scope of the parallelism.

As mentioned, CXPACKET waits can be addressed through indexing, which is paired with query tuning. In order to address the indexing for queries running in parallel, you need to first identify the queries that are using parallelism. There are two methods to do so. The first approach is to examine execution plans that have used parallelism in previous executions. The second is to retrieve execution plans for the parallel queries that are using parallelism and are experiencing CXPACKET waits.

For the first approach, using the plan cache involves identifying the execution plans that are utilizing parallelism and tuning those that are executed most often to reduce their I/O or remove the need for a parallel query. The need for the parallel query can sometimes be attributed to improper indexing on the underlying tables. The query in Listing 10-44 provides a list of execution plans in the plan cache that utilize parallelism.

Listing 10-44. Execution Plans that Utilize Parallelism

```
SET TRANSACTION ISOLATION LEVEL READ UNCOMMITTED;

WITH XMLNAMESPACES (DEFAULT 'http://schemas.microsoft.com/sqlserver/2004/07/showplan')
SELECT COALESCE(DB_NAME(p.dbid)
    , p.query_plan.value('(//RelOp/OutputList/ColumnReference/@Database)[1]','nvarchar(128)'))
      AS database_name
  ,DB_NAME(p.dbid) + '.' + OBJECT_SCHEMA_NAME(p.objectid, p.dbid)
    + '.' + OBJECT_NAME(p.objectid, p.dbid) AS object_name
  ,cp.objtype
  ,p.query_plan
  ,cp.UseCounts AS use_counts
  ,cp.plan_handle
  ,CAST('<?query --' + CHAR(13) + q.text + CHAR(13) + '--?>' AS xml) AS sql_text
FROM sys.dm_exec_cached_plans cp
CROSS APPLY sys.dm_exec_query_plan(cp.plan_handle) p
CROSS APPLY sys.dm_exec_sql_text(cp.plan_handle) as q
WHERE cp.cacheobjtype = 'Compiled Plan'
AND p.query_plan.exist('//RelOp[@Parallel = "1"]') = 1
ORDER BY COALESCE(DB_NAME(p.dbid), p.query_plan.value('(//RelOp/OutputList/ColumnReference/@
Database)[1]','nvarchar(128)')), UseCounts DESC
```

■ **Warning**   This chapter features a number of queries that are executed against the plan cache. The plan cache is accessed through DMO that provides access to the execution plans that are currently in use by the SQL Server, which allows for investigations into current and recent execution activity on the server. While this information is extremely useful, take care when executing this code on production systems. The plan cache is vital to the performance of your SQL Server and interfering with it can negatively impact performance. Be sure to monitor any queries that are executed against the plan cache and use them in non-production environments before a production environment.

The other method for parallelism waits is to investigate plans that are current executing. There are two ways to retrieve the list of plans. The first is to query the sys.dm_exec_* DMOs to identify what statements are currently using multiple workers, such as the query in Listing 10-45. This query provides a list of currently executing parallel plans.

Listing 10-45. Parallel Queries Currently Executing

```
WITH executing
AS (
  SELECT er.session_id
    ,er.request_id
    ,MAX(ISNULL(exec_context_id, 0)) AS number_of_workers
    ,er.sql_handle
    ,er.statement_start_offset
    ,er.statement_end_offset
    ,er.plan_handle
  FROM sys.dm_exec_requests er
    INNER JOIN sys.dm_os_tasks t on er.session_id = t.session_id
    INNER JOIN sys.dm_exec_sessions es on er.session_id = es.session_id
  WHERE es.is_user_process = 0x1
  GROUP BY er.session_id
    ,er.request_id
    ,er.sql_handle
    ,er.statement_start_offset
    ,er.statement_end_offset
    ,er.plan_handle
)
SELECT QUOTENAME(DB_NAME(st.dbid)) AS database_name
  ,QUOTENAME(OBJECT_SCHEMA_NAME(st.objectid, st.dbid)) + '.'
    + QUOTENAME(OBJECT_NAME(st.objectid, st.dbid)) AS object_name
  ,e.session_id
  ,e.request_id
  ,e.number_of_workers
  ,SUBSTRING(st.text, e.statement_start_offset / 2,
    (CASE WHEN e.statement_end_offset = -1 THEN LEN(CONVERT(nvarchar(max), st.text)) * 2
    ELSE e.statement_end_offset END - e.statement_start_offset) / 2) AS query_text
  ,qp.query_plan
FROM executing e
  CROSS APPLY sys.dm_exec_sql_text(e.plan_handle) st
  CROSS APPLY sys.dm_exec_query_plan(e.plan_handle) qp
WHERE number_of_workers > 0;
```

The second way is to start an extended event session and capture transaction information and then group that information on the available call stack. The session, defined in Listing 10-46, retrieves all of the parallel waits as they occur and groups them by their T-SQL stack. The T-SQL stack contains all of the SQL statements that contribute to a final execution point. For example, drilling through an execution stack can provide information on a stored procedure executing a function which executes a single T-SQL statement. This provides information that can be used to track where the parallel wait is occurring. These statements are grouped using the histogram target, which allows you to minimize the size of the collection and focus in on the items causing the most CXPACKET waits on the system.

Listing 10-46. Extended Event Session for CXPACKET

```
IF EXISTS(SELECT * FROM sys.server_event_sessions WHERE name = 'ex_cxpacket')
    DROP EVENT SESSION ex_cxpacket ON SERVER
GO

CREATE EVENT SESSION [ex_cxpacket] ON SERVER
ADD EVENT sqlos.wait_info(
  ACTION(sqlserver.plan_handle,sqlserver.tsql_stack)
```

```
  WHERE ([wait_type]=(191) AND [sqlserver].[is_system]=(0))
  -- 191 in SQL Server 2012
  -- 187 in SQL Server 2008/R2
  )
ADD TARGET package0.histogram(
  SET filtering_event_name=N'sqlos.wait_info'
    ,slots=(2048)
    ,source=N'sqlserver.tsql_stack'
    ,source_type=(1))
WITH (STARTUP_STATE=ON)
GO

ALTER EVENT SESSION ex_cxpacket ON SERVER STATE = START
GO
```

Once the extended event session has collected data for a while, the sessions with the most waits can be returned queries. Listing 10-47 provides a list of all of the CXPACKET waits that have been collected and the statements and query plans associated with them. Once these are known, investigate the indexes being used to determine which are resulting in low selectivity or unexpected scans.

Listing 10-47. Query to View CXPACKET Extended Event Session

```
WITH XData AS (
  SELECT CAST(target_data AS xml) AS TargetData
  FROM sys.dm_xe_session_targets st
    INNER JOIN sys.dm_xe_sessions s ON s.address = st.event_session_address
  WHERE name = 'ex_cxpacket'
  AND target_name = 'histogram'
)
, ParsedEvent AS (
  SELECT c.value('(@count)[1]', 'bigint') as event_count
    ,c.value('xs:hexBinary(substring((value/frames/frame/@handle)[1],3))','varbinary(255)') AS
sql_handle
    ,c.value('(value/frames/frame/@offsetStart)[1]','int') AS statement_start_offset
    ,c.value('(value/frames/frame/@offsetEnd)[1]','int') AS statement_end_offset
  FROM XData d
    CROSS APPLY TargetData.nodes('//Slot') t(c)
)
SELECT QUOTENAME(DB_NAME(st.dbid)) AS database_name
  ,QUOTENAME(OBJECT_SCHEMA_NAME(st.objectid, st.dbid)) + '.'
    + QUOTENAME(OBJECT_NAME(st.objectid, st.dbid)) AS object_name
  ,e.event_count
  ,SUBSTRING(st.text, e.statement_start_offset / 2,
    (CASE WHEN e.statement_end_offset = -1 THEN LEN(CONVERT(nvarchar(max), st.text)) * 2
    ELSE e.statement_end_offset END - e.statement_start_offset) / 2) AS query_text
  ,qp.query_plan
FROM ParsedEvent e
  CROSS APPLY sys.dm_exec_sql_text(e.sql_handle) st
  CROSS APPLY (
    SELECT plan_handle FROM sys.dm_exec_query_stats qs
    WHERE e.sql_handle = qs.sql_handle GROUP BY plan_handle) x
  CROSS APPLY sys.dm_exec_query_plan(x.plan_handle) qp
ORDER BY e.event_count DESC
```

IO_COMPLETION

The IO_COMPLETION wait type happens when SQL Server is waiting for I/O operations to complete for non-data page I/Os. Even though this wait is related to non-data operations, there are still some indexing related actions that can be taken when this wait is high for the SQL Server instance.

First, review the state of Full Scans/sec on the server. If there is an issue with that performance counter, the operations under that counter could bleed through to non-data pages that are being used to manage the indexes. In cases where the two of these are high, place additional emphasis on analyzing Full Scans/sec issues.

The second action that can be taken is to review the missing indexes' information within the SQL Server instance. That information is discussed in Chapter 7. If there are IO_COMPLETION issues, take care to focus more on missing indexes as well.

Lastly, if the cause of the IO_COMPLETION issues is not apparent, investigate them with an extended event session. This type of analysis is outside the scope of this book since these causes would likely be non-index related. The method used for investigating CXPACKET could apply and would be a place to start the investigation.

LCK_M_*

The LCK_M_* collection of wait types refer to waits that are occurring on the SQL Server instance. These are not just the use of locks, but also the times when locks have waits associated with them. Each wait type in LCK_M_* references a distinct type of lock, such as exclusive or shared locks. To decipher the different wait types, use Table 10-4. When the LCK_M_* wait types increase, they will always be in conjunction to increases in Lock Wait Time(ms) and Lock Waits/sec, allowing these counters to help investigate this wait type.

When investigating increases in either the performance counters or the different lock types, see Table 10-4. Use the combination of the wait types and the performance counters to hone in on specific issues. For instance, when the performance counters are pointing to Lock Wait Time(ms) issues, look for long running waits on LCK_M_*. Use the wizard in SQL Server Management Studio to create the Count Query Lock session and determine which lock and which queries, through the query_hash, are causing the issue. Similarly, if the issue is with Lock Waits/sec, look for those with the most numerous locks.

***Table 10-4.** LCK_M_* Wait Types*

Wait Type	Lock Type
LCK_M_BU	Bulk Update
LCK_M_IS	Intent Shared
LCK_M_IU	Intent Update
LCK_M_IX	Intent Exclusive
LCK_M_RIn_NL	Insert Range lock between the current and previous key with NULL lock on the current key value
LCK_M_RIn_S	Insert Range lock between the current and previous key with Shared lock on the current key value
LCK_M_RIn_U	Insert Range lock between the current and previous key with Update lock on the current key value
LCK_M_RIn_X	Insert Range lock between the current and previous key with Exclusive lock on the current key value

(continued)

Table 10-4. *(continued)*

Wait Type	Lock Type
LCK_M_RS_S	Shared Range lock between the current and previous key with Shared lock on the current key value
LCK_M_RS_U	Shared Range lock between the current and previous key with Update lock on the current key value
LCK_M_RX_S	Exclusive Range lock between the current and previous key with Shared lock on the current key value
LCK_M_RX_U	Exclusive Range lock between the current and previous key with Update lock on the current key value
LCK_M_RX_X	Exclusive Range lock between the current and previous key with Exclusive lock on the current key value
LCK_M_S	Shared
LCK_M_SCH_M	Schema Modify
LCK_M_SCH_S	Schema Share
LCK_M_SIU	Shared With Intent Update
LCK_M_SIX	Shared With Intent Exclusive
LCK_M_U	Update
LCK_M_UIX	Update with Intent Exclusive
LCK_M_X	Exclusive

PAGEIOLATCH_*

The final index-related wait is PAGEIOLATCH_* wait types. This wait refers to the waits that occur when SQL Server is retrieving data pages from indexes and placing them into memory. The time in which the query is ready to retrieve the data pages and when they are available in memory is tracked by SQL Server with these counters. As with LCK_M_* waits, there are a number of different PAGEIOLATCH_*, which are defined in Table 10-5.

First, monitor the indexes that are currently in the buffer cache to identify which indexes are available. Also, review the Page Life Expectancy/sec (PLE) counter; which is not currently collected in the monitoring section. Reviewing the allocation of pages to indexes in the buffer before and after changes in the PLE can help identify which indexes are pushing information out of memory. When these indexes are identified, use the techniques in the section "Determining Index Plan Usage" to investigate the plans and tune the query or indexes to reduce the amount of data needed to satisfy the queries.

Table 10-5. *PAGEIOLATCH_* Wait Types*

Wait Type	Lock Type
PAGEIOLATCH_DT	IO Latch in Destroy mode
PAGEIOLATCH_EX	IO Latch in Exclusive mode
PAGEIOLATCH_KP	IO Latch in Keep mode
PAGEIOLATCH_SH	IO Latch in Shared mode
PAGEIOLATCH_UP	IO Latch in Update mode

The second tactic to addressing PAGEIOLATCH_* is to put more emphasis on the Full Scans/sec analysis. Often, indexes that lead increases in this wait type are related to full scans that are in use by the database. By placing more emphasis on reducing the need for full scans in execution plans, less data will need to be pulled into memory, leading to a decrease in this wait type.

In some cases, the issues related to PAGEIOLATCH_* are unrelated to indexing. The issue can simply be a matter of slow disk performance. To verify if this is the case, monitor the performance of the server counters for Physical disk: disk seconds/read and Physical disk: disk seconds/write and the virtual file stats for SQL Server. If these statistics are continually high, expand the investigation outside of indexing to hardware and the I/O storage level. Besides improving disk performance, this wait statistic can be reduced by increasing the available memory, which can decrease the likelihood that the data page will be pushed out of memory.

Buffer Allocation

The final area to look at when determining the server state with indexing is to look at the data pages that are in the buffer cache. This isn't a typical area that people usually look at when considering indexing, but it provides a wealth of information regarding what SQL Server is putting into memory. The basic question that this can answer for the SQL Server instance is, does the data in the buffer represent the data most important to the applications using the SQL Server?

The first part of answering this question is to review which databases has how many pages in memory. This might not seem that important, but the amount of memory being used by the different databases can sometimes be surprising. Before indexes were added to the backup tables in the MSDB database, it wouldn't be uncommon for those tables to push all of the database in the backup tables into memory. If the data in the tables wasn't trimmed often, this could be a lot of information not critical to the business applications consuming an unnecessary amount of data.

For the second part of the question, you will need to engage the owners and subject matter experts for the applications using the SQL Server instance. If the answers from these folks don't match the information that is in the buffer, this provides a list of databases for which you can focus the index tuning effort.

Along those same lines, many applications have logging databases where error and processing events are stored for troubleshooting at a later date. When issues arise, instead of going to log files, the developers can simply query the database and extract the events they need to perform their troubleshooting. But what if these tables aren't properly indexed or the queries aren't SARGable? Log tables with millions or billions of rows may be pushed into memory, pushing the data from the line of business applications out of memory and potentially causing worse issues.

If the data in the buffer isn't being checked, there is no way to know what is in memory and if it is the right stuff.

Checking the data in memory is a relatively simple task that utilizes the DMO sys.dm_os_buffer_descriptors. This DMO lists each data page that is in memory and describes the information on the page. By counting each page for each database, the total amount of pages and the size of memory allocated to the database can be determined. Using the query in Listing 10-48, you can see in Figure 10-12 that the AdventureWorks database occupies the most memory on the server with the IndexingMethod database currently using 7.63MB of space.

Listing 10-48. Buffer Allocation for Each Database

```
SELECT  LEFT(CASE database_id
          WHEN 32767 THEN 'ResourceDb'
          ELSE DB_NAME(database_id)
          END,20) AS Database_Name
       ,COUNT(*) AS Buffered_Page_Count
       ,CAST(COUNT(*) * 8 / 1024.0 AS NUMERIC(10,2)) AS Buffer_Pool_MB
FROM  sys.dm_os_buffer_descriptors
GROUP BY DB_NAME(database_id)
       ,database_id
ORDER BY Buffered_Page_Count DESC
```

	Database_Name	Buffered_Page_Count	Buffer_Pool_MB
1	AdventureWorks	63307	494.59
2	DQS_MAIN	3755	29.34
3	ResourceDb	2255	17.62
4	tempdb	1103	8.62
5	IndexingMethod	977	7.63
6	msdb	702	5.48
7	master	371	2.90

Figure 10-12. *Results for buffer allocation for each database query*

Once the databases in memory have been identified, it is also useful to determine what objects in the database are in memory. For the similar reason as looking to see what databases are in memory, identifying the objects in memory helps with identifying the tables and indexes to focus on when indexing. Retrieving the memory use per table and index also utilizes sys.dm_os_buffer_descriptors, but includes mapping the rows to allocation_unit_id values in the catalogue views sys.allocation_units and sys.partitions.

Through the query in Listing 10-49, the memory used by each of the user tables and indexes is returned. In the results in Figure 10-13, the table BigTable is taking up a substantial amount of memory. If you are familiar with this database, you know that the table isn't one that is part of this database. This can lead you to other questions, such as where did it come from? Why is it so large? Is the space used by the table impacting the ability of other databases to use memory optimally with their indexes? In these cases, you need to investigate the indexes on these tables because the tables that are most in memory ought to have the most well-honed indexing profile.

Listing 10-49. Buffer Allocation by Table/Index

```
WITH BufferAllocation AS (
  SELECT object_id
    ,index_id
    ,allocation_unit_id
  FROM  sys.allocation_units AS au
    INNER JOIN sys.partitions AS p ON au.container_id = p.hobt_id AND (au.type = 1 OR au.type = 3)
  UNION ALL
```

```
SELECT  object_id
    ,index_id
    ,allocation_unit_id
  FROM  sys.allocation_units AS au
    INNER JOIN sys.partitions AS p ON au.container_id = p.hobt_id AND au.type = 2
)
SELECT  t.name
    ,i.name
    ,i.type_desc
    ,COUNT(*) AS Buffered_Page_Count
    ,CAST(COUNT(*) * 8 / 1024.0 AS NUMERIC(10,2)) AS Buffer_MB
FROM sys.tables t
  INNER JOIN BufferAllocation ba ON t.object_id = ba.object_id
  LEFT JOIN sys.indexes i ON ba.object_id = i.object_id AND ba.index_id = i.index_id
  INNER JOIN sys.dm_os_buffer_descriptors bd ON ba.allocation_unit_id = bd.allocation_unit_id
WHERE bd.database_id = DB_ID()
GROUP BY t.name
    ,i.index_id
    ,i.name
    ,i.type_desc
ORDER BY Buffered_Page_Count DESC
```

	name	name	type_desc	Buffered_Page_Count	Buffer_MB
1	BigTable	NULL	HEAP	60609	473.51
2	DatabaseLog	NULL	HEAP	13	0.10
3	Sales	cx_SalesSales	CLUSTERED	9	0.07
4	Sales	ix_modifiedSales	NONCLUSTERED	7	0.05
5	Sales	IX_Sales_CarrierTrackingNumber	NONCLUSTERED	7	0.05
6	ProductReview	IX_ProductReview_ProductID_Name	NONCLUSTERED	5	0.04
7	SalesOrderDetail	IX_SalesOrderDetail_ProductID	NONCLUSTERED	4	0.03
8	SalesPersonQuotaHistory	PK_SalesPersonQuotaHistory_SalesPersonID_QuotaDate	CLUSTERED	4	0.03
9	ProductVendor	PK_ProductVendor_ProductID_VendorID	CLUSTERED	3	0.02
10	DatabaseLog	PK_DatabaseLog_DatabaseLogID	NONCLUSTERED	3	0.02

Figure 10-13. Results for buffer allocation for each table/index query

Schema Discovery

After investigating the state of the server and its indexing needs, the next step in the Analyze phase is to investigate the schema of the databases to determine if there are schema-related indexing issues that can be addressed. For these issues, you are primarily going to focus on a few key details that can be discovered through catalog views.

Identify Heaps

As discussed previously, it is often more ideal to utilize clustered indexes on tables as opposed to storing tables as heaps. When heaps are preferred, it should be when the use of a clustered index has been shown to negatively impact performance as opposed to a heap. When investigating heaps, it is best to consider the number of rows and the utilization of the heap. When a heap has a low number of rows or is not being used, taking the effort to cluster its table may be rather pointless.

To identify heaps, use the catalog views sys.indexes and sys.partitions. The performance information is available in the table dbo.index_usage_stats_history. It can be used in conjunction to form the query in Listing 10-50, which provides the output in Figure 10-14.

The results show that dbo.DatabaseLog has a number of rows. The next step is to review the schema of the table. If there is a primary key already on the table, it's a good candidate for the clustering index key. If not, check for another key column, such as a business key. If there is no key column, it may be worthwhile to add a surrogate key to the table.

Listing 10-50. Query to Identify Heaps

```
SELECT
  QUOTENAME(DB_NAME()) AS database_name
  ,QUOTENAME(OBJECT_SCHEMA_NAME(i.object_id)) + '.'
    + QUOTENAME(OBJECT_NAME(i.object_id)) AS object_name
  ,i.index_id
  ,p.rows
  ,SUM(h.user_seeks) AS user_seeks
  ,SUM(h.user_scans) AS user_scans
  ,SUM(h.user_lookups) AS user_lookups
  ,SUM(h.user_updates) AS user_updates
FROM sys.indexes i
  INNER JOIN sys.partitions p ON i.index_id = p.index_id AND i.object_id = p.object_id
  LEFT OUTER JOIN IndexingMethod.dbo.index_usage_stats_history h ON p.object_id = h.object_id
AND p.index_id = h.index_id
WHERE type_desc = 'HEAP'
GROUP BY i.index_id
  ,p.rows
  ,i.object_id
ORDER BY p.rows DESC
```

	database_name	object_name	index_id	rows	user_seeks	user_scans	user_lookups	user_updates
1	[AdventureWorks2012]	[dbo].[DatabaseLog]	0	1597	0	512	0	0
2	[AdventureWorks2012]	[Production].[ProductProductPhoto]	0	504	NULL	NULL	NULL	NULL
3	[AdventureWorks2012]	[sys].[sysfiles1]	0	2	NULL	NULL	NULL	NULL

Figure 10-14. *Output for query identifying heaps*

■ **Note** The original inspiration for the duplicate and overlapping index query is from the blog post http://sqlblog.com/blogs/paul_nielsen/archive/2008/06/25/find-duplicate-indexes.aspx by Paul Nielsen.

Duplicate Indexes

The next schema issue to review is duplicate indexes. Expect for rare occasions, there is no need to have duplicate indexes in your databases. They waste space and cost resources to maintain without providing any benefit. To determine that an index is a duplicate of another, review the key columns and included columns of the index. If these match, the index is considered a duplicate.

To uncover duplicate indexes, the sys.indexes view is used in conjunction with the sys.index_columns catalog view. Comparing these views to each other using the code in Listing 10-51 will provide a list of the indexes that are duplicates. The results from the query, displayed in Figure 10-15, show that in the AdventureWorks2012 database the indexes AK_Document_rowguid and UQ__Document__F73921F7B9BAB8A8 are duplicates.

When duplicates are found, one of the two indexes should be removed from the database. While one of the indexes will have index activity, removing either will shift the activity from one to the other. Before removing either index, review the non-column properties of the index to make sure important aspects of the index are not lost. For instance, if one of the indexes is designated as unique, be sure that the index retained still has that property.

Listing 10-51. Query to Identify Duplicate Indexes

```
WITH IndexSchema AS (
  SELECT i.object_id
      ,i.index_id
      ,i.name
      ,(SELECT CASE key_ordinal WHEN O THEN NULL ELSE QUOTENAME(column_id,'(') END
          FROM sys.index_columns ic
          WHERE ic.object_id = i.object_id
          AND ic.index_id = i.index_id
          ORDER BY key_ordinal, column_id
          FOR XML PATH('')) AS index_columns_keys
      ,(SELECT CASE key_ordinal WHEN O THEN QUOTENAME(column_id,';(') ELSE NULL END
          FROM sys.index_columns ic
          WHERE ic.object_id = i.object_id
          AND ic.index_id = i.index_id
          ORDER BY column_id
          FOR XML PATH('')) AS included_columns
  FROM sys.tables t
    INNER JOIN sys.indexes i ON t.object_id = i.object_id
  WHERE i.type_desc IN ('NONCLUSTERED', 'HEAP')
)
SELECT QUOTENAME(DB_NAME()) AS database_name
  ,QUOTENAME(OBJECT_SCHEMA_NAME(is1.object_id)) + '.'
    + QUOTENAME(OBJECT_NAME(is1.object_id)) AS object_name
    ,STUFF((SELECT ', ' + c.name
        FROM sys.index_columns ic
            INNER JOIN sys.columns c ON ic.object_id = c.object_id AND ic.column_id = c.column_id
        WHERE ic.object_id = is1.object_id
        AND ic.index_id = is1.index_id
        ORDER BY ic.key_ordinal, ic.column_id
        FOR XML PATH('')),1,2,'') AS index_columns
    ,is1.name as index_name
  ,SUM(CASE WHEN is1.index_id = h.index_id THEN
    ISNULL(h.user_seeks,0)+ISNULL(h.user_scans,0)+ISNULL(h.user_lookups,0)+ISNULL(h.user_
updates,0) END) index_activity
    ,is2.name as duplicate_index_name
  ,SUM(CASE WHEN is2.index_id = h.index_id THEN
    ISNULL(h.user_seeks,0)+ISNULL(h.user_scans,0)+ISNULL(h.user_lookups,0)+ISNULL(h.user_
updates,0) END) duplicate_index_activity
FROM IndexSchema is1
```

```
    INNER JOIN IndexSchema is2 ON is1.object_id = is2.object_id
    AND is1.index_id > is2.index_id
    AND is1.index_columns_keys = is2.index_columns_keys
    AND is1.included_columns = is2.included_columns
  LEFT OUTER JOIN IndexingMethod.dbo.index_usage_stats_history h ON is1.object_id = h.object_id
GROUP BY is1.object_id, is1.name, is2.name, is1.index_id
```

	database_name	object_name	index_columns	index_name	index_activity	duplicate_index_name	duplicate_index_activity
1	[AdventureWorks2012]	[Production].[Document]	rowguid	AK_Document_rowguid	25	UQ__Document__F73921F7B9BAB8A8	NULL

Figure 10-15. *Output for query identifying duplicate indexes*

Overlapping Indexes

After identifying duplicate indexes, the next step is to look for overlapping indexes. An index is considered to be overlapping another index when its key columns make up all or a part of another index's key columns. Included columns are not considered when looking at overlapping columns; the focus for this evaluation is only on the key columns.

To identify overlapping indexes, the same catalog views, sys.indexes and sys.index_columns, are used. For each index, its key columns will be compared using the LIKE operator and a wildcard to the key columns of the other indexes on the table. When there is a match, it will be flagged as an overlapping index. The query for this check is provided in Listing 10-52 with the results from executing against the AdventureWorks2012 database shown in Figure 10-16.

Decisions on handling overlapping indexes are not as cut and dry as the duplicate indexes. To help illustrate overlapping indexes, the index IX_SameAsPK was creating on the column DocumentNode. This is the same column that is used as the clustering key for the table Production.Document. What this example shows, though, is that a non-clustered index can be considered an overlapping index of a clustered index. In some cases, it might be advisable to remove the overlapping non-clustered index. In all reality, the clustered index has the same key and the pages are sorted in the same manner. You can find the same values in both. The grey area comes in when considering the size of the rows in the clustered index. If the rows are wide enough, if just querying for the clustering key, it will at times be more beneficial to use the non-clustered index. In this manner, you will need to spend more time analyzing indexes. This same grey area will apply to comparisons between two non-clustered indexes as well.

When reviewing overlapping indexes, there are a few other things to note. Be sure to retain an index properties, such as whether the index is unique or not. Also, watch the included columns. The included columns are not considered in the overlapping comparison. There may be unique sets of included columns between the two indexes. Watch for this and merge the included columns as appropriate.

Listing 10-52. Query to Identify Overlapping Indexes

```
WITH IndexSchema AS (
  SELECT i.object_id
      ,i.index_id
      ,i.name
      ,(SELECT CASE key_ordinal WHEN 0 THEN NULL ELSE QUOTENAME(column_id,'(') END
          FROM sys.index_columns ic
          WHERE ic.object_id = i.object_id
          AND ic.index_id = i.index_id
          ORDER BY key_ordinal, column_id
          FOR XML PATH('')) AS index_columns_keys
```

```
   FROM sys.tables t
      INNER JOIN sys.indexes i ON t.object_id = i.object_id
   WHERE i.type_desc IN ('CLUSTERED','NONCLUSTERED', 'HEAP')
)
SELECT QUOTENAME(DB_NAME()) AS database_name
  ,QUOTENAME(OBJECT_SCHEMA_NAME(is1.object_id)) + '.'
    + QUOTENAME(OBJECT_NAME(is1.object_id)) AS object_name
   ,STUFF((SELECT ', ' + c.name
        FROM sys.index_columns ic
           INNER JOIN sys.columns c ON ic.object_id = c.object_id AND ic.column_id = c.column_id
        WHERE ic.object_id = is1.object_id
        AND ic.index_id = is1.index_id
        ORDER BY ic.key_ordinal, ic.column_id
        FOR XML PATH('')),1,2,'') AS index_columns
   ,STUFF((SELECT ', ' + c.name
        FROM sys.index_columns ic
           INNER JOIN sys.columns c ON ic.object_id = c.object_id AND ic.column_id = c.column_id
        WHERE ic.object_id = is1.object_id
        AND ic.index_id = is1.index_id
   AND ic.is_included_column = 1
        ORDER BY ic.column_id
        FOR XML PATH('')),1,2,'') AS included_columns
    ,is1.name as index_name
  ,SUM(CASE WHEN is1.index_id = h.index_id THEN
    ISNULL(h.user_seeks,0)+ISNULL(h.user_scans,0)+ISNULL(h.user_lookups,0)+ISNULL(h.user_
updates,0) END) index_activity
    ,is2.name as duplicate_index_name
  ,SUM(CASE WHEN is2.index_id = h.index_id THEN
    ISNULL(h.user_seeks,0)+ISNULL(h.user_scans,0)+ISNULL(h.user_lookups,0)+ISNULL(h.user_
updates,0) END) duplicate_index_activity
FROM IndexSchema is1
    INNER JOIN IndexSchema is2 ON is1.object_id = is2.object_id
    AND is1.index_id > is2.index_id
    AND (is1.index_columns_keys LIKE is2.index_columns_keys + '%'
    AND is2.index_columns_keys LIKE is2.index_columns_keys + '%')
      LEFT OUTER JOIN IndexingMethod.dbo.index_usage_stats_history h ON is1.object_id =
h.object_id
GROUP BY is1.object_id, is1.name, is2.name, is1.index_id
```

	database_name	object_name	index_columns	included_columns	index_name	index_activity	duplicate_index_name	duplicate_index_activity
1	[AdventureWorks2012]	[Production].[Document]	rowguid	NULL	AK_Document_rowguid	25	UQ__Document__F73921F7B9BAB8A8	NULL
2	[AdventureWorks2012]	[Production].[Document]	DocumentNode	NULL	IX_SameAsPK	10	PK_Document_DocumentNode	37

Figure 10-16. Output for query identifying overlapping indexes

Unindexed Foreign Keys

Foreign keys are very useful for enforcing constraints within a database. When there are parent and child relationships between tables, foreign keys provide the mechanism to verify that child tables aren't referencing parent values that don't exist. Likewise, the foreign key makes certain that a parent value can't be removed while child values are still in use. To support these validations, the columns for the parent and child values between the tables need to be indexed. If one or the other is not indexed, SQL Server can't optimize the operation with a seek and is forced to use a scan to verify that the values are not in the related table.

Verifying that foreign keys are indexed involves a process similar to the duplicate and overlapping indexes process. Along with the sys.indexes and sys.index_columns catalog views, the sys.foreign_key_columns view is used to provide an index template that the foreign key would rely upon. This is pulled together in the query in Listing 10-53 with results from the AdventureWorks2012 database shown in Figure 10-17.

The common practice is that every foreign key should be indexed, always. This, though, is not actually the case for every foreign key. There are a couple things to consider before adding the index. First and foremost, how many rows are in the child table? If the row count is low, adding the index may not provide a performance gain. If the uniqueness of the column is fairly low, statistics may justify a scan of every row regardless of the index. In these cases, it could be argued that if the size of the table is small, the cost of the index is also small and there is nothing to lose from adding the index. The other consideration is whether data will be deleted from the table and when activities that require validation of the foreign key will occur. With large tables with many columns and foreign keys, performance may suffer from having yet another index to maintain on the table. The index would probably be of value, but is it of enough value to justify creating it?

While those are good considerations when indexing foreign keys, the majority of the time you will want to index your foreign keys. Similar to the recommendation for clustering tables, index your foreign keys unless you have performance documentation showing that indexing the foreign keys negatively impacts performance.

Listing 10-53. Query to Identify Unindexed Foreign Keys

```
WITH cIndexes AS (
  SELECT i.object_id
    ,i.name
    ,(SELECT QUOTENAME(ic.column_id,'(')
      FROM sys.index_columns ic
      WHERE i.object_id = ic.object_id
      AND i.index_id = ic.index_id
      AND is_included_column = 0
      ORDER BY key_ordinal ASC
      FOR XML PATH('')) AS indexed_compare
  FROM sys.indexes i)
, cForeignKeys AS (
  SELECT fk.name AS foreign_key_name
    ,'PARENT' as foreign_key_type
    ,fkc.parent_object_id AS object_id
    ,STUFF((SELECT ', ' + QUOTENAME(c.name)
      FROM sys.foreign_key_columns ifkc
      INNER JOIN sys.columns c ON ifkc.parent_object_id = c.object_id AND ifkc.parent_column_id
= c.column_id
      WHERE fk.object_id = ifkc.constraint_object_id
      ORDER BY ifkc.constraint_column_id
      FOR XML PATH('')), 1, 2, '') AS fk_columns
    ,(SELECT QUOTENAME(ifkc.parent_column_id,'(')
      FROM sys.foreign_key_columns ifkc
      WHERE fk.object_id = ifkc.constraint_object_id
      ORDER BY ifkc.constraint_column_id
      FOR XML PATH('')) AS fk_columns_compare
  FROM sys.foreign_keys fk
    INNER JOIN sys.foreign_key_columns fkc ON fk.object_id = fkc.constraint_object_id
  WHERE fkc.constraint_column_id = 1)
, cRowCount AS (
```

```
    SELECT object_id
      ,SUM(row_count) AS row_count
  FROM sys.dm_db_partition_stats ps
  WHERE index_id IN (1,0)
  GROUP BY object_id)
SELECT QUOTENAME(DB_NAME())
  ,QUOTENAME(OBJECT_SCHEMA_NAME(fk.object_id)) + '.'
    + QUOTENAME(OBJECT_NAME(fk.object_id)) AS ObjectName
  ,fk.foreign_key_name
  ,fk_columns
  ,row_count
FROM cForeignKeys fk
  INNER JOIN cRowCount rc ON fk.object_id = rc.object_id
  LEFT OUTER JOIN cIndexes i ON fk.object_id = i.object_id AND i.indexed_compare LIKE fk.fk_
columns_compare + '%'
WHERE i.name IS NULL
ORDER BY row_count DESC, OBJECT_NAME(fk.object_id), fk.fk_columns
```

	(No column name)	ObjectName	foreign_key_name	fk_columns	row_count
1	[AdventureWorks2012]	[Sales].[SalesOrderDetail]	FK_SalesOrderDetail_SpecialOfferProduct_SpecialOfferIDP...	[SpecialOfferID], [ProductID]	121317
2	[AdventureWorks2012]	[Production].[WorkOrderRouting]	FK_WorkOrderRouting_Location_LocationID	[LocationID]	67131
3	[AdventureWorks2012]	[Sales].[SalesOrderHeader]	FK_SalesOrderHeader_Address_BillToAddressID	[BillToAddressID]	31465
4	[AdventureWorks2012]	[Sales].[SalesOrderHeader]	FK_SalesOrderHeader_CreditCard_CreditCardID	[CreditCardID]	31465
5	[AdventureWorks2012]	[Sales].[SalesOrderHeader]	FK_SalesOrderHeader_CurrencyRate_CurrencyRateID	[CurrencyRateID]	31465
6	[AdventureWorks2012]	[Sales].[SalesOrderHeader]	FK_SalesOrderHeader_ShipMethod_ShipMethodID	[ShipMethodID]	31465
7	[AdventureWorks2012]	[Sales].[SalesOrderHeader]	FK_SalesOrderHeader_Address_ShipToAddressID	[ShipToAddressID]	31465
8	[AdventureWorks2012]	[Sales].[SalesOrderHeader]	FK_SalesOrderHeader_SalesTerritory_TerritoryID	[TerritoryID]	31465
9	[AdventureWorks2012]	[Sales].[SalesOrderHeaderSalesReason]	FK_SalesOrderHeaderSalesReason_SalesReason_SalesR...	[SalesReasonID]	27647
10	[AdventureWorks2012]	[Person].[PersonPhone]	FK_PersonPhone_PhoneNumberType_PhoneNumberTypeID	[PhoneNumberTypeID]	19972
11	[AdventureWorks2012]	[Sales].[Customer]	FK_Customer_Person_PersonID	[PersonID]	19820
12	[AdventureWorks2012]	[Sales].[Customer]	FK_Customer_Store_StoreID	[StoreID]	19820
13	[AdventureWorks2012]	[Sales].[PersonCreditCard]	FK_PersonCreditCard_CreditCard_CreditCardID	[CreditCardID]	19118
14	[AdventureWorks2012]	[Sales].[CurrencyRate]	FK_CurrencyRate_Currency_FromCurrencyCode	[FromCurrencyCode]	13532
15	[AdventureWorks2012]	[Sales].[CurrencyRate]	FK_CurrencyRate_Currency_ToCurrencyCode	[ToCurrencyCode]	13532

Figure 10-17. *Output for query identifying missing foreign key indexes*

■ **Note**   It bears repeating that the DTA is a good tool for determining useful indexes to add to a database. While there may be more pride in designing indexes for a database by hand without the need of a tool, it isn't practical to ignore useful recommendations. Use the DTA as a starting point to discover indexing suggestions that would have taken hours to determine without the tool in place.

Database Engine Tuning Advisor

The Database Engine Tuning Advisor (DTA) was discussed in Chapter 7. In that chapter, we discussed the two modes for using the DTA: the GUI interface and the command-line utility. While tuning queries is often a process of reviewing statistics and evaluating execution plans, the DTA provides means to accelerate this analysis by using the trace files from the Monitor phase to identify potentially useful indexing recommendations. This process is able to accomplish the tuning with minimal impact on the production environment, since all of the recommendations are derived from analysis on a non-production environment.

The basic process for using the DTA index analysis can be broken out into five different steps, shown in Figure 10-18.

1. Collect a workload.

2. Gather the metadata.

3. Perform the tuning.

4. Consider recommendations and review.

5. Deploy changes.

Through this process, you can get a jump-start on indexing and begin working with recommendations that relate to existing performance issues.

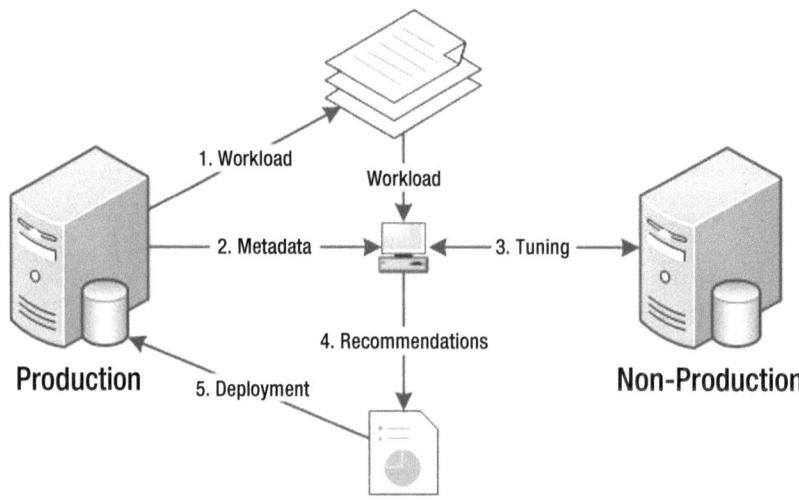

Figure 10-18. Steps for using the DTA index analysis

The first step in the process is to collect a workload. If you followed the process in the Monitor phase, this information should already have been collected. There are two standard scenarios that workloads should represent. To begin, collect a workload that represents a typical day, because even a normal day can have underlying performance issues that tuning can help alleviate. Second, gather a workload during times where performance problems are known to exist. This will be useful for providing recommendations that you may be able to achieve through manual tuning.

After the workload is collected, the next step is to gather the necessary metadata to start the tuning sessions. There are two components to gathering metadata. The first is to create an XML input file for the dta session. The XML input file contains the production and non-production server names and information on where the workload is and what type of tuning options to utilize (a sample is shown in Listing 10-54). For more information on tuning options, see Chapter 7. The second part of this step is the effect on tuning from the first piece. When the tuning occurs, SQL Server will gather the schema and statistics for the database from the production database(s) and move that information to the non-production server. While the database won't have the production data, it will have the information necessary to make indexing recommendations.

Listing 10-54. Sample XML Input File for DTA

```xml
<?xml version="1.0" encoding="utf-16" ?>
<DTAXML xmlns:xsi="http://www.w3.org/2001/XMLSchema-instance" xmlns="http://schemas.microsoft.
com/sqlserver/2004/07/dta">
 <DTAInput>
  <Server>
   <Name>STR8-SQL-PRD</Name>
   <Database>
    <Name>AdventureWorks2012</Name>
   </Database>
  </Server>
  <Workload>
   <File>c:\temp\IndexingMethod.trc</File>
   <File>c:\temp\IndexingMethod_1.trc</File>
  </Workload>
  <TuningOptions>
   <TestServer> STR8-SQL-TEST </TestServer>
   <FeatureSet>IDX</FeatureSet>
   <Partitioning>NONE</Partitioning>
   <KeepExisting>NONE</KeepExisting>
  </TuningOptions>
 </DTAInput>
</DTAXML>
```

■ **Note**   More information on the XML input file configuration can be found in Books Online at `http://technet.`
`microsoft.com/en-us/library/ms173513.aspx`.

The next step is the actual execution of the DTA tuning session. To run the session, execute the dta command using the -ix command-line option, shown in Listing 10-55. Since all of the configuration information for the session is located in the XML file, there is no need to add any additional parameters.

Listing 10-55. DTA Command with XML Input File

```
dta -ix "c:\temp\SessionConfig.xml"
```

After the tuning sessions completes, you will receive a list of index recommendations. This isn't the last step in this portion of the process. Before any recommendation from the DTA can be implemented, they must be reviewed. While using this tool will accelerate the Analyze phase, all of the recommendations need to be reviewed and vetted to verify that they make sense and don't overload a table with more indexes than the SQL Server can support for the workload.

The last step is to deploy the indexing recommendations. This step is technically outside the scope of this phase of the indexing method. At this time, though, you should be familiar with the indexing changes that will be implemented. Add these changes to the existing list of indexing changes from other analysis and prepare them for implementation in the next phase.

Unused Indexes

One of the necessary and potentially dangerous steps in the Analyze phase is the determination of indexes to remove. Some indexes will be removed due to consolidation or because they are duplicates. Often these have less risk than when other indexes are dropped. The indexes in this other category are those that are unused.

The easiest manner for identifying indexes that are not used is to check the list of indexes in each database against the dbo.index_usage_stats_history table in the IndexingMethod database. If there are any unused indexes in the database, the query in Listing 10-56 will identify them. One word of caution with unused indexes: in this analysis, heaps and clustered indexes are ignored, along with any unique indexes and primary keys. Indexes with these properties are often related to other business rules and their removal should be based on other factors. An example of unused indexes in the AdventureWorks2012 database is included in Figure 10-19.

Listing 10-56. Query for Unused Indexes

```
SELECT OBJECT_NAME(i.object_id) as table_name
  ,COALESCE(i.name, space(0)) as index_name
  ,ps.partition_number
  ,ps.row_count
  ,Cast((ps.reserved_page_count * 8)/1024. as decimal(12,2)) as size_in_mb
  ,COALESCE(ius.user_seeks,0) as user_seeks
  ,COALESCE(ius.user_scans,0) as user_scans
  ,COALESCE(ius.user_lookups,0) as user_lookups
  ,i.type_desc
FROM sys.all_objects t
  INNER JOIN sys.indexes i ON t.object_id = i.object_id
  INNER JOIN sys.dm_db_partition_stats ps ON i.object_id = ps.object_id AND i.index_id =
ps.index_id
  LEFT OUTER JOIN sys.dm_db_index_usage_stats ius ON ius.database_id = db_id() AND i.object_id =
ius.object_id AND i.index_id = ius.index_id
WHERE i.type_desc NOT IN ('HEAP', 'CLUSTERED')
AND i.is_unique = 0
AND i.is_primary_key = 0
AND i.is_unique_constraint = 0
AND COALESCE(ius.user_seeks,0) <= 0
AND COALESCE(ius.user_scans,0) <= 0
AND COALESCE(ius.user_lookups,0) <= 0
ORDER BY object_name(i.object_id), i.name
```

	table_name	index_name	partition_number	row_count	size_in_mb	user_seeks	user_scans	user_lookups	type_desc
1	TransactionHistory	IX_TransactionHistory_ReferenceOrderID_Reference...	1	366714	9.96	0	0	0	NONCLUSTERED
2	TransactionHistory	IX_TransactionHistory_ProductID	1	366714	6.71	0	0	0	NONCLUSTERED
3	SalesOrderDetail	IX_SalesOrderDetail_ProductID	1	121317	2.20	0	0	0	NONCLUSTERED
4	SalesOrderDetail	IX_SalesOrderDetail	1	121317	1.85	0	0	0	NONCLUSTERED
5	TransactionHistoryArchive	IX_TransactionHistoryArchive_ReferenceOrderID_Ref...	1	89253	1.71	0	0	0	NONCLUSTERED
6	EmailAddress	IX_EmailAddress_EmailAddress	1	19972	1.51	0	0	0	NONCLUSTERED
7	TransactionHistoryArchive	IX_TransactionHistoryArchive_ProductID	1	89253	1.34	0	0	0	NONCLUSTERED

Figure 10-19. *Output for query identifying missing foreign key indexes*

While this section didn't discuss it, there are two additional scenarios for identifying unused indexes. These are lightly used indexes or no longer used indexes. A similar process can be used for these situations: instead of looking for indexes that have never been used, filter for low usage rates or no use in a period of weeks or months. But don't just remove these indexes automatically. If the index is lightly used, verify how the index is being used before dropping it. It may be used once a day, but it might be tied to critical processes. Also, with no longer used indexes, verify that the index isn't part of a seasonal process. Removing indexes tied to seasonal activity can create more of a burden than just maintaining them in off-peak times.

Index Plan Usage

In previous sections of this chapter, the concept of checking the plan cache to analyze and investigate index usages was discussed. While statistics can show that there was a seek or a scan against an index, it doesn't provide you with enough detail to know what columns to add or what caused the index to use a scan over a seek. To gather this information, you need to turn to the execution plan. And the place where you can get some of the best execution plans for your databases and SQL Server instance is the plan cache. In this last section, in the Analyze phase, you'll be looking at two queries that can be used to retrieve execution plans from the plan cache.

The first query is one that will be used when you need to retrieve all of the plans for a specific index. Suppose you need to determine what processes, or T-SQL statements, are using one of the indexes on a table that is used once or twice a day. For this, you can turn to the plan cache with the query in Listing 10-57 and check if the plan for that query is still in the cache. To use the query, replace the index name in the variable @IndexName and execute it to return a list of plans that use the index. Be cautious if you have a database where there are many indexes with the same name, since index names only need to be unique on a per-table basis. If all of the indexes are named IX_1 and IX_2, you will need to verify the table name in the search to be sure you have the correct index.

Listing 10-57. Query Plan Cache for Index Usage

```
SET TRANSACTION ISOLATION LEVEL READ UNCOMMITTED
GO
DECLARE @IndexName sysname = 'PK_SalesOrderHeader_SalesOrderID';
SET @IndexName = QUOTENAME(@IndexName,'[');
WITH XMLNAMESPACES  (DEFAULT 'http://schemas.microsoft.com/sqlserver/2004/07/showplan')
,IndexSearch
AS (
  SELECT qp.query_plan
    ,cp.usecounts
    ,ix.query('.') AS StmtSimple
  FROM sys.dm_exec_cached_plans cp
    OUTER APPLY sys.dm_exec_query_plan(cp.plan_handle) qp
    CROSS APPLY qp.query_plan.nodes('//StmtSimple') AS p(ix)
  WHERE query_plan.exist('//Object[@Index = sql:variable("@IndexName")]') = 1
)
SELECT StmtSimple.value('StmtSimple[1]/@StatementText', 'VARCHAR(4000)') AS sql_text
  ,obj.value('@Database','sysname') AS database_name
  ,obj.value('@Schema','sysname') AS schema_name
  ,obj.value('@Table','sysname') AS table_name
  ,obj.value('@Index','sysname') AS index_name
  ,ixs.query_plan
FROM IndexSearch ixs
  CROSS APPLY StmtSimple.nodes('//Object') AS o(obj)
WHERE obj.exist('//Object[@Index = sql:variable("@IndexName")]') = 1
```

At other times, searching for just the name of an index will be too broad of a search of the plan cache. In these cases, you can use the query in Listing 10-58. This query adds in the name of a physical operator to the plan cache search. For instance, suppose you are investigating Full Scans/sec and you know what index is causing the spike in the performance counter. Searching for just the index may return dozens of execution plans. Alternatively, you could add in a search for a particular operator, such as an index scan, using the @op variable in the query provided.

Listing 10-58. Query Plan Cache for Index Usage and Physical Operation

```
DECLARE @IndexName sysname = 'IX_SalesOrderHeader_SalesPersonID';
DECLARE @op sysname = 'Index Scan';

;WITH XMLNAMESPACES(DEFAULT N'http://schemas.microsoft.com/sqlserver/2004/07/showplan')
SELECT
    cp.plan_handle
    ,DB_NAME(dbid) + '.' + OBJECT_SCHEMA_NAME(objectid, dbid) + '.' + OBJECT_NAME(objectid,
dbid) AS database_object
    ,qp.query_plan
    ,c1.value('@PhysicalOp','nvarchar(50)')
    ,c2.value('@Index','nvarchar(max)')
FROM sys.dm_exec_cached_plans cp
  CROSS APPLY sys.dm_exec_query_plan(cp.plan_handle) qp
  CROSS APPLY query_plan.nodes('//RelOp') r(c1)
  OUTER APPLY c1.nodes('IndexScan/Object') as o(c2)
WHERE c2.value('@Index','nvarchar(max)') = QUOTENAME(@IndexName,'[')
AND c1.exist('@PhysicalOp[. = sql:variable("@op")]') = 1
```

Both of these queries provide mechanisms for getting in and investigating indexes in their environment and seeing exactly how SQL Server is using them. This information can be easily leveraged to identify when problems are occurring and why, and then provide a path to resolving indexing issues without a lot of the guesswork that many use today.

Implement

The final phase of the Indexing Method is the Implement phase. This phase does as the name implies: implements the indexing changes that were determined as necessary through the Analyze phase. There isn't much to this phase from a process perspective, but there are some important steps that need to be done during the Implement phase that will help build out a successful process. The aim of the entire process is to improve the performance of the database environment. With this aim, there are three key points to remember during implementation.

- Communication
- Source code control (e.g., via deployment scripts)
- Execution

While the last step is the only one where the database is modified, the other two help ensure that the changes will be noticed and that you can continue to use the Indexing Method in the future.

Communication

The first hurdle in modifying the indexes on any database is the need to communicate with management and users of the database your intent to change the database. Modifications to the database can often raise red flags, especially when they are being prescribed by non-owners of the application the database supports. Preparing for and implementing open lines of communication between the owners of applications and the database administration team will help not only in the indexing process, but in other areas of mutual interest. Without this communication, teams can be blindsided by the indexing changes, which may impact something that the analysis did not uncover or a feature that is planned but not yet released.

When it comes to communication, there are basically two items that need to be prepared for the owners of the databases: an impact analysis of the indexing changes and a status report of the changes after implementation.

Impact Analysis

When preparing for changes to indexing on a database, it is important to highlight the intended changes to the application performance. Historically, this has often been a guessing game. There was not a lot of easily accessed information that would indicate where an index is being used, how it is being used, and the frequency of use.

With the processes laid out in the Monitor phase, you gain the ability to confidently know the use of an index. You can determine when it was last used and what operations were included. There is information that can also be used to identify the trend in which an index will no longer be used or is being use more frequently.

Through the Analyze phase, steps were laid out that allow the identification of execution plans that are utilizing different indexes. Use these steps to identify where an index change will have an impact and then perform sample executions of the T-SQL statements before and after the indexing changes are made.

In the end, the impact analysis will function in two important roles during the Implement phase. First, it will communicate to managers and peers the intent of the indexing changes, informing them of the changes to validate what is being done along and allowing them the chance for feedback. Second, the impact analysis provides an insurance policy in case an index change has an unexpected negative impact. This isn't to say that there won't be negative repercussions to poor indexing recommendations, but with others involved and the impact documented, it is more likely a negative impact can be mitigated quicker and possibly identified before actual implementation.

Status Report

On the opposite end of the Implement phase is the status report. As the name implies, the status report is a document that provides feedback to managers and peers about the actual impact of indexes. This document does not need to be very deep, but it does need to cover some key points.

The status report should cover the following information:

- List of all index changes made.

- Status on deployment of changes.

- Brief performance review.

- Information on any regressions noted.

- What was learned in the deployment process.

- Summary of issues encountered.

Don't get too mired in the details while writing the status report. If all goes well, there will be another Monitor and Analyze phase in the near future. In the end, the status report needs to communicate two things. First, it provides an honest assessment of the successes and failures in the indexing deployment. Second, and most importantly, it lists what benefits are now being realized by the indexing changes. This is most important because it is the ROI that managers need to see to be able to justify the time and effort spent on indexing.

Deployment Scripts

The primary deliverable from the Analyze phase is a list of index changes that are planned for the databases in your environment. During the Implement phase, those indexes need to be reviewed and prepared for deployment. As part of preparing the indexes for deployment, three steps need to occur.

- Prepare deployment and rollback of schema.

- Save index changes to source code control.

- Share results of peer review with impact analysis.

Prepare Deployment and Rollback of Schema

Usually, at the completion of the Analyze phase you have a list of the index changes that are being proposed. This list typically is not in state that can be used for deployment at the end of the phase. Between that point and the execution of the changes, the indexing changes need to be put into a state that can be used for their deployment.

When building the deployment scripts, be sure to observe the idea of "doing no harm" to the database. In other words, you need to build scripts that are intelligent enough that they can be executed multiple times with the identical results. Also, this means that scripts should be available to reverse any indexing changes being made. Never assume that the previous indexing state of a table is being stored in source code control. Check to be certain that the existing state is known and develop scripts to revert to that state if needed.

The deployment scripts also need to be aware of the edition of SQL Server that is being used. For instance, if you are using Enterprise Edition, leverage online index rebuilds for indexes that are being rebuilt with new characteristics. If appropriate for the index, Enterprise Edition also allows for compression on the index, which can save space and improve performance in many cases.

Save Index Changes to Source Code Repository

As mentioned, the current state of the indexes on tables should be in a source code repository. If they are not, then with this iteration through the Implement phase, it's time to do so. Source code repositories offer a place to store the code, or schema, for a database to allow your organization to determine what the index, table, or store procedure schema was at a specific date and time. Source code is often well managed from application perspective. Developers are usually quick to choose a tool and leverage it for their applications.

Source code repositories allow you to recover to a point in time for the database schema.

Peer Review with Impact Analysis

The last thing to do before the Execution step is to seek a peer review of the indexing changes. There is nothing worse than working in a vacuum and not understanding the whole impact of the changes that are being proposed against the applications that use the databases. It is easy to get tunnel vision by focusing on the indexing goal and miss the business goals of the current deployment or overlook something that wasn't apparent in the index analysis.

The best way to avoid these pitfalls is to find a peer to review the indexing changes. Bring the peer the index deployment scripts and the impact analysis and go over the changes. Your peer doesn't necessarily need to know everything about the environment, just a basic understanding of indexing. The aim of the peer review is to explain each change. In this dialogue, your peer serves as a sounding board as you explain the indexing need. This serves a dual role. First, your peer will be able to provide feedback on the indexing change. And second, by discussing the changes you may hear yourself describe an indexing change that doesn't sound correct when it is explained.

In some environments, you may not have a peer that you can turn to review the indexes. In these cases, consider going to your manager for the peer review. If that is not possible, talk to your manager about leveraging peers in your technical network. Leverage the forums and social networks to find either a peer or group of peers that will be willing to review your changes with you. Using social networks, such as Twitter, to connect with a technical peer and review some indexing changes is much better than not having a peer review at all.

With the peer review complete, the indexes are ready for the next step in the Implement phase: the step where the indexes are actually applied to the databases.

■ **Note**   Within the SQL Server community, Twitter is one of the more active social networking tools. Use hash tags #sql and #sqlserver to find general information on SQL Server. When looking for answers to questions specifically about SQL Server, you can utilize the hash tag #sqlhelp. Twitter also allows you to add people to your conversation by including their Twitter handle in the tweet. For instance, the authors of the this book, Jason Strate and Ted Krueger, are available through the handles @stratesql and @onpnt, respectively.

Execution

The last piece of the Implement phase is the execution of the T-SQL scripts that will apply the indexing changes to the database. These scripts should already be prepared through the Deploy Scripts step and the scope of the changes should be well known from the Communication step. Thus the Execution step should be relatively painless as the preparation work is already completed.

From an execution standpoint, the manner of execution is completely dependent on your organization's change control process. In some environments, there are automated processes where scripts can be loaded to a deployment mechanism and executed on a schedule. In others, the DBAs simply open SQL Server Management Studio and execute each script in order until all of the changes are completed. Whatever the mechanism, the key is that at this stage, the indexes get deployed.

As the deployment progresses, be sure to catalog the changes made and any issues that arise during execution. Pay attention to unintended blocking on the databases. If indexes are being deployed in an offline state, be sure to select an execution window that is during the database maintenance window. Remember, even online index operations can cause short-lived blocking.

Repeat

In the beginning of this chapter, the discussion started by looking at the three phases of the Indexing Method. The diagram for the process (Figure 10-1) shows the three phases in an endless loop with each phase leading to the next. This choice in layout was intentional. Indexing is not a fixed-point activity. Once the first round of the Indexing Method is completed, it is important to start the next round of indexing.

It can be tempting, when databases are properly tuned, to let the practice of indexing to slip and to focus on other priorities. Unfortunately, new features are often added to applications as frequently as new data is added to the database. Both of these events will change the way in which indexes are used by the database and the effectiveness that the current state of "good" indexes.

In order to maintain the desired performance of the database platform, indexes must be continuously reviewed. This isn't to say that a full-time resource always needs to be assigned to monitoring, analyzing, and implementing indexes. There does, though, need to be an acceptance that at some interval an evaluation of the state of indexing will be completed.

Summary

As this chapter showed, the Indexing Method is quite similar to the scientific method. Within your database platform, statistics can be collected on indexes in order to identify where indexing issues may exist. These statistics can then be further utilized to determine what types of indexes to modify and where. Indexing tools such as the Database Engine Tuning Advisor and Missing Index DMOs can be leveraged to discover "the low hanging fruit," giving you a head start on analysis that you may not have discovered otherwise. By following the phases laid out in the Indexing Method, you can build a stable, repeatable indexing process that can help improve the performance of your database platform and achieve stable performance over time.

Index

■ A

Analyze phase, indexing method, 278
    description, 278
    layout, 278
    schema discovery
        duplicate indexes, 310–312
        heaps identification, 309–310
        overlapping indexes, 312–313
        unindexed foreign keys, 313–315
    server state review, 279
        buffer allocation, 307–309
        description, 279
        performance counters, 279–299
        wait statistics, 299–307
Automatically maintaining statistics, 158
    creation, 158
    prevention, 159
    properties, 158
    updation, 158–159

■ B

Balance index count, 133
Bulk Changed Map (BCM)
        page, 20

■ C

Clustered index, 2, 190
    ever-increasing, 191
    foreign key, 194
        IDENTITY property, 194
        multiple header row, 197
        single header row, 196
    GUID pattern, 202
        NEWID function, 202
        NEWSEQUENTIALID function, 203
        page counts, 204
        script, 203
    identity column, 191–192
    multiple column, 198–202
    narrow, 191
    static, 190
    surrogate key, 192–194
    unique, 191
Column-level statistics. *See* Index-level statistics
ColumnStore index, 223
    guidelines, 223
    limitations, 223
    performance improvements, 223–225
    statistics IO results, 224, 225
Command-line utility, 178
    description, 173
    first scenario, 183–184
    output report, 186
    scenario setup, 182–183
    second scenario, 185
    utility arguments, 179–182
    utility syntax, 178–179
Compression
    description, 7
    page-level, 7
    row-level, 7
Concatenation, query strategies, 238
    description, 238
    execution plan, 239
    query, 238
    removed, 240
    STATISTICS IO, 239
    without spaces, 239
CXPACKET wait type, 301
    extended event session, 303–304
    parallel queries currently executing, 303
    parallelism, 301
    utilize parallelism, 302

■ D

Database Engine Tuning Advisor (DTA), 172, 315–317
    capabilities, 172
    command-line utility, 178
        description, 173
        first scenario, 183–184
        output report, 186
        scenario setup, 182–183
        second scenario, 185
        utility arguments, 179–182
        utility syntax, 178–179
    description, 172
    GUI tool, 174
        configuration screen, 174
        default selections, 175
        description, 173
        indexes options, 177
        progress screen, 176
        recommendations, 177
        tuning options configuration screen, 176
        workload options, 175
    index analysis steps, 316
    limitations, 172
    modes, 315
    PDS items options, 173
    physical design structure options, 173
    process, 316
    table partition
        DDL Statement, 174
        options, 173
    XML input file, 317
Database level fill factor, 133–134
Data conversion, query strategies, 244
    implicit data conversion, 245–247
    setup, 245
Data definition language (DDL), 7
    alter index, 10
    creat index
        index options, 8–9
        syntax options, 8, 9
        type, 8
        UNIQUE keyword, 8
    description, 7
    drop index, 10
        index options, 11
        syntax, 11
Data storage, 15, 187
    clustered indexes (*see* Clustered index)
    ColumnStore index (*see* ColumnStore index)
    extents, 16
        mixed, 17
        uniform, 17
    heaps (*see* Heaps)
    non-clustered indexes (*see* Non-clustered indexes)

page compression, 228
    benefits, 229
    dictionary compression, 229
    implementation, 229
    output, 230
    prefix compression, 229
    query, 230
    row compression, 229
    setup, 229
pages (*see* Pages)
row compression, 226
    fixed-length character data, 226
    implementation, 227
    metadata changes, 226
    numeric data types, 226
    output, 227
    query, 228
    setup, 226
DBCC PAGE
    parameters, 36
    print option
        hex data, 40–41
        hex rows, 39–40
        page header, 37–39
        row data, 42–43
    syntax, 35
Defragmentation, 146
    drop and create, 149
    index rebuild, 147–148
    index reorganization, 148–149
    strategies, 149
        maintenance plans, 149
        rebuild index task, 150–152
        reorganize index task, 149–150
        T-SQL scripts, 152–156
Differential Change Map (DCM) page, 20
DMOs. *See* Dynamic Management Objects (DMOs)
DTA. *See* Database Engine Tuning Advisor (DTA)
Dynamic Management Objects (DMOs), 165, 256
    accuracy, 166
    categories, 165
    data cleanup, 273–274
    depth of analysis, 165–166
    description, 256
    explanation, 166
        sys.dm_db_missing_index_columns, 167–168
        sys.dm_db_missing_index_details, 166–167
        sys.dm_db_missing_index_group_stats, 168, 169
        sys.dm_db_missing_index_groups, 168
    index operational stats, 260
        snapshot population, 263–268
        snapshot tables stats, 261–263
    index physical stats, 268
        history population, 269–270
        history table, 268–269

index usage stats, 256
    snapshot population, 258–260
    snapshot tables stats, 257–258
size of the queue, 165
types of indexes, 166
usage, 169
    execution plan, 170
    impact calculation, 170
    query, 171
    score calculation, 171
    SQL statements, 170
wait statistics, 270
    history population, 272–273
    index related, 271
    snapshot and history table, 271
    snapshot population, 272

■ E

Extensible Markup Language (XML) indexing, 91
    benefits, 91
    categories, 92
    creation, 92
        query() function, 94
        secondary_type, 95
        secondary_type_desc, 95
        sys.dm_db_index_physical_stats query, 95
        Typed XML, 93
        using_xml_index_id, 95
        Well-formed XML, 92
        XMLTable, 93–94
    description, 91
    execution plans effects, 95–97
    exist() Method, 96
    primary index effects, 97
    secondary index, 97
        benefit, 98
        execution plan results, 100
        IDX_SEC_VALUE index, 98–99
        index seek operation, 98
        PATH and PROPERTY indexes, 100

■ F

Fill factor, 133
    database level, 133–134
    description, 133
    fragmentation, 156–157
    index level, 134
Filtered indexes, 6–7
Foreign keys, 313–315
Fragmentation, 135
    default values, 157
    defragmentation, 146
        drop and create, 149

        index rebuild, 147–148
        index reorganization, 148–149
        strategies, 149–152
    events, 135
    issues, 144
        contiguous reads, 146
        index I/O, 144–146
        reasons, 144
    NEWID() function, 136, 157
    NEWSEQUENTIALID() function, 157
    operations, 135
        delete, 140–141
        insert, 136–138
        shrink, 142–144
        update, 138–140
    prevention, 156
        data typing, 157
        fill factor, 156–157
FTS indexing. *See* Full-text search (FTS) indexing
Full-text search (FTS) indexing, 5, 112
    catalog
        creation, 113
        views and properties, 118–120
    description, 112
    index creation, 113
        key indexes, 115
        population, 115
        StopLists, 115–118
        syntax, 113, 115
    index options, 114
    index syntax, 113, 115
    noise words, 115
    table and INSERT statements, 112–113

■ G

Global Allocation Map (GAM) page, 19–20
Graphical user interface (GUI) tool, 174
    configuration screen, 174
    default selections, 175
    description, 173
    indexes options, 177
    progress screen, 176
    recommendations, 177
    tuning options configuration screen, 176
    workload options, 175

■ H

Heaps, 187
    scenarios, 189–190
    temporary objects, 187–189
        clustered index, 188–189
        execution plan, 188
        EXISTS, 189

Heap tables, 2
Implement phase, indexing method, 320
    communication, 320
        impact analysis, 321
        status report, 321
    deployment scripts, 322
        impact analysis review, 322–323
        preparation and rollback, 322
        source code repository, 322
    description, 320
    execution, 323

■ I, J, K

Index(ing), 1
    balance index count, 133
    change managerment, 134
    characteristics
        clustered index, 48
        column store index, 49
        heap index, 48
        non-clustered index, 48–49
    clustered indexes on primary
        keys, 133
    compression, 7
        description, 7
        page-level, 7
        row-level, 7
    DDL, 7
        alter index, 10
        create index, 8–9
        description, 7
        drop index, 10–11
    description, 1–2
    fill factor, 133
        database level, 133–134
        index level, 134
    foreign key columns, 134
    FTS, 112
        catalog creation, 113
        catalog views and properties, 118–120
        description, 112
        index creation, 113–118
        table and INSERT statements, 112–113
    maintenance, 135
        fragmentation (*see* Fragmentation)
        statistics (*see* Statistics maintenance)
    meta data, 11
        sys.column_store_dictionaries, 12
        sys.column_store_segments, 12
        sys.index_columns, 12
        sys.indexes, 11–12
        sys.spatial_indexes, 12
        sys.xml_indexes, 12
    myths, 121

    clustered indexes, physical order
        records, 129–130
    column filteration, in multicolumn
        indexes, 127–129
    description, 121
    fill factor, 130–131
    indexes needs, 122–123
    online index operations, 125–127
    primary keys, 123–124
    table, heap/clustered index, 131–132
spatial data, 101
    cells-per-object rule, 102
    covering rule, 102
    creation, 102–107
    deepest cell rule, 102
    description, 101
    geometry index, 101–102
    grid storage representation, 101
    restrictions, 111
    statistics, properties and information, 109–111
    supporting methods, 107–109
    tessellation process, 102
    visual representation, 102
tools, 165
    DMOs (*see* Dynamic Management
        Objects (DMOs))
    DTA (*see* Database Engine Tuning Advisor
        (DTA))
types, 2
    clustered indexes, 2
    column store indexes, 3
    full-text search, 5
    heap tables, 2
    nonclustered indexes, 3
    spatial indexes, 4–5
    XML indexes, 4
variations, 5
    filtered indexes, 6–7
    included columns, 6
    partitioned indexes, 6
    primary key, 5
    unique index, 5–6
XML, 1
    benefits, 91
    categories, 92
    creation, 92–95
    description, 91
    execution plans effects, 95–97
    primary index effects, 97
    secondary index, 97–100
Index Allocation Map (IAM) pages, 21
Indexed views, 231
    benefits, 234
    considerations, 232
    summary information, 231

Indexing method
  analyze phase, 278
    description, 278
    DTA, 315–317
    index plan usage, 319–320
    layout, 278
    schema discovery, 309–315
    server state review, 279–309
    unused indexes, 318–319
  cycle, 250
  description, 249–250
  implement phase, 320
    communication, 320–321
    deployment scripts, 322–323
    description, 320
    execution, 323
  monitoring phase, 250
    description, 250
    DMOs, 256–274
    performance counters, 251–256
    SQL trace session, 274–277
  repeat, 323
Index level fill factor, 134
Index-level statistics
  cardinality, 51
  catalog views
    sys.stat_columns, 56
    sys.stats, 56
  DBCC SHOW_STATISTICS, 1
    density vector, 55
    histogram, 52–55
    stats header, 52
  DDL statements, 57
  query optimization, 57
  STATS_DATE, 57
Index operational statistics, 66
  compression, 82–83
  DML activity, 67–70
  header columns, 67
  latch contention, 76
    page I/O latch, 77–78
    page latch, 79–80
  LOB access, 83–85
  locking contention, 72
    lock escalation, 75–76
    page lock, 74–75
    row lock, 73–74
  page allocation cycle, 80–82
  parameters, 66
  SELECT activity, 70
    forwarded fetch, 71–72
    range scans, 70–71
    singleton lookup, 71
  syntax, 67
Index physical statistics, 85

  fragmentation statistics, 88–89
  header columns, 86–87
  parameters, 86
  row statistics, 87–88
Index statistics, 51
  index usage statistics (*see* Index usage statistics)
  index-level statistics (*see* Index-level statistics)
  operational statistics (*see* Index operational statistics)
  physical statistics (*see* Index physical statistics)
Index usage statistics
  dynamic management view, 57
  header columns, 58
  system columns, 64–66
  user columns, 58
    user_lookups, 62–63
    user_scans, 61–62
    user_seeks, 59–60
    user_updates, 64
IO_COMPLETION wait type, 305

■ L

Large Object (LOB) Pages, 21–22
LCK_M_* wait type, 305–306
LIKE comparison, query strategies, 235–238

■ M

Manually maintaining statistics, 159
  maintenance plans, 159–161
  methods, 159
  T-SQL scripts, 161
    DDL command, 161–162
    stored procedure, 161
Meta data, index, 15
  sys.column_store_dictionaries, 12
  sys.column_store_segments, 12
  sys.index_columns, 12
  sys.indexes, 11–12
  sys.spatial_indexes, 12
  sys.xml_indexes, 12
Monitoring phase, indexing method, 250
  description, 250
  DMOs, 256
    data cleanup, 273–274
    description, 256
    index operational stats, 260–268
    index physical stats, 268–270
    index usage stats, 256–260
    wait statistics, 270–273
  performance counters
    baseline table, 255–256
    description, 251
    index-related, 252

Manually maintaining statistics (*cont.*)
    populate counter baseline table, 254–255
    snapshot script, 253–254
    snapshot table, 252
  SQL trace session, 274
    add events and columns, 275, 276
    add filters, 277
    creation, 274
    description, 274
    start, 277
    stop, 277

■ N, O

Non-clustered indexes, 3, 204
  considerations, 205
  covering index, 211–212
  filtered indexes, 216–219
  foreign keys, 219–222
  included columns, 212–216
  intersection pattern, 207–210
  multiple columns, 210–211
  search columns, 205–207

■ P

Page Free Space (PFS) pages, 19
PAGEIOLATCH_* wait type, 306–307
Page-level compression, 7
Pages
  BCM page, 20
  boot page, 19
  B-tree structure, 24–25
  column store structure, 25–26
  components, 16
  data files, 18
  data pages, 21
  DBCC EXTENTINFO
    allocation information, 29–31
    output columns, 28
    parameters, 28
    syntax, 27
  DBCC IND
    allocation information, 33–35
    benefits, 33
    output columns, 32
    page type mappings, 33
    parameters, 32
    syntax, 31
  DBCC PAGE (*see* DBCC PAGE)
  DCM page, 20
  extents
    mixed, 17
    uniform, 17
  file header page, 18

  GAM page, 19–20
  heap structure, 22–23
  IAM page, 21
  index pages, 21
  LOB page, 21–22
  organizational structures, 22
  PFS page, 19
  row placement and offset array, 16
  SGAM page, 20
  SQL Server, 43
    forwarded records, 44–45
    page splits, 45–48
  uses, 3
Partitioned indexes, 6
Performance counters, indexing method
  analyze phase, 279
    Forwarded Records, 280–283
    FreeSpace Scans, 283–285
    Full Scans, 285–287
    Heap Script, 283
    Index Searches, 287–289
    Lock Wait Time, 293–295
    Lock Waits, 295–297
    Number of Deadlocks, 297–299
    Page lookups, 291–293
    Page Splits, 289–291
  monitoring phase, 251
    baseline table, 255–256
    description, 251
    index-related, 252
    populate counter baseline table, 254–255
    snapshot script, 253–254
    snapshot table, 252

■ Q

Query strategies, 235
  computed columns, 240
    description, 240
    execution plans, 241
    indexed computed column
      execution plans, 241–242
    indexes, 242
    queries, 241
  concatenation, 238
    description, 238
    execution plan, 239
    query, 238
    removed, 240
    STATISTICS IO, 239
    without spaces, 239
  data conversion, 244
    implicit data conversion, 245–247
    setup, 245
  LIKE comparison, 235–238

scalar functions, 242
  execution plans, 243–244
  queries, 243
scenarios, 235

■ R

Row-level compression, 7

■ S

Scalar functions, query strategies, 242
  execution plans, 243–244
  queries, 243
Shared Global Allocation Map (SGAM) page, 20
Spatial data indexing, 101
  cells-per-object rule, 102
  covering rule, 102
  creation, 102
    CITY_GEOM column, 103
    database, 103–104
    index options, 103
    MakeValid() function, 106
    query against ZIP code data, 105
    Shape2SQL importing census
      ZIP code data, 105
    STDistance() function, 107
    ZIP code data, 106
  deepest cell rule, 102
  description, 101
  geometry index, 101–102
  grid storage representation, 101
  restrictions, 111
  statistics, properties and information, 109
    procedures, 110–111
    views, 109–110
  supporting methods, 107
    geometry type lists, 107
    statement creation, 108
    STDistance() method, 107
    tuned execution plan, 108
  tessellation process, 101
  visual representation, 102
Spatial indexes, 4–5
SQL trace session, indexing method, 274
  add events and columns, 275, 276
  add filters, 277
  creation, 274
  description, 274
  start, 277
  stop, 277
Statistics maintenance, 158

automatic, 158
  creation, 158
  prevention, 159
  properties, 158
  updation, 158–159
manual, 159
  maintenance plans, 159–161
  methods, 159
  T-SQL scripts, 161–162
sys.column_store_dictionaries catalog view, 12
sys.column_store_segments catalog view, 12
sys.index_columns catalog view, 12
sys.indexes catalog view, 11–12
sys.spatial_indexes catalog view, 12
sys.xml_indexes catalog view, 12

■ T

T-SQL scripts, 152–156, 161
  fragmentation
    build index defragmentation
      statements script, 155–156
    collect fragmenation data script, 154
    guidelines, 152
    identify fragmented indexes script, 155
    index defragmantion script template, 153–154
    index defragmentation statements, 156
    rebuild index task properties window, 154
  manually maintaining statistics
    DDL command, 161–162
    stored procedure, 161

■ U, V, X, Y, Z

Unique index, 5–6
XML indexing. *See* Extensible Markup Language (XML)
      indexing
Wait statistics analysis, indexing method
  analyze phase, 299
    CXPACKET, 301–304
    description, 299
    IO_COMPLETION, 305
    LCK_M_*, 305–306
    output, 301
    PAGEIOLATCH_*, 306–307
    query, 300
    query column definitions, 301
  monitoring phase, 299
    history population, 272–273
    index related, 271
    snapshot and history table, 271
    snapshot population, 272